W9-ADP-799

UNTYING
THE TONGUE

UNTYING
THE TONGUE

Gender, Power, and the Word

Edited by
Linda Longmire and Lisa Merrill

Prepared under the auspices of Hofstra University

Contributions in Women's Studies, Number 164

Greenwood Press
Westport, Connecticut • London

Library of Congress Cataloging-in-Publication Data

Untying the tongue : gender, power, and the word / edited by Linda
  Longmire and Lisa Merrill ; prepared under the auspices of Hofstra
  University.
      p. cm.—(Contributions in women's studies, ISSN 0147–104X ;
  no. 164)
   Includes bibliographical references and index.
   ISBN 0–313–30686–9 (alk. paper)
   1. Communication and sex. 2. Power (Social sciences)
  3. Feminism. I. Longmire, Linda, 1949– . II. Merrill, Lisa.
  III. Hofstra University. IV. Series.
  P96.S48U58   1998
  155.3′3—dc21   97–44837

British Library Cataloguing in Publication Data is available.

Library of Congress Catalog Card Number: 97–44837
ISBN: 0–313–30686–9
ISSN: 0147–104X

First published in 1998

Greenwood Press, 88 Post Road West, Westport, CT 06881
An imprint of Greenwood Publishing Group, Inc.

Printed in the United States of America

The paper used in this book complies with the
Permanent Paper Standard issued by the National
Information Standards Organization (Z39.48–1984).

10 9 8 7 6 5 4 3 2 1

Contents

Introduction

Linda Longmire and Lisa Merrill

This volume grew out of an ongoing conversation among teachers, practitioners, and theorists in many disparate fields, all of whom are interested in the intersection of gender and communication. As convenors of the conference on Communication, Language, and Gender, held at Hofstra University, we were eager to present and share one moment of this dialogue. And, as we have worked with the contributors, we came to feel, more strongly than ever, that a crucial factor at the intersection of studies of communication and gender was the unarticulated variable of a mediating conception of power—a vision of power that informs our title, *Untying the Tongue: Gender, Power, and the Word*.

This book explores some of the ways in which power and its expression (or repression) is gendered. The contributed chapters seek to discover contexts and patterns within which power is articulated, reproduced, and ultimately transformed. There are at least three dimensions or approaches to this work that are presented in this wide array of papers, written at a variety of different theoretical levels. Although some of the chapters are primarily descriptive examinations of presumed gender differences, others seek to critique or deconstruct these supposed meanings associated with gender and power relations. Thus, one of the major tasks of this volume involves interrogating our conceptions of power and another is reconceptualizing them in ways that are more inclusive and diverse than in traditional masculinist categories. At a third level of analysis, some of the theorists recognize that these descriptions and attempts at definition are embodied in concrete discursive practices that overtly or transparently configure our experience of gender.

The intersection of three phenomena—communication, gender, and power —calls up a multiplicity of associations. For some, following anthropologist Edward Hall's (1981) notion that "culture *is* communication," all attempts to derive, discover, or create meaning come out of a given cultural context and thus are both shaped by the beliefs about gender that are operative in that sphere and also serve to constitute those beliefs—shaping, framing, limiting what is perceived as possible or desirable for women and men. Individually each of these terms—communication, language, and gender—as linguists and semioticians would tell us, is arbitrary. Their meanings have changed over time, and they connote different things in different contexts.

The symbolic exchange implied by the term *language* has historically reflected the values of a given linguistic group; thus, some theorists claim that women and men use language differently. As members of an historically oppressed and marginalized group, women's experience with communication and language has been marked by their subordinate status. Some of the chapters in this volume are informed by a perspective that attempts to document and describe different communicative strategies employed by women and men. At an earlier stage in this research communicative strategies employed by men were hegemonically regarded as "normative" whereas women's communicative behaviors were seen as deficient. At a later stage some feminist researchers posited that the behaviors, values, and characteristics that they observed in women were, in fact, preferable and the result of some essential difference between men and women. Current research has increasingly acknowledged the multiple subject positions (e.g., race, class, ethnicity) from which people can speak, challenging the assumption that there are essential differences between men and women and contending that most observed differences are social constructions.

Some contributions in the field which have focused on the centrality of *gender* as the key variable in understanding human behavior assume a bipolar gendered experience. More recent research posits myriad intersecting variables that are operative in a given context and moment. In this volume we have included research that reflects each of the above positions.

As we explore in Part I, much research on communication and gender has centered on language structure and use. Women's and men's conceptions of themselves and their identities may be shaped by the language available to them. As psychologist Jerome Bruner (1990) explains, from a very young age we learn to know ourselves, to create a "self" and experience our subjectivity through language. Over the past two decades, theorists influenced by feminist discussions of psychoanalysis have questioned whether the nature and acquisition of all language is patriarchal; thus they describe women's "exclusion" from language in psychic and psychosexual terms. Other linguists have studied biases inherent in a given lexicon, to see what the omissions and symbols present in a given language system reflect about the values of those cultures out of which it has come.

In Part II we broaden our focus on the gendered meanings invoked in given language systems and their usage to look at the implications about gender that have been "read" in the images constructed by a selection of writers, cartoonists, and filmmakers. Creators of images, whatever their intentions, construct artifacts that are assigned meanings by their readers. Some readers and viewers in this collection examine the depictions of women and men—heterosexual, lesbian, and gay—in several mainstream popular venues, such as novels, *New Yorker* cartoons, and popular films, to see what message they derive about the presence or absence of gender stereotyped behavior and the inflection of other axes of power, such as socioeconomic class and ethnicity. We recognize that no one reading of a text makes available all of its meanings but is rather a reflection of what interests and concerns an individual reader brings to the work. The chapters in this section are a sampling of reactions to mainstream artifacts and point out, by their presence or omission, some of the ways that gender and power are represented. Each of the authors discusses specific features, such as depictions of male and female characters' sexuality, intellect, career choice, material conditions, and so on, that are present or problematic in the texts they examine, though no one chapter investigates all of these features.

Within popular mediated culture the interests of those with power are generally reflected as though they are the "normal" and "desirable" state of affairs; but it is often possible for subjugated groups to read against these dominant codes. In Part III we present some possible recuperative "readings" of popular films, television programs, and music videos. Whether films or television programs present victims of violent acts of perpetrators and spectators of acts of violence, sexually objectified entertainers, or power-inflected heterosexual couples, they are targeted at specific audiences who are assumed to share the values implicit in their codes. Some of the chapters in this section explore the intentional use of these mediated artifacts as pedagogical tools with which students can—by interrogating rather than merely consuming these commodified images—challenge their own values.

In Part IV we examine another critical arena of communication—the pedagogical contexts in which the interplay of power and gender can be vividly seen. All of us have been shaped, to some extent, by hierarchical, patriarchal educational systems, constructed, in part, to replicate in both the teaching style employed and the material selected to be "taught," the values that have framed dominant educational enterprises. We discover that not only are learning institutions socially constructed, but so too the roles, relationships, and experiences in these formal environments. Even our ways of knowing, believing, and learning are replete with markings about gender and power. A critical feminist pedagogy that seeks to transform repressive gendered patterns, both external and internal, challenges the very definition of education and notions about ultimate intentions of teaching and learning. By understanding the ways in which the roles, rules, and even the structure of academic disciplines are value laden with messages about power and gender, we can begin the task of transformation.

In Part V we further explore the intersection of gender, power, and communication in the context of relationships, both in the home and in the workplace. All of these relational patterns are undergirded by the assumption that power is typically equated with mastery, control, and domination—over self, others, or the environment. Examining the communicative behavior of men and women at work, in their families, and in friendships helps us not only to unearth these patterns but also to cultivate alternative types of power that emphasize cooperation, integration, and equality.

In the final section we examine the transformative process of "untying the tongue" which challenges some of society's stereotypic assumptions about power and gender. Empowerment takes place at many levels, some of which are more political and others of which are focused on more personal sites of struggle. These chapters examine a number of fundamental definitions and expressions of empowerment that affect self-esteem, physical well-being, and rhetorical effectiveness. Although each of the authors brings her or his own interpretations of empowerment to their work, we recognize that the socially constructed nature of the values and attributes privileged in modern western society is marked by gendered notions of power. By exploring personal narratives as well as some of the larger paradigmatic narratives that influence our understandings of selfhood, health, spirituality, and politics, we begin to create a space within which new voices, energies, and visions can emerge.

In this volume we have attempted to give voice to an interrogation of some of the traditional discursive practices that influence understandings of communication, power, and gender. Recognizing the power that communication has to not only interrogate but to liberate, we appreciate the multiplicity of perspectives presented in this text. A truly transformative dialogue creates a climate that empowers all of us, particularly those whose voices have been most muted, to "untie our tongues."

REFERENCES

Bruner, Jerome. 1990. *Acts of Meaning*. Cambridge, MA: Harvard University Press.
Hall, Edward T. 1981. *The Silent Language*. New York: Doubleday (originally 1959).

Part I

Gender and the Word

In the first part of *Untying the Tongue: Gender, Power, and the Word*, we examine language. The words and grammatical structure of a given language are the most basic building blocks of thought and communication, reflecting the ways speakers of a language conceptualize themselves and their world and communicate with others. Since language reflects a culture's biases and inequities, a socially constructed, gendered power differential between men and women may lead each to have very different relationships to language. Some feminist theorists consider language to be the paradigmatic organizing structure that serves to reinforce, if not construct, women's oppression. In other words, if our native language depicts the universal, the normative, the generic as "male," women are necessarily defined as "other." In *Feminism and Linguistic Theory*, Deborah Cameron (1992) offers: "In the context of feminist linguistic theory, the question of power is a question about who controls language in what way and to what extent. Does power in language derive from other kinds of power (physical, political, economic)? Or is linguistic power the power to define reality and thus the key to all other forms of domination?" (p. 219). The four chapters in this section explore connections among gender, language, and power.

As we see in Lou Ann Matossian's chapter, which opens this section, the nineteenth-century feminist activists and orators in the United States confronted the male generic in their rhetorical arguments for women's rights. If "man" is to mean all people, both male and female, as in "mankind," then rights that are afforded men should apply to women as well. Similarly, as Matossian notes, in Susan B. Anthony's famous speech, "Are Women Persons?" Anthony cited the rights afforded to citizens and persons born in the United States and claimed those for women. The court's rejection of Anthony's claim made it clear that although the word *person* is not marked for gender in the English language, the unmarked assumption was that "person" referred to male persons. Matossian demonstrates how "first-wave" (nineteenth-century) feminists "challenge[d] exclusionary language in institutional settings." In setting out an historical context for feminist studies of language, Matossian reminds us that overtly political struggles for women's basic rights over a century ago were framed in terms that continue to be contested in our contemporary questioning of linguistic constructs.

Grammatical and syntactical structures are the focus of both Gail M. Schwab's and Katherine Stephenson's work as well, but Schwab and Stephenson investigate the language that women and men use rather than the language used to describe or dismiss them. Much contemporary work in fields as diverse as philosophy, linguistics, and communication draws on an exploration of women's and men's discursive behaviors as a metaphor for or evidence of an individual speaking subject's perception of her or his own agency. In her experimental work with French speakers, linguist and psychoanalyst Luce Irigaray found that women and men use language differently; for example, she observed that women were less likely than men to use the pronoun *I* and present themselves as subject of a sentence. Adapting the empirical linguistic research Irigaray conducted in France to American English speakers, Schwab and Stephenson explore whether women and men in their studies indicate a subjective sense of self similarly.

As members of an international team of researchers applying Irigaray's work to speakers of other languages, Schwab and Stephenson have each translated and adapted some of Irigaray's linguistic tests. Schwab's chapter outlines the theoretical foundation for Irigaray's analysis of utterances produced when female and male respondents were instructed to compose sentences that include specific key words. As Schwab describes, Irigaray studied both the utterances of men and women and the enunciation of those utterances (their expression in actual spontaneously produced speech), as well as the relationship between what a speaker says and the person to whom the message is directed. Schwab conducted such studies in English and offers explanations for what the difference she observed in male and female respondents' usage might "mean." Stephenson explored subjects' choice of the possessive term (*hers, his,* or *its*). Both researchers attempt to determine whether men and women in their studies use language differently from each other and from their counterparts in the French studies. As with all empirical research, there are many variables to consider—each of which points toward a direction for possible further study. Both Schwab and Stephenson focus on subjects' written responses or utterances rather than on their enunciations of spontaneous speech. Schwab recognizes that cultural contexts and untranslatable linguistic ambiguities may elicit and account for different responses; in this context Schwab notes that university-student and faculty respondents may experience themselves as more empowered linguistically than would a more random population. From this study we might conjecture that language usage reflects the respondent's experience of her or his subjectivity.

The relationship among gender, culture, and language is the arena for investigation in the last chapter of this section. Following Kuang-Chung, Kathleen G. Williamson and Huang Pang contend that "the semantic and structural logic of language reveals how social relations are produced and reproduced." Williamson and Pang further assert that "the expression of identities in vocabulary parallels the realities of social stratification." By breaking down Chinese pictographic characters into morphemes (units of meaning), Williamson and Pang uncover symbols for female and female-related activities that historically have pejorative associations. They note that in Chinese, as in English, "the symbols we use to communicate are marked for gender." Just as the earlier meanings of such historically matched pairs of English terms as *governor/governess* and *mister/mistress* have changed over time, so Williamson and Huang Pang tell us, the Chinese lexicon has changed as well. Tracing the pictographic radicals (elements that indicate meaning) for "female" in a number of terms, Williamson and Pang lead us on an associative trail that verbally reflects the historical circumstances of ancient Chinese women's status. Finding symbols for "female" embedded in characters for "slave" or "evil," Williamson and Pang speculate about the etymology and the contemporary impact of such associations.

Feminists concerned with the intersection of gender, power, and language may disagree about the extent to which grammatical features embedded within the structure or lexicon of a given language reflect or determine historical or contemporary inequities for women and men in a given culture. Whether one believes that we are born into and grapple with a predetermined symbolic order (encoded in language that existed before us, which shapes how we experience ourselves as gendered subjects), or that the language and symbol systems we use reflect our experience and can (or must) be shaped by us to transform the existing order, the intersections of gender, power, and language are important sites for investigating the societal consequences of communication practices of women and men.

REFERENCE

Cameron, Deborah. 1992. *Feminism and Linguistic Theory*, 2nd ed. London: Macmillan.

1

Masculinist Generic Language and the U.S. Woman's Rights Movement, 1850–1920

Lou Ann Matossian

Dictionaries, as well as men, need revolutionizing, that justice be done woman.
(Prentice Mulford, Letter to *The Revolution*, 26 January 1871)

The role of language in women's subordination has been energetically discussed by feminist activists, as well as by scholars in a variety of disciplines, for more than twenty years. Comparatively little attention has been paid, however, to the politics of language in the nineteenth- and early-twentieth-century woman's rights movement. Yet it was these reformers who, after claiming a public voice for women, went on to challenge exclusionary wording in institutional settings —such as religion and law—whenever such language stood in the way of women's advancement. In particular, gaining the right to vote, to enter the professions, or to hold office meant confronting the selective ambiguity of legal terms such as *person*, *man*, and *he*, which routinely excluded women from rights and opportunities while including them in responsibilities and penalties. From Ernestine Rose, who observed that *society* meant the male sex only, to Charlotte Perkins Gilman, who imagined a completely woman-centered language, feminists insisted that women were *people*, in the fullest human sense. In their rhetoric they sought to recast the very terms of American political discourse.

The existence of the generic masculine has posed an active challenge to English-speaking feminists for at least a century and a half. To make this observation is, however, to stake a claim that still needs documenting, since, with few exceptions, feminist studies of language tend not to be historical and most historians do not concern themselves with language as a topic of inquiry.

This essay follows the nineteenth- and early-twentieth-century U.S. woman's rights movement as it contended with just one of many linguistic issues, the interpretation of "generic" language, especially as used in public settings. Because its ambiguity could be and often was used to marginalize women—effectively denying them social and political rights, in particular the right to vote—feminists found themselves engaged in the politics of language as a matter of practical necessity. At first they maintained that the masculine generic should be considered truly generic, that statements such as "all men are created equal" did include women in the scope of humankind. By the twentieth century, however, feminists had come to regard the generic masculine as an expression of what Charlotte Perkins Gilman, as early as 1911, called "our androcentric culture."

THE WOMAN'S RIGHTS MOVEMENT

The interpretation of generic language was made a feminist issue at the second national woman's rights meeting, held in Worcester, Massachusetts, in 1851. One resolution, citing the Declaration of Independence, concluded with the following statement:

[W]e charge that man with gross dishonesty or ignorance, who shall contend that "men," in the memorable document from which we quote, does not stand for the human race; that "life, liberty, and the pursuit of happiness," are the "inalienable rights" of *half* only of the human species. (Stanton, Anthony, and Gage 1881–1886: 826)

Although some feminists were beginning to analyze the position of women in legal writing, others went on to consider sexism in other forms of public language. Ernestine Rose, a noted lecturer originally from Poland, reported that a member of the British Parliament, Mr. Roebuck, had recently advocated voting rights for tenement dwellers. When asked whether his proposal included both sexes, he demurred on the grounds that the "happiness of society" depended on excluding women from the vote. "Society!" exclaimed Rose. "What does the term mean?"

As a foreigner, I understand by it a collection or union of human beings—men, women, and children, under one general government, and for mutual interest. But Mr. Roebuck, being a native Briton and a member of Parliament, gave us a parliamentary definition, namely: *society means the male sex only*. (Stanton et al. 1881–1886: 538)

At the Massachusetts Constitutional Convention in June 1853, Thomas Wentworth Higginson spoke in favor of woman suffrage, citing the state bill of rights. Remarkably, Higginson drew a connection between women's status and the language of daily life.

Politically speaking, in Massachusetts all men are patrician, all women plebeian. All men are equal, in having direct political power, and all women are equal, in having none. . . .
We see the result of this in our general mode of speaking of women. We forget to speak of her as an individual being, only as a thing. A political writer cooly says, that in

Massachusetts, "except criminals and paupers, there is no class of persons who do not exercise the elective franchise." Women are not even a "class of persons." And yet, most readers would not notice this extraordinary omission. I talked the other day with a young radical preacher about his new religious organization. "Who votes under it?" said I. "Oh, (he said, triumphantly,) "we go for progress and liberty; anybody and everybody votes." "What!" said I, "women?" "No," said he, rather startled; "I did not think of them when I spoke." Thus quietly do we all talk of "anybody and everybody," and omit half the human race. . . . Indeed, I read in the newspaper, this morning, of some great festivity, that "all the world and his wife" would be there! Women are not a part of the world, but only its "wife." (Stanton et al. 1881–1886: 251)

RECONSTRUCTION DEBATES

By the end of the Civil War, women's legal status had begun to improve; however, the restrictive word *male* continued to limit their civil rights in every state. Reconstruction introduced a new obstacle: the proposed Fourteenth Amendment, which would introduce the word *male* into the federal Constitution as well. Seeing a threat to nearly twenty years of feminist progress, Elizabeth Cady Stanton and Susan B. Anthony lobbied vigorously against the measure. Their efforts to substitute gender-neutral wording failed, however, as neither party was willing to endorse full civil rights for black women.

Caught in the middle, reformers briefly maintained a single demand for "universal suffrage." By 1869, however, the growing frustration of woman suffragists was evident. Ernestine Rose, who seventeen years earlier had remarked that "society means the male sex only," now warned that once again women's interests were being obscured:

I understand the word universal to include ALL. Congress understood that Universal Suffrage meant the white man only. Since the war we have changed the name for Impartial Suffrage. When some of our editors, such as Mr. [Horace] Greeley and others, were asked what they meant by impartial suffrage, they said, "Why, man, of course; the man and the brother." Congress has enacted resolutions for the suffrage of men and brothers. They don't speak of the women and sisters.

They have begun to change their tactics, and call it manhood suffrage. I propose to call it Woman Suffrage; then we shall know what we mean. . . . I am a foreigner. I had great difficulty acquiring the English language, and I never shall acquire it. But I am afraid that in the meaning of language Congress is a great deal worse off than I have ever been. I go for the change of name; I will not be construed into a man and a brother. (Stanton et al. 1881–1886: 396–397)

THE NEW DEPARTURE

The passage of the Fourteenth Amendment was first regarded as a grave setback for women's constitutional rights. In October of 1869, however, Francis

Minor, an attorney, outlined an argument that the measure had in fact *already* enfranchised women.

The logic behind this "New Departure" relied heavily on Section 1 of the amendment, which declared: "All persons born or naturalized in the United States . . . are citizens of the United States and of the State wherein they reside." American women, being "persons," were therefore citizens, whose "privileges and immunities" states were forbidden to abridge.

WOMAN SUFFRAGE IN THE COURTS: ANTHONY

Susan B. Anthony tested this approach in 1872, when she and about fifty other women registered—and actually cast ballots for president—in Rochester, New York. Arrested and released on bail, Anthony lectured throughout two counties on the theme, "Is It a Crime for a United States Citizen to Vote?" This speech recapitulated every point made by feminists during twenty years of contending with masculinist generics in the law, including the New Departure theory that women were "persons" under the Constitution. Anthony also highlighted the absurdity of sexist language:

[I]t is urged [that] the use of the masculine pronouns he, his, and him, in all the consitutions and laws, is proof that only men were meant to be included in their provisions. If you insist on this version of the letter of the law, we shall insist that you be consistent, and accept the other horn of the dilemma. (Stanton et al. 1881–1886: 635–636)

"There is no she, or her, or hers, in the tax laws," said Anthony. "The same is true of all the criminal laws." Did these not apply to women?

In the law of May 31, 1870, the 19th section of which I am charged with having violated, not only are all the pronouns masculine, but everybody knows that that particular section was intended expressly to hinder the rebels from voting.

(So much for legislative intent.)

. . . Precisely so with all the papers served on me—the U.S. Marshal's warrant, the bail-bond, the petition for habeas corpus, the bill of indictment—not one of them had a feminine pronoun printed in it; but to make them applicable to me, the Clerk of the Court made a little carat to the left of "he" and placed an "s" over it, thus making she out of he. Then the letters "is" were scratched out, the little carat placed under and "er" over, to make her out of his . . . and I insist if government officials may thus manipulate the pronouns to tax, fine, imprison, and hang women, women may take the same liberty with them to secure to themselves their right to a voice in the government. (Stanton et al. 1881–1886: 636–637)

WOMAN SUFFRAGE IN THE COURTS: MINOR

Although many such cases were argued—and lost—at the state level, *Minor v. Happersett*, in 1875, became the only woman suffrage case ever to be heard in the U.S. Supreme Court (88 U.S. 162). This historic decision at last acknowledged that women were indeed "persons" and therefore citizens. Citizenship, however, did not confer suffrage. Some citizens had the right to vote, while others did not. As Joan Hoff has shown, the concept of "second-class citizenship" enshrined in this decision became the basis for "Jim Crow" laws in later years (Hoff 1991: 175).

WOMAN AS "PERSONS": LOCKWOOD

Minor v. Happersett brought to an end all hope of gaining the vote under the Fourteenth Amendment. Over the next several decades, however, other female "persons" challenged the scope of generic terms. A landmark case of 1894 (*In re Lockwood*, 154 U.S. 116) concerned Belva Lockwood, the first woman attorney admitted to the Supreme Court (Hoff 1991: 183). Although she was a "person" licensed to practice law in several states, Lockwood was denied reciprocal membership in the Virginia bar. According to Hoff:

The historical and legal importance of *Lockwood* lies in the fact that the Supreme Court chose to allow states to confine their definition of a "person" to males only. This, of course, was exactly the same question that Anthony had first posed in Rochester, New York, when she had voted in 1872. From 1894 until 1971 [*Reed v. Reed*, 404 U.S. 71], states could maintain that women were not legally "persons" by virtue of this single Supreme Court decision. (1991: 184)

Thus during the two centuries of constitutional history since 1787, the Supreme Court has recognized women as legal "persons" for only forty years.

GRAMMAR AND GENDER

In the decades after the Civil War, journalists and educators also concerned themselves with the masculine generic, as discussions of proper usage became a popular literary pastime. Kenneth Cmiel (1990) has shown that "verbal criticism," as it was then known, was first written by educated gentlemen concerned about the erosion of class distinctions. For this very reason, however, advice on grammar appealed to the upwardly mobile. Using the generic masculine instead of singular *they* was thus promoted as a mark of social status.

At the same time, verbal critics were also interested in improving the English language, and some felt that an entirely new pronoun was needed. Richard

Meade Bache, whose *Vulgarisms and Other Errors of Speech* appeared in 1869, thought it might be "a great convenience" (Baron 1986: 190–216).

Richard Grant White (1868), a newspaper columnist and one of the most prominent verbal critics, took the opposite view. "First, the thing can't be done; last, it is not at all necessary or desirable that it should be done," he wrote in 1868, responding to readers' queries. Speakers "of common sense and common mastery of English" would use *man*, as in the word *mankind*, along with the pronoun *he*. White's tone then turned sarcastic, and explicitly antifeminist. "Any objection to this use of *man*, and of the relative pronoun," he sneered, "is for the consideration of the next Woman's Rights Convention, at which it may be discussed with all the gravity beseeming its momentous significance."

Meanwhile, in the pages of *The Revolution*, a radical feminist newspaper, an alternative "verbal criticism" took shape between 1868 and 1871 (see Rakow and Kramarae 1990 for excerpts). Several contributors discussed the *man . . . he* construction, as in this meditation on Christianity and chivalry:

Let those who boast of the royal position which civilization has given to woman, look for additional light in the very use of the words man and woman. While her name has become the synonym of frailty, fickleness, and levity; a little word of only three letters has been made to embrace in its signification every human being that has ever lived on the planet. In science, literature, and art, *man* is the central word around which the word woman revolves as a mere nebulous satellite. In Holy Writ, also, man is all in all. . . . It is man that fell and man that is to be redeemed, but who ever heard of the fall of woman! . . . How is all this explained? Is it that man and woman are one? Unfortunate[ly] for women, man is always the *one*. (quoted in Rakow and Kramarae 1990: 182–183)

These commentaries, like those of Rose, Higginson, and Stone, are certainly intriguing to us today. How widely such opinions were shared remains an open question, however. Available evidence suggests that the woman's rights movement *as a whole* was never particularly interested in changing the language of daily life. On the other hand, *antifeminists* such as Richard Grant White did occasionally raise the issue as a means of ridicule. As late as 1919, the lexicographer James Fernald could write: "The masculine has stood as the representative gender for a 'time whereof the memory of man runneth not to the contrary,' and that immemorial prescription still holds good, even in this period of militant feminism" (quoted in Baron 1986: 203).

RADICAL VOICES

Toward the end of the century, *The Woman's Bible*, written by Elizabeth Cady Stanton, drew heavily on the religious as well as the political roots of U.S. feminism. As a commentary, rather than a translation, *The Woman's Bible* drew critical parallels between the sexism of Scripture and contemporary American society. For example:

Our civil and criminal codes reflect at many points the spirit of the Mosaic [law]. In the criminal code we find no feminine pronouns: as "He," "His," "Him," we are arrested, tried and hung, but singularly enough, we are denied the highest privileges of citizens, because the pronouns "She," "Hers," and "Her," are not found in the constitutions. It is a pertinent question, if women can pay the penalties of their crimes as "He," why may they not enjoy the privileges of citizens as "He"? (Stanton and the Revising Committee 1898: 74)

Although the radicalism of *The Woman's Bible* was quite alarming to moderate and conservative suffragists, the even more visionary work of Charlotte Perkins Gilman found a ready audience among feminists at large. Gilman often alluded to language issues in her fiction and social theory, particularly in *Herland*, published serially in 1915 (Matossian 1987).

In this novel, set on the eve of World War I, three male explorers discover a feminist utopia, a peaceful and cooperative world of women who reproduce parthenogenically. In exchange for information about the outside world, the men are allowed to tour the country. They also learn the women's language, which, as one might expect, does not use masculine generics. After more than a year in Herland, Van, the most progressive of the men, analyzes the issue as follows:

When we say *men, man, manly, manhood*, and all the other masculine derivatives, we have in the background of our minds a huge vague crowded picture of the world and all its activities . . . of men everywhere, doing everything—"the world."

And when we say *women*, we think female—the sex.

But to these women, in the unbroken sweep of this two-thousand-year-old feminine civilization, the word *woman* called up all that big background, . . . and the word *man* meant to them only male—the sex. (Gilman 1915/1979: 137)

By the end of their stay, recalls Van, "we were now well used to seeing women not as females, but as people, people of all sorts, doing every kind of work."

CONCLUSION

After 1920, as women's legal situation improved, masculinist generic language waned in importance as a feminist topic. Although gender-neutral pronouns were still occasionally proposed, most writers on language were silent about sexism for the next half century. With the exception of Mary R. Beard (1946), not until feminism's second wave was the topic of language and woman's place reinvented, beginning with the masculine generic. By that time, however, few realized what had gone before.

Whether one considers women's efforts to build organizational communication—through public speaking and assembly, literacy and publication—or ponders the social definitions that kept women silent in the churches and denied them a voice in the laws, linguistic issues can be seen to permeate the history of the U.S. woman's rights movement from its inception (Matossian 1990).

REFERENCES

Bache, Richard Meade. 1869. *Vulgarisms and Other Errors of Speech*. Cited in Dennis Baron (1986), *Grammar and Gender*.

Baron, Dennis. 1986. *Grammar and Gender*. New Haven, CT, and London: Yale University Press.

Beard, Mary R. 1946. *Woman as Force in History*. New York: Macmillan.

Cmiel, Kenneth. 1990. *Democratic Eloquence: The Fight over Popular Speech in Nineteenth-Century America*. Berkeley: University of California Press.

Gilman, Charlotte Perkins. 1911. *The Man-Made World: Or Our Androcentric Culture*. New York: Charlton Co.; New York: Johnson Reprint 1971.

————. 1915. *Herland*. Rpt. 1979, New York: Pantheon.

Hoff, Joan. 1991. *Law, Gender, and Injustice: A Legal History of U.S. Women*. New York: New York University Press.

Matossian, Lou Ann. 1987. "A Woman-Made Language: Charlotte Perkins Gilman and *Herland*." *Women and Language 10*(2) (Spring): 16–20.

————. 1990. "Language and Linguistics." In Angela Howard Zophy, ed., with Frances K. Kavenik, *Handbook of American Women's History*, Vol. 696. New York: Garland Reference Library of the Humanities, p. 314.

Rakow, Lena, and Cheris Kramarae. 1990. *The Revolution in Words: Righting Women, 1868–1871*. New York and London: Routledge.

Stanton, Elizabeth Cady, Susan B. Anthony, and Matilda Joslyn Gage. 1881–1886. *History of Woman Suffrage*, Vols. I–III. Rpt. 1985, Salem, NH: Ayer.

Stanton, Elizabeth Cady and the Revising Committee. 1898. *The Woman's Bible*. Rpt. 1974, Seattle: Coalition Task Force on Women and Religion.

White, Richard Grant. 1868. "Words and Their Uses." *The Galaxy 6*: 235–244. Rpt. 1899 in Richard Grant White, ed., *Words and Their Uses: A Study of the English Language*. Boston: Houghton Mifflin.

2

The French Connection: Luce Irigaray and International Research on Language and Gender

Gail M. Schwab

THE THEORIZATION OF FEMALE SUBJECTIVITY

Since the French publication of *This Sex Which Is Not One*[1] in 1977, Luce Irigaray's name has been at the center of the "women's language" controversy. Misunderstandings of her position abound, among both French and nonfrancophone readers, and among feminists and nonfeminists alike. In this chapter, I would like, first, to try to clarify or even to dispel some of these misunderstandings and, second, to put Irigaray's work on language and gender into a perspective through which Anglo-American linguists and communication theorists can begin to familiarize themselves with this body of very important work. I believe it can be a fruitful source of insights into language and gender, and further that the methodology involved can be implemented for new research in English into gender's relationship to language.

One of the few feminist linguists to take Luce Irigaray's work on language seriously is Deborah Cameron. Unlike many anglophone theorists, Cameron appreciates continental feminist theory's dense philosophical grounding, and in her book *Feminism and Linguistic Theory*, she gives quite a good accounting of Irigaray's position in the late seventies.[2] Although Cameron does not seem to be aware of Irigaray's empirical research on linguistic gender—possibly because this aspect of Irigaray's work has not been translated into English—what she has clearly understoood is Irigaray's importance as a philosopher of subjectivity.[3] Following in Jacques Lacan's footsteps, not as an adoring disciple but as one of his most rigorously serious critics, Luce Irigaray addresses the problem of how the individual takes up a subject position, or a subjective position, in a preexisting language, and more generally in a preexisting symbolic order—that is the problem of how the individual comes to occupy a fixed place as a subject "I" who speaks, as opposed to a "you" who is spoken to, or to a "she" or a "he" who is spoken about in the language of others. Subjectivity is a place from which to speak, and to listen. Failure to take up the subjective position in language results in exclusion from the entire symbolic order—that is, not only from language but from society and culture as a whole.

In order for the subject to come into existence, for the space of a subjectivity to be opened up, carved out of the symbolic order, a split must occur. The potential subject must split, distinguish, differentiate itself from its mother, from the mother-child dyad. To accede to subjectivity the child must learn the self/other distinction, and understand its own position in that dichotomy. The experience of images of the body built up during what Lacan calls the mirror stage (ages six to eighteen months),[4] images of the body as a separate, unified, distinct entity, coupled with and verified by the extravisual sensory experience of the body, makes the self/other split possible. According to Lacan, there is no entry into the symbolic without passage through the mirror, through body/self images.

Irigaray differs from Lacan in many ways. In general terms, one might say that, unlike Lacan who relates accession to the symbolic order to the phallus, and thus to male images, Irigaray insists on the specificity of female body/self images, and on the role they play in the *girl's* entry into the symbolic. The hole that opens up in the symbolic as a subjectivity comes into being takes on a particular shape, a "morphology" to use Lacan's and Irigaray's term, and this morphology cannot *not* be related to the sex of the individual body. Irigaray accepts Lacan's premise that male and female children enter language, society, and culture differently—but not his conclusion that this result in both cases from a relation to the Phallus, or to the penis and the threatening possibility of its undergoing castration.

The whole of *Speculum*[5] and of *This Sex Which Is Not One* are critiques of the use in western culture of the phallus, of the male body, of the masculine, as universals. To use Irigaray's own metaphor, western philosophy and psychology have blindsided the feminine. The possibility of any plurality in sexuality or subjectivity has been repressed out of all theoretical discourse, which unquestioningly and monologically sets itself up as universal, as generic. There is one universal truth, one human subjectivity, and one generic sexuality—an oxymoron to be interpreted as meaning that there is only one sex—male. Irigaray does insist that western society as a whole is homosexual, that there is no heterosexuality.[6] The considerable body of Irigaray's philosophic work is strategically calculated to expose the "universal" and the "generic" as the masculine, and then to go one step further and create an alternative, an alternative enabling us to begin to think of female subjectivity and sexuality in positive terms rather than as the negative of male subjectivity and sexuality.

It was precisely in relation to Irigaray's insistence on foregrounding in the female body that many of the misunderstandings surrounding her work on language arose. Her persistence in returning repressed elements of the female body, like the mucous or the placenta, to consciousness, and in downplaying its fetishized parts like breasts or buttocks, her blatant eroticism when describing lingeringly and lovingly the female organs of sexuality, and most particularly, her metaphoric equation of the labia to the lips,[7] inspired intepretations of her work as "biological," as "biology is destiny" inverted and idealized into a glorification of the female body, and its mystical powers of life.

Irigaray was assumed to be a proponent of a utopian "women's language" of irrationality, based on a woman's body and her sexuality. It is not difficult to see why this connection was initially made, particularly in view of the paucity of translated texts available to foreign readers. However, the creation of a mystical women's language does not correspond to what Irigaray was and is doing. What she has done is to demonstrate, both poetically and philosophically, women's exile in language as we currently know it, and to make the claim that accession to a true female subjectivity requires that our use of language be changed, and further that these eventual changes would necessarily transform the entire symbolic order, thus creating a new language and culture, or even more appropriately, new languages and new cultures. She is to that extent linguistically utopian.

WORKING IN AND ON LANGUAGE

The Linguistic Tests

There is no question that the opening up of a place from which to speak as a woman is of paramount importance for Irigaray, and has been one of her principal contributions to feminist linguistic concerns. But it is essential now to recognize that she has not confined her political strategies to philosophical deconstruction. Before Irigaray ever became a feminist theorist she was a psycholinguist and a psychoanalyst. Her initial research, presented in her 1973 doctoral dissertation, *Le Langage des déments* (The language of dementia),[8] and published in various articles appearing in French journals, and finally collected in the 1985 anthology *Parler n'est jamais neutre* (To speak Is never neuter)[9] was in psycholinguistics, and in the construction of models of linguistic performance for pathological populations in whom the linguistic function had been significantly impaired by senility, aphasia or schizophrenia.

Building on their previous research into the relationship between grammatical-syntactical structures and semantico-lexical categories,[10] and using a Chomskian model of transformational grammar, Irigaray and her frequent collaborator, the linguist Jean Dubois, devised a series of linguistic tests designed to simulate the generation of utterances by proposing to respondents cue words on which certain linguistic operations were to be performed according to given instructions. For example, one test instructs respondents to integrate words into a sentence, words chosen precisely to bring into play syntactic, lexical and semantic considerations. For example, the cue words "red-see-horse" can be integrated into a sentence by the respondent in a variety of ways. How does he or she rearrange the given material to form a syntactically correct sentence? Do respondents try to form a subject for their sentence with the first word given, the adjective "red," a rather difficult linguistic operation requiring some thought, or do they pair up the adjective with the noun "horse" and use horse as a subject, or do they add in a noun more appropriately modified by "red" and make it the subject of the sentence? There are many possible solutions. The respondent must also deal with the lexico–semantical problems posed by the cue words. Horses aren't really red, although it would be perfectly correct grammatically to say that you "saw a red horse." If you were particularly sensitive and scrupulous about the semantic content of your response you might perform a negative transformation and say that you "never saw a red horse." Analysis of the data then deals with the way these problems are solved, or in some cases avoided, by the respondents.

Irigaray and Dubois also designed tests to simulate the activity of the speaking subject by instructing the respondent to carry out certain transformations on given linguistic material—for example, asking the respondent to give the opposite of a word or a phrase. This type of linguistic test asks for the opposites of adjectives, like "deep" or "hot," or of verbs like "to love" or "to die." Such words have multivalent meanings, and can often be interpreted either literally or metaphorically.[11] Respondents are usually very much aware that the opposite of "deep" can be "superficial" as in the opposite of "profound," like a deep poem or deep book; or the opposite of "deep" can be "shallow," as in a shallow hole in the ground. How does the respondent disambiguate the cue in order to perform the transformation? How does the respondent form the opposite of a sentence like "He closes the door"? The transformation can take place at the level of the subject—which would give "She closes the door" or, at the level of the predicate, "He opens the door" or, at the purely morphological level, "He does not close the door."[12]

Another test calls for the production of synonyms for potentially ambiguous nouns, like "master," or verbs, like "to live,"[13] and yet another calls for the respondent to define a particular term presenting either a phonological or a semantic ambiguity, for example: "body," "mirror," or "mother."[14] There is in fact a whole battery of tests, each designed to isolate certain characteristics of linguistic performance, but it would be superfluous to explain them all here in this introductory chapter.[15] The linguistic tests are in any case best understood in the context of a corpus and its analysis.[16] The tests I have described are the ones which have most often been used by Irigaray and her collaborators, and are still in use in the ongoing research on gender differences in language.

With this extensive empirical and clinical work behind her, Irigaray went on to publish *Speculum*, and from that point on into the mid- to late-1980s, a period of ten years more or less, she devoted herself to more theoretically philosophical problems of subjectivity. It was in part the violent opposition to these theoretical works that finally decided her, forced her, to return to some of the empirical research she had done previously, and to begin to apply it systematically to feminism. Her empirical research can be seen as a proselytyzing instrument, as well as a response to critics. The linguistic tests described above had produced cogent and persuasive models of linguistic performance for the pathological populations studied. They had already revealed certain gender differences in language use which Irigaray had not initially pursued to any great extent.[17] So when she encountered resistance to the ideas that men and women have different relationships to language, that they use language differently, she understood that she would have to demonstrate their validity, and was well prepared to do so.

She went out and organized a research team to gather data using the linguistic tests and write up conclusions. To date, three conferences, one in Italy and two in France, as well as a seminar at the International Summer Institute of Structuralist and Semiotic Studies in Toronto, have taken place, where members of the international team have shared the results of their work and planned future projects. Two major publications have also appeared: the volume *Le Sexe linguistique*, a special issue of the French journal *Langages*, edited by Irigaray, which has been translated into Italian,[18] and the book *Sexes et genres à travers les langues* (Sex and gender: A translinguistic approach), currently being translated into English.

Models of Data Analysis

What types of models of linguistic gender differences can be constructed using the data gathered in response to the lingustic tests? How can we determine what they have to tell us? There are different types of analytic methods that can be brought to bear on the data at different linguistic levels. For the purposes of this introduction I have isolated three specific levels: (1) the utterance, (2) the enunciation, and (3) the relationships between utterance and enunciation.

Level 1: The Utterance. If the analysis concentrates on the utterance, on the statement produced, a kind of textual hermeneutics can discern differences in the performances of the respondents. This work is taxonomic in nature and consists, when analyzing sentences, in the distribution of the structural parts of speech into different general categories: like positive–negative–neutral, active–passive, animate–inanimate, human–nonhuman, male–female, and so on.[19] Simply stated, subjects are grouped and counted, verbs are grouped and counted, etc., and then classified. This type of analysis can also be practiced on tests calling for single word answers like synonyms or antonyms, and even for tests producing definitions of terms.

I have practiced this type of taxonomic analysis of the utterance extensively, classifying the types of subjects and direct objects, as well as the types of verbs and adjectival expansions, used by respondents in answer to the cue "make a simple sentence using the words 'mother–daughter.'"[20] I cannot re–present my data or my conclusions here at length, but I can affirm that I found many differences between men's and women's use of language in response to this cue, using the interpretive type of analysis. The most salient gender differences emerged in the area of subject choice, men choosing most often the word "mother" as subject, with women showing more variety in subject choice. The respondents' use of direct objects was also illuminating. Men tended to use far more direct objects than women did, with their corresponding active verbs. They also tended to place "daughter" in the direct object position, thus casting the daughter in the role of passive object to be acted upon by a subject, in most cases her mother.

Careful researchers would of course hesitate to draw many firm conclusions from the analysis of one data sample, generated in response to one linguistic test, in one language. My observations, based on a data sample of 287 respondents, the majority of whom were college students from the New York metropolitan area, will undoubtedly strike the reader as isolated and inconclusive, perhaps even idiosyncratic. However, the statistics and conclusions of one researcher become more convincing when corroborated by the statistics and conclusions of others, this being one of the most significant advantages of working as an international research team. The other significant advantage being that methodological oversights and over-hasty conclusions on the part of one member of the team are often rectified in the work of other group members. I am attempting to emphasize that the entire body of the group's research has the weight and "critical mass" lacking in one linguist's analysis of the results of one particular test.

Level 2: The Enunciation. If the enunciation itself is the focus of study, rather than the utterance, linguistic convention generally seems to indicate the use of spontaneously produced corpuses. Can testing for linguistic gender using semi–induced data generated by linguistic tests have any advantages? Can the results it produces justify the loss of the spontaneity and the so–called authenticity of, for example, corpuses of taped conversations? Irigaray frequently used spontaneous taped conversations as source material in her research into the language of pathology. However, she concluded that when the researcher intends to deal specifically with grammar itself, or with certain lexical or semantic ambiguities, it is much more profitable to control and delimit the respondents' output.[21]

Irigaray has written of the psychoanalytic relation between analyst and patient as a source of "pure language," divorced from immediate social and worldly considerations. In psychoanalysis

nothing is authorized but the order of the word. . . . Nothing else will be produced there, at least nothing explicitly permitted. . . . The merciless character of the analytic frame, of its *staging*, requires that everything which is habitually given as the foundation of discourse be suspended, be treated parenthetically: the referent or the communicable object, the coherent statement . . . , etc. With all of this suspended, the functioning of the enunciating machine or manufacture is uncovered.[22]

This "pure language" of psychoanalysis reveals the very mechanism of enunciation to the analyst, who is forced to listen to it, as well as to its content, in order to recuperate the working of the unconscious. The linguistic tests present a similar type of clinical, experimental situation through which to study the production of language at the level of the structures of grammar. In linguistic research the experimentor is not listening for the unconscious of a particular analysand but rather the grammatical structures produced by many different respondents. Obviously two individuals who come face to face, as do researcher and respondent, cannot help but react to each other if only in a minimal way. Respondents, particularly male respondents, will often try to joke or make light of the situation, in order to alleviate the embarrassment of having to respond "on the spot." One might argue, however, that this "minimal reaction" is still in some ways more objective and clinically impersonal than the psychoanalytic situation, because none of the emotional complexities of the transference come into play between linguistic researcher and respondent.

At the level of the enunciation, generative and transformational grammars, applied to the semi–induced data produced by the linguistic tests, can reveal differences in the activity of the speaking subject with respect to the proposed cues. They articulate the types of transformations the cue material undergoes in the process of becoming an utterance. I have not myself yet used this analytic perspective to any great extent, but it is the principle method used by Irigaray herself in her article "Representation and Self–Affection of the Feminine."[23] Using transformational grammar, she discerns multiple differences in the types of transformations used preferentially by men and women, noting in particular that the negative transformation is used predominately by men and that the interrogative transformation is used predominately by women. It would be impossible to re-present her data and arguments here, but I do think it would be useful, in order to illustrate the types of linguistic gender differences brought to light by this method of data analysis, and in fact by the entire research project in general, to summarize some of her conclusions:

1. Women represent far more often the relation to the *other sex*, whereas men remain amongst themselves.
2. Women are in general far more interested in others—this is especially obvious in the much more frequent use of prepositions indicating relations between persons, for example, *with*.
3. Women are far more interested in the question of *place*; they are close to things, to other people.
4. Women are far more interested in the *qualities* of persons, of things, of actions, and their discourse contains many more adjectives and adverbs than men's.
5. Women are more interested in the *present* and *future*; men, in the *past*.
6. Women are more attentive to the *message* sent than men are; they always make an effort to say something, whereas men are stuck in linguistic inertia, unless their message expresses their own states of mind.[24]

Level 3: The Relationship between Utterance and Enunciation. It is possible to study the relationship between the utterance and the enunciation, by pinpointing the relationships of difference and identity between the subjects of the utterance and the subjects of the enunciation. For example, the "I" of the utterance bears a complex relationship to the "I" of the enunication—as anyone knows well who has ever taught a first-person narrative to an undergraduate class. By the same token the "he," "she," or "they" of a third-person narrative bear a complex relationship to the "I" of the subject of the enunciation, and this relationship is very different depending on whether the "I" of the enunciation is a woman or a man. These dynamics also provide insight into the relationships among the speaker, the interlocutor, and the referent. To whom does the "I" of the utterance address him or herself? To a same-sex interlocutor? To an opposite-sex interlocutor? Are they referring to a third party of the same or of the opposite sex? The relationships within the utterance as well as the implied relationships to the subject of the enunciation are very different in each case. The analytic thrust of Katherine Stephenson's "The Possessive, Gender and Subjectivity," also appearing in this volume, is directed mainly at the relationships among the subjects of enunciation and the subjects of the utterance, and this particular level of analysis also seems to be the one Irigaray herself is most concerned with at the moment. It is the predominate analytic method used in her most recent book, *J'aime à toi*, and it was the focus of the presentation she made in Paris in the spring of 1992, and relates directly to her theoretical work on subjectivity. Her latest research, which has confirmed her initial conclusions about linguistic gender, first reported back in 1967, and supported in the 1987 "L'Ordre sexuel du discours," leads her to conclude that men speakers generally represent themselves, or other men, in statements addressed to themselves, or to other men. Women speak of others (mainly male others) as opposed to themselves, and address their discourse to men in the majority of cases. Irigaray, based on her work with obsessives and hysterics, proposes as paradigmatic male statement "I wonder if I am loved" and as paradigmatic female statement "Do you love me?"[25]

- Women seek communication, and particularly dialogue, but they address themselves mainly to him/he who is interested in other things more than in intersubjective exchange, and who is oriented more towards the past than towards the present or the future.
- Men are interested in concrete objects if they are their own (my car, my watch, my pipe . . .), in abstract objects insofar as they are appropriate to men or consecrated by an already existing community of men, in their psychological states, in their genealogical and family problems; they rarely seek dialogue and remain within a vaguely determined collectivity marked by the masculine gender.[26]

CONCLUSION

Much of the feminist work done in English to date on gender and language—work like Robin Lakoff's, Dale Spender's, Cheris Kramarae's, Deborah Tannen's, and the Candace West and Don Zimmerman studies of interruptions—does not deal so much with actual grammatical structures as with pragmatics, the dynamics of conversation—its economy and politics.[27] There have also been a number of studies of phonological gender differences.[28]

This is very important work, but it does not investigate language as a grammatical structural system, and it does not address the problem of gender differences within the system. I would cite here the admirably rigorous, technically linguistic studies in the 1987 Susan Philips, Susan Steele, and Christine Tanz collection entitled *Language, Gender, and Sex in Comparative Perspective* as an exception to the generalization I have just made, noting however that, as the title indicates, much of it does not really deal with English but with other languages—Japanese, Samoan, Mexican, and so on.[29]

This brings up my next, and final point—the international research promised in the title of this chapter. The linguistic tests, properly understood and properly translated, or transposed, can be used across many different languages.[30] It is important to emphasize here the "properly understood and translated." I myself have misunderstood the objective of certain tests and consequently mistranslated them, and then run into trouble in analysis, as has my colleague Katherine Stephenson.[31] There is a whole cultural context, as well as certain untranslatable linguistic ambiguities, which must be taken into account when the tests are applied in different languages. Nevertheless, properly conceived and translated, the tests can produce data that can be compared translinguistically with quite a high degree of efficiency. In the future, given extensive further research in many different languages, we can perhaps envision broad–based models of linguistic gender differences on an international scale.

NOTES

1. Luce Irigaray, *Ce Sexe qui n'en est pas un* (Paris, 1977), translated *This Sex Which Is Not One*, Catherine Porter, trans. (Ithaca, 1985).

2. Deborah Cameron, *Feminism and Linguistic Theory* (New York, 1985), pp. 127–129, 162–173.

3. *Sexes et genres à travers les langues* (Paris, 1990), the first major book-length publication on linguistic gender compiled by Irigaray and the international research team, is currently being translated by Gail M. Schwab and Katherine Stephenson for Routledge.

4. See Jacques Lacan, "Le Stade du miroir comme formateur de la fonction du Je," *Ecrits* (Paris, 1966), pp. 93–100.

5. Luce Irigaray, *Speculum de l'autre femme* (Paris, 1974), translated *Speculum of the Other Women*, Gillian Gill, trans. (Ithaca, 1985). See in particular the first essay, "The Blind Spot in an Old Dream of Symmetry."

6. Irigaray refuses to acknowledge the current sexual norm as heterosexuality, claiming it is based on an exclusively male model, thus homosexual, or rather *hommosexuel*, a pun on the French word *homme*, "man." See "Woman on the Market," in *This Sex Which Is Not One*, pp. 170–191.

7. For the mucous see Luce Irigaray, "La difference sexuelle," *Ethique de la différence sexuelle* (Paris, 1984), pp. 13–25; and Margaret Whitford, "Luce Irigaray and the Female Imaginary: Speaking as a Woman," in *Radical Philosophy 43* (summer 1986): 3–8. For the placenta, see Irigaray, *La Croyance même* (Paris, 1983), also published in *Sexes et parentes* (Paris, 1987), pp. 35–65; Irigaray, "A Propos de l'ordre maternel," in *Je, tu, nous* (Paris, 1990), pp. 45–54; and Gail Schwab, "Mother's Body, Father's Tongue: Mediation and the Symbolic Order," in *Engaging with Irigaray* (New York, 1994), pp. 351–378. For the labia, see Irigaray, "When Our Lips Speak Together," in *This Sex Which Is Not One*, pp. 205–218.

8. Luce Irigaray, *Le Langage des déments* (Paris, 1973). The English title given in the text is my translation.

9. Luce Irigaray, *Parler n'est jamais neutre* (Paris, 1985). The English title given in the text is my translation.

10. See the seminal article with initial results of the research using the tests. Jean Dubois and Luce Irigaray, "Approche expérimental des problèmes intéressant la production de la phrase noyau et ses constituants immédiats," *Langages 3*: 90–125.

11. See Irigaray, *Parler n'est jamais neutre*, pp. 35–36, for the basis for the foregoing discussion of the linguistic tests.

12. Ibid., p. 191.

13. Ibid., p. 197. It should be noted here that these examples are direct translations from the French where phonological ambiguities are present which do not necessarily come into play in English. The English word "master" is a translation of the French *maître*, but *maître* sounds in French like the verb *mettre*, "to put" or "to put on" or "to place." "Master" is, however, an ambiguous word in English, even if not in the same ways as in French. The English "to live" does present some of the same ambiguities of the French *vivre*, because it can be interpreted in the sense of "to be alive" or "to inhabit."

14. As noted above these ambiguities are not always translatable. The English "body," for example, translates the French *corps* but does not exhibit the homophony of the French word which sounds just like *cor* ("horn"). "Body," however, can refer in English to an abstract, metaphorical referent like a "body of knowledge," or to a concrete, literal referent. "Mirror" in English is one possible translation of the French *glace*, which can also mean "ice" or even "ice cream." "Mother" is the English term for *mère*, but the French is ambiguous in that *mère* sounds just like *mer* ("sea") or *maire* ("mayor"). "Mirror" and "mother" can be nouns in English, but they can also be verbs, and are to that extent ambiguous.

15. For further detailed information on the linguistic tests, see in particular the article "Idiolecte ou autre logique" in *Parler n'est jamais neutre*, pp. 189–211 and passim.

16. In this volume see Katherine Stephenson's "The Possessive, Gender, and Subjectivity" for an analysis of a specific corpus.

17. See in *Parler n'est jamais neutre*, "Approche d'une grammaire de l'énonciation de l'hystérique et de l'obsessionnel," pp. 55–68. These results became the basis for Irigaray's study of the language of hysterics and of obsessives reported in "L'Ordre sexuel du discours," *Langages 85* (March 1987): 81–123.

18. *Le Sexe linguistique*, Luce Irigaray, ed. *Langages 85* (March 1987).

19. Irigaray, *Parler n'est jamais neutre*, pp. 35–37.

20. Gail Schwab, "Dialogue et communication entre mères et filles en américain du nord," *Langages 111* (Fall 1993): 58–67. For further discussion in English of the linguistic tests, and for an illustration in English of the "hermeneutic-taxonomic"

method of data analysis, see Katherine Stephenson, "Luce Irigaray: Theoretical and Empirical Approaches to the Representation of Subjectivity and Sexual Difference in Language Use," *Semiotics 1988: Proceedings of the 13th Annual Conference of the Semiotic Society of America* (New York, 1989).

21. Irigaray, *Parler n'est jamais neutre*, p. 105.

22. Ibid., p. 171. My translation.

23. Luce Irigaray, "Représentation et auto–affection du féminin," *Sexes et genres à travers les langues*, pp. 31–82.

24. My translation. Ibid., p. 64.

25. Irigaray, *Sexes et genres*, p. 63, and "L'Ordre sexuel du discours," passim.

26. Luce Irigary, *J'aime à toi* (Paris, 1992), p. 150.

27. This work is rather well known. I will simply reference some of the principle titles. Robin Lakoff, *Language and Women's Place* (New York, 1975); Cheris Kramarae, *Women and Men Speaking* (Rowley, MA, 1981); Dale Spender, *Man Made Language* (London, 1980); Deborah Tannen, *You Just Don't Understand* (New York, 1990); Candace West and Don Zimmerman, "Sex Roles, Interruptions, and Silences in Conversation," *Language and Sex: Difference and Dominance* (Rowley, MA, 1975); Candace West and Don Zimmerman, "Small Insults: A Study of Interruptions in Cross–Sex Conversations Between Unacquainted Persons," *Language, Gender and Society* (Rowley, MA, 1983).

28. Jennifer Coates, *Women, Men and Language* (New York, 1986); and Jennifer Coates and Deborah Cameron, eds., *Women in Their Speech Communities* (New York, 1988).

29. Susan Philips, Susan Steele, and Christine Tanz, eds., *Language, Gender, and Sex in Comparative Perspective* (New York, 1987).

30. It is the hope of Irigaray, and of all members of the research team, that collaborators will come forward to extend the work into non-European languages.

31. See, for example, Katherine Stephenson's discussion of problems with the cue "dress-self-see" in her article "L'Instance visuelle: analyse syntagmatique d'un corpus anglais," in *Sexes et genres à travers les langues*, pp. 117–163.

SELECTED BIBLIOGRAPHY

Cameron, Deborah. 1985. *Feminism and Linguistic Theory*. New York: St. Martin's.

Cameron, Deborah, and Jennifer Coates, eds. 1988. *Women in Their Speech Communities*. New York: Longman.

Coates, Jennifer. 1986. *Women, Men and Language*. New York: Longman.

Irigaray, Luce. 1967. "Approche d'une grammaire d'énonciation de l'hystérique et de l'obsessionnel," *Langages 5* (March). Reprinted in *Parler n'est jamais neutre*.

———. 1974. *Speculum de l'autre femme*. Paris: Minuit. Translated as *Speculum of the Other Woman*, Gillian Gill, trans. Ithaca, NY: Cornell University Press, 1985.

———. 1977. *Ce Sexe qui n'en est pas un*. Paris: Minuit. Translated as *This Sex Which Is Not One*, Catherine Porter, trans. Ithaca, NY: Cornell University Press, 1985.

———. 1983. *La Croyance même*. Paris: Galilée. Reprinted in Luce Irigaray, *Sexes et parentés*. Paris: Minuit, 1987.

———. 1984. *Ethique de la différence sexuelle*. Paris: Minuit.

———. 1985. *Parler n'est jamais neutre*. Paris: Minuit.

————. 1987. "L'Ordre sexuel du discours," *Langages 85* (March): 81–123.

————, ed. 1987. *Le Sexe linguistique. Langages 85* (March).

————. 1990. *Je, tu, nous.* Paris: Grasset. Translated as *Je, Tu, Nous,* Alison Martin, trans. New York: Routledge, 1993.

————. 1990. *Sexes et genres à travers les langues.* Paris: Grasset.

————. 1992. *J'aime à toi.* Paris: Grasset.

Irigaray, Luce, and Jean Dubois. "Approche expérimental des problèmes intéressant la production de la phrase noyau et ses constituants immédiats," *Langages 3*: 90–125.

Kramarae, Cheris. 1981. *Women and Men Speaking.* Rowley, MA: Newbury House, 1981.

Lacan, Jacques. 1966. *Ecrits.* Paris: Seuil.

Lakoff, Robin. 1975. *Language and Women's Place.* New York: Harper and Row.

Philips, Susan, Susan Steele, and Christine Tanz, eds. 1987. *Language, Gender, and Sex in Comparative Perspective.* New York: Cambridge University Press.

Schwab, Gail. "Dialogue et communication entre mères et filles en américain du nord," *Langages 111* (Fall 1993): 58–67.

————. "Mother's Body, Father's Tongue." In Carolyn Burke, Naomi Schor and Margaret Whitford, eds., *Engaging with Irigaray.* New York: Columbia University Press, 1993, pp. 351–378.

Spender, Dale. 1990. *Man Made Language.* London: Routledge.

Stephenson, Katherine. 1991. "Luce Irigaray." In Eva Sartori and Dorothy Zimmerman, eds., *Fifty French Women Writers.* Westport, CT: Greenwood, pp. 22–43.

————. 1989. "Luce Irigaray: Theoretical and Empirical Approaches to the Representation of Subjectivity and Sexual Difference in Language Use." In Terry Prewitt, ed., *Semiotics 1988.* New York: University Press of America, pp. 412–417.

Tannen, Deborah. 1990. *You Just Don't Understand.* New York: Morrow.

Whitford, Margaret. 1986. "Luce Irigaray and the Female Imaginary: Speaking as a Woman," *Radical Philosophy 43* (summer): 3–8.

Zimmerman, Don, and Candace West. 1975. "Sex Roles, Interruptions and Silences in Conversation." In Barrie Thorne and Nancy Henley, eds., *Language and Sex: Difference and Dominance.* Rowley, MA: Newbury House, pp. 105–129.

————. 1983. "Small Insults: A Study of Interruptions in Cross–Sex Conversations Between Unacquainted Persons." In Barrie Thorne, Cheris Kramarae, and Nancy Henley, eds., *Language, Gender and Society.* Rowley, MA: Newbury House, pp. 103–117.

3

The Possessive, Gender, and Subjectivity

Katherine Stephenson

Thanks to feminist criticism and research on language, it is now widely accepted that women and men use language differently. There are, however, substantive differences in American, English, and French theoretical and empirical research on language and gender. As Gail M. Schwab demonstrates in her chapter "The French Connection: Luce Irigaray and International Research on Language and Gender," it is Irigaray's focus on the relationship between language and an always gendered subjectivity that distinguishes her work from anglophone research on language, as well as the international scope of her research project "Différence sexuelle et communication(s)" to more comprehensively explore and document the sexualization of discourse as a cross-cultural phenomenon. The present study is a companion piece to Schwab's chapter detailing the theoretical basis of Irigaray's empirical research on language and gender in that it presents results obtained from the English version of the linguistic survey developed by Irigaray, in which subjects are asked to compose sentences using third person singular possessive adjectives.

The use of the possessive is particularly interesting to study in order to identify how the sexualization of discourse is manifested differently in various languages given that it presents a fundamental difference between Romance and Germanic languages. In Romance languages, third-person singular possessive adjectives and pronouns do not reflect the gender of the possessing subject but rather agree in gender with the noun they modify or replace; for example, "her book" in French is translated as *son livre*, using the masculine form *son* of the possessive adjective as *livre* is a masculine noun. In English, however, since substantives (nouns or word groups used as nouns) have no explicit grammatical gender, possessive adjectives and pronouns are marked by the gender of the subject who possesses rather than by that of the object which is possessed.

This grammatical difference concerning possessives in Romance and Germanic languages offers particular insight into the question of the linguistic representation of subjectivity, a phenomenon to which women have had difficult access in the phallocentric discourses of patriarchal society. Beginning with her work *Speculum of the Other Woman*, Irigaray has demonstrated that, in the West, the subject of truth and knowledge has consistently been "appropriated" by the masculine and presented a masculine view of the self, the other, and the world. Through her deconstruction of the dominant discourses of the Western tradition, she has detailed the relative paucity of resources women have for linguistically representing their sexed subjectivity, given the domination of the masculine gender in language.

Specifically pertinent to this chapter are Irigaray's theories on the difficulty for women in accessing an autonomous female subjectivity representable in language. If we are to look at the linguistic representation of subjectivity, then we must look beyond the subject's use of the pronoun "I," for subjectivity entails the relationship to the self as a constructed identity, and since there is no identity without the other, the relationship to the sexed other is an integral component of subjectivity. To break this down along sex lines, the construction of male identity is based in large part on the development of a boy's relationship to his mother: he is a male other to a female mother, and she, in turn, validates his relationship to the culturally valorized male subject "he."

Female identity, however, is constructed in the "you/I" relation to a mother of the same sex, a sex which is devalorized in its relationship as other to the culturally dominant male. Female identity remains intrinsically tied to the "you/I" relationship originally developed with the mother as, during the acculturation process, the "you" position is taken over by the culturally validated male subject, since there is insufficient representation of a culturally validated "she." Thus subjectivity as a sexed phenomenon is instrinsically tied not only to being able to represent the self as "I" but also in being able to represent the other of the same sex as "he" or "she." The problem for women, then, is insufficient cultural validation of female subjects, in language as well as in society, for the development of an autonomous female subjectivity, that is, development beyond the "you/I" relation so that women can think of themselves as a "she."

As Irigaray indicates in her book *Je, tu, nous*[1] it will take "a transformation of language" in order for women to be able to share equitably sexed rights, and this transformation "can only take place if we valorize the feminine gender once more" (p. 71). For languages like English, however, in which there is no explicit grammatical gender for substantives, it will necessitate a revalorization of everything that is associated with women, the devalorization of which operates at an implicit level in language. But the fact that in English women can "demand equality in relation to the possession of goods," since they can "mark them with their gender" (p. 72), it offers them the possibility of representing a feminine subjectivity in language not only in the use of the feminine subjects "I" and "she" but also in the use of the possessives "her" and "hers."

This appropriation of subjectivity through possession which Irigaray sees as problematic for English-speaking women is the focus of my analysis of data on sentences using the possessive in English. Although I will be treating differences in the responses among men and women, our most common focus in this research, my analysis will concentrate on certain of those aspects of the data which shed light on the representation of feminine subjectivity in language. The database consists of 287 surveys, 158 (or 55 percent) of which were taken by women, and 129 (or 45 percent) of which were taken by men. The majority of test subjects are students from the University of North Carolina at Charlotte and Hofstra University. The remaining subjects are professors at these two universities. All the surveys were given in written format, and an initial analysis of the data was done by computer to isolate statistically significant differences among the responses of women and men using the chi-square test of independence. The cue for the third section of the English version of the survey is as follows:

III. Complete the first part of the sentences below. Choose *one* of the words separated by slashes *by circling it*.

_____	his/her/its dog.
_____	his/her/its child.
_____	his/her/its mother.
_____	his/her/its garden.
_____	his/her/its shoe.
_____	his/her/its book.

The cue induces a response which provides, at minimum, a subject and a verb to precede the given possessive adjective and noun it modifies; for example, for the first sentence, some typically simple responses from the data are "He walks his dog," "He feeds his dog," and "She loves her dog." Furthermore, the cue requires the respondent to deal with question of gender by demanding that one of the possessive adjectives "his," "her," or "its" be chosen for each of the six sentences. The choice of possessive adjective generally leads to the production of a sentence with a gendered subject. However, though the cue induces a gendered subject for sentences using the possessive adjectives "his" and "her," it is possible for the respondent to avoid such a choice through the use of the pronouns "it," "this," or "that," as in the response "It is her child." Avoidance of a gendered subject can also be effected by using a generic noun and the possessive adjective "its," as in the response "The child lost its book." Thus the cue is structured so as to induce responses that show how women and men represent gender in language and allow us to make certain interpretations regarding the linguistic representation of sexed subjectivity.

For the first part of my analysis I concentrate on the choice of possessive adjective, and I include here all uses of "his," "her," or "its," whether the sentences in which they appear follow the cue or not, as they can be interpreted as representing an intentional choice of gender. My statistical analysis of the possessive adjectives respondents used reveals that a large majority of women and men chose "his" and "her" rather than "its," for 70 percent to 80 percent of their answers. Only with the cue word "mother" is there a more significant usage than elsewhere of the possessive adjective "its." There are several explanations for this difference, which merit a brief summarization: (1) It is easier semantically to use "its" with the cue word "mother" because we can talk of animals having mothers (e.g., "The kitten loves its mother") but not of animals as having dogs, children, gardens, shoes, or books. (2) The generic nouns "child" or "baby" have a much stronger association with "mother" than with any of the other cue words, as in the response "A child loves its mother." (3) Given the order of the words in the cue, with "it" as the third possessive adjective listed and "mother" as the third cue word, respondents who wanted to use "its" at least once in this section, whether to avoid "his" or "her" or to allow for an equal distribution in their choice of gender, could logically have chosen to do so with "mother" given its position. The χ^2 test of independence, however, seems to indicate that the order of the cue words did not significantly influence the choice of possessive adjective.

Looking at how women and men used "his" and "her," there is a pattern that emerges across the six sentences. Although men chose most often the possessive adjective "his" for an average of 39 percent, women chose "her" for an average of 51 percent. Thus women used the possessive adjective marked by their gender 12 percent more than did men, the percentages for men's use of "his" ranging from 28 percent to 49 percent of total possessive adjectives used, and those for women's use of "her" ranging from 42 percent to 60 percent. The women's percentages are higher because they consistently used "her" about one and a half times more than "his," except with the cue word "shoe," where there is an equal usage of "her" and "his" (42 percent). Though men used "his" also on an average of one and half times more than "her" for four of the cue words, they actually used "her" more often than "his" for the cue words "child" and "book." Thus, women clearly used "her" the most often, whereas men used "his" most often for four cue words, and "her" most often for two. The averages for use of the possessive adjective marked by the opposite gender are also revealing. While women on the average used slightly more "his" than men did "her"—women's usage of "his" averaging 34 percent and men's usage of "her" averaging 32 percent—there was a considerably wider margin among women in their usage of the two possessive adjectives: women used "her" 17 percent more than they used "his," whereas men used "his" only 7 percent more than they used "her." A general characterization would be that in men's responses there was more of an alternation among the three possessive adjectives "his," "her," and "its" than in women's responses.

Looking at the percentages in the order of the six cue words, men's highest percentages were "his" for "dog," "her" for "child," back to "his" for "mother"—but with a second-place split between "her" and "its" in which men used three times as many "its" as with any other cue word—"his" for "garden," "his" for "shoe," and "her" for "book." Women, however, always used "her" at least as often as the other possessives and, with five out of the six cue words, from 7 percent to 34 percent more than "his." Furthermore, women used "her" the most often in the first two sentences, with "dog" and "child," indicating a conscious choice of the feminine possessive adjective in spite of the listed order of the possessive adjectives—which presents "his" first—or the meanings of the cue words, since "dog"—the first cue word—certainly has no special association with women. Thus although more of the men seemed to be concerned with a relatively equal distribution between "his" and "her," and occasionally "its," the majority of women clearly opted for using "her," a pattern that indicates that the women were committed to representing feminine subjectivity through marking nouns by the feminine possessive adjective.

I also did a statistical analysis of possessive adjective use which did not include incorrect usages of "his," "her," or "its" as possessive pronouns, multiple possessive adjectives within a sentence, or the use of a possessive adjective with a word other than the cue word. This analysis breaks down the usage of possessive adjectives with the cue word according to the latter's grammatical function in the sentence as either subject, direct object, object of a preposition, predicate noun, or object of a possessive phrase.

The majority of the cue words are used most often as direct object by men and women, with two exceptions which I will treat presently. This usage as direct object is influenced by the cue format, which directs respondants to complete the first part of a sentence ending with the cue words, although any other grammatical usage except that of subject would also be possible. Typical responses for the six cue words are "She loves her dog," "I watched her child," "She respected her mother," "He waters his garden," "The baby lost its shoe," and "She reads her book."

The first exception to the most common usage of the cue word as direct object must also be considered as being induced by the cue. Women and men used the cue word "garden" most often as the object of a preposition—usually the preposition "in"—in sentences like "He works in his garden" and "That woman has flowers in her garden." The other exception, however, is in direct contradiction of the cue format.

Women used the word "mother" most often as subject, whereas men used it most often as direct object. This difference, which could be described as a distinction between an active female subject represented more often by women and a passive female object represented more often by men, corresponds to one found in a previous study I did of another section of this survey,[2] which found that women respondents used "mother" in sentences that characterized her as an active subject whereas men used "mother" in sentences that characterized her as a passive subject.

This exception also reflects one of the few relatively large differences among the responses of women and men. After the most frequent usage of the cue word as direct object, the second most frequent grammatical position chosen by women is that of subject, whereas for men it is that of predicate noun (e.g., "It is his dog"). Although the predicate noun, linked to the subject as it is by the verb "to be," functions as a synonym or mirror of the subject, it amounts to a representation of subjectivity at a second degree. Moreover, these sentences most often represent a simple, almost mechanical response of the type "It's her dog," "That's his mother," more common among men's responses than women's. The fact that women used the cue word modified by a possessive adjective as subject in all six sentences much more often than men—two to four times more than men—and used them as subject one and a half times more often than men used them as predicate nouns, indicates a tendency on the part of women to focus more on the subject than the predicate, on representing subjectivity linguistically. Moreover, women used "her" most often with these subjects (15 percent "her" versus 11.7 percent "his").

The extensive usage of the feminine possessive adjective and the frequent use of subjects marked by the feminine possessive adjective manifest an effort to represent feminine subjectivity in the relationship between the object possessed and the subject who possesses. However, Irigaray demonstrates in her book *Je, tu, nous* that in order for women to gain "access to a status of individual and collective *subjectivity* that is valid for them as women" we must put an emphasis on "the difference of rights between male and female subjects" instead of on "equal rights in relation to the possession of goods" (pp. 72–73). The fact that in English the mark of "gender is expressed in subject-object relations" (p. 72) through the use of possessive adjectives can lead American women to be satisfied with this "appropriation" through possession, and to "abandon their right to denote gender in relation to the subject" (p. 72). I therefore did a statistical analysis of all the grammatical subjects used by women and men to compare their use of a subject marked by their own gender. These subjects include the pronouns "she" and "he," feminine and masculine nouns such as "woman," "sister," "boy," and "man," male and female proper names, and the pronoun "I." The percentages for women and men are generally the same: women used feminine subjects an average of 35 percent of the time and men used masculine subjects an average of 34 percent of the time, a difference of only 1 percent. However, when you add to the feminine and masculine subjects the use of possessive adjectives with a noun subject, the percentages increase to 46 percent of subjects marked by the feminine for women and 40 percent of subjects marked by the masculine for men. Women's greater usage of subjects marked by their own gender than men was not at the expense of women's usage of subjects marked by the opposite gender, however, for women used 28 percent of masculine subjects compared with men's usage of 24 percent of feminine subjects.

The breakdown of these subjects reveals another interesting difference between women's and men's responses. Although there is only an average 1 percent difference in women's and men's use of subject nouns (4 percent vs. 5 percent) and proper names (2 percent vs. 1 percent) marked by their own gender and in their use of the pronoun "I" (5 percent vs. 4 percent), men used the pronoun "he" 24 percent of the time to women's use of "she" 20 percent of the time. The most pronounced difference is in the use of possessive adjectives, with men using a subject noun modified by "his" only 6 percent of the time compared with women's usage of one modified by "her" 15 percent of the time. Thus, women relied much more on the possessive adjective to represent their subjectivity than did men; women used the pronoun "she" only 5 percent more than a subject modified by the possessive adjective "her" whereas men used "he" four times more often than a subject modified by "his." Women also relied much more on the possessive adjective to represent male subjectivity than men did to represent female subjectivity: women used a subject noun modified by "his" 12 percent of the time compared with men's usage of one modified by "her" only 5 percent of the time. Although one might argue that the cue influenced these choices through its requirement of the use of a possessive adjective, these statistics are for the subject of the sentence whereas the cue induced usage of the possessive adjective with an object, either of the verb or a preposition. Thus these results would seem to validate Irigaray's fears that in Germanic languages women may tend to appropriate subjectivity more through possession, through subject-object relations, than through assumption of an autonomous subjectivity.

In conclusion, these statistics seem to show that the majority of women respondents didn't hesitate to represent a feminine subjectivity in sentences produced from a cue where the choice of gender is the focus. Given this choice, the male respondents, who used the feminine possessive adjective in percentages close to those for their use of the masculine, but also used the neuter more often than women, seemed to opt for a more relatively equal, though still somewhat hierarchical, distribution of gender than women. But when this same choice was given to women, they chose the feminine in the highest percentages and used subjects marked by the feminine most often. This tendency on the part of the women respondents to foreground feminine subjectivity seems to reinforce the results of a previous study,[3] where I found that other American women respondents represented feminine subjectivity through the use of the pronoun "I" much more often than French women respondents. Indeed, Irigaray's analysis of the French women's responses revealed the deployment of numerous strategies on their part to avoid saying "I." However, though this analysis of the section on the possessive indicates a marked tendency on the part of the American women surveyed to choose the feminine more than the masculine, or the neuter, when specifically given a choice of gender, it remains to be seen whether they would exhibit a general tendency to spontaneously represent most often a feminine subjectivity in other circumstances. It is the hope of our research team that analysis of other aspects of the responses[4] and of other survey cues will shed light on such questions. Nevertheless, I feel that one can conclude from the present analysis that the American women of this study, the majority of whom are university students it must be remembered, are conscious at some level of what is at stake in equally representing the feminine in patriarchal society and of their responsibility concerning that representation.

NOTES

An earlier version of this paper in French was presented at the conference "Genres culturels et interculturels," organized by Irigaray at the Centre National des Recherches Scientifiques in Paris, France, June 1992, as the second biannual conference of the international research project "Différence sexuelle et communication(s)." For tables of responses and breakdown of statistical analyses, see this author directly. This work was also supported in part by funds from the Foundation of The University of North Carolina at Charlotte and from the State of North Carolina.

1. Luce Irigaray, *Je, tu, nous: Toward a Culture of Difference*, trans. Alison Martin (New York: Routledge, 1993). Originally published as *Je, tu, nous: pour une culture de la différence* (Paris: Grasset, 1990).

2. Katherine Stephenson, "Luce Irigaray's 'L'Ordre sexuel du discours': A Comparative English Study on Sexual Differentiation in Language Use," *Semiotics 1987*, ed. Terry Prewitt (New York: University Press of America, 1988), pp. 257-266. This study includes, among others, an analysis of responses to the cue "Make a single, very simple sentence with the words 'house-mother,' 'table-mother.'"

3. Stephenson, p. 265. The analysis of the use of the pronoun "I" treats responses to the cue "Make a single, very simple sentence with the words 'red-see-horse,' 'dress-self-see,' and 'bore-say-him/her.'"

4. See chapter 2 in this volume by Gail M. Schwab, "The French Connection: Luce Irigaray and International Research on Language and Gender," for examples of other survey items and their analysis.

4

Chinese Sexist Language, Behavior, and Cultural Attitudes*

Kathleen G. Williamson and Huang Pang

The everyday world in which the members of any community move, their taken-for-granted field of social action, is populated not by anybodies, faceless men without qualities, but by somebodies, concrete classes of determinate persons positively characterized and appropriately labeled. And the symbol systems which define these classes are not given in the nature of things—they are historically constructed, socially maintained, and individually applied. (Clifford Geertz *The Interpretation of Cultures: Selected Essays*, 1975: 363-64)

Language is a mediator between physical conditions and the superstructure of human society (Kuang-Chung 1988: 136). In sociolinguistics, the adherents of the Sapir/Whorf hypothesis have been interested in the connection between language structures and human social behavior. For Sapir the "real world" is generally constructed unconsciously upon the language conventions of a group. Through linguistic expression we realize the arrangements between classifications of individuals and groups. The semantic and structural logic of language reveals how social relations are produced and reproduced. Language provides the infrastructure of interpretation and, consequently, forms the foundation of culture (Kuang-Chung 1988: 139).

Geertz posited that a distinctive trait of ideology is its dualism: the virtuous "we" opposed to the evil "they" (1975: 197). Lévi-Strauss (1963) submitted that human societies segregate their semantic worlds into bifurcated "culture and nature" binary oppositions. "Culture" refers to something accepted whereas "nature" refers to what is rejected (Kuang-Chung 1988: 140). The exterior manifestation of this deep binary structure can be subsumed under various differing categories: sacred/worldly, superior/subordinate, masculine/feminine, external/internal, and so on. Lévi-Strauss called this capacity for perceiving

---

realities in binary opposition "the universal structure of the human mind" (1963).

Binary opposition, however, is consistently manufactured in discourses of power. Nature is perceived through culture; "nature" is invariably described and defined by the dominant "culture," just as "female" is always defined by the dominant "male."[1] Kuang-Chung uses a broad definition of ideology not limited to political agendas but, rather, one that is more inclusive by accommodating various spheres of human action. He does not conceptualize the notion of "ideology" as the traditional product of politics. "As a process in which various meanings are reproduced by the established order," Kuang-Chung writes, "ideology should hence be seen as a mental set toward the world in which certain sign systems are privileged as necessary" (1988: 133). As in the Geertzian tradition, he also puts heavy emphasis on language. Kuang-Chung relies on Louis Althusser, who presents ideology as "a representation of the imaginary relationship of individuals to their real conditions of existence" (as cited in Kuang-Chung 1988: 134).

In fact, language should not be dismissed simply as the medium of our thought, it is thought itself. . . . It [language] is the means with which we express, experience, and structure the world as lived by us. Above all, the study of language enables us to transcend and uncover the unconscious "rationality" underlying people's acts and thoughts, which have been denied any worthwhile evaluation, to see how it operates in the process of meaning production. (Kuang-Chung 1988: 135)

The expression of identities in vocabulary parallels the realities of social stratification. The vocabulary of a language system provides evidence of culturally appropriate gender roles and behaviors. Semantic features are related to the cultural and social matrices they represent. The English language contains an overabundance of references to women as objects that relate sexually to men. These appear constantly in terms which are specialized, pejorated, and metaphorically extended for the purpose of objectification and subordination (Schulz 1975).

Likewise in Chinese, we see a long stable history of a written pictophonetic vocabulary revealing cultural values degrading women, despite a display of revolutionary attempts in this century to disband sexist institutions. The traditional and contemporary ideographic language continues to maintain obvious dysphemisms regarding women's role in society.

Written Chinese has been in the hands of a privileged few for thousands of years. The earliest extant representatives of Chinese scripts are from about 2000 BCE; the first large set of examples, preserved mostly on oracle bones and shells, comes from the time (about 1400 to 1200 BCE) when the writing system had basically reached its final stage of development.

There is clearly a relationship between the system's classification and description of source features; the encoding into pictures is necessarily inspired by the unique cultural process which perceives and evaluates the source.

Although the Latin alphabet and script units were ultimately allocated more or less to phonemes, the one-to-one correlation between character script units and meaningful Chinese linguistic units is that between characters and morphemes. Chinese script is pictographic in origin but has not developed as completely ideographic or pictographic due to the inclusion of symbolically associative phonetic characters. This morphemic writing is a stable system historically because the morphemic is a level of language that develops and changes a great deal more slowly than the phonemic system. In its present form, Chinese is older than any modern European script. "Morpheme awareness" in Chinese, which in the West is limited to those who are interested in etymology, is common for the literate Chinese (Kratochvil 1968: 157). Chinese tradition is projected into the morphemic script, the authority of which continues to operate as an essential part of the cognizant language behavior of the literate speakers (Kratochvil 1968: 162).

Basic spoken Chinese pronouns are not obligated to distinguish gender (Chao 1972, 1976). This would appear to be the ideal answer for the centuries old gender-neutral debate that continues in English (Bodine 1975; Wolfe 1980). Studies of the English language have found, however, that generic terms such as "adult" and "child" are loaded with reference to the unmarked male (Wise and Rafferty 1982). This suggests that language may be so ingrained with a convention of inferred masculine referents that even the presumably neutral words now in fashion ("person," "adult," "they," "he," or "she") may result in masculine inferences. The problem is not merely misunderstood referents for language (as in double meaning for "man") but also results from the greater dominance and presence of males throughout our culture and history.

Western feminists should not assume that Chinese culture is more gender egalitarian because of the neutral pronoun in spoken Chinese language. Although we know of no studies regarding inferred referents of gender neutral terms in Chinese languages, other aspects of Chinese sociolinguistics inform us of a language system expressing a sexist, if not misogynistic, culture.

Cultural attitudes about gender differences, subordination, and the legitimated lower social status of women are revealed in the morphemic symbols. If language, at the least, is a correlative factor of culture and thought (the minimum proposition of Whorf) or, more likely, is a cybernetic causative factor in evolving culture-thought, then the spoken language of Chinese must be considered as it rests on the symbology and logic of the written language. Consider the following characters, each containing the pictographic radical for "female."[2] It is important to note that there is a different radical for "human" and no radical that signifies "male."

female 女

1. Nu 奴   slave

2. Bi 婢   slave, maid

3. Ji 嫉   jealous

4. Du 妒   mutual jealousy (between women)

5. Ji 妓   sing-song girl, prostitute

6. Gou 媾   (sexual) intercourse

7. Jian 姦   rape

8. Jian 奸   wicked, evil

9. Pin 姘   extramarital or nonmarital sexual affair

10. Fu   woman, wife

   original form 婦   female 女

   simplified form 妇   broom 帚

11. Qi 妻   wife—original meaning: children of a slave

12. Yao 妖   evil

13. Fang 妨   harmful, to abstract

14. Biao 婊   prostitute

15. Lan 婪   greedy, repacious

16. Chang 娼   prostitute
                                     original form: 倡

17. Piao 嫖   go whoring

18. Xie 媟   disrespectful behavior

19. Mei 媚   appearance of a base person

20. Xian 嫌   suspicious, dissatisfaction

21. Bi 婆   easy to be mad

22. Wang 妄   chaos, false blame

1. *Nu* means "slave." On the early bone inscriptions, this meant slave exclusively. Later, during the Sung or Yuan Dynasty (tenth century), this character also became the traditional word for the female "I" first-person pronoun. The written language is symbolically a different language than spoken Chinese with its ungendered pronouns. Li (1988) posits that the assertive English "I" has a foreign effect on female language users since they are psychosocially blocked from the confident stance that this first person pronoun suggests in a double standard culture.[3] This English language instance is infinitely subtle in comparison to the Chinese female "I/Slave."

2. *Bi* means "slave" and/or "maid." Both *Nu* and *Bi* meant "offender" in ancient Chinese law (700 BCE to 200 BCE). Under that historical jurisdiction, if a man committed a crime, his wife and children would be seized and marketed as slaves.

3. *Ji* means "jealous," with the radicals for "woman" and "disease" (literally, "women's disease").

4. *Du* is "mutual jealousy" between women. "Intramammary abscess" was originally represented by *du* because it was believed that jealousy caused "blocked energy."[4]

5. *Ji* is also a character for "beautiful girl": a "sing-song girl" who pleased people with her singing and dancing. This term degenerated to signify "prostitute" or "whore."

6. *Gou* is the classical form for "intercourse." Note that the radical which symbolizes "human" is not a part of this ideograph. The three radicals here represent "interchange," "female," and "hoe." What is intended is that woman, like the field, is passive and meant to be cultivated.[5]

7. *Jian* signifies "rape." Here we see the radical for "female" three times. Other meanings include "selfish," "excessive" or "loose behaviors," "robber" or "rob," and "false." Ancient Chinese law had a crime called *jianfei*, which referred to the commission of sex out of wedlock.

8. *Jian* is interchangeable with the previous *jian*. The common character of the former is "wicked," "evil," "traitor," "self-seeking," and "wily."

9. *Pin* is the character for "extramarital or nonmarital sexual affair."

10. *Fu* means "woman" or "wife." The left side is the radical for "female" and the right is the radical meaning "broom." Also, according to the oldest Chinese dictionary,[6] the original character for "woman" in the inscriptions on bones and shells represented a female kneeling with a broom in her hand. This character communicates that a woman is a servant by her nature. Furthermore, the pronunciation of the character is the same as the spoken word meaning "service." In traditional households, women were required to remain unseen and unheard. Chinese language was not even equipped with a vocative with which to designate or address a female conjugal partner. In traditional Chinese, a man tended to use the term *neiren*, meaning "inside-the-house-person," when referring to his wife. Women employed *nanren*, "male person," to indicate a definite "my man" or "my husband." The comparable term, *nuren* ("female person"), did not identify a specific person; it could mean wife or a number of women including concubines, mistresses, or prostitutes (Hong-Fincher 1987). Interestingly, *furen* is a modern corruption of an ancient vocative for wives of high status men. Classic Confucianism defines the term: *furen* means "one who follows a gentleman" (Hong-Fincher 1987). The character for this *fu* morpheme is "one who elevates the gentleman/husband to the heavens."

11. *Qi*, for "wife," is a character which originally meant the "children of a slave."

12. *Yao* means "evil." Something abnormal and which harmed people was called *Yao*. Derivative words include: *Yaoyan*, "evil words," and/or "harmful words"; *Yaofen*, "evil environment"; *Yao shu*, "evil trick"; and *Yao mo*, "evil ghost."

13. *Fang* in ancient times was a verb; now people use it as an adjective describing "harm/ful" or as the verb "to abstract" (meaning an intentional act to confuse, slow down or block somebody: as in *fangai* "you abstract me").

14. *Biao* is a common word for prostitute.

15. *Lan* means "greedy" or "rapacious."

16. *Chang* is a "prostitute" or a person who makes a living by selling sex. The character is the common way of writing "娼," which used to designate "prostitute." The older version has the radical for "human," which may be referring to a historical time when prostitution had been performed by people of both sexes. Currently, people

prefer to use the character with the female radical, as it is socially more prohibitive for a man to become a prostitute.

17. *Piao* means to "go whoring," as in a man "visiting prostitutes," which is considered the most intolerable of carousing activities, such as drinking and gambling. Such a man is regarded as thoroughly despicable. However, note the use of the female radical to represent this verb.
18. *Xie* is "disrespectful behavior" and/or "indecent."
19. *Mei* is "the appearance of the base person."
20. *Xian* means "suspicion," "dissatisfaction," and "hatred."
21. *Bi* is defined as "easy to be mad" or "the appearance of a frivolous person."
22. *Wang* signifies "chaos," "false blame," and "illegally."

CONCLUSION

Sexism is not unlike chauvinistic ethnocentrism, racism, or nationalism. Judge the structural and discursive similarities in the manufacture of hegemonic sexism while reading the following excerpt from Kuang-Chung on chauvenistic ethnocentricism:

Being related to ethnocentricism chauvinism is the glorification of one's own group along with fear and hatred of others. Such conceptions reveal that either the group, or its collective consciousness as an "ism," is not a fixed category or entity, but a process within which people live and represent their experience through interaction and signification. . . . Despite the positive/negative ideological feelings of these secondary evaluations, in its very basic essence what is "inside(r)" is determined by its "outside(r)" in an unconscious manner. (1988: 132)

The most widespread and continuous social formation we have seen in human history is the barbarous political stratification which subordinates women. The Chinese written language provides evidence of a sexist campaign which has continued unabated for at least 4,000 years. With this paper, we have attempted to awaken and instigate the reader to suspect and challenge the status quo of the debilitating chauvenism expressed in everyday language.

NOTES

The authors thank Lisa Otey, Dr. Banisa St. Damian, and Dr. Susan U. Philips for their help and guidance with this project and paper.

1. Kuang-Chung also suggests that Lévi-Strauss's studies "need to be extended and tested in considering the thinking of other societies, especially those with a sophisticated tradition of written 'history.' In simple societies, people tend to binarize their vision of the world in the model of natural species, while in complex societies, cultural products are used instead as models of projection. Simply claiming this structure of human mind is 'universal' cannot hold without examining different cultures such as Chinese society. . . . Lévi-Strauss hesitated to apply this structure to Chinese

civilization because such an old and complex culture may not possess a totalizing structure . . . the polarized Culture/Nature binary becomes insufficient to account for highly developed and complex societies" (Kuang-Chung 1988: 141). With the ancient and enduring binary yin/yang cosmology in Chinese philosophy, physics, medicine, and law, it would appear that Kuang-Chung has fallen subject to the chauvinistic ethnocentrism he descried. It should also be noted that, despite a critical analysis of ethnocentrism and binary oppositions, Kuang-Chung, along with many Chinese scholars and linguists that precede him, is guilty of sex-based writing, using "man" and "he" in every case. Yuen Ren Chao wrote in the fifties when androcentrism was less questioned. Kuang-Chung is writing in 1988. It would seem that the Chinese male academic writers consistently and persistently ignore the female inclusion of neutral inference in their writings, something I believe is symptomatic of the cultural syndrome outlined in this paper.

2. Examples belonging to a pictophonetic character with one element indicating meaning (a radical) and the other pertaining to a sound are *biao*, *chan*, and *piao*. Examples of characters belonging to associative compounds, which are formed by combining two or more radicals, each with a meaning of its own, to create a new meaning are *ji*, *jian*, and *fu*.

3. Virginia Woolf examined the seemingly gender-netural pronoun "I" for usage by women of the English language. The presence of Chinese ideographic dysphemisms would seem to magnify this phenomena for Chinese women:

Indeed, it was delightful to read a man's writing again. It was so direct, so straightforward after the writing of women. It indicated such freedom of mind, such liberty of person, such confidence in himself. . . . But after reading a chapter or two a shadow seemed to lie across the page. It was a straight dark bar shaped something like the letter "I." (Woolf, *A Room of One's Own*, cited in Li 1988: 504).

4. One Chinese medical belief is that within the human body there are twelve routes along which energy circulates. When the route is blocked, energy cannot penetrate and will cause the ill part of the body to either swell or fester.

5. The passivity of the female is represented in English by the omission of the female; although there is a countless proliferation of words representing intercourse, all are neutral (e.g., to have sex, to have intercourse, to have an orgasm), or necessitate male subjects (e.g., ejaculate, rape, plow, bang, screw, nail, shove it to her), maintaining the role of the human male as an aggressive warrior who masters a woman in sexual conquest (Wolfe 1980). The negative insinuations of terminology like "emasculate" and "effeminate" expose the rank of traits allocated to the woman's role. Chinese behavioral and linguistic attitudes toward women are reflected in the expression "Fuck your mother!" which is employed in situations (for instance, when someone hammers their thumbnail) where English speakers might say "Shit!" or "Goddamn it!"

6. Shuowei Jiezi, first Chinese dictionary, written by Xu Shen during Northern and Southern Dynasties (AD 420–581).

REFERENCES

Bodine, Ann. 1975. "Androcentrism in Prescriptive Grammar: Singular 'They,' Sex-indefinite 'He,' and 'He or She.'" *Language in Society* 4(2): 129–146.
Chaika, Elaine. 1982. *Language: The Social Mirror*. Rowley, MA: Newbury House.

Chao, Yuen Ren. 1972. *Mandarin Primer: An Intensive Course in Spoken Chinese*, 6th ed. Cambridge, MA: Harvard University Press. (Originally published in 1948.)

————. 1976. *Aspects of Chinese Sociolinguistics*. Stanford, CA: Stanford University Press.

Fenn, Henry C., and T. Gardner Tewksbury. 1967. *Speak Mandarin: A Beginning Text in Spoken Chinese*. New Haven, CT: Yale University Press.

Fisk, William R. 1985. "Responses to 'Neutral' Pronoun Presentations and the Development of Sex-Biased Responding." *Developmental Psychology 21*(3): 481–485.

Fromkin, Victoria, and Robert Rodman. 1988. *An Introduction to Language*. Chicago: Holt, Rinehart and Winston.

Geertz, Clifford. 1975. *The Interpretation of Cultures: Selected Essays*. London: Hutchinson.

Hanquin, Fang. 1983. "Social Changes and Changing Address Norms in China." *Language in Society 12*(4): 495–507.

Hong, Beverly. 1985. "Politeness in Chinese: Impersonal Pronouns and Personal Greetings." *Anthropological Linguistics: Exploring the Languages of the World 27*(2): 204–213.

Hong-Fincher, Beverly. 1987. "Implications of the Changing Status of Women in Modern Standard Chinese Terms of Address." In Donald C. Laycock and Werner Winter, eds., *A World of Language: Papers Presented to Professor S. A. Wurm on His 65th Birthday*. Australia: Pacific Linguistics, pp. 265–273.

Huang, Parker Po-fei, and Hugh M. Stimson. 1976. *Spoken Standard Chinese* (Vol. I). New Haven, CT: Yale University Press, Far Eastern Publications.

Kratochvil, Paul. 1968. *The Chinese Language Today: Features of an Emerging Standard*. London: Hutchinson University Library.

Kuang-Chung, K. C. Chen. 1988. "Nation, Nationalism, and Ideology Reconsidered." *Studies in Symbolic Interaction 9*: 127–144.

Lévi-Strauss, Claude. 1963. *Structural Anthropology*. New York: Basic Books.

Li, Charles N., and Sandra A. Thompson. 1979. "Third Person Pronouns and Zero-Anaphora in Chinese Discourse." In Talmy Givon, ed., *Discourse and Syntax (Syntax and Semantics 12)*. New York: Academic Press, pp. 311–335.

Li, David Leiwei. 1988. "The Naming of a Chinese American 'I': Cross-Cultural Sign/ifications in *The Woman Warrior*." *Criticism 30*(4): 497–515.

Schulz, Muriel. 1975. "The Semantic Derogation of Woman." In Barrie Thorne and Nancy Henley, eds., *Language and Sex: Difference and Dominance*. Rowley, MA: Newbury House, pp. 64–75.

Wang, William S-Y. 1982. *Human Communication: Language and its Psychobiological Bases: Readings from Scientific American*. San Francisco: W. H. Freeman.

————. 1982. "The Chinese Language." In Wang, *Human Communication*, pp. 53–62.

Wise, Erica, and Janet Rafferty. 1982. "Sex Bias and Language." *Sex Roles 8*(12): 1189–1196.

Williamson, Kathleen G. 1992. *Pronouns in Mandarin Chinese*. Unpublished paper, University of Arizona, Tucson.

Wolfe, Susan J. 1980. "Constructing and Reconstructuring Patriarchy: Sexism and Diachronic Semantics." *Papers in Linguistics: International Journal of Human Communication 13*(2): 344–388.

Part II

Gender and the Image

Literary and visual images, like words and grammatical structures, are symbols that can be "read," texts and cultural artifacts to which readers and spectators respond and from which we attempt to attribute meaning. In the previous section we explored some ways in which the communication of language users may be affected by gendered assumptions embedded or inscribed within language systems. In the next two sections we turn our attention to the receivers of messages. The contributors to the sections examine the messages about gender and power that they uncover as they deconstruct images located in novels, cartoons, film, and television.

As readers, listeners, and spectators addressed by a variety of cultural artifacts, we need to be aware of which images are present and which are missing from the texts we encounter. What subtle demonstrations of power lead to the presentation of hegemonic interests of dominant groups (i.e., men, heterosexuals, persons of European background, etc.) as though they are normative, while images of women and other marginalized groups are excluded or represented stereotypically? Are female and gay and lesbian characters absent, or represented only in depictions that trivialize or ridicule their concerns, and so reinforce a heterosexist patriarchy? Silences and absences tell us much about both the values and rhetorical strategies of artists, novelists, filmmakers, and the discursive structure in which they operate (for example, popular novels, magazines, or Hollywood films). As Barry Brummett (1994) notes in *Rhetoric in Popular Culture*, "Power is the ability to control events and meanings" (p. 4). The contributors in this section demonstrate ways to interrogate images as "resisting" readers or spectators, uncovering values and ideologies implicit in the texts, and thus constituitive of some of its possible "meanings."

Sylvia Bailey Shurbutt's chapter serves as a bridge between this and the previous section. Shurbutt's investigation of the work of writer Zelda Fitzgerald raises important questions about the "ownership" of images as she recounts ways in which Zelda Fitzgerald's writings, even in her personal diary, were seen by her husband, F. Scott Fitzgerald, as his property to be employed in his own writing. As Shurbutt reads the corpus of Zelda Fitzgerald's work, she "reads it against" the context of Zelda's life and the Fitzgeralds' tumultuous marriage, helping us to see how the crafting of language into fiction is an act that occurs within a social and political context in which the words of women and the words of men have been valued unequally.

Patricia A. Brieschke discusses Cynthia Ozick's novel *The Cannibal Galaxy* and explores how a reader's identification with the male and female characters in the novel leads her to interrogate the gendered values characters embody. In the act of reading, Brieschke notes how "questions of sexual asymmetry, dominance, and hierarchy differences in language, subjectivity, and identity are inscribed, represented, and reproduced in this novel." She examines the position of a reader addressed by the text.

Phyllis R. Randall's study of the presence and absence of female images in the cartoons published in the *New Yorker* reveals that in 1990 (the year she examined), the urbane, sophisticated worldview constructed by the cartoonists and editors of the *New Yorker* (by way of their selection process) was still deeply sex-role stereotyped. Images of women, their occupational options, and the arena in which women were depicted were still largely restrictive. Those representations of women that did appear on the pages of the *New Yorker* frequently tended to trivialize women's attempts at assertion or independence, subjecting these to ridicule. Randall's research points to the paucity of images of women, the limited contexts in which images of women were located, and the ways in which mainstream and misogynist values are reified in the name of comedy.

Michael P. Kelley also examines the presence and absence of images of marginalized groups in popular culture; his chapter focuses on depictions of lesbians and gay men in mainstream film. Kelley explores the dearth of images of homosexual characters in loving, supportive relationships coupled with the portrayal of gay men and lesbians as murderous and pathological characters in Hollywood films. Although in recent years several low-budget and independent films such as *Priscilla, Queen of the Desert, Go Fish,* and *The Incredible Adventures of Two Girls in Love* have been released, Hollywood films, for the most part, continue to present homosexuality as aberrant. As Brummett (1994) notes, "The empowerment and disempowerment of whole groups of people occurs bit by bit, drop by drop, in the moment-to-moment experiences of popular culture" (p. 76).

REFERENCE

Brummett, Barry. 1994. *Rhetoric in Popular Culture.* New York: St. Martin's Press.

5

Writing Lives and Telling Tales: Visions and Revisions

Sylvia Bailey Shurbutt

Words have long been credited for their power to mold and subvert our lives, for their ability to create the myths and visions of possibilities that shape our lives. The patriarchal establishment has jealously guarded access to the written word, aware of the particular power that printed language has in creating "reality"—hence the traditional hostility toward women who presumed to tread into such sacred territory as "publication." Hawthorne's ruing of that damned bunch of "scribbling women writers" is perhaps the most famous example of male anger toward presumptuous women writers.

Women have always been uniquely aware of the power of the printed word; and women writers, from Amelia Lanier to Virginia Woolf, have made a concerted attempt to rewrite or revise the myths and to seize for themselves the language that constructs and reconstructs the lives of women. The process is called "revisionist mythmaking," and one can discern a sizable portion of nineteenth- and twentieth-century women's writing as an attempt to revise and reconstitute those tales, legends, and stories by which we live our lives. British writer Margaret Drabble (1977) has her poet-protagonist Jane Gray in *The Waterfall* (a revisionist work in which Drabble dramatizes her ideas about the difficulties of female authorship) lament the damaging effect of an androcentric literature which has created many of the myths that misguide our lives: "I blame Campion," says Jane, "I blame the poets, I blame Shakespeare" (p. 92).

In *Writing a Woman's Life*, Carolyn Heilbrun (1988) asserts that we can "only retell and live by the stories we have read or heard. We live our lives through texts" (p. 37). Language, she continues, "may be read, or chanted . . . or come to us, like the murmurings of our mothers, telling us what conventions demand. Whatever their form or medium, these stories have formed us all; they are what we must use to make new fictions, new narratives" (p. 37). In other words, what the woman writer must learn to do, according to Hélène Cixous (1976) and *écriture féminine*, is to "write her self" (p. 881). In this chapter I examine the process of creating and recreating myths through language and how some revisions of those myths have been attempted by nineteenth- and twentieth-century women writers, writers who saw the unique potential and power of language to shape human lives.

It would first do well to look at the creative process in the writer/artist, as defined by Harold Bloom (1973), a process that Bloom calls "revisionist rereading." Gilbert and Gubar (1979) have analyzed Bloom's practice of "applying Freudian structures to literary genealogies" in exposing and articulating the creative process in writers. Bloom's paradigm is one of historical relationships between "father and son"—the Oedipal struggle of one poet's "warfare with his 'precursor,'" the son's rejecting or "rereading" the language and myth of his literary father and revising and refining it into a new mythic vision. A prime example would be the Romantic generation's reaction against their neoclassical predecessors. Bloom's model for the creative process is interesting and helpful, but Gilbert and Gubar question this model: if the paradigm is defined in terms of a "crucial warfare of fathers and sons, . . . [w]here, then, does the female poet fit in?" (p. 47). They answer the question by asserting that the woman writer "does not 'fit in.'" Indeed, according to Gilbert and Gubar, Bloom's "male-oriented theory" of what he calls the "anxiety of influence" has no application to the woman writer, nor can her creative process be explained in reverse Freudian terms of an Electra complex; hers is less a revolt from her female literary predecessors as it is an attempt to discover some (p. 48). Specifically, Gilbert and Gubar define the driving force behind female creativity as an "anxiety of authorship" rather than an "anxiety of influence":

And just as the male artist's struggle against his precursor takes the form of what Bloom calls revisionary swerves, flights, misreadings, so the female writer's battle for self-creation involves her in a revisionary process. Her battle, however, is not against her (male) precursor's reading of the world but against his reading of *her*. In order to define herself as an author she must redefine the terms of her socialization. Her revisionary struggle, therefore, often becomes a struggle for what Adrienne Rich has called "Revision—the act of looking back, of seeing with fresh eyes, of entering an old text from a new critical direction . . . an act of survival." (p. 49)

Thus we come to the process of revisionist mythmaking in the writing of women: their masking, encoding, and subversive use of language in order to create—or recreate—themselves through words; and in so doing, they are able to create not just of a literature of their own but a mythic life of their own.

Annette Kolodny, in "A Map for Rereading: Gender and the Interpretation of Literary Texts" (1985), suggests that the vast majority of women's writing of the past be reread, that readers—male and female—embark upon a "revisionist rereading" of this important literary heritage in order to appreciate more fully the woman writer's use of language and the unique contexts of her life which she expresses through often subtle and sometimes masked use of language. Kolodny uses as an example of such "rereading" of women's texts the current feminist interpretation of Charlotte Perkins Gilman's "The Yellow Wallpaper," which for years was interpreted as gothic horror in the tradition of Poe. Such misreading is less likely when we are aware of the revisionist intent of women writers like Gilman. Kolodny despairs of such "terrible confessions" as Norman Mailer's, "I have nothing to say about any of the talented women who write today. . . . I do not seem able to read them" (pp. 59–60).

Alicia Ostriker explains in "The Thieves of Language: Women Poets and Revisionist Myth-making" (1989) how that "rereading" which Kolodny speaks of can be accomplished. She asserts, "Women writers have always tried to steal the language . . . throughout most of her history, the woman writer has had to state her self-definitions in code form, disguising passion as piety, rebellion as obedience. Dickinson's 'Tell all the Truth but tell it slant' speaks for [women] writers who in every century have been inhibited both by economic dependence and by the knowledge that true writer signifies assertion while true woman signifies submission" (p. 315). Thus, by reconstituting traditional images employed by patriarchal literature (for example, "water" or "earth" as employed in Kate Chopin's *The Awakening*) and by seizing traditional myths which shape the visions and possibilities that we imagine for ourselves, the woman writer can create a more compatible literary landscape, one more in line with her own reality as "she" sees it rather than as her literary fathers see it. The female writer, Ostriker continues, "simultaneously deconstructs a prior 'myth' or 'story' and constructs a new one which includes, instead of exclud[es], herself" (pp. 315–16). Specifically, Ostriker explains revisionist mythmaking in this way:

Whenever a poet employs a figure or story previously accepted and defined by a culture, the poet is using myth, and the potential is always present that the use will be revisionist: that is, the figure or tale will be appropriated for altered ends, the old vessel filled with new wine, initially satisfying the thirst of the individual poet but ultimately making cultural change possible . . . old stories are changed, changed utterly, by female knowledge of female experience, so that they can no longer stand as foundations of collective male fantasy. Instead . . . they are corrections; they are representations of what women find divine and demonic in themselves; they are retrieved images of what women have collectively and historically suffered; [and] in some cases they are instructions for survival. (pp. 316–318)

What are some of the revisionist attempts by women writers, attempts to seize the language and myths of the patriarchy and recast into a form which empowers the female rather than debilitates her? One has only to open the pages of any standard anthology (and happily today they do contain works by women) to find such examples—some obviously revisionist, such as Mary Shelley's recasting of the misogynistic intent of *Paradise Lost* in *Frankenstein*, some more subtly revisionist such as Jane Austen's rewriting of the standard gothic horror story in *Northanger Abbey*.

Austen (1817), whose fascination with the subtleties of language is well documented, was also aware of the question of literature's creating a "reality" greater than reality, of language creating images and myths more potent than real life: "How are [you] . . . to understand the tenour of your life," questions Henry Tilney of Catherine Morland in *Northanger Abbey*, without those words which shape life?" (pp. 48–49). The way Austen deals with this issue is to allow her heroine to revise or rewrite that most popular of literary genres, one destined to make swooning, helpless victims of its heroines and of its (principally female) readers—the gothic romance. As Austen "redefines" or "rewrites" the gothic tale, she reveals in the process that Catherine is trapped not necessarily inside General Tilney's abbey but inside his "fiction of her"—a fiction that she is a wealthy young heiress suitable as a match for his son and the novel's hero, Henry Tilney. One reason Catherine becomes obsessed with the story of the dead Mrs. Tilney is that she sees her own image in that of the general's deceased wife; in searching for and constructing a fiction for Mrs. Tilney, Catherine will discover one for herself as well—a fiction or "literature of her own" distinctively different from that which the men in the novel have constructed for her or which fill the pages of the conventional gothic romance. Thus Austen's purpose for writing *Northanger Abbey* goes further than mere satire of the gothic genre, conventional interpretation of the story: she takes the gothic genre and recasts it as a vehicle for self-discovery for the heroine—a heroine attempting to create or "write" her own story.

Although the twentieth century has given us a diverse range of women writers whose works have been in the revisionist mold—from poets like H. D., Sylvia Plath, and Adrienne Rich, to novelists like Margaret Drabble—one of the most poignant and intriguing revisionist women writers is Zelda Fitzgerald, whose novel *Save Me the Waltz* is her attempt to create a literary life of her own and to revise the archetypal heroine that her husband, F. Scott Fitzgerald, was creating in such novels as *The Great Gatsby* and *Tender Is the Night*.[1] What makes Zelda Fitzgerald's example so interesting is that both she and Scott were simultaneously writing "her story" in 1931—she while recuperating at Johns Hopkins from a breakdown, and he while struggling to pay the bills mounting from those breakdowns.

Zelda's is the classic example of what Carolyn Heilbrun refers to as the most crucial attempt at revisionist mythmaking—the process of "writing a woman's life." Heilbrun agrees with Nancy Miller, who writes in *Subject to Change: Reading Feminist Writing* that the "plots of women's literature are not about life" but rather about the "plots of literature itself, . . . [about] rendering a female life in fiction" (Heilbrun, 1988, p. 45). Zelda's brief efforts to become an author—to become the artist rather than the work of art—can be looked at precisely in these terms.

From the beginning hers was not calculated to be an easy road to author-ship. Even her own daughter admitted that the men in Zelda Fitzgerald's life did not make it an especially easy or comfortable experience: ". . . she was the classic 'put down' wife," writes Scottie Fitzgerald Smith in the introduction to her mother's *Collected Writings* (1991), whose literary efforts were thwarted by her "male chauvinist husband (except that authors are the worst kind, since they spend so much time around the house)" (p. v). Nonetheless, for twelve years, from 1922 until 1934, Zelda Fitzgerald managed to produce a small but in many ways exquisite body of writing, much of her short fiction published under joint byline or under Scott's name, though Scott meticulously credits her authorship in his *Ledger*. When Scribner's agreed to publish, under her own name, *Save Me the Waltz*, Zelda's only finished novel, a clause was added to the contract designating half the royalties toward Scott's debts (Milford, 1970, p. 226); for this, Zelda's major published work, she realized the heady sum of $120.73 (Milford, 1970, p. 264).

Save Me the Waltz is a touching *Kunstlerroman* (narrative of an artist's "becoming") about a young woman's finding an identity separate from that of her famous artist husband and about her own journey into the world of art as she attempts to make herself into a dancer.[2] The book also records heroine Alabama Knight's attempt to create her own story, to write or "play" her own life rather than to follow the script created by father or husband David (the Dick Diver/F. Scott Fitzgerald of the story). To a friend who remarks to Alabama that she is as "good as a book," the heroine replies: "I am a book. Pure fiction." "Then who invented you?" the friend questions, and Alabama's blithe answer belies the fact that it has now become her painful task to create herself (Fitzgerald, 1991, p. 70).

As Alabama and David wend their way through a series of adventures in Paris and the Riviera, it is clear that David adores her more as an appendage, a beautiful decoration, than as the complex person she is: he displays her to friends and acquaintances as if she were "one of his pictures," Zelda writes (p. 138). It also becomes clear that David has no interest in encouraging her to discover a sense of self apart from him: he insists that a woman's place is "with the wine" (p. 78). Yet David is not blind to the hollowness of her position. On a night he returns from an unchaste interlude, the night Alabama tells him that she is going to become a dancer—a goal he cannot take seriously—it is David who articulates the dimensions of her life with him: "I understand," he says, "It must be awful just waiting around eternally" (p. 112).

Although the novel possesses a lushness of imagery that is reminiscent of Scott's writing, *Save Me the Waltz* is written in a style and with a use of language distinctly different from his. Often the language is full and sensuous with the detail of a pre-Raphaelite painting. Describing the exquisite Mediterranean setting as David and Alabama begin a southern holiday, Zelda's prose is finely tuned to the lushness of the landscape and the richness of its antiquity (pp. 71–72). At other times the style is broken and disjointed like a surrealist canvas.[3] When Alabama is overcome by the pain of blood poisoning, her career brought to a halt, Zelda's prose is fractured and halting:

Nebulous weeds swung on the current . . . [and] crows cawed from one deep mist to another. The word "sick" effaced itself against the poisonous air and jittered lamely. . . . "Sick" turned and twisted about the narrow ribbon of the highway like a roasting pig on a spit, and woke Alabama gouging at her eyeballs with the prongs of its letters. (p. 180)

Always, however, Alabama's story is told in a rich and fragmented style, like the chaotic bits and pieces of a woman's life divided between work, family, and love—or between the reality of her actual world and the male artist's fantasy or fiction of her world.

When Scott learned that Zelda had written a novel drawing from their shared experiences, he was furious accusing her of "appropriating" *his* material destined for his current manuscript *Tender Is the Night*. It also galled him that she had finished the work in just three months, whereas he had agonized over his book for seven years (blaming the distractions and delays on her illness). He ordered her editor to consult him first before going any further with publication of her book (Fitzgerald, 1991, p. 199) and complained: "Turning up in a novel signed by my wife as a somewhat anemic portrait painter with a few ideas lifted from Clive Bell . . . puts me in an absurd [and] Zelda in a ridiculous position. . . . [M]y God, my book made her a legend and her single intention in this somewhat thin portrait is to make *me* a non-entity" (pp. 3–4). Yet Scott conceded that Zelda's talent was real and that hers was a good novel, perhaps a "very good novel" (p. 4). Zelda defended herself with touching eloquence, writing to Scott that she did not wish to interrupt his work for her own slight efforts: "I did not want a scathing criticism such as you have mercilessly—if for my own good given my last stories, poor things" (p. 467).

In the year following publication of Zelda's book, she and Scott were in therapy at La Paix with Dr. Thomas Rennie, of the Phipps Clinic. From their candid discussions with Rennie of their problems, a 114-page transcript of their conversation was produced by a stenographer; it is a telling account of their troubles and gives some insight into the different versions of Zelda's story that both she and Scott would produce. Scott is very defensive and blames Zelda for the fact that he has not been able to publish a novel for eight years. He admits, "It is a perfectly lonely struggle that I am making against other writers who are finely gifted and talented. You are a third rate writer and a third rate ballet dancer." Zelda responds, "You have told me that before." Scott continues, "I am a professional writer, with a huge following. I am the highest paid short story writer in the world. I have at various times dominated—" and Zelda interrupts: "It seems to me you are making a rather violent attack on a third rate talent then" (Milford, 1970, pp. 272–273).

Scott's version of Zelda's story, as most are aware, is markedly different from her own, and it is important to emphasize that not only did he utilize their shared experiences and discuss at length his stories with her during their composition,[4] he appropriated her words as well—through her letters and diaries—not only for *Tender Is the Night* but for *This Side of Paradise*, *The Beautiful and the Damned*, and many of his short stories (Milford, 1970, p. 35).[5] For the *New York Tribune* in April 1922, Zelda herself points to this particular habit Scott had of borrowing her words; her tone is light, but the meaning is clear:

It seems to me that on one page I recognize a portion of an old diary of mine which mysteriously disappeared shortly after my marriage, and also scraps of letters which,

though considerably edited, sound to me vaguely familiar. In fact, Mr. Fitzgerald . . .
seems to believe that plagiarism begins at home. (Fitzgerald, 1991, p. 388)

It is important also to note that Scott was determined to render his version
of "Zelda" not only in his novels and stories but in real life as well. Scott used
up a good deal of his energy writing copious accounts and personal analysis of
Zelda's mental problems for her various doctors (Milford, 1970, p. 253). What
is more, Scott was convinced that his version of Zelda was the only true one;
writing to a friend shortly after one of her confinements, he confesses: "In an
odd way, perhaps incredible to you, she was always my child . . . my child in a
sense that Scottie isn't. . . . I was her great reality, often the only liaison agent
who could make the world tangible to her" (p. 308). Milford points to the importance of Scott's controlling the women in his life, noting that in 1940 he was
simultaneously at the helm for mistress, wife, and daughter: "Scott, at the same
time he advised Scottie, was making plans for Zelda, and forming what Sheilah
Graham has called their 'College of One,' setting out to give Miss Graham a
liberal education based upon carefully drawn lists of recordings, books, and
paintings. In this Scott revealed a penchant for making Galateas of his women"
(p. 347).

To read the letters and the novel of Zelda Fitzgerald is to be touched by the
poignancy of her and Scott's dilemma. In the end, when family and mental
stability seemed beyond her reach, all she asked was to be able "to work"
(Milford, 1970, p. 257). More than anything, she wished approval and validation as an artist from the man she most admired in the world: she wrote to Scott
in the fall of 1930, when he had phoned to praise something she had written,
that she was "heavy with happiness" (Fitzgerald, 1991, p. 458). In the end,
however, husband and doctors won the battle over whether she would discover
the artist within herself. Zelda writes to Scott in March 1934 that she was not
trying to transform herself into a "great artist or a great anything." She
continues that she does what interests her but if he wished her to "give up
everything," she would "do so willingly" (pp. 470–471). Ironically Zelda began
a new novel after Scott's death, *Caesar's Things*, finishing only seven chapters
before she died, like Brontë's mad Bertha, in an asylum fire on March 10, 1948.

What Zelda Fitzgerald (and so many women writers before her) attempted
to do was to seize the language and create her own story or "fiction"—rather
than continue to be the fiction itself, fiction as conceived by an androcentric
literature and language. If she failed to become the artist she wished, she did at
least succeed in rendering her own story with a language that was uniquely hers
and a style distinct from her husband's. Perhaps the vehemence with which
others resented her seizing her story as her own resulted from her too direct, too
honest retelling. If she chose not to wear a mask and not to achieve her ends
through indirection, as so many women writers before her had done, one can
only applaud Zelda's effort, while lamenting the sacrifice of her sanity she had
to offer as tribute. Gilbert and Gubar (1979) have written of the lamentable
necessity for women writers to employ the mask in their fiction: "For the

woman writer . . . concealment is not a military gesture but a strategy born of
fear and disease" (p. 74). Employing the paradigm and metaphor of Milton's
rebellious daughters—the Mary Shelleys and Emily Brontës of literary history—Gilbert and Gubar posit the choice of the woman writer either to submit
docilely to male myths about women or, figuratively speaking, to rewrite
"*Paradise Lost* so as to make it a more accurate mirror of female experience.
This way of coping with Miltonic patriarchy is the modus operandi chosen by
. . . the woman [writer] . . . who teaches herself the language of myth, the
tongue of power, so that she can reinvent herself and her own experience while
seeming innocently to read to her illustrious father. . . . [Thus she] produces a
palimpsestic or encoded artwork, concealing female secrets within male-
devised genres and conventions" in order "to write" her own life (p. 220).
Certainly, Carolyn Heilbrun (1988) has articulated an important idea when she
asserts, "There will be [real] narratives of female lives only when women no
longer live their lives isolated in the houses and [in] the stories of men" (p. 47).

NOTES

An earlier version of this paper, titled "Creating a Woman's Life Through Words: A
Language of Their Own," appeared in *Women and Language 17*(1) (spring 1994): 38–
42. © 1994 *Women and Language*. Reprinted with permission of publisher.

1. Dale Spender delivers a severe indictment of F. Scott Fitzgerald in her brilliant
and energetic work *The Writing or the Sex? or Why You Don't Have to Read Women's
Writing to Know It's No Good* (1989).

2. In her own failed search for the artist in herself, Zelda Fitzgerald first worked as
feverishly as her fictional character Alabama to turn herself into a ballerina. Indeed on
September 23, 1929, she was invited to join the San Carlo Opera Ballet Company and
school in Naples, where she was offered a dance solo in *Aïda* as her debut. As Milford
reports, "It was Zelda's chance and it was not such a bad one, but inexplicably she did
not take it. Scott never acknowledged that Zelda had come this close to a serious career
as a ballerina" (pp. 156–157).

3. Zelda created some extraordinary and critically praised paintings in the surrealist
style, enjoying her own one-woman show in 1942 at the Museum of Fine Arts in
Montgomery (Milford, 1970, p. 369).

4. Scott candidly confided in a 1921 magazine interview: "I married the heroine of
my stories. I would not be interested in any other sort of woman" (Milford, 1970, p. 77).
Scott's friend Alexander McKaig recorded in his diary Zelda's influence on the actual
composition of his stories: "Fitz confessed this evening at dinner that Zelda's ideas
entirely responsible for 'Jelly Bean' & 'Ice Palace.' Her ideas largely in this new novel
[*The Beautiful and the Damned*] . . . She is without doubt the most brilliant & most
beautiful young woman I've ever known" (Milford, p. 81).

5. George Nathan remembered that he thought Zelda's diaries so extraordinary that
he wished to publish them and spoke with Scott about doing so. Scott replied that he
"could not permit" their publication because "he had gained a lot of inspiration from
them and wanted to use parts of them in his own novels and short stories" (Milford,
1970, p. 71).

REFERENCES

Austen, Jane. 1972. *Northanger Abbey*. New York: Penguin Books. (Originally published posthumously in 1817.)

Bloom, Harold. 1973. *The Anxiety of Influence*. New York: Oxford University Press.

Cixous, Hélène. 1976. "The Laugh of the Medusa." Keith Cohen and Paula Cohen, trans. *Signs 1* (summer): 875–893.

Drabble, Margaret. 1977. *The Waterfall*. New York: Popular Library.

Fitzgerald, Zelda. 1991. *The Collected Writings*. Matthew J. Bruccoli, ed. New York: Charles Scribner's Sons.

Gilbert, Sandra M., and Susan Gubar. 1979. *The Madwoman in the Attic: The Woman Writer and the Nineteenth-Century Literary Imagine*. New Haven, CT: Yale University Press.

Heilbrun, Carolyn. 1988. *Writing a Woman's Life*. New York: Ballantine Books.

Kolodny, Annette. 1985. "A Map for Rereading: Gender and the Interpretation of Literary Texts." In Elaine Showalter, ed., *The New Feminist Criticism: Essays on Women, Literary, and Theory*. New York: Pantheon Books.

Milford, Nancy. 1970. *Zelda: A Biography*. New York: Harper and Row.

Ostriker, Alicia. 1989. "The Thieves of Language: Women Poets and Revisionist Myth-making." In Showalter, *The New Feminist Criticism*.

Spender, Dale. 1989. *The Writing and the Sex? or Why You Don't Have to Read Women's Writing to Know It's No Good*. New York: Pergamon Press.

6

Reading Our Selves in *The Cannibal Galaxy*

Patricia A. Brieschke

I have written about Cynthia Ozick's *The Cannibal Galaxy* before, from the perspective of a teacher who uses literature to study and teach about school administration.[1] I am intrigued by this rare, compelling, accessible novel about a man who administers a Jewish day school and his relationship with a woman who writes scholarly books. In the story a male administrator is outwitted by a woman at his own game. Principal Joseph Brill is defeated by two women, mother and daughter, Hester and Beulah Lilt, who triumph over a patriarchal educational system. This is the triumph of ideology and methodology over a traditional male perspective and value system. More subtly, I am drawn to this story of split consciousness, where the apparent binary opposition of male/female—the desire for autonomy and authenticity versus the desire for intimacy and love—is explored in all its wild contradictions through the characters of Hester and Joseph.

My first two readings of the novel preceded the search for theoretical ways to think about reading a text. Without any theoretical framework, during a relatively naive and unschooled reading, unexpectedly a flood of connections from my own personal preoccupations with human relationships came together in the characters of Hester Lilt and Joseph Brill. My perceived self, expressed along conspicuously male and female poles, a new awareness of the contradictions and tensions of this polarity, and my preoccupation with uniting these presumed oppositional elements suddenly were illumined in this slim, dense, elegant novel.

A GENDERED READING

I wondered, What might an explicitly feminist reading of *The Cannibal Galaxy* uncover? At first this seemed like a sacrilegious project. I had encountered the sensibilities, feelings, ideas, creation, and vision of another woman—the author—revealed to me through my own selves. My smatterings of knowledge about historical criticism, reader response theory, psychoanalytic theory, and others only increased my pleasure, allowing multiple spheres of meaning and understanding as I encountered recognition of my experience of dual consciousness in fictive reality. However, I'm also aware that Ozick has spoken and written about her work in the context of Judaic culture and traditions, speculating on the possibility of creating an endogenously Jewish culture, in part through a new kind of literature, a "liturgical" Jewish literature. She has even considered the art of fiction writing as a Jewish calling, never a feminist calling.[2] The tensions in her work between the antirational and rational are associated with Jewish mysticism, the religious imagination, and the magic of the Kabbalah, not with a feminine or feminist consciousness.

Ozick is a Jewish writer who happens to be female. She is not, by her own definition, a woman writer or a feminist writer. How she sees herself and her work *does* influence how I read her texts,[3] even if such knowledge is extrinsic to the text. Knowledge is a filter, inviting particular interpretations, obscuring others. Still, if feminism is about improving the situation of women in the world, and if a feminist interpretation of text might simply mean exploring the human reality of woman's life, then *The Cannibal Galaxy* can be considered a feminist text.[4] Ultimately, Ozick's concern is reparative—repair of the world through recognition of the intrinsic value of both women and men, the source of which Ozick locates in the Torah.

One might say that there is nothing overtly feminist about this novel: there is no discernible intent to end the subordination of women; no explanation of the essential "truth" of female experience; no abstract model of gendered identity or invitation to link the text to everyday life practices in the hope of affecting social change; not even the basis for an academic feminism with rigorous intellectual analysis. Yet the novel fulfills Rita Felski's broad definition of feminist literature in that it reveals "a critical awareness of women's subordinate position and of gender as a problematic category."[5] And subtly developed in the characters of both Beulah and Hester Lilt is a theory of resistance.

The term *gender* is used to stand for the social, cultural, and psychological meaning imposed upon biological sexual identity. In *Sea Changes*, Cora Kaplan states that "a feminist literary criticism that privileges gender in isolation from other forms of social determination offers us a similarly partial reading of the role played by sexual difference in literary discourse, a reading bled dry of its most troubling and contradictory meanings."[6] Yet questions of sexual asymmetry, dominance and hierarchy, differences in language, subjectivity, and identity are inscribed, represented, and reproduced in this novel. The Jewish, the European, and the cross-cultural experiences provide context for gender considerations.

A feminist aesthetic that posits a privileged relationship between femaleness and literary structure or style, or attempts a reductionist feminist analysis of the relationships between gender and literature, is a disservice to Ozick, *The Cannibal Galaxy*, and women. Concerned primarily with my own sense making, I'm approaching this text not as a critic or theoretician but as a reader—a reader with shifting polar voices or identities seeking clarification or enlightenment through an inter-textual dialogue with the novel.[7] This readerly stance has led me to a vast subtext of feminist thought in the novel that emerges beyond the author's stated conscious deliberate intentions, outside of all reviews, critical analyses, or scholarly interpretation of the novel, and simultaneous with other social, psychic, political, and cultural contexts. These meanings become available through a variety of textual juxtapositions, including my own autobiography in dialogue with the text.

I have not read this novel for positional meaning and I do not have a political agenda. Not only do I read without a political agenda, but I also do not have a unified theory. I would be quite content to do without theory or politics if this would allow me the freedom to enjoy my relationship to *The Cannibal Galaxy*—its story, language, layered meanings, authorship, and craft. Theoretical frameworks of abstract indeterminacy, absent authors, identity-less writing and reading, and of the lie of a unified voice do not consider the dual/dialectical selves of a reader.

My perspective is circumscribed by my status as a white academic woman—bounded by culture, geography, time, class, race, and gender, by my resistance to politics and theory as if they in themselves are oppressive social forces, and by my belief that interpretation does not transcend very far beyond the experience of one human being or group. All interpretation reflects the desires and ideals of the interpreter. My purpose here is *ad hoc*, personally contextual, and pragmatic. I simply want to understand those desires and ideals.

What is the state of being "woman" and "man"? In what group and with what other identities might our selves be considered part of an us?

Jonathan Culler considers:

If the experience of literature depends upon the qualities of a reading self, one can ask what differences it would make to the experience of literature and thus to the meaning of literature if this self were, for example, female rather than male. If the meaning of a work is the experience of a reader, what difference does it make if the reader is a woman?[8]

What difference does it make, I ask, if the reader is a bifurcated self? When I read a text written by a woman I approach it differently from the way I approach a text written by a man: I anticipate a certain kind of intimacy.

Patrocinio Schweickert[9] discusses the woman reader, the possibility of immasculation by the text, and the role of her own subjectivity in allowing that to happen. Apparently, a feminist consciousness, commitment to emancipatory praxis, and a dialectical rather than a dualistic subject-object relationship with the text—in other words, *choosing* not to submit to the power of the text—will enable the woman reader to take control of the text, and, by extension, her life. This normative injunction presupposes a rather sophisticated unified reader.

In *The Cannibal Galaxy*[10] I encounter a text that I read with my dual consciousness, and I feel an extraordinary, disturbing bond with the author. The interpretive acrobatics of my split consciousness are mirrored in the painful opposition of woman's point of view/man's point of view in the text. It is a leap to assume that this duality is a characteristic of Ozick's own consciousness, but even if she does not embody it, she recognizes and creates it.

My bifurcated self feels strong identification with Joseph, a man who works as an administrator and who methodically destroys all that is feminine, nurturing, and reciprocal within himself. He embodies these dual tensions, whereas Hester—the writer, author, scholar, visionary woman—represents for me a romantic figure who attempts to transcend duality and Joseph's efforts to immasculate her. She maintains her differences and her authentic self but consequently is exiled to isolation, idealization, misunderstanding, condemnation, and a loveless existence. My other self identifies with Hester. My masculine self, like Joseph, defines herself in terms of separation, individuation, autonomy, even isolation. My feminine self seeks affiliation and love in the context of authenticity, as Hester would have liked, on her own terms. The desire for autonomy versus the desire for intimacy finds expression in the text through the characters of Hester and Joseph.

READING JOSEPH

Joseph Brill is emotional, conflicted, afraid, destructively idealistic, and sexually confused. He disengages and detaches in order to escape the pain of feeling deeply, but only succeeds in isolating and dehumanizing himself. He yearns to unite the contradictory elements of his psyche, but instead negates and destroys the feminine element so that he is no longer creative, responsive, tender, or nurturing. He is left hard, dominant, controlling. His spirit disintegrates long before his body settles into passive retirement before a television set. In one scene he leads the child Beulah to three photographs in his office of Freud, Spinoza, and Einstein and asks her if she knows who they are. "Men," he says, "who were never in contradiction with themselves."

But Joseph recognizes early in the novel that self is only a "Partial Reality." Hester Lilt represents another Partial Reality, and my other self. It is almost as if Hester is created to transcend the stereotype of woman, to portray a new woman who embodies both feminine and masculine qualities. On the surface, she appears rather masculine, yet the content of her writing and lectures, as least the select passages that are revealed in the novel, appear to express a woman's consciousness: she discredits mechanistic predictive thinking, the mythos of cause and effect, the idea of reality-as-given, the hoax of pedagogy. She does not believe in hierarchy. Unlike Joseph, she can see the structure in silence. Her language is rich with metaphor and parody, analysis and allusion, myths and stories. Hester, "the dreaming rationalist," also embodies contradictions.

Joseph's contradictions are rooted in his childhood, in the internalized values of American and European societies (e.g., Americans value manual over mental labor; his parents, French Jews, unlike the intellectuals he idolizes, prefer that he learn a trade over a discipline). His mother, the first woman in his life, had made him afraid of ecstasy and beauty, and of Claude, the young friend of his early manhood who scares Joseph with his homosexuality. Joseph never recovers from these first losses. Later, as a middle-aged principal, he allows rumors to circulate that he is the victim of a tragic love affair. In his own mind he almost comes to believe the fantasy, in which his lost love sometimes takes the form of Claude, who represents beauty, scholarship, and poetry, and sometimes Berthe, his older sister.

Joseph's objective and subjective realities conflict along the bifurcated poles of his mind. Part of him values the abstract, the disengaged, while the other self-conscious subject is slowly destroyed by the very objectivity he purports to value. He has the sensibilities of a dreamer that stand in opposition and contradiction to his male or masculine approach to the world. He is fascinated by facts—not what they are, how they got to be, and how he constructs or interprets them—but he believes that they are merely out there. It never occurs to him that every fact has a factor, or a maker. He is torn between two worlds, two continents, two cultures, two ways (the direct path and "the roundabout way"), and two apparently oppositional aspects and expressions of sexuality: masculinity/femininity.

Even the school that he founds has two sides—or contradictory natures: the beach side, waters with a history of turbulence, and the field side, where buses lined up in the tumble-down weed-filled meadow. He feels more at home on the beach side where there is imagination, history, and possibility. Between these two sides he feels himself "not so much a school-master as a man of almost sacral power" (p. 4). He is aware of his power but, at the same time, he exhibits contempt for his own work. He had given up the study of astronomy; school administration is a fall from the heights. He is full of self-debasement and believes that Hester recognized his low status. He sees himself at times as "Captain of fleas and midges, warrior among the mothers!" In the beginning of the novel I meet Joseph tortured with a sense of a lost future. He has a sense of himself as not having achieved even a fraction of which he is capable. Perhaps he is nothing more than a "rough alternative" of another possibility or incarnation. Over the years Joseph reflects on life less and less.

Joseph's contradictions are manifested in a major way in the school situation: through his Dual Curriculum, which focuses both on western culture and the scriptures; through his ambivalence about teachers; and through his intolerance of children. Brill also felt contempt for Gorchak, his best teacher, who "kept up a military pace," who believed only right and wrong answers, who declared that children who did not excel were lazy, that a lazy pupil was a dreamer, and that "the dreamers were worthless" (p. 42). The school is Joseph's whole life, yet he disparages it at every turn. He likes to tell the lesson that he learned from his father: "When the teacher begins, *khapt men a dremele* . . . that's the time for a nap" (p. 3).

Joseph views administration as an absolute autonomous practice, not as a fundamentally social construction, a way of being and relating created by social arrangements. He is an insider who pretends to be objective and apolitical. Yet his values have no counterpart in reality. For example, he yearns for the opportunity to nurture genius, but perceives all the children as ordinary, "commoners" and "weeds." Rather than question this discrepancy, he chooses to misread or ignore it. His poor judgment is itself a political act, operating on the interest of some and at the expense of others. He will recognize genius only in children who look and perform a certain way. Never does he acknowledge his subjectivity as human observer in making the judgments that affect his interaction with students, teachers, parents, and ultimately with his polar self. This interplay reinforces the contradictions that shape his vision of reality.

Joseph Brill's life is circumscribed by women: an unsympathetic mother who sees his studies as "futilite"; a secret infatuation in the Musée Carnavalet with a nearly nude stone statue of an insane voluptuous Frenchwoman, Madame de Sevigne; a disturbing friendship with the feminine, dreamy, homosexual aesthete, Claude; a rich benefactress who enables him to found his school; his little sisters Michelle, Leah-Louise, and Ruth, who, with his mother, father, and brothers, are murdered by the Nazis; his three older sisters, Anne, Berthe, and Claire (the ABCs), who reconstruct their lives; the nuns, "holy women," who hide him in the subcellar of their convent school; the mothers, "these *women*," or, in Yiddish, "di vayber," as if "the word had long been pickled in gall"; women teachers who he could not count on; the clerk-receptionist, Iris, whom he marries but whose name he forgets; the child Beulah who he dismisses as dim-witted; and Hester Lilt, the woman and mother whose faith he experiences as his destruction.

Joseph does not particularly like women. His perceived relationship to them is generally one of master to subject: ". . . he saw them as nature's creatures, by which he meant vehicles instinct with secretion. . . . Even when he yielded he mastered them, because they had arrived as petitioners, as suppliants, and to yield was to consummate mastery—it was the sign of his scepter" (p. 40).

Women make him feel like a potentate, the ruler of an entire society. But Hester is not like other women. Certainly not like the mothers of the children in his school: "From morning to night they were hurtled forward by the explosions of internal rivers, with their roar of force and pressure" (p. 64). Hester is "Madame de Sevigne in the middle of America" (p. 53), the stone woman for whom he first experienced ecstasy, who is also a mother—the stupendous, insane mother of the "extraordinary *fille*," Comtesse de Grignan. He elevates her even beyond that comparison and sees her as a brilliant enigma who scorns him or is indifferent to him and whose indifference he deserves. As he begins to study her work in earnest, he feels that he is entering her mind—"it was very serious in there, and very splendid" (p. 54), and it reminds him again of being with Claude. He experiences her frightening clarity, honesty, and logic, and perceives that she has renounced lyricism, poetry, originality, and everything "expressive." It is almost as if he must, at all costs, interpret her as masculine and deny her femininity, particularly her maternity. This may be the desire of his unconscious to regain Claude.

READING HESTER

Hester does not consciously assert a sexual identity. Joseph imposes this on her. He is attracted to Hester, in part, because she does not embody stereo-typical female characteristics: "She did not go to a hairdresser or contemplate her clothes" (p. 48), and she wore sensible, laced shoes. In Hester, he believes he has found a soulmate. This identification, too, may signal Joseph's use of Hester as an instrument to re-experience his repressed love for Claude. He locates this rupture in her and calls it a brokenness. "She was a looking-glass for him" (p. 49). An important question here is, what does it mean to be broken? To be split into binary opposition?

Joseph identifies with Hester at first, feeling camaraderie. He considers her an equal, a "primary thinker." Talking with her was different from talking to other women: "her voice was a man's voice: full and low." Her signature also was like a man's, not the usual female hand. Hester is cool, aloof, direct, ironic, satirical; she addresses Joseph as "Mr. Brill," using his name "without the plosive preface of his title!" She is humble and does not call herself "Doctor." Joseph associates her with beauty and burnished hope, the motherland. She makes him long "for the child Joseph he had once been" (p. 53). Talking to Hester, he is "not in control." Not since Claude had he felt this way. His dual selves yearn alternately to submit to her and to dominate her. Ultimately, she must be mastered because the masculinity in her female self inflames in him the desire he felt for the femininity in Claude's male self. Consider that early in the novel, when Claude kissed him, "he was unsure whether he liked it; it frightened him terribly; it made him think of Leviticus" (p. 15). Yes, he is unsure, and he continually reconstructs his past, re-examining history as a way of constructing his present reality. Hester's past remains a secret, just as her name, Joseph Lowin points out,[11] describes "the hiding of the face of God . . . hester panim." In the novel, her surname, "Lilt," reminds him of unarticulated images from the past (reminiscences of Claude?). "He wanted to detain her until he could learn what there was in her of *déjà vu*" (p. 51).

Hester presents Joseph with an alternative vision of woman. She is an intellectual, writer, and lecturer who, he perceives as having more power than he because he does not value the power to make decisions regarding the fate of children. Creating a false hierarchical structure, he places her in a superior position, with himself as the subordinate intellect. Yet he wants an affiliative collegial relationship with her. She resists. With so much of her unknown to his contradictory selves, he becomes frantic to decode her, to decide what her desires are: desire like ambition, desire "to bring form into being . . . to make a frame for every idea," to mimic "every rational scheme" (p. 64). The self who desires domination is disappointed when she does not cooperate in his fantasy.

Hester's behavior appears masculine, which is what draws Joseph, but he is misled by appearances. He wants to treat her like one of the boys, different from other women, but she rejects his invitation, refuses to renounce her femininity, even while she has no interest in compliance. It is not merely a coincidence that Hester Lilt is "an imagistic linguistic logician," that one of her celebrated books is called *The World as Appearance*.

Hester provides opportunities for Joseph to reevaluate the meaning of various feminine and masculine qualities, but habitually he "stops too soon," choosing instead to define her according to his own reality. She objects to his perceptions as an attack. She has formed herself into the person she wants to be—"I've become what I intended to be" (p. 45). Her actions are not mediated by others; she does not put herself in the service of others. Her sense of self does not appear to be dependent on affiliations and relationships. Although Hester is never seen interacting with other women, she tells Joseph repeatedly that she is no different from the other mothers. She expresses some disdain or contempt for Iris when Joseph announces his marriage. "Principal Brill's bride," she murmured with this new scoffing passion of hers. "The secret of *my* brain? Why not tell the secret of the bride's? Or is there no secret because there is no—" (p. 113). Even if she would have liked a reciprocal relationship with Joseph, he does not offer it: "What you are made me stop. You're too elevated. You're too clever. You're too acute" (p. 113). He praises and flatters her, subordinating her to an idealized status. He insists on her idiosyncratic masculine self as opposed to her collective female identity. Joseph will allow her to be a man, but he will not allow her to be a woman. He denies her authenticity.

Hester responds to Joseph's idealization with a counterattack. She chides and taunts him, confronts and ridicules him. Understanding him precisely, she shows little mercy: "You *are* a coward . . . you want to know everything in advance—every twist, every contingency . . . how to manage fate, only because once upon a time fate managed you" (p. 112).

In a dramatic attempt to "unite his two minds," Joseph makes a choice to fulfill Rabbi Pult's and an old writer's prediction: he has become a teacher; now he will marry. His future wife, Iris, is the school clerk–receptionist. He likes the idea of marrying "a clerk–receptionist: the odd humble hierarchical stammer of it" (p. 87). Iris becomes his ideal woman because he can fertilize and impregnate her. Consistent with his vision of women's nature, his wife/secretary is disqualified from education and professional status, and fit only to bear his child, to reproduce the race. She bestows on him the kind of personal attention and services that men are used to receiving from their mothers, wives, lovers, and sisters. Eventually, he comes to see Iris as "the most trivial woman on earth" (p. 142).

In the end, all women fail Joseph. "Only Madame de Sevigne could outlast time" (p. 130), but a stone statue is a poor substitute for a real woman. When the illusion is stripped bare and he sees that Hester is, after all, as she has said all along, a woman and a mother, he becomes rejecting, cruel, punishing, and dismissing. Her womanhood is unimportant, for "what had her womb brought forth but Beulah" (p. 138). He values only the part of her that he idealizes. He thinks that he has deciphered her, decoded her, and broken the enchantment. He accuses her of being nothing, empty, "a barren pot," of using Beulah as her subject matter, the thesis of her work: "You need her to be nothing, so you can be something." He accuses her of cannibalizing her own child.

READING THE TEXTS OF OUR OWN LIVES

The story of Hester Lilt is a narrative about a fictional woman's experience at a particular moment in time across particular cultures, in relation to a particular fictional man, created by an actual woman with her own historical experiences. For Ozick, Hester and Joseph are a site upon which to structure meaning. Religion, nationality, class, culture, and accidents of personal history are inextricably bound to Joseph's experiences, but they appear less important than gender to my understanding of Hester, perhaps because Ozick purposefully obscures them.

Ozick is not interested in the revolutionary potential of the novel form as an arena for feminist politics. *The Cannibal Galaxy* is not text as ideology. Yet there are themes in the novel surrounding the question of unity and contradiction—of bifurcated selves—that address the human experiences as one of split consciousness. The very essence of this postmodern novel is the problem of the unified self—the self in struggle for unity and integrity.

In the novel, Joseph perceives the world as "a vale of interpretation."[12] He is obsessed with interpreting Hester; she devotes her writing and scholarship to decoding meaning. I looked for signs in the novel of female and/or male language to construct interpretation and was not surprised to find that Ozick uses language singularly and playfully, but never differentially, in revealing the split consciousness of Joseph and Hester.[13]

Originally, I asked the question, What if *The Cannibal Galaxy* were interpreted as a feminist text, a story of the human reality of women's life in relation to man's? Or as a dialectical text in which the apparent binary opposition of male/female roles are explored by the author in the site of the characters—where one pole is not privileged to assume dominance over the other? The only way to answer this question is to accept the wild contradictions—not only of the novel and its characters but, more important, of ourselves. Both men and women reveal interior oppositional selves that struggle with phenomena of intimacy, desire, emotion, spirituality, self-understanding, expression, and identity. One small step toward the project of reparation, if this is desirable, or toward understanding the ambiguous, troubled, shifting order of dual consciousness, is offered by the novel: in reading, we can choose to be complicit in our own immasculation or opt for authenticity.

NOTES

1. I discuss my use of Cynthia Ozick's *The Cannibal Galaxy* (New York, 1983) in "The Administrator in Fiction: Using the Novel to Teach Educational Administration," *Educational Administration Quarterly 26*(4) (September 1990).

2. In her extraliterary writing and speaking, particularly in her essay "Literature and the Politics of Sex: A Dissent" (*Art and Ardor* [New York, 1983], p. 285), Ozick indignantly rejects the term "woman writer." In "Dissent," she argues that "woman writer has no meaning—not intellectually, not morally, not historically." She says: "When I write, I am free. I am, as a writer, whatever I wish to become. I can think myself into a male or female, or a stone, or a stick of wood, or a Tibetan, or the spine of a cactus. . . . In life, I am not free. In life, female or male, no one is free."

3. I respect the teaching of Roland Barthes ("The Death of the Author," *Image, Music, Text*, Stephen Heath, trans. [New York, 1977]); Michel Foucault ("What Is an Author?," Josue V. Harari, trans., in Paul Rabinor, ed., *The Foucault Reader* [New York, 1984]); Edward Said (*Beginnings: Intention and Method* [New York, 1975]); and others to set authorial presence aside in order to free the text for multiple uses, but I reserve the right to restore her to the picture as needed. I cannot kill off Ozick, or any other author, even if this defiance of postmodern feminist practice damns me, in Toril Moi's perspective (*Sexual/Textual Politics: Feminist Literary Theory* [London and New York, 1985]), as a slave to the patriarchal practice of authority.

4. Several of Ozick's stories appear ironically feminist; for example, in "Virility" (*The Pagan Rabbi and Other Stories* [New York, 1971]), a nephew publishes his Aunt Rifke's poetry under his own name and receives critical acclaim for the "virile" work. When the hoax is discovered and the aunt's poetry is published in her own female name, it is received as weak, sentimental woman's writing.

5. Rita Felski, *Beyond Feminist Aesthetics* (Cambridge, MA: 1989), p. 14.

6. Cora Kaplan, *Sea Changes: Culture and Feminism* (London, 1986), p. 148.

7. I agree with Roland Barthes ("Death of the Author", pp. 147–148) that the text is not dependent exclusively for its meaning on either the author's subjectivity or any individual characteristic that I, the reader, might have; as a reader, I am appropriating the text, but the text itself and my reading of it can always be reinterpreted, and must and will be reinterpreted, since no text is available to anyone outside of interpretation. I bring to my reading the text itself; my knowledge of the author; information on various schools of literary thought; awareness of the audience to whom I'm reporting my understanding; and, not least important, my self-reflexive stance and readerly needs.

8. Jonathan D. Culler, *On Deconstruction: Theory and Criticism after Structuralism* (New York, 1982), p. 42.

9. Patrocinio P. Schweickert, "Reading Ourselves," in Elaine Showalter, ed., *Speaking of Gender* (New York, 1989).

10. For readers unfamiliar with the novel, I provide a brief summary, with the understanding that plot summaries of primary texts are in themselves gestures of interpretation: *The Cannibal Galaxy* is the story of Joseph Brill, a French-born Jew who, while hiding from the Nazis during World War II, decides to trade his desire to study astronomy for a school principalship. Upon emigrating to America, he becomes a

visionary leader of a midwestern Jewish day school where he implements a dual cur-riculum integrating Western European and Jewish studies. Brill meets the brilliant philosopher and writer Hester Lilt, mother of Beulah, a student in his school. A tension is set up in the principal between his longing for a lost past (genius, beauty, family, his friend Claude, his feminine self) versus the ordinariness of a middling existence. Beulah, whose education Brill sees as the rare opportunity of his pedagogic career, is considered dull-witted, conforming, and ordinary. Brill is obsessed with the mother's excellence, disappointed by her commonplace child. Hester Lilt condemns Brill as a man who "stops too soon," who gives up on the child, who settles for second rate in his own life. Brill is horrified by mediocrity and by the unendingness of the ordinary, but while worshipping genius he fails to recognize it. His relationship with himself deterio-rates. He elects to become "normal" by marrying the school secretary and producing his own prodigy. His son, Naphtali, is intellectually quick and shows great promise. Following Beulah's graduation, Hester and Beulah move to Europe, Brill retires to Florida, and Naphtali becomes a business administration major. Beulah becomes a Parisian painter and theoretician of the avant-garde. When interviewed about her childhood in America, she cannot remember anything about Principal Brill's school. This is the final blow to Brill, who, in a moment of clarity, feels that his life is a sad, dismal failure and that he has "been ambushed by Hester Lilt." He thinks of her as a cannibal galaxy, "those megalosaurian colonies of primordial gases that devour smaller brother galaxies."

11. Joseph Lowin, *Cynthia Ozick* (Boston, 1988).

12. It helps me to be reminded that every written work, whether fiction or nonfiction, is a kind of mask, both an interpretation and an interpretable cultural artifact, and that each interpretation is again another written work which itself must be interpreted, and that each intepretation along the way gives up or obscures some meaning and acquires new meaning. This point is made strongly in Cheryl Walker's discussion ("Feminist Literary Criticism," pp. 557–561) of Toril Moi's *Sexual/Textual Politics*. Joseph Lowin (*Cynthia Ozick*, p. 81) discusses the use of different frames for interpreting *The Cannibal Galaxy*.

13. I could almost consider that Ozick's playfulness simultaneously pokes fun at contemporary feminist critics with their linguistically based methods of analysis such as semiotics and deconstruction, and upholds its importance by legitimating Hester's form of discourse—academic writing, scholarship, public speaking in an institutional frame-work that traditionally has been exclusionary to women. Hester pushes language to its boundaries, takes pleasure in its abstraction, and plays with the mystery of the absence of language, for example, in her article "On Structure in Silence": "Silence is not random but shaping. It is like the empty air around the wing, that delineates the wing" (p. 101).

7

Females and Feminism in *New Yorker* Cartoons

Phyllis R. Randall

The cartoons in the *New Yorker*, "America's best graphic comedy" (Inge, 1984, p. 72), are literate, topical, and funny in that *New Yorker* fashion, "approaching the neurotic" (Blair and Hill, 1978, p. 426). From the beginning, the *New Yorker* was designed not for the little "old lady in Dubuque," as Harold Ross, the founding editor put it (quoted in Pinsker, 1984, p. 192), but rather for a decidedly upscale market—business and professional people, well educated, "well-heeled," and well informed—not only about "culture of the past and present" but also about "the latest trends in society, politics, and the mass media" (Inge, 1984, p. 71). Since humor is "culture based" (Apte, 1985, p. 16), requiring "psychical accord" (Freud, quoted in Barreca, 1988, p. 12) and "shared values" (Merrill, 1988, p. 276), it would seem likely that the cartoons would be a reflection of that world.

I wondered what notions the cartoons would reflect toward gender and sexism. Knowing that, from the beginning, the *New Yorker* had some female cartoonists, I further wondered if contemporary cartoons might manifest female or even feminist humor: would a magazine geared to the sophisticated reader contain cartoons reflecting such security in the world of the liberated woman that humor about or addressed to that kind of woman would be included?[1]

To determine the answers to these questions, I examined all the cartoons for the year 1990, 1,025 cartoons in all.[2] Of these, 164 depicted either inanimate objects or animals. Though many of the animals were anthropomorphized and hence might have been included in my count, there were relatively few of them, and so for fairness in the statistical results, I thought it better to eliminate all animal cartoons. With the remaining 861 cartoons, I began by counting which sex appeared in each cartoon in a primary position (that is, not as a bystander but as a participant in the central action or interaction): male(s) alone, female(s) alone, or both in the same cartoon. Separately, I did the same with cartoons that pictured historical or fictional characters.

The results of this first statistical analysis demonstrated that, over-whelmingly, *New Yorker* cartoons showed either men and women together (48.5 percent) or men alone (43.4 percent); only 8.1 percent of the cartoons showed women only. Men, to put it another way, appeared in 91.9 percent of the cartoons, women in 56.6 percent. If a woman were to appear in a cartoon, she was overwhelmingly more likely to appear with a man than alone or with other women. A man, however, was nearly as likely to appear alone or with other men as with women. There were forty-four cartoons of historical or fic-tional characters, 5.8 percent of the total number of cartoons. Of these, 75 percent showed only men, 15.9 percent showed only women, and 9.1 percent showed both sexes together. From this simple head count in the cartoons, then, one might reasonably conclude that the *New Yorker*'s cartoon world belongs to men, with women shown as part of that world principally when accompanied by men.

Before I turn to other statistical data that support that conclusion, it is worth looking further at the subcategory of historical/fictional characters. In the forty-four cartoons in this category there were fifty-seven different male and twenty-nine different female characters. It is no surprise that there were many more allusions to male historical figures than to female (twenty-five to seven—the latter included Judith, Salome, Coco Chanel, Marianne Moore, and George Sand), for the target readership would have received a traditional education in history, and the political and economic nature of that history focuses mainly on males. One could suppose that fictional characters would be about equal by gender, since in literature female characters appear about as often as male characters. The figures fail to bear out this assumption, however, with twenty-nine (55.8 percent) different male characters and twenty-three (44.2 percent) different female ones. What is most noticeable about this category, however, is who is pictured. More than half the time males are heroes of some sort (eighteen of the twenty-nine)—Captain Nemo, Hercules, Paris, Hector, Ulysses, for example—whereas the females are overwhelmingly from children's tales, particularly fairy tales (fourteen of twenty-three)—Alice in Wonderland, Dorothy of Oz, the Little Mermaid, Sleeping Beauty, Snow White, Mother Goose. Within this historical/fictional category I have also included pop culture figures, and here again, the males are more often heroes of some sort—Uncle Sam, Dick Tracy, Superman (three times), Santa, the Lone Ranger and Tonto, Batman, Spiderman, Roy Rogers. But the pop culture females pictured include such titillating titans of womanhood as Barbie, Charlie's Angels, and Madonna.

With 43.4 percent of the cartoons of male characters only and 75 percent of the fictional/historical cartoons with males only, one might reasonably conclude that the world of *New Yorker* cartoons is overwhelmingly a male one (a conclusion reached by Swords, 1992, about cartoons in general).

Skewing by gender is revealed also in the workforce of the cartoons. Those who work in *New Yorker* cartoons are primarily males, not females. Of the thirty-six different occupations discernible in the cartoons, males occupy thirty-one whereas females occupy just nineteen. More striking, perhaps, are the

Table 1
One-Sex Occupations

Female	*Male*	
secretary	physician, counselor	hairdresser
nurse	lab scientist	clergy
model	explorer	bartender
fortune-teller	professional sportsmen	butler
book editor	decorator	musician
	police officer	taxi driver
	military personnel	farmer
	computer operator	other blue collar

occupations that only one sex is found in. The data in Table 1 show only females in the role of secretary, nurse, model, fortune-teller, and, more surprising, book editor. The list of occupations in which only males are shown is not only far more extensive but also far more surprising: four hairdressers appeared as well as two decorators; three police officers; seventeen doctors, psychiatrists, or counselors of some sort—all male!

The additional data on occupations in Table 2 show the six occupations that males and females appeared in most frequently. That business is the top occupation for both sexes comes as no surprise. Considering the evidence noted so far, what is a surprise is that some of the women depicted in business situations are clearly businesswomen: they are carrying a briefcase or are seated with men around a conference table. Nevertheless, most often the women appearing in business settings are aides of some sort. The other females shown working are in traditional occupations—secretaries, waitpersons (diners had only female waitpersons; all fancy restaurants had only male), teachers (all elementary classes), and bank clerks/tellers.

These *New Yorker* data are particularly revealing compared to the data from the *Statistical Abstracts of the United States 1990*, which show that nearly half or more than half in many of these occupations are female, including teachers at all grade levels (49.6 percent), bartenders (49.6 percent), psychologists (55.8 percent), painters (51.2 percent), authors (56 percent), editors and reporters (51.1 percent). Even in occupations in which women are less represented, *Statistical Abstracts* data far exceed *New Yorker* data: doctors (18.2 percent), lawyers and judges (19.5 percent), musicians (29.6 percent), police (13.4 percent), and media announcers (16.7 percent).

Such a lopsided *New Yorker* view of the work world led me to consider also nonwork settings in the cartoons. Table 3 shows the number of males and females in each of the ten most frequently pictured settings. Initially, I did not intend to do a statistical analysis of settings until I noticed many that showed men at home alone. The figures of Table 3 illustrate that whether at home

Table 2
Seven Most Frequent Occupations

Female	*Male*
business—20	business—213
secretary—9	artist—23
waitperson—7	lawyer—22
teacher—6	journalist, mostly TV—20
bank clerk—6	doctor, counselor—17
artist—4	military personnel—14
journalist, mostly TV—3	cowboy—14

Table 3
Sex of Characters in Setting

	Male	Female	M/F
Domestic	58	23	143
Outdoors	94	10	78
Office	61	2	19
Restaurant/bar	31	6	35
Doctor's office	12	4	5
Court/law office	12	—	5
Store	11	1	7
Heaven/Hell	7	—	1
TV, including studio	6	—	4
Bank	2	—	7

or outdoors or at a restaurant or, indeed, whether in afterlife in Heaven or Hell (four such cartoons), for the *New Yorker* in 1990, it was a man's world. Females were far more likely to appear at home, outdoors, in a restaurant, or in Heaven accompanied by a male than alone or with another female.

Since so few women are pictured on their own at the center of the cartoon interaction—or, indeed, pictured at all—I was led to another search. Of the 861 cartoons, 30 depicted groups or crowds of some sort. I reasoned that here at last women should begin to appear in about the same numbers as men. Table 4 gives details on the number of recognizably male and female characters appearing in crowds in one of six settings that occurred two or more times. Only in classrooms (three cartoons) and in stores (two cartoons) were the crowds about evenly divided by sex. The store-scene cartoons were particularly interesting since both of them showed parents standing in the Santa Claus line with their

Table 4
Number of Characters by Sex in Crowds

	Male	Female
Classroom	13 (54.2%)	11 (45.8%)
Street scene	47 (72.3%)	18 (27.6%)
Restaurant	25 (64.2%)	14 (35.8%)
Court, mostly jury	19 (73.1%)	7 (26.9%)
Art gallery	12 (85.7%)	2 (14.3%)
Store, with child	8 (53.3%)	7 (46.7%)

children. In that line more than half (53.3 percent) of the parents were male (a sight I have never seen). But then none of the other statistics match my reality either.

The most telling evidence of all that the world of *New Yorker* cartoons is male, indeed, that in that world women are barely visible, is found in the count of pedestrians on ordinary street scenes in New York, almost half of them in neighborhoods or parks, all in daylight. And there, on the streets of *New Yorker* cartoons, 72.3 percent of the people one will pass are male!

To sum up, by statistical evidence, the ordinary woman (that is, discounting the historical/fictional figure) will, if she appears at all, not work, but if she does, it will be in a traditional service occupation. She is sometimes found at home alone, but not as often as her husband is, despite his work. If she does venture to a store, a doctor's office, her church, her hair salon, a decorator shop, or a bar, she will be waited on by men. If she takes a taxi (driven by a male) to go to a concert, the musicians will be male. But she does not get in a taxi often, apparently, because she isn't seen much in restaurants (unless, of course, with a man). Certainly she does not venture outdoors without the protection of some man, not even in broad daylight. Indeed, she is not even to be found at home as frequently as her husband. So, she doesn't work, she isn't at home or in restaurants, the streets, the art galleries. Where are all the women of the *New Yorker* cartoon world? They must be there; their presence is implied everywhere. But they are mostly invisible.

Turning to a content analysis of the cartoons provided little relief from the bleak picture created by the statistical evidence. I culled from the 861 cartoons all those which depended for their humor either in text or subtext on some depiction or interrogation of women's roles.[3] Only twenty-six cartoons (3 percent) qualified. Not all of these twenty-six cartoons, of course, revealed a positive view of either females or feminism.

Among the 835 other cartoons the old stereotypes of women, especially *New Yorker* stereotypes, were still present, left over from the James Thurber battle-of-the-sexes days, where "meek, docile men are browbeaten by large, scowly, aggressive females" (Blair and Hill, 1978, p. 447). Specifically, eighteen cartoons presented "situations that pitted frail and defenseless men against menacing big women" (p. 424). An example would be the cartoon which has an overpowering woman declaring her husband to be an excellent mouser—he's shown on all fours tracking a mouse down (June 15, 1990, p. 40). Other stereotypes include women as money grubbers, as bargainers, as dimwits, as the woman behind the man, and as inveterate shoppers. Two of these last are worth noting. In the first, one woman explains to another over tea that she wants her "ashes scattered over Bergdorf" (April 30, 1990, p. 52). This cartoon perpetuates the stereotype, true, but with that gentle self-mocking, self-deprecating tone that both Merrill (1988, p. 273) and Walker (1988, pp. 123–124) find characterizing female humor. In the other (July 16, p. 35), two women dressed exactly alike pace off with the caption, "Chanel bags at dawn." This cartoon, too, perpetuates a stereotype of women, but though it mocks the stereotype, it might be read as taking a potshot at male aggression. Females, the subtext says, can be just as aggressive as males, but they would not be so ludicrously aggressive as to kill someone, the way men have done—hence Chanel bags, not guns. Because the humor can be read without the subtext, however, I do not include it among the feminist cartoons. Instead, both cartoons, by Victoria Roberts, may stand as examples of female, not feminist, humor.

In addition to these cartoons with female stereotypes, others show putdowns of men by women. Not one of them, however, shows any satire or repressed aggression that might have been stimulated by ideas from the feminist movement. (Indeed, none of these cartoons is by a woman.) Instead, they picture women as the dominating force in keeping men in their place, not by being harridans but by controlling. Some examples: a woman explains that she is recharging her husband's batteries—he's plugged into an outlet (January 1, 1990, p. 24); another confides to a friend that her husband is the best entertainment available under $1.79 (January 15, 1990, p. 83). Another, surveying her living room decor, remarks to her friend that she thinks her husband looks "better in here" (February 12, 1990, p. 33).

So the battle between the sexes goes on in the pages of the *New Yorker.* Now, however, and to my surprise, the battle is sometimes literal. Much humor, of course, is based in aggression, including the put-down stereotypes just reviewed (Barreca, 1988, pp. 5–10; Merrill, 1988, pp. 274, 278), but the two cartoons that showed literal aggression are a different matter. The first (January 1, 1990, p. 77) shows a heterosexual couple squaring off in a boxing ring while the announcer introduces them and their disagreement over the color for the dining room. Since decorating the home is a traditional female bailiwick, the stereotype of a woman's domain is broken. Moreover, the man is fighting to get his way, breaking the code of chivalry forbidding physical attacks on females. Of course the wife is shattering a stereotype as well, since she is willing to match his aggression, breaking the code of submission. Perhaps this cartoon reveals life in which the breakdown of stereotypes results in all hell breaking loose, where no codes are agreed upon. The second cartoon (November 12, 1990, p. 47) shows two couples having a food fight in a restaurant while the waiter asks, "How is everything?" Though less provocative than the earlier cartoon, both break the stereotype in portraying the tension that underlies much male/female interaction. Since the humor is directly related to that shattering, I count both of these among the twenty-six feminist-influenced cartoons.

Seven other feminist-based cartoons rely on language influenced by the feminist movement for the humor. For example, a woman coming upon a crowd around a man with a spilled briefcase says, "Let me through! I'm a businessperson!" (August 13, 1990, p. 40). In another, a large-breasted female at a bar, obviously at home in it, says, "I'm a bachelor myself" (July 9, 1990, p. 68). Though the sexiness of the woman continues one stereotype, her awareness of the sexism in the language—the choice of the male term *bachelor* rather than *spinster*—reveals that she is a woman influenced by feminist notions of equality. Likewise with the man depicted in a Christmas cartoon inviting a guest "to share some holiday thought with us on the subject of gender-neutral toys" (December 24, 1990, p. 43). Also aware of a feminist agenda is the woman in the art gallery who turns to her male partner and asks, "Do you really like Rembrandt, or do you simply identify with him as a white heterosexual male?" (August 20, 1990, p. 58). Three of these cartoons, however, present demeaning depictions of the feminist movement. In one (April 23, 1990, p. 33), a woman is plucking petals off a daisy, saying, "I'm empowered, I'm not empowered." The concept of empowerment, an integral aspect of many feminist ideologies, is too fundamental to be left to chance. The second cartoon (December 3, 1990, p. 54) shows a fortune-teller asking a woman, "Career track or mommy track?" Again, the two-track system is a serious problem, but to ally the issue to fortune-telling is to demean the seriousness of the problem.

The third cartoon, which shows language influence but is ultimately demeaning, reveals two women in a Laundromat, one saying, "The great leveler" (January 29, 1990, p. 36). There is a hint of gender-based solidarity in that remark, but the setting demeans the concept of sisterhood, which is based on ideology, not laundry. This cartoon, unlike the two mentioned above, is by a woman, Victoria Roberts; nevertheless, all three fail to reveal that double-edge Walker notes as typical of the humor of minorities and women (1988, pp. 101–138). Walker writes that these groups, aware of their oppression, tend to treat lightly what they consider profoundly important, like empowerment, career advancement, and a level playing field of opportunity in this world. I do not believe that these cartoons show awareness of the underlying importance of the issues.

In addition to the language cartoons are ten cartoons showing a "new man" and a "new woman" (five of each), both outcomes of a feminist consciousness. Two of these reveal the self-mockery so typical of female humor. For example, two cartoons show a woman literally transforming herself from the skin out. In one a heavyset matron in a bustier, net stockings, and outré hairdo presents herself to her husband, who comments, "Jeepers creepers! It's Madonna, but it's you, too, Margaret" (June 4, 1990, p. 34). This cartoon, by Victoria Roberts, is reminiscent of the Helen Hokinson society matron cartoons from early *New*

Yorker days, gently self-mocking, but with no social or ideological agenda. Sheppard notes that Hokinson's women are "well-intentioned but imperceptive and self-deluding—qualities which render them fully likeable" (1984, p. 44). Made in that mold, this woman is bold enough to adventure but foolish enough to follow the wrong road. Moreover, she still seems to need a husband's approval. The other cartoon, also by a woman, Roz Chast, shows a "before" picture of a stereotypically fashionable woman transformed by the switch from boots to sensible shoes, from a fire-engine red clown suit to a nondescript navy dress into an "after" picture of a plain, "no-nonsense" woman. Though the humor lies in the reversal of the direction of the usual makeover job, the subtext seems to allude to the price to be paid for participating (working?) in the everyday world rather than being a clown in it. Mocking the artificial dichotomy, cartoonist Roz Chast might be saying, "What price feminism, eh?"

By contrast, the "new male," the one who has assimilated a feminist agenda, is presented more favorably: one cartoon has a man explain to a friend that he pays alimony to two women but collects it from two others, so "It equals out" (January 8, 1990, p. 31); another drinks a toast to women, "the gatekeepers" (January 22, 1990, p. 58); and a third shows a woman telling her date that he is as "caring, sensitive, warm, witty, emotionally available," and so on, as his ad had promised (April 2, 1990, p. 73). But at least one "new male" cartoon is less flattering: a man explains to his buddy, "Women want more these days, Bill. It's not enough to be a jerk anymore" (February 26, 1990, p. 43).

Three of the "new woman" cartoons, however, go beyond self-mockery to positive images of feminist figures. There is no ambiguity in reading the cartoon showing two women saluting each other at a bar with a toast, "Wine. Men. Song" (February 26, 1990, p. 115). Another shows a woman liberated enough to defy the stereotype: in a May 14, 1990, cartoon a grandmother at the dinner table thanks everyone for coming but announces that starting next year, "Mother's Day will find me at the Desert Palm Spa" (p. 37). In an October 22, 1990, cartoon a father holds his baby daughter up to watch a car mechanic since he wants her "to know something about engines" (p. 51). (It should be noted that all three of these cartoons were created by men.)

By contrast, three cartoons had decidedly negative depictions of feminist concerns; a fourth is somewhat ambiguous. In the first (February 19, 1990, p. 39), a male patron at a restaurant has called for the chef and discovered that the chef is female and stereotypically attractive; he says, "My compliments anyway." The humor in this kind of cartoon relies on the male perspective of the incongruity of a female, let alone an attractive one, being able to cook professionally. A November 12, 1990, cartoon shows a man at a cocktail party telling three women, "Hey! Love the way woman are beginning to laugh at themselves" (p. 42). None of the women is laughing. Feminists, knowing the ubiquity of the charge that women have no sense of humor (see Barreca, 1988; Crawford, 1992, pp. 29, 35–36; Merrill, 1988, pp. 273–274; Swords, 1992, pp. 66–67; Walker, 1981, 1988, pp. 78–80), might have a hard time laughing at that cartoon. Nor might they find funny the cartoon showing a board meeting of many Uncle Sams deciding that, in the interest of "equal opportunity," they should admit an "Aunt Sam" (June 4, 1990, p. 40). True, equal opportunity is a feminist goal, but these Uncle Sams are an embodiment of inequity, not opportunity.

Another cartoon in this category shows, among a panel of pictures of people who "Have an Influence on Me Now," a picture of "My Boss" (August 6, 1990, p. 70). She turns out to be a seductive female in a form-fitting black evening gown with a slit in the skirt up to her hip and lots of décolletage. This panel acknowledges both a female in a supervisory position and that person's influence. But the implication that the influence has much to do with sex and little to do with brains or ability is particularly demeaning to women.

This cartoon could be contrasted to another depicting a similar situation which shows a positive feminist viewpoint. It too shows a female boss influencing a male subordinate, but she is complimenting him on a job well done, suggesting that he take the afternoon off and go shopping (September 10, 1990, p. 87). Reversing the stereotype, that is, applying the female stereotype to the male, the female boss not only asserts her power in the situation but also reveals the shallowness of the stereotype. Her handling of the situation reveals an emancipated woman creating the new norms that Toth writes about, the woman who has "warmth and spunk and vitality" (1984, p. 211), or as Walker puts it, the woman who is "gutsy, self-determined, clear-eyed" (1981, p. 8). If she is not quite "subversive," at least she breaks the "current cultural and ideological frames" (Barreca, 1988, p. 9).

She is in direct contrast to the woman depicted in another cartoon which I also find, nevertheless, profeminist. This cartoon involves a double whammy of sexist undergirding so thorough as to end up making fun of the very stereotypes it portrays (see Walker, 1988, pp. 118–130). Labeled "The Judgment of Paris," though using the central figure from Botticelli's *The Birth of Venus* (August 27, 1990, p. 33), it shows Paris interviewing a nude Venus standing on her shell. She says, "I'm fluent in Greek and Trojan and I can type sixty words a minute." The undergirding of the humor in this cartoon is, as is true for all humor, shared audience culture: the knowledge of the Paris story, choosing a woman just for her beauty, the reference to Venus as the goddess of love, the knowledge of the interviewing of beauty contestants, and the application to the business world where secretaries can be hired by Paris's standard. But only women share the code of being consigned to the typing pool, no matter what their other qualifications. Thus the layers of cultural and occupational restrictions and stereotypes can be seen as ridiculous.

As one could expect in the *New Yorker*, however, even the most positive feminist cartoons tend to be mild, not overtly assertive or aggressive. Though some of the cartoons reveal a collective consciousness and a sense that all women are part of a group with problems and interests in common, few proceed to the next step. Walker (1988, pp. 13–14) notes that the "collective consciousness" kind of humor can lead to outright feminist humor, which she finds of two types: humor with a double text to challenge the stereotype that it presents and humor that directly challenges the discrimination that leads to the stereotypes.

One cartoon shows rather clearly the "collective consciousness" of feminist humor (July 16, 1990, p. 41). It reveals a panel labeled "Up-to-Date Career-Specific Romance Novels," which shows three such books: *Prognosis: Passion*, in the Jenny Thompson, M.D., series; *Split-Level Love*, in the Lorraine Lewis, Realtor, series; and *Brent Kane, Target Audience*, in the Amy Scott, Media Planner, series. The surface stereotype is obvious: women as lightweight readers interested in the never-never land of romance. Yet all three series are about professional women, women who work (which in light of the statistical analysis for the year is fiction in itself). Though the surface text makes fun of females, the subtext recognizes "our shared socialization" (Merrill, 1988, p. 275) and hence turns the stereotype to a different end.

The most forceful feminist cartoon of the year, the one that directly challenges the discrimination that leads to the stereotyping, was created by Robert Weber (November 19, 1990, p. 53). It shows a man and woman talking as they leave a business conference together. She is responding to him, "No, Mr. Kurlander, I don't have, nor have I ever had, a recipe for cranberry muffins." Professionally dressed and coiffed, not stereotypically pretty enough (by cartoon standards) to have obtained her job on looks, the heroine is obviously a woman of accomplishment. Emancipated and assertive, she holds her own with Mr. Kurlander, looks him straight in the eye, and responds politely but firmly in language which echoes that of the notorious McCarthy hearings. She knows his inquiry was a condescending question on a topic he (stereotypically) believes her to be an authority on just by virtue of her gender. So while she answers his surface question, by using language reminiscent of the McCarthy hearings she at the same time responds strongly to Mr. Kurlander's subtext that renders all women stereotypically domestic by virtue of being female.

To summarize the content analysis, of the 3 percent of the cartoons that showed some assimilation of feminist ideas, most (7) relied on language or on depicting a "protofeminist" new man (5) or new woman (5). Of these twenty-six cartoons, six were decidedly negative. Most of the rest revealed self-mockery. A few others moved into the category of feminist humor, promoting a shared consciousness, and, less often, attacking the stereotypes and discrimination. Of the seven cartoons which depicted feminism in a positive light, six were created by men. (Swords, 1992, also presents evidence of feminist cartoons by males.) Perhaps that fact is the brightest part of the otherwise bleak picture of females and feminism in *New Yorker* cartoons. Feminism has indeed permeated the consciousness of a few of the magazine's cartoonists; for those few, male and female alike, the liberated women they depict are not the objects of the humor but the perpetrators of it.

NOTES

1. Since my focus is on assimilation of feminist culture, not male-female differences in humor (for which see, among others, Apte, 1985, chap. 2; Barreca, 1988, pp. 5–10; Mitchell, 1977, 1985; Crawford, 1992; and Swords, 1992), I was not concerned with the gender of the cartoonist in this study and analyzed the content of the cartoons irrespective of the sex of the cartoonist. Only afterward did I check names of the cartoonists. (Some cartoons had plainly legible signatures, but most could not be deciphered.? The sex of the cartoonist is mentioned in text only if it is relevant to the analysis.

2. Because the editorship of Tina Brown began in 1992 and I wanted to avoid any changes she might be responsible for, I choose a year before her presence could have exerted any influence.

3. The key here is the dependence-for-their-humor idea. I did not count, for example, cartoons with women pictured in nontraditional occupations unless the humor of that cartoon depended on that depiction.

REFERENCES

Apte, Mahadev L. 1985. *Humor and Laughter: An Anthropological Approach*. Ithaca, NY: Cornell University Press.

Barreca, Regina. 1988. "Introduction." In Regina Barreca, ed., *Last Laughs: Perspectives on Women and Comedy*. New York: Gordon and Breach Science, pp. 3–22.

Blair, Walter, and Hamlin Hill. 1978. *America's Humor: From Poor Richard to Doonesbury*. New York: Oxford University Press.

Crawford, Mary. 1992. "Just Kidding: Gender and Conversational Humor." In Regina Barreca, ed., *New Perspectives on Women and Comedy*. Philadelphia: Gordon and Breach, pp. 23–37.

Inge, M. Thomas. 1984. "The *New Yorker* Cartoon and Modern Graphic Humor." *Studies on American Humor 3*(1) (spring): 61–73.

Merrill, Lisa. 1988. "Feminist Humor: Rebellious and Self-Affirming." In Regina Barreca, ed., *Last Laughs: Perspectives on Women and Comedy*. New York: Gordon and Breach Science. (Originally published in *Women's Studies 15*: 271–280)

Mitchell, Carol A. 1977. "The Sexual Perspective in the Appreciation and Interpretation of Jokes." *Western Folklore 36*(4) (October): 303–329.

———. 1985. "Some Differences in Male and Female Joke-Telling." In Rosan A. Jordan and Susan J. Kalcik, eds., *Women's Folklore, Women's Culture*. Philadelphia: University of Pennsylvania Press, pp. 163–186.

Pinsker, Sanford. 1984. "On or About December 1910: When Human Character—and American Humor—Changed." In William B. Clark and W. Craig Turner, eds., *Critical Essays on American Humor*. Boston: G. K. Hall, pp. 184–199.

Sheppard, Alice. 1984. "There Were Ladies Present: American Women Cartoonists and Comic Artists in the Early Twentieth Century." *Journal of American Culture 7*(3) (fall): 38–48.

Statistical Abstract of the United States. 1990. Washington, DC: U.S. Government Printing Office.

Swords, Betty. 1992. "Why Women Cartoonists Are Rare, and Why That's Important."
    In Regina Barreca, ed., *New Perspectives on Women and Comedy*. Philadelphia:
    Gordon and Breach, pp. 65–84.
Toth, Emily. 1984. "A Laughter of Their Own: Women's Humor in the United States."
    In William Bedford Clark and W. Craig Turner, eds., *Critical Essays on American
    Humor*. Boston: G. K. Hall, pp. 199–215.
Walker, Nancy A. 1981. "Do Feminists Ever Laugh? Women's Humor and Women's
    Rights." *International Journal of Women's Studies* 4(1) (January/February): 1–9.
———. 1988. *A Very Serious Thing: Women's Humor and Culture*. Minneapolis:
    University of Minnesota Press.

8

Basic Instinct: Does Hollywood Instinctively Marginalize Lesbians and Gays?

Michael P. Kelley

The homosexual extras and gay businessmen cooperated fully. They didn't know, of course, that the bad guy in the film was a homosexual that had just murdered nine people on a city bus. But then you rarely explain to extras what a whole scene is about.[1]

The year 1992 presented a flood of films that have ostensibly challenged the traditional gender roles that dominate American culture. From *Silence of the Lambs* to *Fried Green Tomatoes* to *Basic Instinct*, critics found characterizations wanting, lacking, and deplorable. Major campaigns were mounted against the film industry by such groups as ACT UP, Queer Nation, and GLAAD (Gay and Lesbian Alliance Against Defamation). The purpose of this chapter is to trace the highlights of these criticisms, assess the effects of them, and place them within the perspective of previous and similar efforts. In so doing, the possibilities as well as the limitations of such protests may become clearer.

THE OBJECTIONS

According to media critic Michael Medved, a 1989 poll reported that 82 percent of Americans "felt that movies contained too much violence, 80 percent [contained] too much profanity and 72 percent . . . too much nudity."[2] Despite these audience sentiments, the sixty-fourth Annual Academy Awards' Best Actor category honored "three murderous psychotics: Anthony Hopkins in *Silence of the Lambs*, Warren Beatty in *Bugsy*, and Robert De Niro in *Cape Fear* . . . a delusional homeless psychotic (Robin Williams for *The Fisher King*), and a depressed neurotic (Nick Nolte for *The Prince of Tides*)."[3]

Silence of the Lambs, "an FBI trainee's hunt for a serial killer" involving a "deliciously sadistic psychiatrist-turned-cannibal,"[4] might have been less disturbing had it been a less successful film. *Silence of the Lambs*, however, garnered five *major* Oscars, a feat accomplished only two other times in the sixty-four year history of the awards.[5] The gender criticism of *Silence of the Lambs* is twofold. Some critics objected to the film's character Buffalo Bill, "a cross dressing, misogynistic serial killer," because "the character embodies anti-homosexual stereotypes."[6] Other objections, however, focused on the film's divergence from the novel. As a GLAAD representative noted, "*Silence of the Lambs* is homophobic . . . because the psycho character is portrayed as a homosexual, even if he's not really in the book."[7]

Similar objections were raised about other films during 1992. When *Fried Green Tomatoes* diverged from the original story by *not* depicting the lesbianism inherent in the novel, *Advocate* critics attacked Jon Avnet, the movie's director, for "whitewashing . . . lesbian themes"[8] and "apparently think[ing] of lesbianism as an optional extra, like bucket seats in a sports coupe."[9] Although the lesbian relationship may have been clear to some viewers of the movie,[10] in a discussion of the film in a college class on sex roles, not one student who had previously viewed the movie recognized a lesbian theme. In response to the question of whether or not the film's main characters were lesbians, director Avnet is reported to have said "People can postulate what they want. . . . What I wanted to deal with was intimacy between two women. As to whether or not they are gay . . . who gives a shit?"[11]

There were a variety of other films that were attacked for their gender portrayals. *JFK* was criticized by GLAAD/LA for "a gratuitous and overwrought drag/bondage sequence that did not advance the story line" and for creating the "feeling that the gay community is twisted, pathetic and dangerous"; in short, GLAAD concluded that "the only gay characters [in *JFK*] were child molesters, racists, or just plain evil."[12] *The Prince of Tides* was criticized for presenting a "stereotypically flamboyant" gay male who asks Nick Nolte to dance at a party and won't take no for an answer, "enhanc[ing] the notion that gay men have raging hormones and must target all males."[13] *Father of the Bride* was criticized for "trot[ting] out every imaginable stereotype . . . commonly associated with effeminate men" in their portrayal of the wedding coordinator hired by Steve Martin for his daughter's wedding.[14]

By far, however, the most vitriolic criticisms of the film industry in 1992 were reserved for the Michael Douglas–Sharon Stone movie *Basic Instinct*. Unlike some other movies, from its inception *Basic Instinct* was subject to criticism and pressure from representatives of the lesbian and gay community. *Basic Instinct* depicts "a hard-drinking, psychologically unstable detective who falls in love with . . . a bisexual female novelist [and ice pick murderer], whose female lover is [likewise] presented as a violent . . . figure."[15] When the film was in production in San Francisco, local GLAAD representatives working with the original scriptwriter Joe Eszterhas obtained Eszterhas's concurrence "that the script contained 'certain insensitivities.'"[16] Director Paul Verhoeven, however, "refused to even consider" the scene changes proposed by Eszterhas and "certain lesbian, gay, and bisexual groups staged protests near the film site aimed at interrupting production."[17] This "marked the beginning of year-long protests in major metropolitan cities"[18] and mounting pressure on Eszterhas, director Verhoeven, producer Alan Marshall, and Carolco Pictures, all of which "came to very little"[19] change among the major participants to the dispute.

The objections, of course, were as varied as the objectors. As one Queer Nation member said, "We see ourselves [portrayed in film] as freaks, killers, psychopaths and perverts. We see ourselves as lonely victims. We see ourselves made to reflect straight anxieties about sexuality and gender."[20] According to the author of a critique that appeared in a Los Angeles–based, lesbian-oriented magazine, *Basic Instinct* is "not really about lesbians (or bisexual women, for that matter) at all. It's a woman-hating plot that's simply a twist on the classic Madonna/whore complex."[21] The National Organization for Women called *Basic Instinct* "one of the most blatantly misogynist films in recent memory."[22] Jack Garner, writing for Gannett News Service, noted almost as an afterthought that "*Basic Instinct* also deals with homosexuality and bisexuality in somewhat confused and confusing ways."[23] Chris Fowler, executive director of GLAAD/LA, wrote that "The lesbian portrayals [in *Basic Instinct*] are cardboard at best, derogatory and defaming at worst . . . the whole film reinforces the myth that lesbians hate men. . . . It is probably the most misogynistic film I have ever seen."[24]

David Ehrenstein may have encapsulated much of the criticism of the film when he reported that "*Basic Instinct* exists in a testosterone-crazed never-never land in which women, groomed to *Cosmo*-girl perfection, bark obscenities, smirk defiantly, and strike Valkyrie-like poses, only to melt into a puddle of feminine submissiveness when placed in the masterful arms of a 'real man.'"[25]

THE STRATEGIES AND TACTICS OF THE PROTESTERS

The aim, however, of gay activist groups such as ACT UP, Queer Nation, and GLAAD is not clearly discernible. Often the stated goals of these groups depended upon who was making the statement. One goal was to effect a boycott of the film *Basic Instinct*. Another goal was to stage an outdoor demonstration at the Dorothy Chandler Pavilion site of the Academy Awards as well as a visible protest during the award ceremony itself. It was reported "[i]n a news release issued in February, [that] the Los Angeles chapter of . . . Queer Nation . . . would 'shut down the Oscars and put an end to Hollywood's homohatred.'"[26] The New York *Daily News* reported that there would be "massive covert action" and that "[p]eople had 'infiltrated' at all levels. There was going to be a 'powerful' disruption."[27]

The tabloid press picked up where the activists left off. A front-page headline of the *National Enquirer* announced "Gays Plot to Ruin Oscar Night . . . by

Exposing Stars," and a front-page headline in the *Star* proclaimed "Gays Plot to 'Out' 60 Stars at Oscars" and, in smaller print, "Militants Smear Best Actress Nominee Jodie Foster."[28]

With this and much other coverage in the media, the actual results were less than overwelming. The Associated Press reported that *Basic Instinct* opened "at 1,500 theaters throughout the nation" and "[p]rotests occurred in San Francisco, Los Angeles, New York, and other cities" with "approximately 50 protesters" counted in the San Francisco demonstration."[29]

A visual editorial appearing in the April 10, 1992, issue of the Los Angeles–based *Frontiers* magazine pictured a theater poster ad for *Basic Instinct* that had been "defaced" or had its consciousness raised by the superimposition of Queer Nation–style bumper stickers.[30]

Then, as the Academy Awards drew closer, the *Los Angeles Times* reported that "articles were published in the show-business trade newspapers and elsewhere, suggesting that a disruption could occur at the . . . Oscars," that there were "plans to 'stop cars from getting to the Oscars,'" and that "maps to the homes of gay stars" would be distributed.[31] Two days before the Oscars, in an apparent warm-up to the big event, "about 100 activists demonstrated outside the Los Angeles offices of the Directors Guild of America."[32] And Aslan Brooke, writing in *Frontiers*, reported that "Queer Nation . . . did raise some eyebrows by passing out a map to 'Hopefully Hetero Stars' Homes,' which listed a large number of actors who 'have done nothing to promote queer visibility in film.'"[33]

Contrariwise, Judy Sisneros, a member of Queer Nation, was quoted as stating that her group decided against distribution of the maps "fearing that it would focus media attention on identification of closeted celebrities rather than on the depiction of gays and lesbians in film."[34]

EFFECTS OF THE PROTESTS

Although some of these events came to pass, others did not, and others may or may not have occurred. Queer Nation's claim to "shut down" the Oscars did not materialize and no protests occurred inside the Music Center. A protest rally did, however, materialize on the street. The protest crowd, estimated at "hundreds" by the *Advocate*, gathered well in advance of the award telecast. According to that reporter, police officers moved in on the crowd two and a half hours before the ceremony began. The *Los Angeles Times* added other details: "[d]ozens of police officers on foot and horseback" maintained their vigil and "[a]t least 10 people were arrested."[35] According to Annette Gaudino, one of the protesters, the arrests "took the leaders," which impacted on the subsequent demonstration: "The energy [of the protest] wasn't focused."[36]

One of the hopes of many activists was that Jodie Foster, the star of *Silence of the Lambs*, would "out" herself either prior to or at the Oscars by unequivocally declaring her lesbian sexual orientation. The gay publication *Frontiers* reported that "protesters chanted 'Dyke! Dyke!'" when "one Oscar nominee arrived."[37] The story was also reported by the *Los Angeles Times,* which guardedly reported that a banner that read "Quick, get out of the closet, there's a big moth in there" was hoisted at one point in the obvious hope that one actress would notice. But when she arrived—about a half-hour later—the actress got out on the other side of her car and walked diagonally away from the protesters. She did not appear to see the banner.[38]

In a different article on the same page, the *Times* reported Foster's reaction to the protests: "I think protest is good. . . . It's American, not against the law. It's in the Constitution." In an apparent allusion to the protesters' "outing" tactics, revealing names of purportedly gay actors, she added: "Criticism helps people learn . . . but anything else falls into the category of *undignified.*"[39]

Michael Szymanski's "Outing Oscar" article in the relatively obscure *Square Peg Magazine* was atypical in that it clearly identified "the actress" as Jodie Foster. It was also the only source that this author found that reported "publicists' rumors that gay radicals were going to throw blood on [Foster] and *Basic Instinct* star, Sharon Stone." The article also reported that each actress "had two security guards following their every step."[40]

Many of the announced actions of the various gay activist groups did not come to pass. There were no disruptions inside the music center. Gay maps to the homes of the stars may or may not have been distributed. Yet the media had *carried* the message. And if the sampling of letters to the editor published by the *Los Angeles Times* are at all representative, many viewers were offended by Jodie Foster's reference to her character as "feminist" and to the "rationalized cannibalism" of the film.[41]

Even *People* magazine noted in its review of *Basic Instinct* that "Gay activists . . . [had] launched a crusade against [the movie], arguing that the film is homophibic because it portrays lesbians and bisexuals as psychopathic killers."[42] As one Queer Nation member reportedly announced: "This is a post-modern demonstration: We announce the action. The media creates it. And then whatever happens happens."[43]

Not all coverage was welcomed in all quarters. A gay man residing in Orange County, California, objected to the "film at eleven" which began with "some guy in a tu-tu waving his arms in the air shrieking 'We're here, we're queer, and so are some of you.'" He also expressed vociferous objections to the telecast of

an interview with a man wearing white pancake make-up, eyelashes from here to Rhode Island, and a huge red hat. The words coming from his mouth were these: "I'm here to protest the negative images of gays by Hollywood." . . . Was I on vacation when we elected members of Act-Up [*sic*] and Queer Nation as the national gay and lesbian spokespeople?[44]

Another writer objected to GLAAD/LA's "nonexistent coverage of the actions surrounding this year's Academy Awards" in their May newsletter, claiming that "GLAAD had gone to great lengths to disassociate itself from the 'radical' techniques employed by some of the demonstrators, and from the forecasts of mass outings, telecast disruptions, and blood throwing (none of which occurred)."[45]

BROADER ISSUES

The protests against many of our current, popular movies may, at the least, have raised the public's gender consciousness. To some critics, the issue is simple: "If there's to be a gay killer, then we want to see a gay cop stop that person."[46] "*My Own Private Idaho* is about gay and sexually ambivalent male characters; then the videocassette's cover jacket should not picture the films' two male stars each with a woman!"[47]

The baseline objection seems to be that "homosexual men and women are almost never portrayed as real people with real jobs living real lives."[48] Lesbian, gay, and bisexual people are, nonetheless, portrayed in numerous films. When Vito Russo published the revised edition of his seminal study of homosexuality in film, *The Celluloid Closet* in 1987, he noted that "more than a hundred films [had] dealt with gay issues or featured gay characters" since the first edition that was published in 1981.[49]

The critique of gender portrayals in film is not recent. Russo first published his study in 1981. Since 1987 GLAAD has been working to "confront public expressions of homophobia or heterosexism, and to promot[e] the fullest possible understanding of the breadth and diversity of gay and lesbian lives."[50]

Moreover, it has been more than a generation (1973) since the Gay Activists Alliance joined the National Gay Task Force to issue media guidelines under the title "Some General Principles for Motion Picture and Television Treatment of Homosexuality." At that time, according to *Variety*, gay activists met with representatives from the Association of Motion Picture and Television Producers to effect a change in the depiction of homosexuals in the media.[51]

Although it has been more than twenty years since these two gay groups released their joint statement of principles, it is instructive to review their principles: First, homosexuality in itself is not humorous. Second, gender slurs such as "fag, faggot, dyke, queer, lezzie, homo, fairy, mary, pansy, [and] sissy" are insulting and their usage should be no different from such ethnic slurs as "kike, wop, spic, [and] nigger." Third, the same equitable treatment that should be applied to language should likewise be applied to the portrayal of behaviors. Fourth, though stereotypes are real, overreliance on stereotypes conceals the "broad spectrum of the gay community." Fifth, homosexuality is not an illness but rather "a natural variant of human sexuality. If all blacks or Jews or Irish or Chicanos were portrayed as anguished, oddball or insane, they'd be [as] angry [as gays]." Sixth, the industry has "an obligation to do [its] homework and free [itself] from . . . myths." Seventh, there is considerable choice in gay-themed material that can relate to general audiences and should be used. "Gays do not want to return to media invisibility." Last, though there is an advisory panel "available to the industry," there are gay people *in* the industry. The industry must "provide a climate in which they feel free to speak out openly."[52]

HOMOPHOBIA AS SYMPTOM

Rather than view homophobia in the media as the disease, it may be more useful to view homophobia as part of the larger whole of *stereotyping* and *heterosexism*. As Vito Russo observed, "Homosexuals are convenient scape-goats but their shabby treatment is only the most ostentatious aspect of a wider problem—that the diversity of American life has never been reflected in popu-lar films." Russo goes on to assert that "[t]here are virtually no black faces on the American screen . . . [except] the faces of clowns—Richard Pryor, Whoopi Goldberg, Bill Cosby, and Eddie Murphy . . . there are no black romantic leads of either sex . . . [n]or do we see Asian faces . . . except . . . as psychopathic drug runners or nymphet newscasters."[53]

In addition to the symptom of stereotyping, homophobia in film may also be interpreted as an example of heterosexism. As the British observer Mark Finch argued, "the attention to homosexuality in . . . films is also a delving deeper into the heterosexual gender system—a sort of inspection of the timbers for dry rot. . . . It is only through images of homosexuality that these films can afford to contemplate what really interests them"—namely, heterosexuality.[54]

Robert Hanke takes the argument for homophobia as heterosexism one step further in his analysis of hegemonic masculinity. In his essay on the subject, he labels the phenomena "in which any changes in images of male and female characters are taken as the displacement of dominant gender ideologies" a "progressive fallacy. . . . Put simply, hegemonic masculinity *changes* in order to remain hegemonic."[55]

Thus, in the few areas where gender ideologies seem to shift, the shift is apparent. The "feminist" statement that Jodie Foster saw contained in *Silence of the Lambs* character Clarice Starling is vitiated by the dominant masculine culture of the FBI as well as the grossly distorted sexualities of the antagonist characters Hannibal Lecter and Buffalo Bill. What is then reasserted in the film is the dominant, heterosexist ideology that cannot comprehend homosexuality, cross-dressing, body piercing, and tattooing in anything but a pathological sense. Indeed, the only efforts to humanize are directed at developing sympathy for the cannabilistic Lecter who yearns for the bucolic, for a window with a view of nature!

SUMMARY

To return, then, to the original question: Does Hollywood marginalize gays and lesbians? The only answer seems to be an unqualified yes. Hollywood reflects and re-creates the dominant gender ideal. And the maintenance of the dominant gender ideal necessities for its survival the marginalization of different gender ideals. As observers of gender, we may also need to acknowledge the hegemonic inclinations of other sexual orientations. For instance, hegemonic homosexuality is inclined to co-opt the ideals of monogamy from heterosexuality leading to a marginalization of multiple sexual encounter behavior into the classification of "promiscuity." Further, hegemonic homosexuality is inclined to accept mutually exclusive definitions of heterosexuality and homosexuality leading to a denial of the validity of bisexuality.

In the search for legitimacy and validity, the defender often asserts the claim of similarity. Thus, homosexuals may claim that they are "just like heterosexuals" in spite of the obvious, as well as less obvious differences, in sexual orientation, lifestyle, values, and so on. The search for acceptance can inadvertently foster denial and marginalization which, in turn, fans the flames of homophobia and misogyny.

NOTES

An earlier draft of this chapter was presented at the Fifteenth Annual Conference of the Organization for the Study of Communication, Language, and Gender, Hempstead, NY, October 16, 1992.

1. Bruce Dern discussing *The Laughing Policeman*, 1974, as quoted in the *Advocate* #613 (October 6, 1992), p. 22.

2. Michael Medved, "Has Hollywood Gone Too Far?" *USA Weekend* (March 27–29, 1992), p. 4.

3. Ibid.

4. Terry Pristin, "How Orion Kept Its *Lambs* Alive," *Los Angeles Times* (April 1, 1992), pp. F1, F6.

5. Terry Pristin, "*Silence of the Lambs* Sweeps 5 Major Oscars," *Los Angeles Times* (March 31, 1992), p. A1.

6. Ibid., p. A22.

7. Jehan Agrama, "Co-President's Column," *GLAAD/LA Reports* 4(5) (May 1992): 2.

8. "Shitty Lesbians," *Advocate* #603 (May 19, 1992), p. 91.

9. David Ehrenstein, "*Fried Green Tomatoes* Caps a Banner Year for Delesbianization," *Advocate* #596 (February 11, 1992), p. 67.

10. See Jehan Agrama's quote ("While some people feel the movie was very denatured, it *was* a lesbian film. We're claiming this one as our own.") in "Shitty Lesbians," p. 91; and the *GLAAD/LA Reports*' claim ("The producers may not think they have produced a 'lesbian love story,' but the emotional tie between the women speaks to the lesbian experience.") in "*Fried Green Tomatoes* Lesbian-Positive Picture," *GLAAD/LA Reports* 4(1) (January/February 1992): 5.

11. "Shitty Lesbians," p. 91.

12. "Stone Unturned by *JFK* Gay Portrayals," *GLAAD/LA Reports* 4(1) (January/February 1992): 3.

13. "*Prince of Tides*," *GLAAD/LA Reports* 4(1) (January/February 1992): 3.

14. "*Father of the Bride*," *GLAAD/LA Reports* 4(1) (January/February 1992): 4.

15. David J. Fox, "*Instinct* Sizzles at the Box Office," *Los Angeles Times* (March 23, 1992), p. F6.

16. Ibid.

17. Chris Fowler, "GLAAD News: Executive Director's Report," *GLAAD/LA Reports* 4(3) (April 1992): 10.

18. Aslan Brooke, "Basic Oscar," *Frontiers* (Los Angeles), (April 24, 1992), p. 13.

19. Fowler, "GLAAD News," p. 10.

20. Brooke, "Basic Oscar," p. 13.

21. Lynn Harris Ballen, "The Queers Who Cried Wolf?" *Square Peg Magazine* (May 1992): 25.

22. Brooke, "Basic Oscar," p. 13.

23. Jack Garner, "*Basic Instinct* Reveals Some Naked Truths about Sex," *Desert Sun* Special Section (March 20, 1992), p. 10. For what it's worth, he also observes that Sharon Stone's character is "a fascinating look at an ultra-manipulative, take-charge woman that is rarely seen on the screen."

24. Fowler, "GLAAD News," p. 10.

25. David Ehrenstein, "*Basic Instinct*: This is a Smart, Hot, Sexy, Commercial Film?" *Advocate* #601 (April 21, 1992), p. 87.

26. John Gallagher, "Protest Threats Raise Visibility at Academy Awards," *Advocate* #602 (May 5, 1992), p. 14.

27. Michael Signorile, "Hollywood Homophobia Was a Story Madly Spinning Out of Control," *Advocate* #602 (May 5, 1992), p. 31.

28. Graphics reprinted in *Advocate* #602 (May 5, 1992), p.31.

29. "*Basic Instinct* Opens to Protests from Homosexual Groups," *Desert Sun* (March 22, 1992), p. G1.

30. *Frontiers* (April 10, 1992), p. 64.

31. David J. Fox, "What Impact on Oscar for Gay Protest?" *Los Angeles Times* (March 16, 1992), pp. F1, F8. See also Chris Woodyard, "Officials Confident of Security for Oscars," *Los Angeles Times* (March 30, 1992), pp. B1, B3.

32. Gallagher, "Protest Threats," p. 14.

33. Brooke, "Basic Oscar," p. 13.

34. Gallagher, "Protest Threats," p. 15.

35. Robert W. Welkos and Eric Malnic, "Gay Activists Rally on Streets Outside Music Center," *Los Angeles Times* (March 31, 1992), p. F2.

36. Gallagher, "Protest Threats," p. 14.

37. Brooke, "Basic Oscar," p. 13.

38. Welkos and Malnic, "Gay Activists Rally," p. F2.

39. Elaine Dutka and David J. Fox, "*Lambs* Flock Revels in Success," *Los Angeles Times* (March 31, 1992), pp. F1, F2.

40. Michael Szymanski, "Outing Oscar," *Square Peg Magazine* (May 1992): 21–22.

41. "Oscar Letters: Feminism and Foster's Character in *Silence of the Lambs*," *Los Angeles Times* (April 4, 1992), p. F16.

42. Mark Goodman, *People* (March 30, 1992), p. 17.

43. Signorile, "Hollywood Homophobia," p. 31.

44. Peter Campione, "Gays, the Media, and Who's in Charge," *Orange County Blade* (July 1992): 8–9.

45. Tom Mertz, "Does GLAAD Promote 'Bland' Gay and Lesbian Images?" *Edge Magazine* #233 (June 17, 1992), p. 70.

46. Christ Uszler, head of the now-defunct Alliance for Gay and Lesbian Artists, in Brooke, "Basic Oscar," p. 13.

47. "The Degaying of *Private Idaho*," *GLAAD/LA* (August 1992): 5.

48. Joe DeChick, "*Instinct* Ignites Some Basic Controversies," *Desert Sun Weekend* (March 20, 1992), p. 12.

49. Vito Russo, *The Celluloid Closet*, rev. ed. (New York: Harper and Row, 1987), p. 248.

50. "GLAAD/LA Profile," a publicity release of GLAAD/LA (summer 1992).

51. Russo, *Celluloid Closet*, p. 220.

52. Ibid., pp. 220–221.

53. Ibid., p. 258.

54. Mark Finch, "Business as Usual: Substitution and Sex in *Prick up Your Ears* and Other Recent Gay-themed Movies," in Simon Shepherd and Mick Wallis, eds., *Coming on Strong: Gay Politics and Culture* (London: Unwin Hyman, 1989), p. 87.

55. Robert Hanke, "Hegemonic Masculinity in *thirtysomething*," *Critical Studies in Mass Communication* 7(3) (September 1990): 245.

Part III

Gender, Power, and the Media

Media images are enormously powerful. The gendered, sexed, raced, classed lives we see portrayed in popular culture are "larger than life" whether we see them on movie screens, billboards, or on television sets in the intimacy of our homes. As spectators we do more than passively witness visual messages presented to us through the mediums of television and film. In this section we continue to examine mediated messages, but we turn now from an examination of images represented in or absent from mediated artifacts to an examination of the politics of the representational process itself, exploring critically how spectators are addressed by mediated texts and what are the implications of this address.

In order to enter into the world of a given film or video text, viewers are enjoined to take on a role: we are addressed by the text in a particular language or vernacular; we are constructed by the text as a certain kind of assumed viewer, with a specific set of values, experiences, and identities. But the spectator to whom a text is directed may not resemble the actual viewer at all. When, for example, as feminist spectator subjects, we resist a text's "preferred" or hegemonic readings, seeing through its codes to the implicit assumption of a male, white, middle-class, or heterosexual viewer, we become strategically aware of what Teresa de Lauretis refers to as the complex relationship between ideologies of gender called up by representation of Woman and actual women as social subjects.[1] Similarly, it is not merely the absence or muting of mediated images of people of color, of working-class people, of gays and lesbians, or of any marginalized group that serves to reproduce the ideologies that oppress them. Rather, we need to deconstruct how such images are deployed and consider from what positions of power and points of view the texts are constructed. Are images of women and people of color presented as exoticized "others" depicted voyeuristically for a "mainstream" audience? Given that any text's meanings are arbitrary and contested, we can resist these meanings and ask when it is possible/desirable to reappropriate images, to use them intentionally, strategically for purposes other than those for which they were designed.

In Lisa Merrill's chapter, "Spectatorship and Complicity," she examines the implications of spectatorship in films that depict violence against women. By questioning who is assumed to be addressed by these films, Merrill interrogates a particular narrative structure wherein the plight of a female character is narrated to viewers by a male character who has witnessed her victimization. In examining the responsibilities, assumed complicity, or necessity for active resistance on the part of the spectator-characters, Merrill raises questions about everyday-life performances of aggressive masculinity and the ethics of spectatorship. How are spectators implicated in the acts they witness? To what extent is gender a performative act? How might we read violence against any member of a marginalized group as a "performance," and for whom? Given that both the films Merrill discusses are purported to depict "real-life" events, how has the shaping power of these narratives influenced audience members' experiences of the "news stories" that suggested them?

Patricia A. Sullivan's chapter also explores "the communication processes through which some voices become dominant and some voices become muted." Sullivan examines MTV as the site of her investigation, seeing beyond the question of whether and how a particular music video addresses predominantly male or female viewers, to the political implications and stereotypes invoked by such a construction. Because Sullivan recognizes that "the power to name extends to the power to control visual images," she chooses to encourage her college students to "develop resistive reading practices in response to media messages that marginalize the voices of women and people of color." Like Merrill's analysis of male characters who goad other men into a particular sexist and heterosexist treatment of women, Sullivan explores the construction of a male character in a Billy Idol video as a "nerd" because he does not exploit sexual opportunities with women. Because the "story" in this video is told through the first-person point of view of the male rock singer, female characters, though depicted, are again spoken for (as they are in the films Merrill discusses) by a male storyteller who addresses audience member/listeners who are assumed to share his values.

Lynn H. Turner also acknowledges the profound effect of popular media in shaping cultural values. As in Sullivan's chapter, Turner investigates "television programs as sites of struggles for meanings" rather than venues in which mainstream culture is unproblematically reflected. As with the resisting or oppositional readings Sullivan makes possible for her students, Turner asserts that "feminist critical theory takes on the task of examining how the dissemination of cultural values through art, literature, and popular culture devalues and reproduces the dominant ideology that oppresses women." Turner introduces her students to a variety of feminist theoretical positions, and then employs a popular situation comedy, *Coach*, as a text within which they can witness these contested "meanings" exemplified.

Although many cultural critics bewail the passivity assumed of viewers who uncritically take in popular culture messages from mainstream television, Deborah Petersen-Perlman intentionally employs television as a teaching tool in service of her self-professed feminist pedagogy. As with Sullivan and Turner, Petersen-Perlman takes as her project showing student spectators "how to be actors rather than settling for being acted upon" by the media. Her chapter presents both her rationale for teaching critical viewing of images of "the family" as it is presented in prime time television, and her methodology in setting up collaborative group projects, wherein college students take on responsibility for different aspects of the analytic process.

Each of these contributors attempts to meld theory and practice, recognizing, as critical spectators to popular media, that to "read" the narrative of visual texts on only their most literal, accessible terms would necessitate reifying the gendered values and attitudes represented. Yet the "meanings" of any symbol, artifact, image are open to question. One can provide alternative or oppositional readings. Each of these chapters presents a model for encouraging and teaching that critical practice.

NOTE

1. This reading of de Lauretis on the process of subjectivity is influenced by Jennifer Terry's "Theorizing Deviant Historiography" in Ann-Louise Shapiro, ed., *Feminists Revision History* (New Brunswick, NJ: Rutgers University Press, 1994), p. 299.

9

Spectatorship and Complicity: Who Is the "Accused" in Popular Film Depictions of Gender and Violence?

Lisa Merrill

In her book, *Terrifying Love: Why Battered Women Kill and How Society Responds* (1989), psychologist Lenore E. Walker states:

We live in a violent world, and in a society riddled with violent images. Through the media, through advertising, and in many other ways, we've become perpetual observers—if not actual perpetrators—of violence. Such exposure does not necessarily make a person abusive, but it can and does enable her or him to grow more accepting of brutality in the environment, to perceive it as normal. (p. 3)

As Molly Haskell, E. Ann Kaplan (1983), and others have noted, "two main cycles of films have dominated commercial cinema since the mid-1960s in the wake of the women's movement. The first excluded women (these were the so-called 'buddy' films); . . . while the second . . . showed women being raped and subjected to [other] violence" (Kaplan 1983, p. 73).

In this chapter I explore the relationship between traditional mediated depictions of masculinity and violence against women in two contemporary popular films. I investigate ways in which spectators to violence are depicted within the films, and how male characters are encouraged by other males to identify with perpetrators rather than victims. Finally, I explore the connection between homophobia and misogyny that underlies this identification and how the depiction of spectatorship on the screen reifies the position of the actual male spectator.

Mass-mediated narratives, like literary narratives, are presented from a specific point of view and directed to assumed spectators. Whether the film professes to present an account of actual violent acts, as in *Casualties of War*, a fictionalized account of actual acts, as in *The Accused*, or a wholly fantasized depiction of violence, as in *Clockwork Orange*, *Last Tango in Paris*, *Straw Dogs*, *Looking for Mr. Goodbar*, *Blue Velvet*, *Thelma and Louise*, and *Pulp*

Fiction, spectators are addressed in a way which assumes their vicarious identification with either perpetrator or victim of violence.

As Keya Ganguly (1992) asserts:

we need to scrutinize cultural representations to question the pleasures of the text, and also to expose how representations . . . can mute women's subjectivity. To an extent, then, the enterprise of feminist criticism must be to *re-present* to our audiences the strategies by which representations (in popular culture, for example) are effective in reproducing patriarchy. (p. 69)

Many contemporary films depict women characters victimized by misogynistic violence. The two films examined below, *The Accused* (1988), directed by Jonathan Kaplan, and *Casualties of War* (1990), directed by Brian DePalma, represent within the film the reactions and responses of spectators to acts of violence against women. Thus, in these films the medium of representation is being employed strategically in a reflexive manner which may illuminate the relationship between spectatorship and complicity in violence against women.

Although there are many differences between the two films, set respectively in the 1980s in Massachusetts and in the 1960s in Vietnam, there are numerous similarities. Both films depict actual brutal gang rapes committed against oppressed and marginalized women. Furthermore, in each film there is a male character who witnesses, but refuses to take part in, the crimes. In each film, male protagonists coerce, or attempt to coerce, each other into acts of violence against women through homophobic strategies of humiliation. In other words, the dynamic overtly displayed in these films is the connection between homophobia and misogyny. For a man to refuse to participate in acts of violence is to risk being perceived as homosexual. Both films are presented through the point of view of the male spectator-protagonist who observes, but does not participate in, the crimes.

CASUALTIES OF WAR

In many ways, Brian DePalma's *Casualties of War* is the more stereotypical of these two mainstream films. The opening credits tell us "This film is based on an actual incident that occurred during the Vietnam War. It was first reported by Daniel Lang in the *New Yorker* magazine in 1969."

The film opens with a shot of a young, clean-cut man (played by actor Michael J. Fox) riding a subway train in California. We see people get on and off, but there is a strangely hollow absence of sound as the camera fixes the viewer's gaze (and by implication, Fox's) on a young Asian woman sitting across from him. Then we see, as if fading into a blackout, the jungles of Vietnam momentarily superimposed. The daylight train scene fades to the blues and blacks of the jungle as the film flashes back in time to Private Ericksson's (Fox) experience in Vietnam. We see Ericksson's unit bombed and him stuck in a ditch, until rescued by Sergeant Meserve (Sean Penn). Meserve's character is macho and jaded. He embodies a masculinist depiction of bravado in the physical attitudes he assumes and in the degree to which he objectifies the Vietnamese people, whom he does not even acknowledge as human. In contrast, Ericksson tries to befriend the Vietnamese children, and speaks tenderly of his wife and baby at home. Meserve trusts none of the Vietnamese, and after he witnesses the death of his friend and fellow soldier, Brownie, Meserve decides to "requisition" a Vietnamese girl for "a little portable R and R to break up the boredom and keep up the morale." For Meserve (whose name easily translates into the blind acceptance of militarism, "me-serve"), the Vietnamese are objects, whether they are to be protected or to be used and destroyed.

Ericksson vehemently opposes the abduction and subsequent rape of the young woman. The film's spectators cannot help but identify with him. As the camera peeks into the various rooms where her family is sleeping, the viewer's gaze becomes Ericksson's as we, through the eye of the camera, are brought along for this expedition. When the young woman is awakened, screaming, and torn away from her family, the camera moves out for a long shot so that we see Ericksson's disgust and powerlessness as he proclaims, "We're supposed to be here to help these people." Diaz, the newest member of the unit, confides to Ericksson that he is "not going to rape anybody," but he soon gives in to pressure from the group. When Ericksson refuses, members of the unit taunt him, saying, "Maybe he's queer" and "Maybe when I'm done humping her, I'll hump you."

Apparently DePalma was accurate in his depiction of the attempt within the military to equate resistance to violence with male homosexuality. In a study of military men's stories, Helen Michalowski (1982) noted this equation was a recurring theme; for example, Wayne Eisenhart, a marine, reported:

During basic training, the man's insecurity about his own sexuality is manipulated so as to link sexuality with aggression and violence. . . . [O]ne is continually addressed as "faggot" or "girl." . . . By associating qualities that are stereotypically considered common to women and homosexual men with all that is undesirable and unacceptable in the male recruit, misogyny and homophobia are perpetuated in the military and in society at large. (pp. 329–332)

However, in Michael J. Fox's character, Private Ericksson, DePalma has constructed a protagonist most likely to refute the homosexual association. Ericksson is an enlisted man who chose to belong to the military rather than a draftee taken into the military against his will; Ericksson is married and father of a baby daughter. Hence the homophobic taunts do not threaten him. It is Ericksson's moral code which is threatened, first by the rapes and then by the murder of the Vietnamese woman. Even loyalty to his fellow soldiers takes second place to his adherence to his own religious and moral values.

As the film progresses, Ericksson's insistence on reporting the incident takes on a heroic quality. Despite the threats on his own life, and the apparent indifference of his commanding officers, Ericksson continues to confront Meserve, at one point saying with frustration: "Nobody cares, Meserve. I told everybody. You don't have to try to kill me, because nobody cares." Yet he persists and finally confides in a chaplin. The film then jumps to the court martial of the other members of Ericksson's unit. As the camera fades from one face to another, we hear them interrogated in a tone of sarcasm and incredulity: "So you don't feel responsible for the crimes of rape and murder?" and "You involved yourself in rape to avoid being ridiculed?" Each is found guilty and sentenced to many years of incarceration.

Casualties of War ends with Ericksson back on the subway, waking from the dream and running after a young Asian woman who asks, "Do I remind you of someone? You had a bad dream, but it's over now." The reassurance delivered by this nameless, anonymous female character in an open public space, at the end of Ericksson's ride, is doubly ironic: first, because her statement negates the degree to which violence has been used to construct race, gender, and sexuality in Ericksson's experience of Vietnam; and second, because, despite Ericksson's efforts, the nightmare is *not* over. Although Ericksson—and through him, the actual film spectators—did recognize the humanity of the brutalized young Vietnamese woman and the horrors of her rape and murder, titles at the very close of the film, before the credits, read, "Although this film is based on an actual incident, the names of the participants have been changed. Herbert Hatcher was found not guilty of murder. On appeal Hatcher's rape conviction was reversed and on retrial he was acquitted, his confession having been disallowed on constitutional grounds."

Although *Casualties of War* presents spectators with a protagonist who consciously and successfully resists the pressure exacted upon him to commit acts of violence against women, despite threats of humiliation, we are presented as well with what E. Ann Kaplan (1983) refers to as the oppression of women through representation itself (p. 73). For the story as it is told in *Casualties* is Ericksson's story, not the story of the nameless Vietnamese woman whose words we (and Ericksson) never understand. It is *his* dilemma, whether or not to accede to the power and threats of his male peers, and not her dilemma as she is raped and murdered, with which the audience is assumed to be concerned. In *The Feminist Spectator as Critic*, Jill Dolan (1991) asserts that "[p]erformance usually addresses the male spectator as an active subject, and encourages him to identify with the male hero in the narrative. The same representations tend to objectify women performers and female spectators as passive, invisible subjects" (p. 2).

Thus the "action," in terms of narrative story line in *Casualties*, takes place within the frame of the mind and memory of the male protagonist; and through him, to the film's (male) spectators. As Suzanne Kappeler (1986) notes in *The Pornography of Representation*, when consumers of mediated messages move from a content orientation to an analysis of the process of representation, we see that the "history of representation is the history of the male gender representing itself to itself" (p. 52). Actual spectators, whether male or female, heterosexual or homosexual, whether of European, Asian, or African descent, are addressed in mainstream U.S. films as if we were all male, heterosexual, white, middle-class, U.S. citizens. In *Casualties of War*, the "victim" whose concerns are most palpable to the audience is Ericksson, the white, straight male protagonist.

THE ACCUSED

Jonathan Kaplan's *The Accused* also concerns the rape of a woman by a group of men, as witnessed by a male spectator. But the narrative construction of *The Accused* highlights and calls into question the nature of spectatorship and representation from the opening frames. As the film begins, we (and the camera) are outside of a rundown local bar at the edge of an overpass of a major highway. Suddenly a young woman (Jodie Foster as Sara Tobias) bolts out of the door, screaming and clutching her clothes just as we see a young man in a phone booth, calling the police to report, "There's a girl in trouble . . . it's a rape . . . there's three or four guys . . . there's a whole crowd." He refuses to give his name. The camera cuts between the male character in the phone booth and Sara running into the road, desperately trying to flag down a motorist to get help. Through the windows of the phone booth, we watch the male character see Sara's escape.

As the film progresses, from Sara's examination in the hospital to her meeting with the deputy District Attorney (Kelly McGillis as Kathryn Murphy) assigned to represent her, viewers see Sara observed and spoken for by her attorney and later by the television reporters who broadcast details of the case on the news. Sara is a working-class client represented by an attorney and an object of representation to those spectators within the film who "see" her. Kathryn first surveys Sara through the window of the hospital examining room before meeting her. Later, when Sara is out of the room, Kathryn remarks to the nurses that, despite Sara's obvious bruises, she has so much liquor on her breath that it will be hard to get a conviction. As the film demonstrates, one must look like a sympathetic victim to secure the identification of the jury.

Sara is a working-class, hard-talking, hard-drinking woman who unabashedly describes to Kathryn her experiences with drugs, alcohol, and men. Kathryn determines that a jury will not find Sara a credible witness on her own behalf; so while discussing the case at a violent hockey game with her boss, Kathryn decides to "make a deal and put them away," to allow a plea bargain for a lesser charge. The class differences between the characters are further explored when we see Sara and one of the rapists, a college student named Bob, and his friend, Ken (the young man who called the police in the opening frame), all learn about the lesser charge while watching the local news broadcast on television. The camera cuts between Sara, at work as a waitress, glancing up at the screen; Ken, at work in the college cafeteria; and Bob, at the fraternity, relaxing and watching the TV news report as his fraternity friends cheer. Clearly, the working-class characters, muted and spoken for by the society at large, are doubly exploited. They work in service industries whereas the legal and academic institutions that shape their fate are constructed to serve the interests of privileged consumers. Sara, watching while she works, is informed of her fate in a manner that further reinforces her passive and objectified status; although her victimization is the subject of a news story, she must survey it, and herself, through the hegemonic frame of the network news broadcast.

Sara's despair escalates as soon as the decision to go to trial is taken from her. She has been silenced, deprived of her opportunity to tell her story by the woman assigned to speak for her. At this juncture in the film, class allegiances are stronger than those between these two women. Sara Tobias and Kathryn Murphy's relationship is characterized by a lack of reciprocity. Although Sara Tobias is portrayed as forthright and direct, their are few mutual gazes between the two women. Kathryn, conscious of how a jury would "see" Sara, appropriates and identifies with the male gaze as well, never fully acknowledging the other woman. Kathryn Murphy is more male identified and concerned with prosecuting a "winning" case than empowering the female victim to tell her own story.

The turning point of the film occurs as Sara accidentally encounters one of the male customers in the bar who watched and cheered while she was being attacked. At first, not recalling in what context he saw her last, the man attempts to flirt with her. When he recognizes her and becomes verbally abusive, reminding her of the incident, and of her powerlessness, she intentionally crashes her car into his truck repeatedly. This act of extreme frustration leads to injuries requiring her to be hospitalized.

While visiting her at the hospital, Kathryn observes the arrogance of this male witness, who characterizes Sara's rape as a "live sex show." He has conflated the rape, which he encouraged for his specular pleasure, with a "live sex show" performed by willing participants and is sexually aroused in a similar manner by either. This character embodies Catherine MacKinnon's (1993) notion that: "[i]n terms of what men are doing sexually, an audience watching a gang rape in a movie is no different from an audience watching a gang rape that is reenacting a gang rape from a movie, or an audience watching any gang rape" (p. 28).

MacKinnon has claimed that spectators' arousal by pornography contributes to a climate in which real acts of violence against women are tolerated, encouraged, witnessed as entertainment. Like MacKinnon, the film's fictional attorney Kathryn Murphy is appalled by this response. She finds those male spectators who perpetuated and encouraged the rape of Sara Tobias for their entertainment culpable, and she determines to prosecute them.

Kathryn returns to the bar where the rape occurred and sees the pinball machine on which Sara was attacked. As the camera pans the room, along with Kathryn, viewers discover pictured on the pinball machine an illustration of a scantily clad woman sitting in a basketball hoop. The game is called "Slam

Dunk." All the institutions of popular culture, even the material object of the pinball machine, contribute to the objectification and sexualizing of women. At a nearby videogame, Kathryn sees the date of Sara's rape illuminated with a name and score: "Ken" played this video game the night of Sara's attack and thus witnessed the crime. Ken is the witness who called the police in the opening scene of the film. Kathryn locates him, and, after some misgivings, he agrees to testify to observing a room full of men "induce, entreat, and encourage" Sara's attack. However, during a prison visit to one of the assailants, his classmate, Bob, Ken briefly loses his courage to testify. Negotiating between the peer pressure of gender identification and his own moral code, Ken temporarily hesitates. Sara acknowledges his fear when she confronts him after he withdraws from the case. "Are you scared?" she asks. When he nods his head, she replies, "Me, too." For the men in the bar to be found guilty, the rape must be witnessed by someone who was not complicit in the act. Resisting the patriarchal readings of representation is risky, but Ken agrees when faced with Sara's courage.

Up until this point, the film audience, like members of a jury, have heard characters describe events that occurred in the past. The film proceeds in a linear, realistic manner until Ken takes the stand. Then, with Ken's testimony at the trial, he starts to explain, "This girl walked in; she was sexy . . . ," the film flashes back to the bar and the night of the attack. It is only now, toward the end of the film, that viewers are to see the violent events that have been discussed as they "happened." Through the technique of flashback, Ken's experience of the rape is authorized as the "true" account, which viewers now see enacted before them. Thus we are again seeing a woman attacked through a convention that presents her story as seen through the eyes of a male witness. Sara is portrayed as a flirtatious, seductive woman who is conscious of being watched by every man in the bar. However, when Danny, the man with whom she is dancing, starts to force himself on her, it is clear that she is being attacked. The other men in the room demonstrate callous disregard for her welfare, shouting with excitement, "He's going to fuck her right there!" as Danny rips her clothes, and "Go for it, Danny!" Then one of the witnesses encourages others to rape her, saying, "Get the frat boy in there," "Go on, you might learn something," "Hold her down," and ". . . needle dick, are you a faggot?"

After the depiction of the multiple rapes in flashback, the film returns to its present time frame, in the courtroom. After a recess, as the jury's decision is read, we see Kathryn turn around to make eye contact with Sara. When the "witnesses" who encouraged the attack have been found guilty, both women and Ken exchange an appreciative look. At the close of the film, titles read, "One out of every four rape victims is attacked by two or more assailants."

DISCUSSION

What are we to make of the depiction of rape and the representation of sexuality and gender identity in the two films discussed above? First, as Gamman and Marshment (1989) explain in their book, *The Female Gaze: Women as Viewers of Popular Culture*, it is within popular culture that women and men are offered the culture's dominant definitions of themselves (p. 2). In the two films discussed above, and numerous others in which aggression against women is depicted, we see male characters pressuring other males to *act* in specific ways to "prove their manhood." Thus, it is through specific acts and behaviors that men are enjoined to perform their gender for each other.

In *Gender Trouble*, Judith Butler (1990) claims that "[g]ender is . . . an identity instituted through a stylized repetition of acts. . . . What is called gender identity is a performance accomplishment compelled by social sanction and taboo. In its very character as performative resides the possibility of contesting its reified status" (pp. 270–271).

The failure of one man to "act like a man" threatens the reified status of maleness as natural and innate, rather than a social construction. If one can choose to act like a man, one could just as well choose to act differently. But the choice of acting or representing gender, though not biologically determined, is reinforced by strong social sanctions. Butler (1990) claims that "gender performances in non-theatrical contexts are governed by [even] more clearly punitive and regulatory social conventions" (p. 278). Hence, one man's choice to act differently demonstrates that all gender-identified behavior is, in fact, chosen rather than innate. This may be enormously threatening to men, especially since such behavior has been afforded more social status, wheras behavior associated with women is historically devalued.

What are the qualities which characterize stereotypical masculine sexuality? Bruce Kokopeli and George Lakey (1982) argue that masculine sexuality has been shaped by the patriarchy to express domination, the oppression of women, competition among men, and homophobia (p. 231). Men who depart from this "ideal" are frequently portrayed as traitors to the male cause. Since women are devalued—and men who are perceived to be like women, or effeminate, are similarly devalued—men may go to extreme lengths to prove their manliness rather than endure the social humiliation that such refusal may engender.

But in the performance of extreme forms of "macho" behavior men are, in fact, performing for other men. Thus the male performer demonstrates his masculinity for the male spectator(s). Similarly, in mass-mediated communication, as in all forms of representation, the two active subjects, or participants, are the author of the act and the spectator. Both of these subject positions are frequently assumed to be male (Kappeler 1986, p. 51).

Whether individual male "actors" in real life "perform" acts of violence against women for the consumption of other actual male viewers, or male filmmakers employ the cinematic apparatus to capture and convey images of female victimization for assumed male spectators, many of the same voyeuristic impulses are implied. A voyeuristic response to violence against women may account, to some degree, for some of the success of mainstream films. In other words, even if the plot casts these actions as despicable, the camera's lingering presentation of each specific act depicted may "encourage, induce, and incite" a way of seeing women that further objectifies and victimizes them.

Yet, as the very text of *The Accused* illustrates, looking at a violent act may not in itself be a crime, but "watching" in such a way as overtly to encourage the performance of that crime for one's visual consumption renders the spectator culpable.

The complex interrelationship among spectatorship, objectification, and violence in popular culture and everday life is clearly illustrated in the circumstances of the actual rape on which *The Accused* was based. In the early 1980s *Hustler* magazine featured a photo essay entitled "Dirty Pool" in which a young woman was gang-raped on a pool table in a working-class neighborhood bar, held down and repeatedly penetrated by penises and pool cues. As Ann Russo (1992) notes, three months after the publication of this issue, a twenty-one-year-old woman was gang-raped in a bar in New Bedford, Massachusetts. While she was raped, the rest of the customers watched and cheered. Although the rapists and witnesses who condoned the actual incident may not have been directly influenced by the magazine, Russo notes that "in the subsequent August 1983 issue of *Hustler* a 'picture-postcard' appears which is said to come from New Bedford. It features a woman laying across a pool table waving to the audience with the statement, 'Greetings from New Bedford, Massachusetts, the Portuguese Gang-Rape Capital of America'" (p. 158). As Russo indicates, this publication both trivializes completely the specific woman's rape and makes an ethnic slur against the Portuguese community, specifying the act as "Portuguese" rather than an act of violence potentially committed by males of any class and ethnicity. The waving woman in the postcard further distances viewers from the pain of actual rape victims. Thus the depiction of a woman's victimization and male spectators' complicity with the act was constructed by and reflected within cultural artifacts which commodify and fetishize her pain for the consumption of other spectator-readers who are positioned and greeted as voyeurs.

In the two films cited above, viewers are invited to take up positions in which they/we are addressed by male characters who also function as spectators, and yet speak on behalf of the woman violated. In re-presenting fictionalized narratives of incidents known to have actually occurred and been reported in the news media, they problematize the ethics of spectatorship and complicity and foreground the construction of gender and sexuality implicit in the "telling" of both stories. Both films feature male characters who resist the peer pressure to demonstrate their heterosexuality by abusing women; yet both filmmakers employ narrative frames that empower and validate the male character, setting him up as an omniscient "spokesperson" who addresses the actual film spectator—also assumed to be male.

What is the experience of a *female* spectator to the depictions of acts of violence against women? To the extent that the cinematic apparatus serves to "structure dominance through processes of identification and objectification" (Gamman and Marshment 1989, p. 7), female spectators may respond by either identifying with male characters or the objectified female victim. Kaplan (1983) claims that "[w]omen are oppressed . . . both [by] the power of the camera to subdue women and the way the camera constructs a masochistic female spectator" (p. 73). Given that, according to Dolan (1991), "The male spectator's position is the point from which the text is most intelligible" (p. 12); "the female spectator is placed in an untenable relationship to representation. . . . If she identifies with the male hero, she becomes complicit in her own indirect objectification" (p. 13). How is it possible to resist this masochistic objectification?

Films that feature, and even fetishize, violence against women often have been read as if addressed to a spectator who is, on the one hand, neutral or "universal," without specifying that that universe is hegemonically constructed as male, heterosexual, and complicitous with this violence. For example, as Susan Brownmiller (1975) observed in *Against Our Will: Men, Women and Rape*, in 1972 *Newsweek* published reviews of both *Clockwork Orange* and *Frenzy* by their senior film critic, Paul D. Zimmerman. In the review of *Clockwork Orange*, Zimmerman asserted that "As a fantasy figure Alex appeals to something dark and primal in all of us. He acts out our desire for instant sexual gratification, for the release of our angers and repressed instincts for revenge, our need for adventure and excitement" (p. 334). With Hitchcock's *Frenzy*, Zimmerman claimed that "Hitchcock's graphic, brutalizing handling of a rape sequence with a crescendo of groans from the killer mixed with the recited prayers of the victim triggers *our own latent excitement* . . . [and makes] his audiences accomplices to his acts of criminal genius" (cited in Brownmiller 1975, p. 335; italics mine).

Zimmerman's readings of these films, though acknowledging spectators' complicity, completely negate the possibility of a female (or male) spectator who identifies with the position of the prospective victim and doesn't feel sexual gratification or latent excitement at witnessing her pain. In the more than twenty years since Zimmerman's misogynist reviews were published, an interrogation and deconstruction of gender and genre categories has afforded critical theorists and spectators perspectives from which to question which points of view and whose interests are privileged, reified, or negated by various techniques of representation.

Regardless of the dominant readings ascribed to a cultural artifact, subversive and oppositional readings *are* possible. As Gamman and Marshment (1989) note, "Popular culture is a site of struggle. . . . [I]t can also be seen as a site where meanings are contested and where dominant ideologies can be disturbed" (p. 1). Women may choose to read against the text of a film, to resist its dominant meanings and foreground instead the experience and relationships of the female characters. In *The Accused*, for example, the growing sense of mutuality and trust that develops in the relationship between the two female characters is depicted through the gradually increasing amount of mutual glances between them. *The Accused* can be seen as a woman's survival story, as a story of female bonding and support, where one woman learns to validate and empower the other.

On the other hand, films that afford spectators such a muted and objectified depiction of a female character's experience that they offer little or no way to identify with any but the male protagonists who abuse her must be uncovered and "read" with resistance. Only by so doing can we uncover the myth of objectivity that casts as "universal" and "human" specifically heterosexual male experiences of the world and negates all other points of view.

REFERENCES

Brownmiller, Susan. 1975. *Against Our Will: Men, Women, and Rape*. New York: Simon and Schuster.

Butler, Judith. 1990. "Performative Acts and Gender Constitution: An Essay in Phenomenology and Feminist Theory." In Sue Ellen Case, ed., *Performing Feminisms: Feminist Critical Theory and Theatre*. Baltimore, MD: Johns Hopkins University Press, pp. 270–282.

Dolan, Jill. 1991. *The Feminist Spectator as Critic*. Ann Arbor: University of Michigan Press.

Gamman, Lorraine, and Margaret Marshment, eds. 1989. *The Female Gaze: Women as Viewers of Popular Culture*. Seattle, WA: Real Comet Press.

Ganguly, Keya. 1992. "Accounting for Others: Feminism and Representation." In Lana Rakow, ed., *Women Making Meaning: New Feminist Directions in Communication*. New York: Routledge, pp. 60–79.

Kaplan, E. Ann. 1983. *Women and Film: Both Sides of the Camera*. New York: Methuen.

Kappeler, Suzanne. 1986. *The Pornography of Representation*. Minneapolis: University of Minnesota Press.

Kokopeli, Bruce, and George Lakey. 1982. "More Power Than We Want: Masculine Sexuality and Violence." In Pam McAllister, ed., *Reweaving the Web of Life: Feminism and Nonviolence*, Philadelphia: New Society, pp. 231–240.

MacKinnon, Catharine. 1993. *Only Words*. Cambridge, MA: Harvard University Press.

Michalowski, Helen. 1982. "The Army Will Make a 'Man' out of You." In Pam McAllister, ed., *Reweaving the Web of Life: Feminism and Nonviolence*. Philadelphia: New Society, pp. 326–335.

Russo, Ann. 1992. "Pornography's Active Subordination of Women: Radical Feminists Reclaim Speech Rights." In Lana Rakow, ed., *Women Making Meaning: New Feminist Directions in Communication*. New York: Routledge, pp. 144–166.

Walker, Lenore E. 1989. *Terrifying Love: Why Battered Women Kill and How Society Responds*. New York: HarperCollins.

10

Evolving Images of Women and Men:
The Construction of Gender Roles on MTV

Patricia A. Sullivan

A radical critique of literature, feminist in its impulse, would take the work first of all as a clue to how we live, how we have been living, how we have been led to imagine ourselves, how the language has trapped as well as liberated us, how the very act of naming has been until now a male prerogative, and how we can begin to see and name—and therefore live—afresh.

Adrienne Rich
(1979, p. 35)

In her essay "Lies, Secrets, and Silence," Adrienne Rich (1979) suggests that feminist critics must enter "old texts from new critical directions" in order to "understand the assumptions in which we are drenched" (p. 35). In engaging texts through feminist critical acts, Rich argues that women not only seek "self-knowledge" but also confront "the self-destructiveness of male-dominated society" (p. 35). My course on communication and gender is designed to encourage female *and* male students to engage in resistive reading practices so that they will be able to challenge "the self-destructiveness of male-dominated society." Early in the semester I establish a theoretical framework that is used throughout the course to examine gender constructions in a number of communication contexts. Gender constructions are examined in the television drama, music television videos (MTV), advertising, and the novel. This essay focuses on my use of MTV in the communication and gender course. First, I map the theoretical framework that informs dialogue in the course, then I turn to a discussion of MTV in terms of that framework.

THE THEORETICAL FRAMEWORK

After I provide students with an overview of research on communication and gender, I develop a theoretical framework that embraces the ideas of Carol Gilligan (1982), Cheris Kramarae (1981), Dale Spender (1992), Mary Field Belenky, Blythe McVicker Clinchy, Nancy Rule Goldberger and Jill Mattuck Rule (1986), and bell hooks (1984). Students are encouraged to reflect on the communication processes through which some voices become dominant and some voices become muted. Although theorists mentioned above foreground the power of language in communication, course discussions emphasize that the power to name extends to the power to control visual images.

Spender (1992), relying on the work of Shirley Ardener and Edwin Ardener (1978), articulates two important statements in *Man Made Language* that become touchstones for the analysis of discourse in my communication and gender course. She explains the process by which women's voices become muted and notes: "Inherent in this analysis of dominant/muted groups is the assumption that women and men will generate different meanings, that is, that there is more than one perceptual order, but that only the 'perceptions' of the dominant group, with their inherently partial nature, are encoded and transmitted" (1992, p. 77). Furthermore, Spender observes that "It is my belief that if women were to gain a public voice, they would in many instances supply very different meanings from those that have been provided, and legitimated, by males" (p. 78).

The emphasis on "different perceptual orders" and "different meanings" also provides the opportunity for me to address dominant and muted voices from an intercultural perspective. I encourage students to be aware that much of the early gender research focused exclusively on the muted voices of white women. bell hooks's theoretical ideas provide a helpful departure point for creating a more inclusive framework for analyzing dominant and muted voices from the vantage point of women and men of color.

The discussion of dominant and muted voices thus establishes the central problem addressed in this course. Because this course relies on a rhetorical critical approach to communication and gender, I address the problem of hearing "different voices" through the filter of traditional rhetorical approaches. Students read an essay that summarizes problems with approaches to rhetorical theory and criticism that exclude the experiences of women. "Toward a Rhetorical Theory Accounting for Gender" by Catherine A. Dobris (1989) identifies three problems that mark traditional rhetorical critical approaches. Because the framers of such approaches—the dominant voices—have been male, the approaches reflect "a male universe of ideas" (p. 151). This "male universe of ideas" "fails women in at least three ways" (p. 149).

First, traditional rhetorical critical approaches overlook "female value systems" (p. 149). As an illustration, Dobris points to standards used to evaluate discourse and says: "Traditional critics may place greatest emphasis on the final impact of a poem, short story or speech, failing to recognize that the author intended a more conjunctive, less goal-oriented style" (p. 149). If narratives written by women violate this "goal-oriented style," they may "be judged inadequate" (p. 149). Second, Dobris indicates that traditional approaches to rhetorical criticism may devalue women as creators and as subjects. Men have set the standards, for example, for appropriate subject matter in speeches, novels, etc. If women speak or write about childbirth or women's rights as opposed to politics or sports, their work may be "labeled as deficient" (p. 149). Additionally, women face a double-bind situation. Even if they choose to write about "important topics" such as politics or sports, they may not be viewed as credible sources because they are women (p. 149). Women are women and their voices are muted even when they decide to play by the rules that frame "the male universe of ideas."

Finally, women's experiences are marginalized by traditional critical models that do not "take female experiences, attitudes, values, and beliefs into account" (p. 149). Traditional critical models do not provide the tools to analyze discourse produced by women.

When the course turns to communication contexts, students are encouraged to develop resistive reading practices in response to media messages that marginalize the voices of women and people of color. "Oppositional Decoding as an Act of Resistance," an essay by Linda Steiner (1988) published in *Critical Studies in Mass Communication*, provides guidance as members of the class work together to develop resistive reading strategies. Steiner argues that readers of *Ms.* magazine, who submitted offensive advertisements and clippings from a range of media sources for republication in the "No Comment" feature, were engaging in oppositional decoding. Readers "read against" those advertisements and clippings and refused to accept what Stuart Hall (1980a, 1980b) refers to as "the preferred readings"—the readings suggested by dominant culture. Steiner proposes that reading against such texts foregrounds marginalized or muted voices—marginalized or muted interpretations.

Additional ideas for resistive reading are provided by Teresa de Lauretis (1984). In *Alice Doesn't: Feminism, Semiotics Cinema*, de Lauretis (1984) offers suggestions for reading against hegemonic cinematic texts. She identifies two approaches for interpreting the cinematic text. When viewers approach a film through the lens of the dominant code, they fill in "gaps"; when viewers approach a film through the lens of the muted or marginalized code, they seek "borders" (p. 99). "Gaps" demand that viewers visualize "preferred readings"; "borders," on the other hand, invite viewers to visualize alternative readings. De Lauretis notes:

Borders are not gaps—in a story, in a chain of signifiers, in a presumed continuity of the drive from excitation to discharge to excitation—that can be filled, overtaken, and thus neglected. Borders stand for the potentially conflictual copresence of different cultures, desires, contradictions, which they articulate or delineate. Like the river between two cities, two countries, two histories, in the surprising last shot of the film, borders mark difference itself; a difference that is not just in or in the other, but between them and in both. Radical differences cannot perhaps be represented except as an experiencing of borders. (p. 99)

During the examination of contexts for communication and gender, students are invited to search for "borders" in challenging "preferred readings" of television programming, advertising, and the novel.

By synthesizing recommendations from Steiner and de Lauretis, I offer suggestions for "resistive reading." When students search for borders, they "read against" expected interpretations and refuse to fill in the "gaps" in predictable ways. Steiner notes a number of possibilities for "resistive reading" as revealed in her analysis of the *Ms.* "No Comment" feature. Resistive readers objected to advertisements that depicted women as men's property. Other "offensive themes" identified by Steiner include: the "mocking or condemning of feminism"; "the social acceptance of sexual exploitation"; "the authority of science against women"; the suggestion "that women enjoy sexual abuse or violence or that beating women is fun and unproblematic"; "gender stereotyping"; the assumption that it is acceptable for "men to presume to speak for women"; the assumption that women are "stupid or silly"; and the trivialization or undermining of "women's work and accomplishments" (pp. 7–10).

Steiner relies on Hall's work but modifies his theoretical ideas to embrace a feminist approach to cultural criticism. She notes that although Hall recognizes possibilities for resistive reading, he does not speculate on why audiences might "read against" dominant codes or how audiences might use information gained from oppositional reading practices.

In her essay Steiner maps the value for audiences engaging in oppositional reading practices. She poses a question: "Why do readers choose to attend to markers of their low social status and of their status as sexual objects and to the hegemonic structures responsible for maintaining that status?" (p. 11). Her response to this "why" informs the logic behind the resistive reading practices advocated in my communication and gender course. She notes that oppositional reading is "therapeutic" (p. 11). However, she suggests that the value of resistive reading goes beyond therapy for those whose voices have been marginalized.

First, Steiner argues that resistive reading serves an important consciousness-raising function. Resistive reading permits the muted group to define itself and its concerns.

Most centrally, the activity gives shape and meaning to experiences, symbolically marking the group's normative boundaries and reconfirming its convictions and commitments. The group must demarcate its world view from that of the dominant culture. The newly produced texts both violate the dominant code and, by extension, the value system it sustains. They also produce and nourish alternative codes and values. (p. 11)

Furthermore, when alternative codes and values are produced and nourished, "converts" promote and continue to work for change that would reflect those alternative codes and values.

Finally, Steiner argues that the collection of materials in "No Comment" serves a vital role in bringing about change. She observes that such collections serve as a reminder that women's rights are violated in a range of communication contexts—not just "pornographic magazines" (p. 12). The spirit of collection dominates my course as I urge students—female and male—to recognize the harm done to women by advertising, newspaper articles, and television programming. Without such a recognition, the voices of women and people of color will remain on the margins of discourse. Steiner comments:

"Political pornography" is readily available, in rural family magazines, and mail-order catalogs. The more salient political battles actually must be waged against and within these areas. These items corroborate feminists' belief that dominant mass media do ideological work and that, regardless of media effects in the behavorial sense, mainstream content must be contested. (p. 13)

Throughout my course on communication and gender, we contest "mainstream content." A focus on MTV provides one context for protesting "mainstream content."

RESISTIVE READING AND MTV

When my course turns to MTV as a communication context, students already have engaged in resistive reading of television dramas (such as *Thirtysomething* and *Northern Exposure*). However, many students seem to assume that the "offensive messages" on MTV will be easy to identify. In other words, they believe that filling in gaps in the "obvious" way, as implied by hegemonic codes, will pose few challenges. Foregrounding "different" or marginalized voices will be a straightforward proposition when viewing music videos.

Two books and one scholarly essay provide departure points to suggest that music videos represent sophisticated communication artifacts. E. Ann Kaplan (1987) remarks in *Rocking around the Clock: Music Television, Postmodernism, and Consumer Culture* that "MTV is more obviously than other programs one nearly continuous advertisement, the flow being merely broken down into different *kinds* of ads" (p. 143).

Lisa Lewis's book, *Gender Politics and MTV: Voicing the Difference* (1990), provides the central focus for analysis of music videos in my communication and gender course. She proposes that powerful female rock artists—such as Madonna—have changed the landscape of MTV by creating videos that resist the patriarchal codes that dominated the channel in its early days. In the early days of MTV (1981–1983), Lewis claims that Warner Amex Satellite

Entertainment Company (WASEC) offered "male-address videos" designed to appeal to male adolescents. In these videos, "'the street' became an overarching sign system for male adolescent discourse" (p. 43). "The street" symbolized "the male adolescent quest for adventure, rebellion, sexual encounter, peer relationships, and male privilege" (p. 43). The patriarchal discourse exploited women and girls by "reproducing coded images of the female body, and positioning girls and women as objects of male voyeurism" (p. 43). MTV thus targeted the male adolescent and exploited stereotypic images of women. The female point of view was missing in the early days of MTV.

Lewis suggests, however, that in 1983 female musicians found a "voice" on MTV and appeared in videos that spoke to female experiences. MTV became more inclusive as female musicians struggled to "rework the ideological stance of male privilege into a redress of grievances for girls by approximating the richness of signification that the image of 'the street' holds for boys and men" (p. 109). "Female-address videos" are marked by what Lewis refers to as "access signs" and "discovery signs" (p. 109). When female musicians rely on "access signs," they appropriate the privileges of the male domain—"the street." In these videos, female musicians invade "male space" and demand "parity with male-adolescent privilege" (p. 109). Female-address videos also contain what Lewis defines as "discovery signs" (p. 109). These "discovery signs refer to and celebrate directly female modes of cultural expression and experience. These signs attempt to compensate for the devaluation and trivialization of female-cultural experience by presenting images of activities that are shared by girls alone" (p. 109).

Thus, Lewis argues that women have found their textual space on MTV. The "discovery signs," in particular, suggest female empowerment. Examination of music videos—a provocative form of mainstream communication targeted for adolescents—provides students with opportunities to practice the resistive reading strategies proposed in the course. Students note links between Lewis's ideas and theoretical constructs proposed by Spender (1992), Kramarae (1981), Gilligan (1982), Belenky et al. (1986), hooks (1984), Steiner (1988), and de Lauretis (1984). Ultimately, this exercise raises questions about Lewis's approach to male-address video and female-address video. I encourage class members to critique music videos with an eye to determining whether women do have a voice on MTV.

A survey of music television reveals that the male-address video continues to dominate programming. "Rock the Cradle of Love" by Billy Idol is used to illustrate the male-address video genre. In this video, an apartment serves as the metaphorical "street," the site where "adolescent boys carve out their own domain" (p. 43). As Lewis notes: "Even when the physical image of the street was absent from the video, it remained an implied presence, for as a sign system it summarized perfectly the male-adolescent quest for adventure, rebellion, sexual encounter, peer relationships, and male privilege" (p. 43).

One reason that I use "Rock the Cradle of Love" to demonstrate the male-address video is that it represents an unusual twist on the genre. Lewis's accounts of male-address videos do not hold explanatory power for one of the most interesting dimensions in "Rock the Cradle of Love." "Rock the Cradle of Love" not only positions women as "objects of male voyeurism," but men who refuse to recognize their "male privilege"; therefore, this video provides special opportunities to engage female and male audience members in resistive reading. David D. Gilmore's (1990) book, *Manhood in the Making: Cultural Concepts of Masculinity* provides a starting point for discussing masculine gender constructions in our culture. Gilmore emphasizes that women are *born* women, but men *become* men through "testing." For example, men become men by demonstrating their sexual prowess. An essay by Bill Kidd (1987), "Sports and Masculinity," provides another reference point for stereotypic constructions of masculinity. "Sports and Masculinity" explores the role that sports play as "men become men." The voyeuristic singer of "Rock the Cradle of Love" mocks the "nerd" who refuses to be tested—in this case sexually tested—and become a man.

In "Rock the Cradle of Love," Billy Idol symbolizes the male who recognizes that he has particular privileges simply because he is male. He has the right to "adventure, rebellion, sexual encounter, peer relationships, and male privilege." He also has the right to mock males who do not exploit their male birthright. The rock singer is the voyeur who invades the apartment of a stereotypical "nerd"—a male who does not have the courage to pursue sexual adventures and to exploit women—and goads him to "Rock the Cradle of Love."

A woman knocks at the "nerd's" door; she is admitted, removes her eyeglasses, and turns into a temptress. After students view this video, a number of the "offensive themes" identified by Steiner emerge during discussion. Indirectly, for example, the video indicts feminism; "Rock the Cradle of Love" communicates that gender relations in our society have not changed; women still want to please men. Because the story is told through the voyeuristic perspective of the rock singer, the message seems to be that men know what women want and can speak for them. Additionally, the video suggests that "real men" know what "real men" want and can speak for them.

When class discussion turns to discovery and access signs in the female-address video, resistive reading centers on Madonna's music videos. Lewis argues that Madonna has exercised extraordinary influence in developing the female-address video. Due to her professional success, she has "creative control over her own representation" (p. 106). Furthermore, Lewis suggests that Madonna's "appropriation and resignification of the standard female representation was a fundamental upset to the standard's ability to function as a strategy to thwart female musician authorship and subjectivity" (p. 106).

Class discussions trace Madonna's works as female-address videos. Her reliance on access and discovery signs is mapped through examination of "Like a Prayer," "Vogue," and "Justify My Love." As we work together during class sessions to unpack the music videos, the limitations of Lewis's genres become clear. Lewis's music television video genres encourage viewers to "fill in the gaps" rather than seek "borders." "Vogue" in particular defies categorization according to Lewis's schema; Madonna forces viewers to engage in resistive reading by mocking stereotypic gender representations.

When class discussion turns to "Vogue," an essay by Cathy Schwichtenberg (1992) provides guidance. "Madonna's Postmodern Feminism: Bringing the Margins to the Center" proposes that the video artist defies gender boundaries because she defies easy categorization.

[She] fracture[s] the notion of an "identity" with a motley pastiche of interests, align-ments, and identities that intersect at decisive moments. Such provisional coalitions could present a formidable challenge to patriarchal moralism, which, lacking the pre-sumed immanence of identity categories, would have a more difficult time maintaining social control over "others" aligned in a disparate unity. (p. 128)

In "Vogue," Madonna juxtaposes images that defy the viewer to fill in gaps in accordance with stereotypic gender constructions.

Although Madonna "vamps" and plays on images of Dietrich, Harlow, and Monroe, she also mocks traditional images of women by donning outrageous breast cones. She urges viewers to resist the image of the "vamp" as she challenges hegemonic images associated with female sexuality. Furthermore, "Vogue" carves out space for homosexuality and bisexuality—provinces not accounted for in Lewis's schema. The video contains so much oppositional coding that viewers cannot simply fill in the gaps; they must seek borders.

As the discussion of MTV as a context for communication and gender closes, students raise questions about Lewis's approach to the analysis of music videos. Her schema cannot account for "Vogue" or any music video that does not trade on stereotypic gender constructions. Lewis's schema helps viewers provide "preferred readings" of music videos, but it does not invite viewers to provide "oppositional readings" of music videos. In addition, students raise questions about Lewis's approach as informed by white heterosexual gender constructions. The discussions of MTV as a communication context push students to take visual constructions of gender in mainstream communication more seriously.

CONCLUSIONS

Throughout my communication and gender course, I urge students to scrutinize their predispositions to fill in textual "gaps." Some texts, such as "Vogue," challenge students to recognize "borders." My course does examine a range of communication contexts; however, I consider the examination of visual communication especially important for my students.

In *Eloquence in an Electronic Age: The Transformation of Political Speechmaking*, Kathleen Hall Jamieson (1988) argues that the success of a public speaker hinges on her or his ability to "evok[e] common visual experiences" (p. 119). Although Jamieson's ideas center on the transformation of public speaking, her observations speak to the importance of educating our students to "read" visual communication. She notes: "Because television is a visual medium whose natural grammar is associative, a person adept at visualizing claims in dramatic capsules will be able to use television to short-circuit the audience's demand that those claims be dignified with evidence" (p. 13).

Encouraging my students to engage in oppositional reading of music videos is especially important. After the discussion of music videos, most students voice a new appreciation for the power of visual communication when viewed through the critical lens that frames the communication and gender course. Additionally, most students indicate that they feel empowered as resistive readers.

REFERENCES

Ardener, Shirley. 1978. *Defining Females*. New York: John Wiley.

Belenky, Mary Field, Blythe McVicker Clinchy, Nancy Rule Goldberger, and Jill Mattuck Tarule. 1986. *Women's Ways of Knowing: The Development of Self, Voice, and Mind*. New York: Basic Books.

de Lauretis, Teresa. 1984. *Alice Doesn't: Feminism Semiotics Cinema*. Bloomington: Indiana University Press.

Dobris, Catherine A. 1989. "Toward a Rhetorical Theory Accounting for Gender." In Kathryn Carter and Carole Spitzack, eds., *Doing Research on Women's Communication: Perspectives on Theory and Method*. Norwood, NJ: Ablex, pp. 137–160.

Gilligan, Carol. 1982. *In a Different Voice*. Cambridge, MA: Harvard University Press.

Gilmore, David. 1990. *Manhood in the Making: Cultural Concepts of Masculinity*. New Haven, CT: Yale University Press.

Hall, Stuart. 1980a. "Cultural Studies and the Centre." In S. Hall, D. Hobson, A. Lowe, and P. Willis, eds., *Culture, Media, Language*. London: Hutchinson, pp. 5–39.

———. 1980b. "Encoding/Decoding." In S. Hall, D. Hobson, A. Lowe, and P. Willis, eds., *Culture, Media, Language*. London: Hutchinson, pp. 128–138.

hooks, bell. 1984. *Feminist Theory: From Margin to Center*. Boston, MA: South End Press.

Jamieson, Kathleen Hall. 1988. *Eloquence in an Electronic Age: The Transformation of Political Speechmaking*. New York: Oxford University Press.

Kaplan, E. Ann. 1987. *Rocking around the Clock: Music Television, Postmodernism, and Consumer Culture*. New York: Methuen.

Kidd, Bill. 1987. "Sports and Masculinity." In Michael Kaufman, ed., *Beyond Patriarchy: Essays by Men on Pleasure, Power, and Change*. New York: Oxford University Press, pp. 252–264.

Kramarae, Cheris. 1981. *Women and Men Speaking: Frameworks for Analysis*. Rowley, MA: Newbury House.

Lewis, Lisa A. 1990. *Gender Politics and MTV: Voicing the Difference*. Philadelphia: Temple University Press.

Rich, Adrienne. 1979. "When We Dead Awaken: Writing as Re-vision." In Adrienne Rich, ed., *On Lies, Secrets, and Silence*. New York: Norton, pp. 33–49.

Schwichtenberg, Cathy. 1992. "Madonna's Postmodern Feminism: Bringing the Margins
    to the Center." *Southern Communication Journal 5* (spring): 120–131.
Spender, Dale. 1980. *Man Made Language*. Reprint ed., London: Pandora, 1992.
Steiner, Linda. 1988. "Oppositional Decoding as an Act of Resistance." *Critical Studies
    in Mass Communication 5* (spring): 1–15.

11

Teaching Theoretical Perspectives in the Gender and Communication Classroom: From Biology to Hegemony in *Coach*

Lynn H. Turner

In gender and communication classes the focus is often on the following two general assertions: (1) women and men are perceived to use different kinds of speech, serving different functions (Kramarae 1981); and (2) women's speech is devalued and restricted reflecting their lesser position relative to men in our culture (Campbell 1991; Hayles 1986). Explaining both speech differences and male dominance requires recourse to theoretical thinking about women's and men's speech as well as about the social structure in which it is embedded. Thus, introducing theoretical constructs and perspectives is a critical task in the gender and communication classroom.

However, students often complain that theory is difficult to understand and far removed from practice. Television programs may, as Vande Berg (1991) argues, be an avenue allowing students to visualize the link between theory and practice. Using television examples in classes may stimulate "students to use theoretical and critical constructs in their leisure television viewing with others, thus rehearsing and learning them" (Vande Berg 1991, p. 106).

In this paper I propose to do the following: (1) discuss three theoretical frameworks that are often invoked to explain gender differences in communication and one theoretical perspective that focuses on male dominance; (2) review the arguments in favor of using televised examples to illustrate these theoretical frames; and (3) provide an extended specific application from the ABC television program *Coach* (1989–).

THEORETICAL PERSPECTIVES

A simple explanation for communication differences between the sexes is a biological one. Several early researchers have argued that "nature not nurture" causes the differences between the genders (Dibble 1976; Jonas and Jonas

1975). Researchers who espouse this theoretical position argue for innate differences between the sexes. One area within the biological perspective that has received attention from researchers involves brain differences between the sexes. In many ways, male and female brains are not significantly different. The area that brain researchers have focused on concerns differentiating the functions of the right- and left-brain hemispheres of the cerebral cortex. It has been hypothesized that each side of the brain serves different functions; the left side processes information in a logical, analytical manner, whereas the right side interprets information holistically (Lesak 1976). Because these two specialties roughly conform to sex differences found in cognitive processing, verbal, and spatial skills, gender differences in brain lateralization were posited (Kimura 1985). Levy (1976) argued that women excel in verbal skills because they are more likely than men to integrate their left and right hemispheres in thinking and learning. Because men are more strongly lateralized than women they excel in spatial performance (Levy and Reid 1978).

This theoretical perspective is controversial and has received ambiguous empirical support (Pearson, Turner, and Todd-Mancillas 1991); consequently, other theoretical frameworks have been advanced. A second perspective involves social learning. This position holds that through a process of observation, imitation of role models, and rewards and punishments for the fidelity of our imitations, we acquire sex-role orientations. Sex-role orientations refer "to the extent to which a person has internalized society's sex-typed standards of desirable behavior for men and women" (Pearson 1985, p. 10). Sex-role orientations include "feminine" (the desirable behaviors for women); "masculine" (the desirable behaviors for men); and "androgynous" (the desirable behavior for both men and women combined). Theorists adopting this framework argue that because society's standards of behavior differ for men and women, internalizing a feminine sex-role orientation will cause a person to speak differently than internalizing a masculine sex-role orientation. The androgynous sex-role orientation purports to explain the instances where men and women do not differ in their communication behaviors.

Three obvious differences between this perspective and the biological position include the following.

1. Sex-role orientation allows for more than the two biological categories of male and female. For example, one may be a feminine male, a feminine female, a masculine male, and so on.
2. Sex-role orientation, with its focus on social standards, allows an understanding of the changes we find over time.
3. Sex-role orientation implies some degree of choice in a person's selection of behaviors, while biology disallows any consideration of choice.

However, the sex-role orientation perspective also received ambiguous empirical support (Pearson, Turner, and Todd-Mancillas 1991) and did not completely explain gender differences. In 1982 Gilligan proposed a third perspective. Gilligan suggested that women and men communicate their moral and ethical choices differently from one another. These differences stem from different ways of seeing the world. According to Gilligan, women and men develop different world views because their early childhood experiences differ. Growing up and developing gender identity is a different psychological process for boys and girls.

Citing the work of Chodorow (1987), Gilligan explains that because mothers generally provide the primary care for children between birth and three years of age, males and females experience a variety of issues, especially those related to intimacy and relationships, in different ways. Gilligan (1982) argues:

For boys and men, separation and individuation are critically tied to gender identity since separation from the mother is essential for the development of masculinity. For girls and women, issues of femininity or feminine identity do not depend on the achievement of separation from the mother or on the progress of individuation. Since masculinity is defined through separation while femininity is defined through attachment, male gender identity is threatened by intimacy while female gender identity is threatened by separation. Thus males tend to have difficulty with relationships, while females tend to have problems with individuation. (p. 8)

Gilligan reasons that these psychological differences between men and women lead them to different orientations toward moral decision making. Men's ethical stance is grounded in rights and responsibilities. Men develop what Gilligan labels a language of justice, where ethical decisions can be made on the basis of principle. The metaphor that is most apt for this male approach is the ladder, where competing principles can be prioritized or rank ordered.

Women's ethical position is situated in context, and thus, it is more equivocal and ambiguous than men's. Gilligan argues that situational factors, especially those relating to interpersonal relationships, inform women's ethical stance. Thus, women develop a language of care and connection. The appropriate metaphor for women's approach is the web. Here connections spread out horizontally, and prioritizing is not relevant because all linkages are equally important to the structure of the web.

Gilligan's work offers a rich framework for communication researchers because of her claims that men's and women's different moral justifications are expressed in the language they use. However, Gilligan has been criticized for many oversights in her theoretical approach; primary among them is the neglect of women's position in the social structure (Hayles 1986). Feminist critical theory focuses attention on the social structure by recognizing gender as the primary social organizer. This "means understanding patriarchy as a pervasive, long-standing but not inevitable means for organizing gender relations as well as other economic and political relations" (Rakow 1985, p. 6). Feminist critical theory takes on the task of examining how the dissemination of cultural values through art, literature, and the popular culture devalues women and reproduces the dominant ideology that oppresses women (Gitlin 1982; Press 1989).

Utilizing a feminist critical approach in the classroom can help focus on some of the problems in the three other theoretical perspectives and can add to the dynamics of discussion about gender and communication issues. One method for introducing this discussion is through the use of television programs as examples of "sites of struggle" (Brummett 1992) for meaning.

TELEVISION IN THE CLASSROOM

Television is a useful tool for introducing and critiquing these theoretical perspectives in the classroom for several reasons. First, television provides clear models of gender issues being negotiated through communication (Vande Berg 1991). These models are recognizable and familiar to students. Further, television is easily available, repeatable, and allows us access to many types of intimate communication that are difficult to observe in life (Haefner and Metts 1989).

Additionally, interaction on television is focused. It does not contain the "noise" that naturally occurring interactions do, and thus allows classroom analysis to center on a single concept. Llosa (1984) states that life "flows without pause, lacks order, is chaotic, each story merging with all stories and hence never having a beginning or ending. Life in a work of fiction is a simulation in which that dizzying disorder achieves order, organization, cause and effect, beginning and end" (p. 40).

Finally, television programs bear an interesting relationship to reality. Television fictions do not necessarily reflect gender interactions as lived by most men and women. Nor does television necessarily influence the way real men and women speak. Instead, television programs "reference" cultural values. As Cantor (1990) suggests, television teaches us ideal and acceptable ways for women and men to interact. Television thus highlights cultural values which may not be enacted by men and women but which provide an index for people's comparison with their own lived experiences. In serving this highlighting function, however, television does not present a single, definitive reading (Dow 1990). Rather, television presents images that allow for divergent readings and enables viewers to struggle over them, emerging with their own preferred interpretation.

COACH: NARRATIVE AND STRUCTURAL BACKGROUND

A brief description of an episode of *Coach* follows in order to clarify the suggestions for using it in class. The episode, which first aired March 26, 1991 (it is now in reruns), begins with Hayden Fox, the head football coach at Minnesota State University, and his fiancée, Christine Armstrong, coming to the University gym on a Sunday night for a swim. Hayden persuades Christine to go skinny-dipping by telling her how sexy it will be. Although Christine is apprehensive that they will be seen by someone, she acquiesces to Hayden's reassurances that no one else uses the pool on Sunday and the building is locked. As they race off to the pool, we see Luther, Hayden's assistant coach, approaching in his bathing suit.

The next scene is in Hayden's office the following Monday morning. Luther is trying to apologize to Hayden for embarrassing Christine and him at the pool the night before. However, Luther cannot keep from complimenting Christine's figure, which irritates Hayden further. While they are talking, Dauber, the other assistant coach, comes in the office with a copy of *Minnesota Life*. This issue has a feature article about Christine, who is the anchor on a Minneapolis nightly newscast.

As Hayden reads the article, he discovers that Christine makes a substantially higher salary than he does. Dauber and Luther tease him a bit about this, and the director of the university band comes in and ridicules Hayden about the disparity between his salary and Christine's. Hayden is extremely upset about the situation, and when Christine surprises him that night by coming out to his cabin with steaks and wine to celebrate the article, he tells her he is unhappy about the difference in their salaries. She cannot understand his position, they argue, and she leaves in anger.

The next day Hayden is still fuming about his "low" pay and is trying to think of a way to earn more money than Christine. Luther suggests endorsing a product and reminds Hayden that he was approached in the past to endorse jock straps. At first Hayden is hesitant, but soon he warms to the idea. He contacts the company, has his picture taken, and signs a release without reading it.

Later, as he is celebrating the size of his check, Dauber comes in with the news that the ad campaign has taken Hayden's face and superimposed it on the body of a man wearing nothing but a jock strap. The picture has been made into life-sized cutouts which are positioned around the campus. The boxes of jock straps also have the same picture on them.

Hayden gets very upset and realizes he has been taken for a fool. Rather than become the laughing stock of the university, he reluctantly gives Dauber and Luther his check and instructs them to buy up all the jock straps and collect all the life-sized posters.

That night Hayden is in the cabin surrounded by cartons of jock straps and cutout statues of "himself." Christine comes in and Hayden explains what has happened. He says he was trying to earn money to "get them even." She tells him she loves him for things that have nothing to do with how much he earns and they have to learn how to support each other if they are going to be married. Hayden looks around the room, dryly notes that he has "support" covered, and they embrace.

CLASSROOM APPLICATION

This episode presents several opportunities for discussing the theories, particularly during the two scenes when Christine and Hayden are at his cabin. The first time she visits and they argue, the differences between them are highlighted. Hayden offers a biological explanation for their differences. He says that his feelings are rooted in "basic biological male/female stuff." He explains why he is upset by saying that it is the male's primitive instinct to drag an animal home to feed his family, "And you sure as hell don't want to come home to your hut and find out that your wife has dragged in something bigger." Hayden's argument is that men and women are inherently, biologically different from one another and Christine's larger salary has violated basic natural order.

As Christine argues back in this scene, she takes a sex-role orientation position. She does this by saying she cannot believe that Hayden is arguing for those strict differences between men and women "in this day and age." In making this comment she implies that sex-role expectations may have been as Hayden describes them "in the Stone Age" but they have changed now. Further, she asserts, "I work damn hard for my money." In this she is embodying a masculine or androgynous sex-role orientation. Later in the episode she states, "I know we are both competitive people," again reflecting that a biological female may adopt a masculine or androgynous sex-role orientation through choice and changing social standards.

The last scene of the episode provides some material for discussing Gilligan's (1982) perspective. When Christine asks for an explanation, Hayden says he took the endorsement to reduce the inequality between them. "I was just trying to get us even, honey." This reveals that Hayden is thinking in hierarchical or rank-order terms, as Gilligan suggests. Hayden says, "Deep down inside my gut I feel like I'm supposed to be the strong one. Like I'm supposed to be the protector." Again this statement reveals thinking predicated on individuation and ranking. Christine's comments are generally congruent with Gilligan's characterization of the female voice. Christine says she wants Hayden with her, not because he is stronger, but because "there's comfort in togetherness." Christine's focus is on their relationship. She expresses that she sees them as a "team," bonded rather than individuated, and therefore it would not occur to her to rank order them in terms of salary or anything else.

In this episode of *Coach*, especially in the two main scenes between Hayden and Christine, we have the opportunity to present vignettes that should enliven theoretical perspectives for classroom discussion. The entire episode can be easily shown in a class period. Students should be encouraged to think about the explanations Hayden and Christine each favored for their different approaches to their problem. Many questions could be addressed to the ways in which Hayden and Christine illustrate Gilligan's voices.

The preceding discussion focused on using *Coach* to introduce three explanatory frames for assumed differences between women and men. Feminist critical theory examines male dominance and this can be introduced in the classroom through a discussion of this episode of *Coach* also.

As Dow (1990) suggests with reference to *The Mary Tyler Moore Show*, television provides "the possibilities for contradiction of feminist premises through hegemonic processes" (p. 262). Dow's argument is that television situation comedies are inherently conservative and though they do show some change over time in response to social change, they do so in a manner that actually protects the dominant cultural ideology from radical change. This perspective can be introduced in the classroom through a careful analysis of *Coach*. A number of hegemonic devices are present in the episode which reinforce stereotypic gender relations despite the fact that Christine embodies a modern woman's choices and speaks in Gilligan's different, womanly voice. Two of these devices are discussed in this section: (1) Hayden and hegemonic masculinity and (2) intragender relationships and the relationship between the public and private domains.

Hayden and Hegemonic Masculinity

Trujillo (1991) reviews five features of hegemonic masculinity in American culture: (1) physical force and control, (2) occupational achievement, (3) familial patriarchy, (4) frontiersmanship, and (5) heterosexuality. Hayden is clearly presented as representing these features, or striving to represent them. Most of them are illustrated in the single episode of *Coach* discussed previously. Some may need the elaboration provided by a familiarity with other episodes in the series.

First, Hayden is associated with physical force because of his profession as head football coach. Certainly football is a highly physical endeavor, and as Trujillo (1991) points out, "American football's hostile takeover of the more pastoral baseball as our 'national pastime' has reinforced a form of masculinity which emphasizes sanctioned aggression, (para)militarism, the technology of violence, and other patriarchal values" (p. 292). Additionally, Hayden represents power and control because his physical presence is much larger than that of most of the other characters. He towers over Christine and Luther.

Second, the episode highlights Hayden's association with occupational achievement by its focus on salary, an American marker of success. Hayden's team has recently become a winning one, and this episode suggests that his concern about his earnings is closely tied to his need for occupational achievement. Further, as Trujillo (1991) argues, the construction of sport as work is a powerful element in reproducing hegemony. With its emphasis on winners and losers, sport is an excellent metaphor for success and failure in capitalist society.

Hayden does illustrate familial patriarchy in *Coach*, although his fatherly role is not much in evidence in this particular episode. His insistence on being the major breadwinner in relation to Christine, however, is a clear portrayal of familial patriarchy.

Hayden is also presented as a frontiersman in *Coach*. By choice he lives in a rustic cabin in the woods. He drives a pickup truck and hunts and fishes.

Finally, the series in general, as well as this particular episode, presents Hayden as a devoted heterosexual partner to Christine. His urging of the evening of skinny-dipping, his compliments about her figure ("I'm not ashamed of my body, and I'm very proud of yours"), and his sensual description of the water lapping at their skin and their bodies touching each other all establish the character's heterosexuality.

Intragender Relationships and the Public and Private Domains

This episode, as most in the series, places Hayden in the context of friends and family. Notably, Hayden's coworkers, Dauber and Luther, also offer him friendship. Christine, on the other hand, is shown as rather isolated. She is incorporated into Hayden's family and friendships, and is rarely shown with friends of her own, particularly not close women friends. Christine is a token woman at work where she is mainly surrounded by men.

As is traditional in the dominant culture, the private and public domains are seen as separate spheres on *Coach*. However, this division is enacted somewhat differently for Hayden and Christine. Hayden is shown moving easily between his work and private, domestic contexts. He has the ability to compete success-fully in the work world as well as the opportunity to perform his private roles of fiancé and father. Hayden is allowed to enjoy fatherhood although he is a divorced father and had virtually no contact with his daughter through her growing up years. Thus Hayden has the best of both worlds. Christine, how-ever, has never married before and has no children, indicating that she has given up some aspects of her personal life to obtain the success she has achieved as a television journalist.

CONCLUSION

Using a feminist theoretical lens illuminates how popular culture creates an image of masculinity, femininity, and humanity that is informed by men's vision. Women's perspectives are silenced and the dominant ideology is reinforced. As Dow (1990) argues, "television is recombinant and . . . strategies proven successful at defusing feminist content in one situation are likely to be used in another" (p. 271).

Additionally, feminist theories provide vantage points for assessing the weaknesses of the other three theoretical frameworks. This is an important function in the classroom. Feminist theories allow us to question the usefulness of perspectives that omit a consideration of social structure. These questions may take many forms. For example, we may ask, how can biological answers account for the fact that women and men have not subscribed to invariant behaviors over time? How does sex-role orientation explain the constraints that women (and men) are subject to if their orientation fails to "match" their biological sex? Do women enact an ethic of care and connection because of a psychological response to their acquisition of gender identity or as a socially accepted strategy that allows them to cope with male dominance?

Television examples such as the episode of *Coach* described in this paper can be extremely useful in the gender and communication classroom. They offer clear models of interpersonal theoretical constructs and perspectives. In so doing, they provide a vantage point for beginning a discussion of these theories. Finally, they offer a text for feminist critical theorizing. In this capacity, classroom discussion can focus on evaluating the efficacy of various theoretical perspectives and illuminate the tension between messages of change and messages co-opting challenges to the status quo.

REFERENCES

Brummett, B. 1992. Personal communication. Milwaukee, WI.

Campbell, K. K. 1991. "Hearing Women's Voices." *Communication Education 40*: 33–48.

Cantor, M. G. 1990. "Prime-Time Fathers: A Study in Continuity and Change." *Critical Studies in Mass Communication 1*: 275–285.

Chodorow, N. 1978. *The Reproduction of Mothering*. Berkeley: University of California Press.

Dibble, H. L. 1976. "More on Gender Differences and the Origin of Language." *Current Anthropology 7*: 744–779.

Dow, B. J. 1990. "Hegemony, Feminist Criticism, and *The Mary Tyler Moore Show*. *Critical Studies in Mass Communication 7*: 261–274.

Gilligan, C. 1982. *In a Different Voice*. Cambridge, MA: Harvard University Press.

Gitlin, T. 1982. "Prime Time Ideology: The Hegemonic Process in Television Entertainment." In H. Newcomb, ed., *Television: The Critical View*, 3rd ed. New York: Oxford University Press, pp. 426–454.

Haefner, M. J., and S. Metts. 1989. "Using Television and Film to Study Interpersonal Communication." Paper presented at the annual conference of the Western States Communication Association, Spokane, WA.

Hayles, N. K. 1986. "Anger in Different Voices: Carol Gilligan and *The Mill on the Floss*." *Signs 12*: 23–29.

Jonas, D. F., and D. A. Jonas. 1975. "Gender Differences in Mental Function: A Clue to the Origin of Language." *Current Anthropology 16*: 626–630.

Kimura, D. 1985. "Male Brain, Female Brain: The Hidden Difference." *Psychology Today 19*: 50–52, 54, 55–58.

Kramarae, C. 1981. *Women and Men Speaking*. Rowley, MA: Newbury House.

Lesak, M. 1976. *Neuropsychological Assessment*. New York: Oxford University Press.

Levy, J. 1976. "Cerebral Lateralization and Spatial Ability." *Behavior Genetics 6*: 171–188.

Levy, J., and M. Reid. 1978. "Variations in Cerebral Organization as a Function of Handedness, Hand-posture in Writing, and Sex." *Journal of Experimental Psychology 107*: 119–144.

Llosa, M. V. 1984, October 7. "Is Fiction the Art of Lying?" *New York Times Book Review 1*: 40.

Pearson, J. C. 1985. *Gender and Communication*. Dubuque, IA: Wm. C. Brown.

Pearson, J. C., L. H. Turner, and W. Todd-Mancillas. 1991. *Gender and Communication*, 2nd. ed. Dubuque, IA: Wm. C. Brown.

Press, A. 1989. "The Ongoing Feminist Revolution." *Critical Studies in Mass Communication 6*: 196–202.

Rakow, L. 1985. "A Paradigm of One's Own: Feminist Ferment in the Field." Paper presented at the annual conference of the International Communication Association, Honolulu, HI.

Trujillo, N. 1991. "Hegemonic Masculinity on the Mound: Media Representations of Nolan Ryan and the American Sports Culture." *Critical Studies in Mass Communication 8*: 290–308.

Vande Berg, L. R. 1991. "Using Television to Teach Courses in Gender and Communication." *Communication Education 40*: 105–111.

12

Toward a Feminist Pedagogy: Using Television to Explore Gender and Communication Issues in the Classroom

Deborah Petersen-Perlman

I am a woman, a wife, a mother, a college professor who specializes in broadcasting studies, and last, but certainly not least, a feminist. All of these facts about who I am inform what I believe about teaching and about my students, what I believe about my content area, and what I believe about the way I teach. The facts of my personhood, together with my pedagogical beliefs have shaped the course of my career, and this chapter. In the following pages I bring together these different threads to discuss the importance of using television as a tool of feminist pedagogy. In particular, I have selected a case study within a case study to illustrate the value of television within a feminist pedagogical frame.

Through television we share a common body of images and stories about who we are. Whatever any of us thinks of television, it is, for many people growing up today, a window to the world beyond the confines of their own households. The images of television, together with the attitudes and values of families, can prove to be a powerful combination in the formation of the next generations' attitude structures. Learning how to use television as a teaching tool can be enormously empowering to young adults who grew up with it as a forceful presence in their lives. This chapter lays a foundation for helping students do this analysis by means of a feminist pedagogical frame, an assessment of an efficacious way to use television in educational settings, and a case study of one such practical application within a particular classroom.

FEMINIST PEDAGOGY

Although I recognize the pedantry implicit in trotting out dictionary definitions, it seems important to establish a feminist pedagogical frame by setting forth terms from which the argument for a new pedagogy can emerge. Pedagogy is "the science of teaching"; science is "knowledge ascertained by observation and experiment, critically tested, systematized, and brought under general principles." Art, on the other hand, is "human skill as opposed to natural agency; skill acquired by study and practice." To me, a more useful definition of pedagogy encompasses both science and art. How, then, can *feminists* adapt these definitions so as to formulate *feminist* pedagogy?

Feminism, as a term, can be defined almost in as many ways as there are people who declare themselves as feminist. I think it is reasonable to suggest that one can forge personal definitions which borrow from the more commonly held and agreed upon definitions. I think this is particularly true when we use "feminist" as an adjective to describe the practice of teaching. To that end, I would like to offer my own beliefs about teaching, my definition of "feminist pedagogy" as derived from the work of writers who have gone before me, and then to demonstrate how I applied this definition to my own teaching.

To begin this endeavor, I offer my pedagogical credo:

- I believe the best climate for learning is one that engenders mutual respect and enthusiasm between teachers and students.
- I believe students learn best when they are actively involved in the process of learning.
- I believe students can teach themselves, their student peers, and me—their teacher.
- I believe collaboration is healthier than competition. I also believe that competition is a natural human motivation and that it is therefore inevitable that humans will compete. I believe that we can use competition to positive ends if we can learn to harness it effectively.
- I believe students need to take responsibility for their own learning in order for them truly to possess knowledge.
- I believe my role as a teacher is to serve as a guide.
- I believe that no one knows, nor should they know, everything.
- I believe that there is no one singular truth.
- I believe that learning happens on many levels that are idiosyncratic to the individual learner.
- I believe humans accomplish more when they feel appreciated. Therefore, I believe in celebrating each individual's accomplishments.
- I believe that standards are important. I also believe that standards are idiosyncratic, dynamic and that they evolve.
- I believe that there is more than one way to do anything. I also believe that some ways are better than others in terms of meeting individual tasks or goals.
- I believe that learning is ongoing.
- I believe that teaching is one of the best ways of learning.

I discovered that this personal pedagogical doctrine was in keeping with the ideas of many who, over the past decade and a half, have taken on the task of redefining the pedagogical pursuit in feminist terms. Nancy Porter described what I perceive to be among the first steps of the new teaching. In keeping with the ideas of Paolo Freire, Porter argues for the liberation of teaching. "To liberate teaching and for teaching to be liberating, the learner in oneself must be freed."[1]

Barrie Thorne wrote in 1984 about the trend in rethinking and revising the curriculum and the ways we teach. She says: "Above all, the process involves taking all people seriously and urging them to take themselves seriously. . . . One of the greatest gifts a teacher can give is to help others find a sense of agency in their lives."[2] In other words, by showing students how to be *actors* rather than settling for being *acted upon*, we give our students directions on the path to self-fulfillment and active citizenship.

Martha Thompson[3] stresses the need for a supportive classroom that acknowledges the "real differences" among students and teachers in areas such as knowledge, social experiences, and literacy skills. Thompson employs techniques that encourage students to work together in pairs or small groups so as to establish a collegial and possibly collaborative spirit among them. Along the same lines of Thompson's ideal classroom, Lynn Weber Cannon[4] has stressed the need for ground rules for class discussion. Such rules help to set the kind of respectful tone that best accommodates open discussion of the "real differences" Thompson alluded to, as well as helping students learn about and hopefully accept each other.

One of the leaders of this new teaching is Peggy McIntosh.[5] McIntosh suggests five phases of perception. In the first three phases McIntosh focuses her discussion on curricular concerns. In the last two phases she includes the teacher-student dynamic.

The first curricular phase begins with the traditional model of (male) teacher as god: he talks and the students listen. The material studied in these traditional classrooms comes from the "sacred" Western canon (consisting mostly of white, male writers, or at any rate "those who had most public power and whose lives were involved with laws, wars, acquisition of territory, and management of power").

The second stage of instruction, according to McIntosh, is the classroom which admits star pupils (mostly male, or females who thrive in a white male mode of instruction and learning) who make contributions on the basis of their superior knowledge. Again, the subject matter studied is from the Western canon, allowing some token women authors (and perhaps even a few non-Western writers).

In phase three, McIntosh tells us, the curriculum ventures "further down from the pinnacles of power toward the valleys." Here students encounter more "normal" women and other "common" people. At this point the political under-girding of the curriculum becomes apparent and students and some teachers begin to challenge the canon. When students and teachers understand that the curriculum is not "pure," but rather that it is the product of the power structure of our social system (that is, of, by, and for elite white males) those who do not fit into or feel comfortable within such a system must first question its legitimacy and authority and then act to change it. There is a bit more participation on the part of the students, but the teacher is still the ringmaster and the degree of student power is somewhat diminished by an overwhelming sense of frustration with the victimization and disenfranchisement of those who are not white males.

The fourth stage is nontraditional, according to McIntosh. The teacher's expertise is diminished and teachers and students approach a new kind of partnership. Power and superiority are devalued and in their place a system of lateral values emerges. Students and teachers learn from each other, without placing a premium on hierarchical knowledge.

The final phase is an ideal yet to be realized, wherein teachers have created a much more inclusive learning environment, both in terms of the material studied and in terms of the role of students. In this stage the texts go beyond the boundaries of Europe and of white North America. Writers of both sexes and all sexual orientations, writers from the East, the Middle East, Africa, Hispanic North America, South America, virtually everywhere are included. The students are confronted with multitudinous "ways of knowing." The students, for their parts, take greater control of their own learning. The teacher is no longer an "all knowing, superior being." Hopefully, the teacher is, at most, a guide for the student who can discover her or his own learning capabilities and strengths. McIntosh's ideal can be realized only if we, as feminist teachers, take on the tasks of expanding the canon and asserting lateral values within our classrooms.

Valerie Swarts wrote in her paper "Feminism and Learning Theories" that "fundamental to incorporating a process of questioning, helping students to embark on their own process of inquiry, and establishing a learning environment that enables students to respond to challenges so that they can develop a grammar of feminism, is a discovery of the ways in which women see and know, relate and respond."[6] In other words, the expanded canon must be more inclusive of different genders, sexual orientations, and ethnic/racial cultures so as to empower and support our diverse student populations.

The basic precepts of a feminist/multiculturalist pedagogy, as I see it, begin with a commitment to collaborative learning, or, at the very least, the kind of cooperative learning which McIntosh characterizes in phases four and five, along with nurturance, and affirmation. Reconceptualizing issues of power and powerlessness are at the center of feminist revisions of pedagogy. For some, me included, feminist pedagogy embraces the concerns of multiculturalism and inclusiveness. Our students come from so many different backgrounds and ethnicities that it is important to celebrate these differences so as to encourage the best from everybody.

Feminist pedagogy, as I interpret it, accommodates worlds beyond empiricism. The pedagogy I want to practice is closely aligned with the ideas of McIntosh in phases four and five of her curricular revision. In this ideal educational world students assume responsibility for and control over their own learning. They respect each other and the ideas of those who are foreign to them. The teacher is a guide, providing access to materials and methods and affirming the originality and insight of each student. The feminist teacher fosters a safe, respectful and encouraging environment for learning and growth. Mistakes and errors are not condemned, but rather are seen as windows of opportunity.

Given the limitations of a system governed by grades and populated by would-be job seekers who see college as a way station before the career, the feminist teacher takes what works and adapts it to the teaching environment. One technique that has worked for me and others is the incorporation of television as a teaching tool and subject of study. Our student population consists, as Shields and Kidd noted in 1973, of people who are very familiar with television and film examples.[7] Because these students already know about television, Vande Berg[8] asserts that students are encouraged to feel confident enough to actively participate in class discussions, thereby meeting a number of goals of feminist pedagogy and the more general goal of active learning. Television then, because it is grounded in the vernacular, is a natural tool of feminist pedagogy. The familiarity of television has an empowering and inclusive potential. Students can feel expert about television, thus approaching the goals of McIntosh's final phase of collaborative learning. Regardless of television's content, and perhaps because of its content, students can discern the way shared meanings are created and in doing so take an active role in interpreting the value of these meanings for their own lives.

USING TELEVISION TO TEACH

From the outset of this discussion, it is important to acknowledge the kinds of negative, prejudicial, and dismissive attitudes academics, intellectuals, and others share about the value of television in the United States. Although the vast majority of people in this country watch television on a regular and substantial basis, television is the bastard "art" form. As Vande Berg and Wenner note: "Television has been blamed for the ills of our society. . . . It's been widely blamed for ruining our children's minds and abilities to read, pushing people to violence, reinforcing stereotypes, serving as a shrine to rampant commercialism, and making it likely that we vote for political candidates more on the basis of their image than on their likely effectiveness in accomplishing goals we believe are important."[9] Regardless of one's position on these issues, it is clear that most people perceive television's impact on daily American life to be quite extensive and mostly negative. Because television is so central to modern life and because of its perceived impact, it is important to study television in a serious and thoughtful way. More to the point, it is important to use television to study our society—particularly in terms of its capacity to socialize young children.

It has been only recently that television has been deemed worthy of inclusion in the classroom, beyond the odd crisis coverage or space shuttle landing. Teaching guru Wilbert McKeachie[10] refers to the use of film in the way many teachers want to make use of television: to illustrate concepts central to the class topic. McKeachie stresses that "As with all instruction a key variable in learning is student involvement—activity which encourages meaningful thought."

Those of us who have studied television from critical, cultural and industrial perspectives need to go much further than McKeachie in stressing and legitimizing the study of television. A number of my colleagues in communication have begun this work. Foss and Kanengieter provide a good foundation for the justification of including the visual media as part of the curriculum. They write: "We no longer live in a logocracy—a culture based on verbal texts—but in a culture characterized by omnipresent visual images in forms such as television, film, billboards, architecture, and dress."[11]

Beyond our visual orientation, we also use television as a foundation for social interaction. Janis argues that "television, like other socializing agents, provides models or "scripts" of social actions."[12] Sometimes, however, these "scripts" are not translated to action. The fear of many scholars and social observers is that television displaces other activities. We are all most familiar with that lumpish phenomenon known as the couch potato. Critical study of the medium requires activity on the part of the viewer. Roth suggested that "college students can become television literate and avoid becoming victims of television—becoming so passive that they do not really want to take responsibility for their own learning."[13] I would suggest that the need for visual literacy is important for everybody, but most particularly it is important for the teachers and care providers of young children (i.e., the students in today's college classrooms).

The concepts of television as a tool of socialization and the need for televisual literacy are actually quite compatible. As Fiske suggests, reality is already encoded.[14] If we can agree that this is the case, the need to take television seriously and to teach students how to use and interpret it becomes more evident.

The first step in this process is learning how to "read" television. Rubin defines media literacy as "making use of the skills of critical viewing and receivership which enable students to identify conventions through which particular meanings and effects are created in visual communication."[15] Schamber identifies three basic skills necessary for visual literacy:

1. Reading—the ability to read and interpret visual grammar and syntax.
2. Writing—visual composition, or the design of visual messages: development of ideas; collection and organization of information; use of tools to prepare the various aspects of the messages.
3. Evaluation of messages—analysis and assessment; the ability to clarify how the features and relationships among them contribute to the effects produced by the images.[16]

Once these skills have been acquired, the real work of using television to talk about social concerns can begin.

What follows is a case study of a classroom in which I implemented as many of the ideas described above as possible.

THE CASE STUDY

The class I have selected as the subject for this paper is titled "Critical Assessments of Television." Obviously, the focus of this class is television, and we use videotaped television programs as a way of studying the medium. Beyond this, however, we focus on television's place within American society. To do this we identify the nature of televised portrayals. We look at issues of race, class, gender, and the kinds of social commentary offered by the medium. Our methods are varied, but the general mode of operation is to read, discuss, watch, and analyze.

Preliminaries

My role as teacher in this class began with the selection of a textbook that I felt used nonsexist language and covered issues of gender, race, and class in a respectful and exploratory fashion. My choice was Vande Berg and Wenner's *Television Criticism*. Before constructing the class, I selected two project options so as to accommodate different learning styles and working preferences among the students—they are described in detail below.

A given week would consist first of class discussion on the assigned reading, as well as additional materials suggested by the class members. At the end of the first period we previewed the critical exercise for the week. Day 2 involved viewing the program on which we would apply the exercise. If time permitted, we watched the program twice—making sure the students had familiarity with the characters, the situation and any other important information for the purposes of analysis. On day 3, the students completed the exercise and then debriefed as a class the nature of the critical experience. Each class exercise was designed to prepare students for their class projects. As a result, we began the quarter by looking at the nature of critical writing. We then discussed genre criticism, followed by various forms of narrative analysis, Marxist analysis, and so on as time permitted.

Class Projects

One option involved independent work, allowing students to write three papers from what I considered incrementally more difficult perspectives. The students selecting this option began by writing a journalistic style essay on a program of their choice. This essay was to be modeled after the kinds of articles which appear regularly in newspapers and weekly periodicals. The focus was on audience analysis and a program's potential popular appeal. The second assignment was a genre analysis that required each student to select and define a particular genre of television programming and then to choose three programs to represent this genre. The students had to watch three episodes each of these programs and then write about what made these programs character-istic of or unique from the genre under study. Their final paper involved whatever mode of analysis the student chose and then the analysis of five episodes of a particular program. At the end of the quarter, each student gave a minipresentation incorporating the use of videotaped excerpts of the program(s) under study.

THE CASE AND ITS ATTENDANT RATIONALE

The second option is the focus of this case study. The subject matter of this second option was the prime time lineup directed at children and their families. The students who selected this option were divided into program groups of four. These groups were guided by my personal research interests which con-cern programming aimed at children and their families. The programs selected were all half-hour sitcoms (with one cartoon) scheduled during the first hour of prime time on each of the networks.

I presented this second option as an invitation to participate in my research project. Rather than my disseminating truths from on high, my students would be teaching me what they learned. Furthermore, the structure of the project necessitated that they learn from each other. (Students in my classes also have the option to formulate their own research agenda, but in so doing they must propose a project that will involve the same workload as their classmates who have selected option one or option two. These projects are subject to my approval.) The responsibilities for option two were structured on a rotating basis so that each student had the opportunity to take on each of the four responsibilities identified as part of the project: videotape/transcript; popular article review, video backup; scholarly criticism abstract and application; analysis paper. Each student received an individual grade for the work com-pleted. For the most part, the students worked for themselves, using the group as a kind of sounding board for their own ideas. The goal here was to encourage the groups to meet outside of class to review and evaluate the various critical modes we discussed as a class. As mentioned above, they also had in-class opportunities by way of exercises designed to illustrate the critical method under discussion in a given week.

The due dates for each part of the project were staggered according to the perceived difficulty of the task. The first rotation task for person A was video-taping the program and preparing a transcript. The transcript is time consuming, but necessary (I thought) for a student to conduct a thoroughgoing analysis. The videotaping/transcription was a potentially problematic part of the scheme. A failure to meet this responsibility was really the only opportunity to adversely affect the work of another group member. To offset that possibility, the person responsible for reading, photocopying, and commenting on the popular coverage of the program under study (person B in the first rotation) had backup taping responsibilities as well.

Person C in the first round was required to find an article of scholarly criticism from academic journals, critical compendia, or other texts, which dealt with the critical methods discussed in class for that particular week. For the first rotation the students would want to select articles dealing with genre criticism—particularly sitcom genre criticism. Because this part of the assignment involved library work (synthesis of the article under scrutiny along with a brief statement applying the ideas from the article to the program and method under study within the class) this work was due the following week.

Person D was given the task of using a particular mode of analysis (the one under study during the first week of any given rotation) to criticize the appropriate episode of the program (the episode videotaped and transcribed for the first week of the given rotation). These papers were extensions and applications of the assigned chapters from the text, the scholarly articles reviewed, and the student's original insights. Students were encouraged to be creative but thorough in making the critical arguments in their papers. This part of the assignment required reading other group members' work and the synthesis of that work, together with assigned readings. The analysis paper was due two weeks after the rotation began.

The teams were then responsible for putting together a twenty-five-minute thematic presentation using videotaped examples of the program and charts or tables from their analyses. Their goal was to present a strong critical argument regarding the program as a tool of social discourse. They were asked to pay particular attention to considerations of race, class, and gender in their analyses.

What the Students Found

Most students opted to do the group project. They selected ten prime time situation comedies as the focus of their work. The list of these programs follows:

The Cosby Show	*The Simpsons*
Who's the Boss?	*Fresh Prince of Bel Air*
Home Improvement	*Brooklyn Bridge*
Full House	*Blossom*
Doogie Howser, M.D.	*The Wonder Years*

It is important to note that *The Simpsons*, though an animated cartoon, can be legitimately included in this genre because it is the domestic sitcom that serves as the basis for the program's satire.

The two most popular modes of analysis were a kind of sociological comparison based on semiological analytical schemes and a study of values, based on the work of Suzanne Williams.[17] In addition, many students were interested in narrative frameworks and, most particularly, discourse analysis.

When I presented the project to the class, I explained that I felt it was important to look at prime time programs because these were the television shows children were most likely to watch with their families. If indeed families are watching these programs together (and the Nielsen ratings data suggest this is true historically) then it is during this kind of viewing that children are most likely to ask their parents and siblings about what it is they are watching (whether or not it is true, good, valuable, beautiful, etc.). I argued that it is important to examine what children are watching because these are the programs that serve as what Schrag[18] calls the "first stories" (the stories told to children and those which establish the narrative paradigm against which they judge subsequent stories). Additionally, these "first stories" play a role in establishing a foundation for attitudes, values, and policies. Further, I suggested that it is important for college students to reflect on how their own values and attitudes were influenced (at least in part) by the first stories they watched on television.

The kinds of questions which shaped the students' analyses can be summarized as follows:

- What does it mean to be a little girl/boy growing up in America?
- Are black children different from white children?
- If there is no mother/father, can you still have a family?
- What do mothers/fathers do for a living?
- Who has more authority: mother, father, siblings, grandparents? Why?
- What is appropriate/good/valued behavior?
- What are appropriate/good values?

In conducting their analyses, the students found that most of these programs portrayed teamwork, conformity, and hard work and a balance between rationality and emotionalism as values central to a healthy and happy family. Traditional, nuclear families depicted parents as essentially rational beings with great problem-solving skills. Nontraditional family structures generally accorded attributes of teamwork, conformity, rationality, and hard work to the chief problem solver.

Students noted that the Huxtable family of *The Cosby Show* were quintessentially "normal" by TV sitcom standards. Dad/Dr. Heathcliff Huxtable is powerful, credible, trustworthy, compassionate, and understanding. When his friend and colleague, Dr. Morgan, comes to talk to Cliff about an upcoming fund-raiser, even he turns to Cliff for advice and a sympathetic ear. Cliff's beautiful and accomplished wife Claire, a lawyer, is his equal on paper, but she does not have the same screen dominance accorded the more powerful Cliff. Even though a verbal description of her attributes shows her to be on a par with her husband, the students noticed that he gets considerably more screen time and therefore he makes the more lasting impression and has the greater impact.

One of the more prominent themes which the students saw emerging from this archetypical sitcom was with regard to the work ethic: "If you want something you have to work for it." Underlying the entire program however, the students perceived an active effort to recode ethnicity by combatting racial stereotypes, many of which have been pervasive on American television (especially the programs viewed by the students when they were younger). The very "normalness" of the Huxtables is meant to serve as a counter statement to the dominant media image of the absentee African American father.

Brooklyn Bridge portrayed the Bergers as a warm, engaging, and eminently moral family. The major themes that emerged from the students' analysis placed family unity at the top of the list. Like the Huxtables, the Bergers teach their children about responsibility. One particular episode which struck a familiar chord with these students dealt with the young protagonist, Alan, failing at a job opportunity. Although father George and grandfather Jules were there to pick up the boys when they failed, the children were not absolved of their obligations to their employer. The boys have learned three important lessons: "Follow through on your obligations; take responsibility seriously; make good when you fail."

Particularly noteworthy for this rather homogeneous group of students was the portrayal of the Bergers as an identifiably Jewish family. These students were motivated by the program to learn about what made the family "typically Jewish" by 1950s standards.

The Wonder Years is another sitcom with a stereotypical, nuclear family structure. Students characterized this program as "monoethnic." Each student analysis paper took note of the absence of African Americans, Hispanics, and Asians from the world portrayed in this program. The patriarch, Jack Arnold, is portrayed as the strong, silent type (read poor communication skills). The mother of the house, Norma, is a submissive and sensitive woman who keeps the household together. Aside from Kevin Arnold's best friend, Paul, this program shows a white (Christian), middle-class world. Paul is Jewish, but students did not learn this from the season during which they were conducting this analysis; Paul's religion was the subject of an episode during an earlier season. Students decided that the show was characteristic of the era depicted (late 1960s/early 1970s) and therefore limited in terms of likely themes and depictions.

Doogie Howser, M.D. also offers up a traditional family structure. Certainly Doogie's role as a child prodigy is unusual, but his family is classically hierarchical. Furthermore, the medical theme of the program casts Doogie and his doctor colleagues as superior beings. What emerges is a world where it is tempting, and often true, to cast the doctor as a white, elite male who is the closest thing to a god on earth. Although the program offers valuable lessons on morality and growing into responsible adulthood, the lasting impression is that of the great white doctor. Two episodes in particular (one featuring Doogie's mother Katherine and the other the African American orderly Ray) led the students to suggest that women and African Americans were condescended to and patronized.

Home Improvement is a variation of the traditional sitcom. This group of students took particular delight in identifying, reviewing, and analyzing the messages about gender roles which serve as the show's raison d'être. Tim Allen's portrayal of Tim "The Tool Man" Taylor pokes gentle fun at traditional American views of masculinity. The character of Tim Taylor is rather dumb and insensitive. Jill Taylor, his wife, is thoughtful, intelligent, sensitive and has a razor sharp wit. The values/behavior analysis (from Suzanne Williams) that students conducted revealed that the typical sitcom family values of teamwork and a respect for hard work were in Jill's domain, rather than in Tim's. Tim, on the other hand, was seen as more of an individualist in that he was shown thinking of himself more than of his family and a conformist in that he tended to go along with the crowd, rather than following a personal ethic. *Home Improvement* departs from the typical sitcom value structure by making the nonconformist character of Jill more sympathetic, whereas Tim's conformity to peer pressure and stereotyped expectations of masculinity are the focus of the program's humor.

The Simpsons is a favorite among many of the college students I know. The satirical program presents a rather sick, dysfunctional family. The traditional values of hard work, teamwork, conformity, and rationalism are ridiculed by the central characters of Bart and Homer Simpson. Marge and Lisa, who are more considerate and conventional, are overshadowed by their male counterparts. As one student put it, "This program mutilates typical family values."

The remaining four programs recoded the family. Instead of the stereotypical nuclear patriarchal family, these shows featured blended families and families altered by death and divorce. This ratio of six "typical" family sitcoms to four "new" family sitcoms seems particularly noteworthy given the recent political debates about family values.

Two of the remaining programs dealt with families of divorce. Both *Who's the Boss?* and *Blossom* feature single-parent households. Both of these shows include a grandparent as a central character. *Who's the Boss?* includes a second single-parent household that has blended together with another family. Both of these programs featured themes that deal with sex and sexuality, as well as gender roles.

The students who watched *Who's the Boss?* were particularly struck by an odd double standard concerning issues of sexuality. The program's matriarch is a modern, hip woman named Mona who talks freely about her sexual desires. As one student put it: "You would think that AIDS didn't exist to observe the way she talks about her sexual exploits." Her daughter, a divorced and attractive advertising executive named Angela, is prudish by comparison. When Angela strikes up a relationship and subsequent engagement with her live-in housekeeper, Tony, they remain chaste. Tony's daughter, Samantha, grows up on the program and remains a virgin until she marries. Essentially, the younger generations in this program seem to be taking a more responsible view toward sex and sexuality than the older generation.

Another double standard that gave the students pause concerned Angela's presence when she was with now-fiancé Tony as contrasted with her behavior in other circumstances. The very title of the program suggests the mixed messages students observed. Angela is portrayed as a good mother and a successful advertising executive who can afford to have a live-in housekeeper. She is savvy in the business world, but when she is with Tony she becomes passive and overly pliant, deferring to Tony's wishes.

Blossom is the story of a divorced dad, Nick, and his family of three, Tony, Joey, and Blossom. Nick's ex-father-in-law and the children's grandfather is a regular character on this show. The central values of the program included honesty, friendship, and communication. The program also features "taking things in stride" as an important value of this family. The students who watched and wrote about *Blossom* noted that, with the exception of Tony—a recovering substance abuser—the men of this family are generally immature. The students suggested that all of these men seem "governed by their groins." Blossom is the youngest member of the family but also the wisest. One student suggested that Blossom had the greatest power in the family. She seemed to be the central problem solver, generally employing logic and rationality in her decision making. Even when she turns to her dad to discuss her problems, she ends up using her father as a sounding board as she solves her own problems.

The two remaining programs portray blended families. Although *The Cosby Show* added a theme similar to *Fresh Prince* during the last season (a poor cousin comes to live with the well-off Huxtables), *Fresh Prince* features cousin Will (the Fresh Prince) as the central character. In the case of *Fresh Prince of Bel Air*, the Banks family takes in their nephew Will as a favor to Vivien Banks's sister. Will and his mother come from Philadelphia. After Will gets into trouble in his old neighborhood, his mother decides he needs the more "wholesome," and certainly less troubled, environment of Bel Air. Will is depicted as a stereotypical African American teenager and offers a sharp contrast to his Bel Air cousins, who are wealthy and who act like their rich, white counterparts. The program's themes include cultural issues such as racial conflict and interracial marriage. Much of the program's humor comes from the contrasts between Will's streetwise approach to language, dress, and behavior, and the more rarified manners of this wealthy Los Angeles suburb and its inhabitants.

Whereas *Cosby* portrayed the African American family as "normal" and essentially just like the white family, *Fresh Prince* underscores differences between white and black culture. Will offers up a celebration of these differences, while still dealing with serious racial issues like black-on-black prejudice. When *Cosby* dealt with black matters, the focus was on black heroes/heroines such as Winnie and Nelson Mandela and Martin Luther King. *Cosby* subtly encouraged black pride by hanging works of art by black artists on the set of the show and making allusions to important black figures in politics, the arts and sciences, and history. These figures and topics tended to be in the background, whereas Will's blackness and representation of inner-city experiences is in the foreground. *Fresh Prince* also deals with issues such as homosexuality, violence, and male/female dynamics. *Cosby* tended to focus on family dynamics. It is fair to suggest that both programs have recoded ethnicity, but in diverse ways.

The final program reviewed by students, *Full House*, also features a blended family. The Tanners include a widowed father (Danny) and his three young daughters, his brother-in-law (Jesse) and his wife (Becky), and a family friend (Joey). This implausible conglomeration nevertheless manages to underscore the values of the typical sitcom: teamwork and conformity dominate as the moral lessons of most episodes. The three adult male characters are identified as the central authority figures. Becky, the only adult female in the regular cast, was a late addition to the program and is clearly a secondary character of lesser importance in terms of authority.

Danny is portrayed as having many stereotypically "feminine" traits. He is the primary caregiver, and hence he has to be emotionally centered and affectionate; but beyond those traits he is also characterized as being a compulsive cleaner. His cleaning fetish (which extends to a general interest in order) is mocked and ridiculed. Jesse, on the other had, is identified as macho—interested in leather, motorcycles, and rock and roll. Jesse is clearly the preferred masculine role model.

One particular lesson emerged from an episode of *Full House* wherein Michelle, the youngest daughter, learns from another child that her household is not "typical/normal." Up to this point in the program, the Tanner children seemed to perceive their own situation as normal. The moral lesson gleaned from this particular plot shows Michelle reaccepting her family as normal.

ANALYSIS OF THE PROJECT

Although I will proudly apply the label of feminist pedagogy to the process of instruction in my "Critical Assessments of Television" course (specifically in terms of collaborative learning, affirmation, and nurturance), I recognize that it is not a perfect application. One of the preliminary pedagogical tasks in my classroom is encouraging students to scrutinize television.

The structure of this assignment required student collaboration. The students became critics, and as such they were actively engaged in and in control of their own learning. They necessarily adopted a process of questioning as they scrutinized these programs for the purposes of writing the final paper and pulling together a class presentation. The presentation involved the use of video clips, which meant that the students had no choice but to support their claims with concrete evidence from the texts they were analyzing. Furthermore, the students had to rely on each other in order to make the presentation. They had to listen and learn from each other, and in so doing they had to respect each other's work and insights. The project as a whole, and the presentation in particular, meant that the students had to assume responsibility for, and control over, their own learning. My role as teacher was to provide a map. The students selected their own paths and reached unique destinations.

The questions posed by the students in their analyses incorporated the vocabulary of inclusion: both in terms of feminism and multiculturalism. By applying this vocabulary to their criticisms, the students were able to take note of the real differences which exist among themselves, but also between the world as portrayed on television and the real world. The students developed a heightened awareness of the implicit messages communicated by entertainment television, with particular regard to who is included and affirmed and who is not. On the one hand, students were alerted to how television's portrayals of different kinds of people can lead to affirmation of previously held beliefs; but on the other hand, they were able to recognize television's potential for expanding the worldview of the audience.

The process of careful scrutiny made students more careful consumers of television. A number of students suggested that the class experience had "ruined" their television viewing. They could no longer engage in mindless viewing. They could no longer be couch potatoes. Furthermore, they were no longer inclined to merely accept what came on television simply for the sake of watching television. Analyzing the programs we watched in class made the students more selective. It is important to note that we might not all select the same programs, nor will our assessments of each program's value/significance be the same. What has happened, however, is that students are able to apply their own critical frame to their own viewing experiences.

NOTES

1. Nancy Porter, "Liberating Teaching," *Liberal Education 68* (summer 1982): 115.

2. Barrie Thorne, "Rethinking the Ways We Teach," in Carol Pearson, Donna L. Shavlik, and Judith G. Touchton, eds., *Educating the Majority: Women Challenge Tradition in Higher Education* (New York: American Council on Education, 1989), pp. 311–325.

3. Martha Thompson, "Diversity in the Classroom: Creating Opportunities for Learning Feminist Theory," *Women's Studies Quarterly 15* (fall/winter 1987): 81.

4. Lynn Weber Cannon, "Fostering Positive Race, Class, and Gender Dynamics in the Classroom," *Women's Studies Quarterly 18* (spring/summer 1990): 129–133.

5. Peggy McIntosh, "Interative Phases of Curricular Re-Vision: A Feminist Perspective," Working paper number 124, Wellesley College Center for Research on Women.

6. Valerie Swarts, *Feminism and Learning Theories: A Unique Voice in the Classroom*, paper presented at the Seventy-seventh Annual Meeting of the Speech Communication Association, Atlanta, GA, November 2, 1991, p. 3.

7. Donald Shields and Virginia Kidd, "Teaching through Popular Film: A Small Group Analysis of *The Poseidon Adventure*," *Speech Teacher 22* (September 1973): 201.

8. Leah Vande Berg, "Using Television to Teach Coursees in Gender and Communication," *Communication Education 40* (January 1991): 106.

9. Leah Vande Berg and Lawrence Wenner, *Television Criticism: Approaches and Applications* (New York: Longman, 1991), p. xi.

10. Wilbert McKeachie, *Teaching Tips: A Guidebook for the Beginning College Teacher*, 8th ed. (Lexington, MA: D. C. Heath, 1986), p. 161.

11. Sonia Foss and Marla Kanengieter, "Visual Communication in the Basic Course," *Communication Education 41* (July 1992): 312.

12. Irving L. Janis, "The Influence of Television on Personal Decision-Making," in Stephen B. Withey and Ronald P. Abeles, eds., *Television and Social Behavior: Beyond Violence and Children* (Hillside, NJ: Lawrence Erlbaum, 1980), pp. 161–190.

13. Audrey Roth, *The Boob Tube and Communication Competencies*, paper delivered at the Thirty-fourth Annual Meeting of the Conference on College Composition and Communication, Detroit, MI, March 17–19, 1983, p. 18.

14. John Fiske, *Television Culture* (London: Methuen, 1987).

15. Rebecca Rubin, "Communication Competence," in Gerald Phillips and Julia Wood, eds., *Speech Communication: Essays to Commemorate the Seventy-Fifth Anniversary of the Speech Communication Association* (Carbondale: Southern Illinois University Press, 1990), p. 94.

16. Linda Schamber, "Core Course in Visual Literacy for Ideas, Not Techniques," *Journalism Educator 46* (spring 1991): 16–21.

17. Suzanne Williams, *A Comparison of Cultural Values in Animated Cartoons Produced for Theatre and Television*, unpublished doctoral dissertation, University of Wisconsin, Madison, 1987.

18. Robert L. Schrag, *Sugar and Spice and Everything Nice Versus Snakes and Snails and Puppy Dogs' Tails: Selling Social Stereotypes on Saturday Morning Television*, paper presented at the annual meeting of the Southern States Communication Association, Memphis, Tennessee, April 1989.

Part IV

Power and Pedagogy

In the following section we explore issues of power and pedagogy and the ways in which observed gendered differences relating to these experiences, relationships, and institutions are socially constructed. In examining different ways of knowing, believing, and learning attributed to gender and biological sex, we want to avoid essentialist explanations that directly or indirectly assume these patterns are fixed, biologically given, universal categories. Although Carol Gilligan (1982) notes that the "different voices" of women "arise in a social context where factors of social status and power combine with reproductive biology to shape the experience of males and females and the relations between the sexes" (p. 2), her research unfortunately can be used to fortify this type of essentialism.

Contributors in this section explore the interplay of power and gender in the ascribed traditional roles of teacher and student by looking at the connection between communication and pedagogy as the site where power differences are expressed. The contributors interrogate the ways in which pedagogy does or does not work as an active process of giving voice to students in order to change the traditional hierarchy in these power relations. Roles that are socially constructed can be socially deconstructed so as to transform gendered educational institutions and pedagogical styles.

Daniel J. Shea discusses the politics of pedagogy: how the power relations in pedagogical contexts are gendered, and what it might mean to transform these patterns. His chapter analyzes the dynamic of what he calls "connected teaching," which is distinguished from the usual "separated" interactions of pedagogical relationships by its emphasis on active caring and the cultivation of personal voice. Shea claims: "The implicit and dynamic grammar of connected teaching is ecological synergy, the holistic perception that the whole of the teaching-learning experience is a unique and unified system of interactive connections greater than the mere sum of its parts, that the whole so created in connected teaching is as evanescent as a Navajo sand painting and as enduring as memory." Shea integrates Peter Elbow's distinction between the "doubting game," a pedagogical style that is logic based, adversarial, and impersonal, with the "believing game," an approach to learning that cultivates listening, context, and the commonality of experience. Rather than seeing learning as the power of reason to control, through abstraction and quantification, unruly feelings, a feminist pedagogy encourages the integration of mind and heart, self and others, and qualities deemed masculine and feminine.

Richard West examines young students' perceptions of their male and female teachers. Although he asks students to identify those aspects of these relationships they consider to be positive, this chapter assumes a pedagogical and societal context of stereotypic gender roles and behaviors. The communications between teacher and student that West explores take place within a set of fairly rigid gender expectations. One of the challenging goals for future research is to define and determine which interpersonal interactions are in fact "positive" for the student. What constitutes a positive and valuable experience for students, and does this reflect or contradict the gendered expectations of the society? Is it helpful to reinforce or to subvert given gender roles in relationships between teacher and student? What are the boundaries and possible consequences of such redefinitions? Though these question are not dealt with explicitly in West's chapter, they are assumed and implied by his work and point to future deconstructive projects.

Cheryl Forbes and Allen Emerson investigate both students' voices and the roles of teachers in various disciplines. Disciplinarity itself is shown to be a gendered phenomenon, constructed by discourse and requiring particular discursive styles. These authors look at the ways in which the discourses of mathematics and English are configured by power relationships and thereby encourage a particular and gendered use of language. Forbes and Emerson explore the kind of talk and other metacommunication students are enjoined to learn as they are initiated into these disciplines. These different voices that practitioners employ are not only gendered but value laden. The areas associated with maleness call upon a particular discursive style marked by a use of the passive voice that indicates a presumed "objectivity" (e.g., "it has been determined that"). There is now abundant research demonstrating the ways in which females are influenced away from mathematics, natural sciences, and other "logico-scientific" thinking whereas males are encouraged to pursue them. The disciplines characterized by this supposed objectivity and value freedom are thus more highly valued because of their association with maleness.

These different discursive styles and their corresponding disciplines are further explored in Janice Koch's chapter. As students acquire the skills and subject matter of these disciplines, they learn how to talk in the language of these fields. Students of math and science (like students of English and education) are also taught critical messages about power and gender as they are initiated into their respective areas of expertise. Koch examines these patterns in order to begin to decouple the disciplines of science and math from their association with masculinity in order to encourage women to enter these fields.

Because educational environments and pedagogical practices are so fundamental to how we learn about who we are as people and what is possible in our world, it is critical to challenge the biases of institutions and relationships that would privilege males and marginalize females.

REFERENCE

Gilligan, Carol. 1982. *In a Different Voice: Psychological Theory and Women's Development*. Cambridge, MA: Harvard University Press.

13

The Grammar of Connected Teaching

Daniel J. Shea

In recent years, women researchers conducting formal inquiries into the core psychological experience and functional reasoning structures of women subjects have critiqued the traditional insistence in developmental psychology on separation and autonomy as the benchmarks of human maturity. These researchers have begun to chart evidence for the assertion that women experience themselves primarily not as isolated subjectivities but rather as selves connected to others.

In 1982 Carol Gilligan published *In a Different Voice*, in which she reported on her discovery of a distinct pattern of reasoning about moral dilemmas which appeared in her women respondents. Although she was quick to point out that this distinction was one of theme rather than gender per se, it is evident from the book's contents that the reasoning pattern Gilligan reported on was clearly more characteristic of her women respondents than of the men.[1]

Gilligan reported that, when presented with an ethical dilemma, her male respondents tended to reason about the dilemma in terms of abstract considerations of rights, whereas her female respondents thought about the dilemma in terms of concrete responsibilities and the actual consequences of a decision. Although the male respondents tended to approach ethical quandries as quantitative problems amenable to solution through a philosophical calculus, the women subjects appeared to place primary emphasis on not sundering existing human relations, on finding a decision point that would resolve the dilemma without failing to include the legitimate interests of all the parties involved. In this respect her work is reminiscent of Piaget's studies of children's games, where it was discovered that boys would interrupt a game to squabble endlessly about interpretations of rules whereas girls, when they reached a similar impasse, would quit the game and engage in another.[2]

On the basis of her work with ethical dilemmas, Gilligan has argued that traditional developmental psychology has been flawed by a tacit male bias. The findings of research conducted on male subjects has been, in this analysis, uncritically extrapolated to pertain to women as well. In the process, women have been measured against a scale not of their own devising, and have been found wanting, due not to any deficiency in themselves but rather to a failure of methodological self-consciousness in the design and execution of the research. If it has been assumed that the way men reason about problems is illustrative of reason itself, an assumption traceable as far back as Aristotle's *De Anima* which asserts that women are inferior to men because they cannot reason like men, and if women fail to achieve like men on certain scales of rational development, such as Kohlberg's stages of moral reasoning, the flaw may well be in the assumption that man is the measure of reason, if not of all things. Gilligan argues that there may be more than one way to reason, another voice that has been historically stilled by domestication and by exclusion from public affairs and philosophical status.

The publication, in 1986, of *Women's Ways of Knowing* by Belenky, Goldberger, Clinchy, and Tarule, dealt with similar issues in the conduct of college education. In addition to postulating a developmental sequence in the cognitive development of women students which paid attention to the effects of differential sex-role stereotyping on the ways in which women construct their self-concepts as knowers, the researchers also noted that college education is organized around an ideology of knowledge that pays homage to the rituals of rigor, objectivity, detachment, separation of the knower from the known and an adversarial style of thinking and communicating which is unconsciously assumed to be equivalent to thinking itself.[3] In addition to the overt and covert forms of sexist bias which manifest themselves in college classrooms—documented both in this book and in the report of the Association of American Colleges titled "The Classroom Climate: A Chilly One for Women"[4]—the authors of *Women's Ways of Knowing* also raise the issue of the psychological ambience of the classroom where feeling tones dominated by authority, competition and win-lose interactions reinforce a sense of higher education as a rite of passage roughly analogous to running a psychological gauntlet. This distinction is made possible from the vantage point of a style of reasoning which the authors call "connected," which they associate with the stylistic preferences of their women respondents and which they contrast with traditional "separated" thinking, the style of reason that Isaac Newton and the other founders of the Royal Society had in mind when they declared, in the society's founding documents, that their purpose was the elaboration of a completely masculine science.[5]

The epistemology of connected reason arises from the roots of conscious experience, in primary, affective object relations which differentiate self from not-self, object relations which instantiate self-consciousness. Related to the manner in which psychic experience differentiates itself is the fact that, until very recent times, women as mothers have been the exclusive identification from which both male and female offspring must distinguish themselves in order to arrive at the experience of ego or I. As Nancy Chodorow has argued, we as women and men experience ourselves the way we do because we both have been mothered by women.[6]

The origin, then, of the structure of sensory perception from which connected thinking arises is a primitive psychic object relation of undifferentiated identity with a female mother. In female children, the development of their gender identity involves psychic separation and individuation in a context of unbroken gender identity with a female caretaker. In the case of male children, however, the development of male gender identity, at least in cultures where women mother, involves a repression and denial of the male child's first affective object relation, that of identity with his mother.

Given that repression is an act of psychic violence, a forgetting in which the act of forgetting is itself forgotten, it can be argued, from an examination of psychoanalytic object relations in the infancy of the mind, that male gender identity as a concious phenomenon depends upon the denial, or the psychic negation, of any identity with femaleness. Speaking philosophically, we can assert that the female child's psychic logic is dualistic in a nondualistic field, while the male child's psychic logic achieves dualism by extinguishing all memory of the nondualistic field of experience into which it was born.

Thus "separated" reason, in which affective relations with an object of study are avoided and in which "objectivity" is defined as detachment and distance, is psychically redolent of its roots in the unconscious male psyche. Alternatively, "connected" reason, in which attachment and closeness are perceived as illuminating, rather than clouding, thought and in which objectivity is perceived in terms of a phenomenological epoche in which the perspective of the object of thought is allowed to manifest itself—Heidegger's notion of truth as *aletheia*, or "unconcealment"—arises from a first psychic experience in which the unity of being, as a felt phenomenon, has never been sundered.

The Swiss psychiatrist Carl Jung, writing early in this century, addressed the issue of the repression of femaleness in the male psyche with his descriptive notion of the anima or contrasexual opposite repressed into the unconscious male mind. In a similar vein, masters of Zen Buddhism argue that women are constitutionally closer to the awakening of their true nature, in which the subject and object of perception are one and not two, than are men. As Lao-Tzu put it: "He who knows the masculine, but abides in the feminine, is the true son of heaven."[7] We are now reaching the point where we can see that wholeness in the life of the mind is a marriage of separated and connected forms of consciousness into something which is neither, a unique synergy beyond gendered form which Coleridge signified in his assertion that "a great mind must be androgynous, having the characteristics of both sexes."[8]

However, the style of interpersonal communications prevalent until just yesterday in the life of the Western academy, and in its teaching praxis, has been exclusively that of separation, or what Peter Elbow calls the "Doubting Game," looking for what is wrong, reasoning in an adversarial way, constructing truth as a calculus of conviction by methods of proof, criticism and disproof of assertions, asserting mastery and control by adherence to impersonal and universal standards of verification and criticism. In an intellectual culture dominated by separated reason, or bluffed into thinking that separated reason is reason itself, negation remains the primary posture.

Elbow contrasts the Doubting Game, as an intellectual posture, with what he calls the Believing Game, driven by a primary impulse to discover the intellectual structure of what is intelligible, an accepting and listening observational style of discrimination in which the basis of intellectual authority is found in a commonality of experience, documented in narrative and contextual systems of signification, rather than by recourse to the methodologies of abstraction and quantification.[9] The Believing Game is what Lao-Tzu called the Valley Spirit, and it is cognate with the structure of connected reasoning as described by Gilligan and a newly emerging host of researchers documenting the meaning of women discovering their own psychological paradigm independently of the authoritative male canon.[10]

Blythe Clinchy has reported that when women students were asked to assess the Doubting Game, the adversarial style of intellectual jousting as they encountered it in their classrooms, they replied that they didn't like it and didn't do it very much. Instead of arguing an oppositional point of view in their heads, they sought to comprehend what would lead a person to assert an idea. They preferred, in other words, to understand the etiology and genesis of an idea, no matter how odious or agreeable, the meaning of the idea in the mind of the person proposing it, to constructing the idea as an assertion requiring criticism as factually correct or false.[11]

Clearly, intellectual integrity and cognitive power are enhanced, and balanced, when both postures of consciousness achieve a behavioral interface. However, connected thinking in Occidental culture, particularly since the rise to dominance of the mechanistic paradigm of Newtonian science, has largely been relegated to subordinate status, to questions of methodology in the social sciences and in psychotherapy. Western intellectual culture, built on the Aristotelian law of noncontradiction, or negation of identity, has, until the advent of post-Einsteinian physics, insisted on a bloodless quest after the grail of objectivity. Now that we know that we cannot study the cosmos without changing it, connected thinking is reasserting itself in scientific reason. Like the artifactual technologies we have created to extend our senses into the microdomain of subatomic phenomena and the macrodomain of the galaxies, we are organic biotechnologies organized to produce self-reflexive self-consciousness in the cosmos. Objectivity does not separate after all; objectivity connects us to the field in which we are a temporary wave and apart from which we would not, indeed could not, be. Meister Eckhart's heretical declaration—"The Eye with which I see God is the Eye with which God sees me"—has been vindicated.

Teaching practice, a channel for the transmission and cultivation of reason, can be organized in either a separated, a connected or a combined style. Women researchers have documented a prevalence and dominance of separated teaching styles, emphasising adversarial, competetitive challenges and impersonal communications styles, as a style of pedagogy which, at certain stages in the construction of a woman student's intellectual self-concept, lead to impasse and frustration.[12] Critical reasoning, hypostasized as reason per se, reasoning against another, is corrosive of human connectedness, a style of verbal disconnection and aggressive detachment. Separation and negation, embodied in an instructor's exhortation to his class to "tear into" his interpretation of a novel as evidence of their ability to think are, in light of the present analysis and the more extensive feminist critique of communications styles in the American academy, sexist in a subtle and pervasive way that fails to recognize, nor to encourage, communications and thinking styles which emphasize vulnerability, imperfection, the surrender of intellectual defenses, humor and the deflation of authority, and the weaving of a communal rather than an individual style of reasoning in which diversity of opinion is welcomed, integrated and valued. As Blythe Clinchy has written: "When a woman (or anybody) with a proclivity toward connected knowing enters an environment that fails to recognize connected knowing as a legitimate way of knowing, she feels disconfirmed as a thinker."[13]

These observations point toward the elaboration of a grammar of connected thinking and teaching in Wittgenstein's sense of grammar as "descriptive not of one experience but of the framework within which our experience can be described."[14] The word *grammar*, therefore, as used in this paper, signifies an organizational structure of immediate perception, leveraged beyond conventional gender dualisms by a self-conscious awareness of the operations of the sex-class system in the life of the mind. Nourished by experiential insights into the masculinist exile of intimacy and identity from intellectual life—a subordinate status mandated by the rules governing separated reason—this perceptual template, or grammar, no longer bound by the limits engraved in language by the normative masculine, liberates consciousness and allows us to articulate our awareness as explicitly feminist thinkers in active, unrehearsed speech, original and unique, outside the limits of traditionally gendered language. Connected thinking arises from a grammar—a perceptual framework enabling a new speech—which springs not from psychological disconnection and distance, but from a relational sense of identity. The connected teacher models this sense of identity in the classroom by her openness to the experience and thoughts of her students, by her willingness to share her own experience, and by entering into active, caring, personal relationships with each student in the class.

Thus, the connected teacher is neither syballine oracle nor Freire's banker actively making deposits in his student's mind banks. The connected teacher models active reason, spontaneous and unrehearsed, as a human, imperfect and attainable activity, as a source of puzzlement, joy, desire, and energy. The connected teacher is focused on the birth of reason in the life of the student's mind. He or she is intent on forging a personal connection to each student, developmentally paced to the student's capacity, which assists, midwife-like, at the ongoing birth of intellect.

In connected teaching the teaching process is the object of thought, a medium of subtle communications including words and behavioral signs, which evokes the critical reflection of both teacher and students, a stream of communal consciousness in which the teacher, by thinking spontaneously and talking together with the students, assists each student to make explicit and thoughtfully to articulate her tacit knowledge. The implicit and dynamic grammar of connected teaching is ecological synergy, the holistic perception that the whole of the teaching-learning experience is a unique and unified system of interactive connections greater than the mere sum of its parts, that the whole so created in connected teaching is as evanescent as a Navajo sand painting and as enduring as memory.

To teach is to live, and to feel alive. As Madeline Grumet puts it:

If I am a teacher I rise early. It may still be dark. I check to see if my children are up. I made their lunches last night. My eldest can't find her shoes. My youngest worries that I will forget to sign her permission slip for the field trip. I worry that I will dash out of the house and leave the stencil that I need for my second period class in the typewriter.

Maybe it will be light when I get to school. Maybe there will be no homeroom announcements, and I can slip out to run off the stencil. Maybe there will be a fire drill and second period will self-destruct. Maybe the entire morning will be drenched in bleary anxiety, filtered through chalk dust, recorded only in the incomplete circles my coffee cup leaves on the cover of my grade book. Or maybe the winter sun will shine with a summer's heat and on the very day we are reading Frost, the world will exhibit its essential paradox in mud and snow and they will feel metaphor seep through the soles of their shoes and know it from the ground up.[15]

Connected teaching assumes that paying close attention to people, and connecting directly with them as individuals, allowing them to give voice to their thoughts in an environment where words are not used as weapons, and students don't lose by being told they are wrong, can draw into existence an intellectual voice even in the most frightened and silent of students. Connected teaching arises out of active caring for the intellectual development of each student, what Noddings has called the reintroduction of the voice of the mother in teaching.[16] As Sarah Ruddick describes it: "The domination of feeling by thought, which I had worked so hard to achieve, was breaking down. Instead of developing arguments that could bring my feelings to heel, I allowed feeling to inform my most abstract thinking."[17] In a connected classroom, feelings do not cloud intelligence, they bring it to life.

Research into the origins, development, and repression of a unique intellectual self-identity in women subjects continues to this day. New developments in the study of young women entering adolescence suggest that adolescence is a time in which girls come not to know what they had known to that time, a time in which their personal voice, their actual identity, is subjected to repression by a cultural system of masculine values and an educational praxis which, in both content and method, models the law of the fathers.[18] Connected teaching seeks to recover that original voice, and to endow it with philosophical status.

The new psychology of women has altered the dominant paradigm in the way we understand human behavior. It has given us a new viewpoint from which to think about issues of epistemology, judgment, and valuation. Man is no longer the exclusive measure of human behavior, nor of reason.

The application of the findings of this research to educational practice generates, in our time, the concepts of connected thinking, connected teaching and the cultivation of a personal voice as correctives to the rigidity which sets into teaching practice due to a monotonous and exclusive reliance on separated styles of thinking and communicating, styles that have been shown to be related to gender identity acquisition and a socialization process which is differentially weighted to give advantage to all that is felt to be masculine. Curiously, in Clinchy's Wellesley study, male respondents demonstrated the same emotional ambivalence toward entering another person's perspective that the women respondents showed toward argument.[19] The terms of the difference have been cast in a women-mothered infancy, the ambivalence is aboriginal but not unbridgeable. In the integration of connected teaching into the classroom lies an opportunity to widen the psychological horizons of students of both sexes and an ancillary opportunity to cultivate in students of each sex the qualities of mind that dualistic sex-role socialization may have denied them.

NOTES

1. Carol Gilligan, *In a Different Voice: Psychological Theory and Women's Development* (Cambridge, MA: Harvard University Press, 1982).

2. Jean Piaget, *The Moral Judgment of the Child* (New York: Free Press, 1965).

3. Mary Field Belenky, Blythe McVicker Clinchy, Nancy Rule Goldberger, and Jill Mattuck Tarule, *Women's Ways of Knowing: The Development of Self, Voice, and Mind* (New York: Basic Books, 1986).

4. Association of American Colleges, Project on the Status and Education of Women, "The Classroom Climate: A Chilly One for Women" (Washington, DC: Association of American Colleges, 1982).

5. See Evelyn Fox Keller, *Reflections on Gender and Science* (New Haven, CT: Yale University Press, 1985).

6. Nancy Chodorow, *The Reproduction of Mothering: Psychoanalysis and the Sociology of Gender* (Berkeley: University of California Press, 1978).

7. Lao Tzu, *Tao Te Ching*, Poem 28.

8. Samuel Taylor Coleridge, quoted by Carolyn Heilbrun, *Toward A Recognition of Androgyny* (New York: Harper Colophon, 1973).

9. Peter Elbow, "The Doubting Game and the Believing Game: An Analysis of the Intellectual Enterprise," Appendix Essay in *Writing without Teachers* (London: Oxford University Press, 1973).

10. See, for example, Jean Baker Miller, *Toward a New Psychology of Women* (Boston: Beacon Press, 1976); Luise Eichenbaum and Susie Orbach, *Understanding Women: A Feminist Psychoanalytic Approach* (New York: Basic Books, 1982); Juliet Mitchell, *Psychoanalysis and Feminism* (New York: Pantheon Books, 1974); and Judith V. Jordan, Alexandra G. Kaplan, Jean Baker Miller, Irene P. Striver, and Janet L.

Surrey, *Women's Growth in Connection: Writings from the Stone Center* (New York: Guilford Press, 1991), to name but a few.

11. Blythe McVicker Clinchy, "Issues of Gender in Teaching and Learning," *Excellence in College Teaching*, Vol. 1 (1990), pp. 52–67.

12. See, again, Association of American Colleges, "The Classroom Climate"; Belenky et al., *Women's Ways of Knowing*; and the Working Papers of the Wellesley College Center for Research on Women.

13. Clinchy, "Issues of Gender in Teaching and Learning," p. 65.

14. Ray Monk, *Ludwig Wittgenstein: The Duty of Genius* (New York: Free Press, 1990).

15. Madeleine R. Grumet, *Bitter Milk: Women and Teaching* (Amherst, MA: University of Amherst Press, 1988).

16. Nel Noddings, *Caring* (Berkeley: University of California Press, 1990).

17. Sara Ruddick, "New Combinations: Learning from Virginia Woolf," in C. Asher, L. DeSalvo, and S. Ruddick, eds., *Between Women* (Boston: Beacon Press, 1984).

18. See Carol Gilligan, Nona Lyons, and Trudy Hanmer, *Making Connections: The Relational Worlds of Adolescent Girls at Emma Willard School* (Cambridge, MA: Harvard University Press, 1990); Carol Gilligan and Lyn Mikel Brown, "The Psychology of Women and the Development of Girls," paper presented at the Laurel-Harvard Conference on the Psychology of Women and the Education of Girls, Cleveland, OH, April 1990; and Elizabeth DeBold, "The Mind-Body Split in Adolescent Girls," unpublished audiotape of a lecture presented at a conference on Women's Ways of Knowing sponsored by the Association for Women in Psychology, Putney, VT, 1991.

19. Clinchy, "Issues of Gender in Teaching and Learning," p. 67.

14

Voices Seldom Heard: A Descriptive Analysis of Female and Male Teachers' Positive Interactions with Young People

Richard West

The American public school system is once again faced with challenges. Educational goals have been indicted, teacher morale is low, and worst of all, students are being negatively affected. In fact, the working conditions of the teaching profession have disenchanted the most dedicated of professionals. Personnel are distressed, equipment is faulty, books are unavailable, and school conditions are adequate at best (Duke 1984; Friedman and Farber 1992; Shanker 1986). Further, female students at all levels continue to be disadvantaged in the classroom, and females are also viewed as powerless in the teaching ranks (Arch and Cummins 1989; Best 1983; Rich 1992). It should become a priority for researchers to discover ways of enhancing the educational process for students and teachers alike.

Because an already overburdened educational system is trying to keep pace with an ever-changing student population, teachers find themselves working more diligently than ever. Today when teachers stand before a class, they can no longer be concerned with just teaching the basics. Teachers must also try to provide their students with an education that will allow them to cope with society's inadequacies and injustices.

What a teacher says in class, then, is integral to the whole learning environment. In most cases, the teacher is the most significant other outside the classroom. The relationship with a student and the way in which a student learns, is directly affected by the way a teacher communicates with the young person (Feezel 1987).

Biological sex plays a role in the teacher-student interaction. Much has been written with respect to the influence of sex in classroom communication (Allen, Willmington, and Sprague 1991; Bate 1992; Cooper 1995; Sadker and Sadker 1990; Stewart, Stewart, Friedley, and Cooper 1990). Little investigation, however, has examined how young children view classrooms taught by females and males. This research is a descriptive attempt to fill that void.

The purpose of this chapter is to discover which interactions in the classroom are perceived as valuable for students. Specifically, this research asks students to consider whether interactions with their female teachers or male teachers emerge as most positive. Further, this investigation draws on elementary and secondary students, an often overlooked population in research.

This research will also provide important information about what teachers are doing right. Too often, teachers are criticized for their performance in and out of the classroom. Identifying students' positive experiences with teachers has benefit for those in educational reform. At the very least, this undertaking will demonstrate what is being perceived as rewarding for students. Clearly, no educator wants to ignore these unheard voices.

RELEVANT LITERATURE

A discussion of interpersonal behaviors of teaching necessitates an explication of what comprises those behaviors. One construct noted to be part of a teacher's instructional repertoire is immediacy (Andersen 1979). "Immediacy" refers to decreased physical and/or psychological distance between interactants; that is, communication that enhances closeness to another (Mehrabian 1969). In essence, immediate teachers are viewed as accessible, involved, and effective (Andersen and Nussbaum 1990) and immediate teachers enhance their likability by students (Bassett and Smythe 1979).

The immediacy literature is clear with regard to its effectiveness in the classroom. Researchers have indicated that immediate teachers elicit student motivation (Christophel 1990) and prompt high levels of cognitive and affective learning (Gorham 1988; Kearney, Plax, and Wendt-Wasco 1985). Further, teachers are aware of their immediacy behaviors (Gorham and Zakahi 1990), and students are more likely to respond reciprocally to immediate teachers (Plax, Kearney, and Downs 1986). That is, students will affirm teachers who affirm them.

The research on teacher immediacy and student responses suggests that (1) teacher immediacy behaviors are critical in student learning, (2) students consistently respond positively to immediacy behaviors, and (3) teacher-student relationships can be enhanced by the integration of immediacy behaviors. It is reasonable to argue, then, that teachers who employ immediate behaviors are promoting positive academic experiences with their students. These instances are paramount in establishing and maintaining teacher-student relations, managing classroom misbehaviors, and embellishing student self-esteem (Brophy and Good 1986; Englander 1986). Teachers who use immediate behaviors are teachers who are positively recalled by students. Previous research has neglected to explore this issue with grade school and high school students, and therefore the following research question is posed: biological sex clearly impacts the classroom setting (Hall and Sandler 1984; Pearson, West, and Turner 1995; Sadker and Sadker 1985). Students may learn more about power relationships than subject matter in their interactions with teachers in the classroom. Teachers do not treat males and females similarly, that is, they evidence bias against women (Stewart et al. 1990). Countless studies demonstrate that when females and males engage in identical behavior, the behavior is devalued for the female. For example, Goldberg (1968), in a classic study, showed that when an identical essay was attributed either to a female or to a male, the essay was given a higher grade when evaluators believed it to be written by the male. Further, both women and men demonstrated the same prejudice.

In another frequently cited essay, Hall and Sandler (1982) argue that females are at a "significant disadvantage" in the college classroom. Female students are less involved in classroom interactions, have less confidence, and have lower expectations. The teachers' communicative behaviors may encourage these outcomes. Teachers provide more disparaging remarks to female students, are more likely to discourage classroom participation from females, and prevent female students from seeking additional help.

Since male and female students are treated differently, it is not surprising that they begin to evidence different interaction patters within the classroom. Research indicates that male teachers may be more responsible for differential treatment of students than female teachers. In two studies, Rosenfeld and Jarrard (1985, 1986) examined classroom interaction and showed that sexism is primarily a "male disease" (p. 161). Student perceptions of the classroom climate were dependent on whether the classroom was liked or disliked and whether the teacher was male or female.

It is clear, then, that biological sex must be considered when discussing teacher-student interaction. Most of the research has focused on college students, and thus, the results have limited application to other academic levels. Further, because positive student experiences have lasting impact on a child's self-esteem and self-concept (Civikly 1992; Cooper 1995), studying these positive experiences with knowledge of who is facilitating these interactions is resourceful.

The foregoing literature review prompts the following research questions:

1. What do elementary/secondary students report to be their most positive interpersonal classroom interaction with a teacher?
2. Are female or male teachers reported to be more positive in their interpersonal classroom interactions with elementary/secondary students?

METHOD

Participants

Participants in this study were 158 (87 males; 71 females) public grade and high school students in a school system located in New England. Nineteen of the participants were in fifth grade, twenty-four were sixth graders, seventeen were seventh graders, and nineteen of the participants were in the eighth grade. The high school respondents included twenty first-year students, eighteen sophomores, twenty-one juniors, and twenty seniors.

Procedures

Data collection procedures for all grades were similar. The principals selected which classes could be visited to minimize disruption of classroom processes. A research assistant entered the classroom and distributed a questionnaire packet that included questions which asked students to recall their most positive interactions with teachers. Basic demographic information was also solicited from respondents. The assistant explained that the survey was not a test, that it would not be graded, and instructed not to mention specific names of teachers in their answers. The students were informed that they could describe any positive/negative experience from kindergarten to their current grade level and told that experiences should be limited to the classroom. Although the question order did not vary across academic levels, the assistant's directions had to be altered to account for misinterpretations and misunderstandings at various academic levels. Originally, 171 students completed the questionnaire. However, due to either an explanation of experiences outside of the classroom or not responding to both questions, thirteen responses were eliminated from the final analyses.

Coding and Reliability

Each of the 158 responses to the open-ended questions was transcribed and unitized by the coders. The phrase, sentence, or paragraph that described each incident of (positive/negative) experience was determined to be the unit of analysis. All descriptions by students were of one positive episode. Coder training was conducted with two graduate students uninvolved with the study. Training using mock data resulted in coders agreeing on twenty-one of twenty-eight comments, achieving a 75 percent agreement level. Differences were discussed and clarified.

To ascertain coder reliability in this study, all responses provided by participants were read by both trained coders. A typological analysis (Goetz and LeCompte 1984) of data was employed to answer the first research question. Using this approach, a coder would independently read the response for each question and place that comment into an particular category. What constituted a category was based upon coder knowledge and intuition, as well as on experience attained in coder training. Subsequent comments were either classified as conceptually similar to a previous comment and placed into an existing category or listed as indicative of a new category. The coders then met to compare their categories and to resolve differences. The coders agreed on a coding system depicting three categories of positive experiences with teachers. Across categories, the coders achieved a 90 percent agreement level.

As a further reliability check, 10 percent of the responses were read by two additional coders unaware of the purpose of the study. The coders independently examined the category schemes identified by students. They then were asked to place a response into one of the corresponding categories. Coders agreed with prior coding decisions, achieving a 96 percent level. These levels of agreement were determined to be sufficient in establishing reliability for this study.

RESULTS

Positive Categories

Although the participants in this study ranged from elementary school through high school students, the results revealed similar experiences across grade levels. Because of the existing similarities and because insufficient information existed at each academic level, comments from all grades were merged. Previous educational researchers examining elementary and high school classrooms defended such an approach in their preliminary analyses of student behavior (Good, Slavings, Harel, and Emerson 1987; Good, Slavings, and Mason 1988). The following results are derived from an analysis of all classrooms.

From the analysis, three categories of positive communicative experience were identified. The three included "helping," "recognition," and "enjoyment via activity." A brief explanation of each is provided below.

Helping referred to teachers assisting the students with personal, family, and school challenges or problems. Comments in this category referred to teachers who would aid students in understanding test questions or make homework more clear. Further, student comments in this category pertained to teachers assisting students in personal issues such as problems with motivation or grades.

Recognition pertained to an awareness that the teacher perceived in the student something of value. Student comments in this category referred to teachers overtly complimenting the student in front of his or her classmates and teachers acknowledging appreciation for student achievements such as receiving an A on a test.

The third category, enjoyment via activity, related to students participating in classroom events that were not associated directly with ordinary school work or that deviated from traditional classroom procedures. These events included preparing food or celebrating a holiday by having a classroom party.

Biological Sex

Of significant interest in this study is the role of biological sex in teacher-student interaction. For purposes of this exploratory study, descriptive analysis was employed. The male student–male teacher interaction emerged as the most frequently cited biological sex pair for positive interaction, accounting for 35 percent of the responses. In descending order, the next three combinations were female student–female teacher, male student–female teacher, and female student–male teacher.

The number of reported instances were fifty-six (male-male), fifty-three (female-female) (34 percent), twenty-nine (male-female) (18 percent), and twenty (female-male) (13 percent).

DISCUSSION

The results of this study suggest that students view teachers helping as a valuable experience in the classroom. Of the 158 responses, seventy-two, or 46 percent, of the students' positive comments were categorized as helping. One student wrote that "the teacher stayed after school with me so that I would understand the math that we covered in class. It helped me on my next test in class." These comments imply that the student would not have understood without the teacher's help. It is likely that this category emerged since teacher assistance contributes to a student's positive self-esteem and students inevitably recognize this important influence (Civikly 1982). Jones (1987) noted that the majority of teacher helping which occurs is in the form of corrective feedback. It is plausible, then, that because feedback has been identified as an effective immediacy behavior (Gorham 1988), corrective feedback in particular can increase student compliance and facilitate student learning. Recognition was the second most frequently mentioned positive interpersonal experience representing forty-five of the 158, or 28 percent of comments. Students were clear in identifying the teacher's role in highlighting a student behavior or accomplishment. For example, the statement "I got to serve as a student teacher because I got the highest on the spelling test" is representative of this category. Inherent in these comments is a sense of pride; students seem very proud of what they did, and their teachers recognized this. Pioneering and classic work by Rogers (1961) on the impact that recognition has on interpersonal growth, contributes to a better understanding of the importance of this category.

Forty-one of the 158 comments, or 26 percent, composed the enjoyment-via-activity category. These comments pertained to teachers integrating games, simulated exercises, or general classroom activities in their lessons. Comments such as "We got to play math bingo and it was better than doing the fractions on the board" or "She [teacher] was cool because we played a grammar game with subjects, nouns, and other stuff" reflect student attitudes in the classroom. Wood (1981) commented that these experiential activities are valuable in a child's academic progress. Darrow (1986) noted that these activities empower students to become participants not spectators in the school.

Biological Sex

The second research question examined biological sex. The results of this analysis proved very intriguing. As previously mentioned, same sex pairs emerged as the most frequently cited positive interaction. Although the male-male interaction was coded as the most frequent pair, both same sex combinations will be considered together. Since more males were examined than females in this study, percentage of difference between the two pairs remains unimportant.

One explanation offered as to why male student–male teacher and female student–female teacher interactions dominate the positive interaction category appears to affirm traditional sex-role thinking. This supports the notion that children identify best with adults of the same sex during their formative years (Davies 1989). Students seem to closely identify with a teacher of the same sex, or at the very least, students are likely to identify with models perceived as similar to themselves (Bandura 1971).

The educational system (and teachers in particular) may communicate traditional ways of thinking, knowing, and behaving (Cooper 1995; Delamont 1990), including traditional sex roles. One sixth-grade boy, for instance, indicated that his male teacher let him "be the bombardment referee [*sic*] in P.E." An eleventh grader revealed that she got to "help [her female teacher] at the Christmas party. I introduced people and hung decorations." This helping behavior corresponds to stereotypical female behavior (Bem 1981). Female and male teachers appear to be reinforcing stereotypic behaviors in their female and male students. Sadker and Sadker (1982) pointed out, "As teachers enter the classroom, they carry with them more than their dittoes and chalk; they also bring socially influenced beliefs of what are appropriate behaviors, values, and careers for girls and for boys" (p. 99). Adler, Kless, and Adler (1992) echoed this sentiment by acknowledging that there are "boy and girl cultures" (pp. 183, 184) in school and teachers foster these subcultures unconsciously.

In this study teachers who were reported as fostering "positive" interpersonal interactions with their students were teachers who subscribed to stereotypical models of relating: these models, however, silence female students, further causing inequalities in time and attention from teachers (Kramarae and Treichler 1990; Measor and Sikes 1992; Smithson 1990). In addition, teachers who perpetuate these expected sex role behaviors are teachers who may thus foster male role strain, anxiety, and even alienation (Sadker and Sadker 1982). It may be, then, that male and female elementary and secondary students in this study have been accustomed to rigid role interpretations and deviating from this orientation would be perceived as confusing (Marland

1983). Thus, interactions supporting this stereotypical perspective were viewed as positive.

Cross-sex pairs emerged as the two next most frequently reported positive interactions. Although these pairs did not constitute a larger number of responses, some explanation is warranted. With regard to the male student–female teacher pair, previous research has concluded that male students have evaluated their interactions with female teachers as positive. For instance, Etaugh and Harlow (1975) concluded that boys were praised more than girls by their female teachers. Dweck, Davidson, Nelson, and Enna (1978) noted that boys received more positive teacher feedback than girls. It is reasonable, therefore, that the male students in this study favorably recall interactions with their female teachers because their female teachers favorably responded to them.

Finally, the results pertaining to the female student–male teacher interaction may best be understood by noting that it was the least reported in all combinations. The results do not imply, however, that male teachers are viewed as more negative. Rather, the findings suggest that male teachers may not have been seen as valuable models for elementary and secondary female students. It may be that male teachers are not "in tune" with girls at these ages. Regardless of his intentions to help, recognize, or employ classroom activities, the teacher may be unable to identify with his female students and in turn, his female students are incapable of identifying with him. The result is girls viewing classroom interactions not as favorably with their male teachers as with their female teachers.

CONCLUSION

Clearly, the results of this study are preliminary. Nonetheless, important points emerge about teaching and education in general. Although educators wrestle with critical educational reform issues for the next century, students might be called on to offer their impressions of their educational experiences.

Future research should expand respondent size, employ follow-up interviews with students, compare respondents at various academic levels, and determine if there are additional biological sex influences in response. In addition, we must continue to study this younger population to determine their impressions of teaching behaviors. The findings provide a descriptive base of understanding for researchers interested in discovering the nature of student-teacher interaction.

ACKNOWLEDGMENT

The author thanks Dr. Victoria DeFrancisco and Dr. Lynn Turner for their helpful suggestions with early drafts of this manuscript.

REFERENCES

Adler, P. A., S. J. Kless, and P. Adler. 1992. "Socialization to Gender Roles: Popularity among Elementary School Boys and Girls." *Sociology in Education 65*: 169–187.

Allen, R. R., S. C. Willmington, and J. Sprague. 1991. *Communication in the Secondary School: A Pedagogy*. Scottsdale, AZ: Gorsuch Scarisbrick.

Andersen, J. F. 1979. "Teacher Immediacy as a Predictor of Teaching Effectiveness." In D. Nimmo, ed., *Communication Yearbook 3*. New Brunswick, NJ: Transaction, pp. 543–559.

Andersen, J. F., and J. F. Nussbaum. 1990. "Interaction Skill in Instructional Settings." In J. A. Daly, G. W. Friedrich and A. Vangelisti, eds., *Teaching Communication: Theory, Research, and Methods*. Hillsdale, NJ: Lawrence Erlbaum, pp. 301–316.

Arch, E. C., and D. E. Cummins. 1989. "Structured and Unstructured Exposure to Computers: Sex Difference in Attitude and Use among College Students." *Sex Roles 20*: 245–254.

Bandura, A. 1971. *Psychological Modeling: Conflicting Theories*. Chicago: Aldine Atherton.

Bassett, R. E., and M. J. Smythe. 1979. *Communication and Instruction*. New York: Harper and Row.

Bate, B. 1992. *Communication and the Sexes*. Prospect Heights, IL: Waveland.

Bem, S. L. 1981. "Gender Schema Theory: A Cognitive Account of Sex Typing." *Psychological Review 88*: 354–364.

Best, R. 1983. *We've All Got Scars*. Bloomington: Indiana University.

Brophy, J., and T. L. Good. 1986. "Teacher Behavior and Student Achievement." In M. C. Wittrock, ed., *Handbook of Research on Teaching*. New York: Macmillan, pp. 328–375.

Cazden, C. B. 1988. *Classroom Discourse*. Portsmouth, NH: Heinemann.

Christophel, D. 1990. "The Relationships among Teacher Immediacy Behaviors, Student Motivation, and Learning." *Communication Education 39*: 323–340.

Civikly, J. M. 1982. "Self-concept, Significant Others, and Classroom Communication." In L. L. Barker, ed., *Communication in the Classroom*. Englewood Cliffs, NJ: Prentice-Hall, pp. 146–168.

———. 1992. *Classroom Communication: Principle and Practice*. Dubuque, IA: Wm. C. Brown.

Cooper, P. J. 1995. *Speech Communication for the Classroom Teacher*. Scottsdale, AZ: Gorsuch Scarisbrick.

Darrow, H. F. 1986. *Independent Activities for Creative Learning*. New York: Teachers College Press.

Davies, B. 1989. *Frogs and Snails and Feminist Tales: Preschool Children and Gender*. Sydney, Australia: Allen and Unwin.

Delamont, S. 1990. *Sex Roles and the School*. London: Routledge.

Duke, D. L. 1984. *Teaching: The Imperiled Profession*. Albany: State University of New York.

Dweck, C. S., W. Davidson, S. Nelson, and B. Enna. 1975. "Sex Differences in Learned Helplessness: II." *Developmental Psychology 14*: 268–276.

Englander, M. E. 1986. *Strategies for Classroom Discipline*. New York: Praeger.

Etaugh, C., and H. Harlow. 1975. "Behaviors of Male and Female Teachers as Related to Behaviors and Attitudes of Elementary School Children." *Journal of Genetic Psychology 127*: 163–170.

Feezel, J. D. 1987. "The Communication Skills of Teachers: A Coherent Conception." In J. McCaleb, ed., *How Do Teachers Communicate? A Review and Critique of Assessment Practices*. Washington, DC: ERIC Clearinghouse on Teacher Education, pp. 29–42.

Friedman, T. A., and B. A. Farber. 1992. "Professional Self-Concept as a Predictor of Teacher Burnout." *Journal of Educational Research 86*: 28–35.

Goetz, J. P., and M. D. LeCompte. 1984. *Ethnography and Qualitative Design in Educational Research*. Orlando, FL: Academic.

Goldberg, P. 1968. "Are Women Prejudiced against Women?" *Transaction 6*: 28.

Good, T. L., R. L. Slavings, K. H. Harel, and H. Emerson. 1987. "Student Passivity: A Study of Question Asking in K-12 Classrooms." *Sociology of Education 60*: 181–199.

Good, T. L., R. L. Slavings, and D. A. Mason. 1988. "Learning to Ask Questions: Grade and School Effects." *Teaching and Teacher Education 4*: 363–378.

Gorham, J. 1988. "The Relationship between Verbal Teacher Immediacy Behavior and Student Learning." *Communication Education 37*: 40–53.

Gorham, J., and W. R. Zakahi. 1990. "A Comparison of Teacher and Student Perceptions of Immediacy and Learning: Monitoring Process and Product." *Communication Education 39*: 354–368.

Hall, R. M., and B. R. Sandler. 1982. *The Classroom Climate: A Chilly One for Women?* Washington, DC: Association of American Colleges.

———. 1984. *Out of the Classroom: A Chilly Campus Climate for Women?* Washington, DC: Association of American Colleges.

Jones, F. H. 1987. *Positive Classroom Instruction*. New York: McGraw-Hill.

Kearney, P., T. G. Plax, and N. J. Wendt-Wasco. 1985. "Teacher Immediacy for Affective Learning in Divergent College Classes." *Communication Quarterly 33*: 61–74.

Kramarae, C., and P. A. Treichler. 1990. "Power Relationships in the Classroom." In S. L. Gabriel and I. Smithson, eds., *Gender in the Classroom: Power and Pedagogy*. Urbana, IL: University of Illinois, pp. 41–59.

Marland, M. 1983. *Sex Differentiation in School*. London: Heinemann.

Measor, L., and P. J. Sikes. 1992. *Gender and Schools*. New York: Cassell.

Mehrabian, A. 1969. "Some Referents and Measures of Nonverbal Behavior." *Behavioral Research Methods and Instrumentation 1*: 213–217.

Pearson, J. C., R. L. West, and L. H. Turner. 1995. *Gender and Communication*. Dubuque, IA: Wm. C. Brown/Benchmark.

Plax, T. G., Kearney, P., and Downs, T. M. 1986. "Communicating Control in the Classroom and Satisfaction with Teaching and Students." *Communication Education 35*: 379–388.

Rich, A. 1992. "Taking Women Students Seriously." In M. Anderson and P. H. Collins, eds., *Race, Class, and Gender: An Anthology*. Belmont, CA: Wadsworth, pp. 390–396.

Rogers, C. R. 1961. *On Becoming a Person*. Boston: Houghton Mifflin.

Rosenfeld, L. B., and M. W. Jarrard. 1985. "The Effects of Perceived Sexism in Female and Male College Professors on Students' Descriptions of Classroom Climate." *Communication Education 34*: 205–213.

———. 1986. "Student Coping Mechanisms in Sexist and Nonsexist Professors' Classes." *Communication Education 35*: 157-62.

Sadker, M. P., and D. M. Sadker. 1982. *Sex Equity Handbook for Schools*. New York: Longman.

————. 1985. "Is the O.K. Classroom O.K.?" *Phi Delta Kappan 66*: 358–361.

————. 1990. "Confronting Sexism in the College Classroom." In S. L. Gabriel and I. Smithson, eds., *Gender in the Classroom: Power and Pedagogy*. Urbana: University of Illinois, pp. 176–187.

Shanker, A. 1986. "Our Profession, Our Schools: The Case for Fundamental Reform." *American Educator 10*: 10–17.

Smithson, I. 1990. "Introduction: Investigating Gender, Power, and Pedagogy." In S. L. Gabriel and I. Smithson, eds., *Gender in the Classroom: Power and Pedagogy*. Urbana: University of Illinois, pp. 1–27.

Stewart, L. P., A. D. Stewart, S. A. Friedley, and P. J. Cooper. 1990. *Communication between the Sexes: Differences and Sex-role Stereotypes*. Scottsdale, AZ: Gorsuch Scarisbrick.

Wood, B. S. 1981. "Speech Communication in the Elementary School." In G. W. Friedrich, ed., *Education in the 80's: Speech Communication*. Washington, DC: National Education Association, pp. 13–21.

15

(Re)telling the Old Tales: The Emerging Voices of Women in English and Mathematics

Cheryl Forbes and Allen Emerson

INTRODUCTION—CHERYL

When I staggered through the math courses my high school and college required, I asked myself, "Why can't math be more like English?", the way Professor Higgins in *My Fair Lady* wondered why women couldn't be more like men. Math implied "male" to me, English female—with all the stereotypes in play. Mathematics is linear, logical, lucid; English is spongy, amorphous, imprecise. So when I wanted math to be more like English, I suppose I was really asking that math be less linear, more circular, that it be more like language and reality as I experienced it. I wanted math to be more female. Because it wasn't, I didn't know how to talk in math. I was silenced.

INTRODUCTION—ALLEN

Strangely enough, I wasn't fond of mathematics until I reached college, when I finally saw what my teachers had been trying to describe the elegance, the beauty, the deep satisfaction of symbols, and their strength. I discovered via physics that mathematics gives us control over nature. The power of mathematics overwhelmed me as I contemplated the flight of a ball defined equationally. The world became a place that could be contained within symbols. Mathematics reduced the world to something I could understand and control. It was heady, offering me independence from the vagaries and uncertainties of nature and human relationships. I also learned that mathematical thinking rewarded individual effort, which naturally meant that math was something a person did by oneself, with oneself, silently. I never wanted math to be anything other than what I had discovered it was, a particular kind of language that left behind the ambiguity and "sloppiness" that poetry seemed to bring out in people. Early on

I asked my teachers, "Why can't poets just come out and say what they mean the way mathematicians do?" Indeed, I see now that I was really asking, "Why can't English be more like math?" I believed that anyone could *do* English; not everyone could master mathematics. I had, one might say, a Professor Higgins view of the two disciplines.

Now that we've heard two versions of the story, we want to bring them together, not as opponents but as partners, collaborators. We want to listen as well as we know how to the emerging voices of women in a developmental mathematics course and a first-year writing course. Belief in gendered stereotypes often results in the voices of women, who are so successful in an open-ended English class, becoming silenced or, at best, defensive in a mathematics class. Yet in a mathematics class, women who may prefer the security of the closed atmosphere of "getting the right answers" may find themselves silenced, defensive, or confused in an English class.

We wondered whether this situation was an inevitable result of the two kinds of discourse we found within the disciplines of English and mathematics. Can we assume that English is more connected to immmediate experience, to the experience of human relationships, than is mathematics, which is considered more "logico-scientific," according to Bruner (1986)? How do women talk in math and English? How can teachers in each discipline make the most of the ways women talk? We hope that these questions will appear in sharper relief as we listen to the emerging voices of the women from a developmental mathematics class and three from a first-year composition class in a four-year, private liberal arts college in the Midwest. The data came from several hours of taped in-class conversations, ethnographers' observation notes of the classroom interaction, teacher conferences with the students, and the students' writing, either in learning logs or in essays.

In our analysis we applied three interpretive approaches: an examination of women's cognitive and affective development, the styles of female discourse, and the construction of narratives. As we discuss each one, please keep in mind that we are analyzing patterns. We are not claiming that *all* women talk as these women do. Nevertheless, it is striking that over the course of the semester—even at times during the course of one conversation—we could hear these students moving back and forth between the stages of "knowing" that Belenky, Clinchy, Goldberger, and Tarule (1986) have claimed are representative of women: silence, received knowledge, subjective knowledge, procedural knowledge, and constructed knowledge. Often, the women seemed caught between silence and "received knowledge" (the kind of knowledge that mathematics and a grammatical approach to writing supposedly privilege), as if they were asking, "What is my voice supposed to sound like as a female student of mathematics? Of writing? What rules do I need to know to get the right answer?" Occasionally, the women ventured into constructed knowledge, suddenly finding themselves listening to their voices, though they never seemed entirely comfortable. Their talk illustrated the claims made in the work of

Tannen (1990) and Lakoff (1990) regarding the characteristics of female discourse: overlapping, interrupting, cooperating.

In keeping with the students' ways of knowing and talking, it was also striking that we could hear their conversations becoming *narratives*, in the sense described by Witherell and Noddings (1991)—narratives that construct an identity and allow for a voice, within both the mathematical and writing communities. More specifically, as the women in the mathematics class constructed narratives of themselves, they came to understand that mathematics as a discipline is not antithetical to narrative but rather is itself a narrative community.

These, then, are the three interpretive strands we tried to hold on to as we entered the maze of conversations before us: an exploration of women's cognitive and affective development, an examination of styles of female discourse, and the construction of narrative. It was not always possible to follow each one separately; we found them braided together, not hanging loose for our easy reach. As we followed them, we became narrators ourselves, telling the stories of these women, and the stories that emerged in the mathematics class and the stories that emerged in the writing class became commentary on and for each other.

The two women in the developmental mathematics class, Ms. A, an art major, and Ms. V, an undecided major, were colleagues in the same group, along with a male student, Mr. C, and were taped every class during their second semester of instruction. All three of them had been in the first-semester developmental math course with Allen, though they had not been members of the same collaborative group. They were, however, familiar with each other and with Allen's approach to mathematical instruction. In addition, Ms. A and Mr. C shared another class, a developmental English class. The conversations that emerged from this group proved so rich and multifaceted that, despite taping two other mixed-gender groups throughout the semester, we have decided to focus on these students.

Ms. A was highly successful in the first-semester course, Ms. V and Mr. C moderately so. Ms. A and Mr. C were articulate in collaboration with each other. However, Ms. V, a student whose first language was not English, was less successful (though not unsuccessful) when collaborating with both Ms. A and Mr. C; nor was she as successful when collaborating with Mr. C only. As we saw, Ms. A and Ms. V at times found the sound of their "mathematical" voices foreign and disconcerting.

Ms. A and Ms. V worked hard, as the transcripts of lesson segments showed. Students at this institution do not receive college credit for developmental math courses, nor do these grades figure into students' grade-point averages. Yet because they are mathematically underprepared they must successfully pass the courses to enter regular college mathematics courses. In such a setting, the most stereotypical perceptions concerning women and mathematics often dominate, particularly on the part of the women themselves.

Mr. C, though he did not work as hard as the women, served as an interesting catalyst and counterpoint to the women, at times allowing their voices to resonate, at other times silencing them. He seemed able to use either a "female" or a "male" discourse style, so much that it is hard to determine—at least in the transcripts we have before us—which style predominated.

The women students in the second-semester, first-year composition course, Ms. J, Ms. L, and Ms. G, were fulfilling their writing requirement when we recorded their conversations. They reflected the "typical" female student in English, and we chose to listen to them for this reason. However, we also chose to listen to them because all three students had shown an aptitude for and an interest in science and mathematics. Ms. J entered college as a premed major though her experience with a biology course during the first semester and her experience in this writing course caused her to change her major to English. At first she found poetry particularly frustrating. Her voice began to emerge as she learned that metaphor and ambiguity could be her friends, not enemies. The second student, Ms. L, entered college as an English major and future teacher. The third, Ms. G, wanted to major in art and German with an English minor. She scored well on college entrance exams in mathematics, yet failed her first-semester mathematics course. These three students spent the first half of the semester in different mixed-sex groups, the last half in a group of their own. There was one other student in this group, Ms. T, who planned to major in nursing. Because she rarely talked, despite the repeated efforts of her colleagues to engage her, we did not hear her enter the conversations from the writing class until a month before the semester ended. Ms. T seemed locked in silence, like many women who are silenced in math. Ms. G addressed explicitly what usually remained only implicit in the discussions the women held in the math class: issues of voice, subjectivity, objectivity, their identity as knowers, and their relationship to the known and to authority. Yet when we compare their conversations with those of Ms. A and Ms. V, the similarities are greater than we would expect, given the supposed dissimilarities of the two disciplines.

We wanted to focus on two classroom sessions, one from math and one from writing, beginning with an excerpt from a transcript between Ms. A and Ms. V one Monday late in the semester.[1] The students in the math class had begun working on a problem the previous Friday. The task required that they work out for themselves a definition of a mathematical function; in the previous lesson Allen had presented an approximate definition. The students were to invent data about five students—their height and weight—a story. The assignment was to decide whether the data they were making up on the heights and weights of the students on their campus represented a mathematical function. They were assigned to determine whether data represented in different forms—ordered pairs, equations, and graphs—supplied different information or whether these representations portrayed reality in different ways and so required different interpretive methods. Janet Emig, researcher in English education, asserts that "changes in medium or symbol affect our thinking; using different symbol systems seems to change what we see or say and thus suggests that we don't have direct access to some fixed reality" (Elbow 1990, p. 50). She could well have been describing the work of these developmental math students. They were confronted with a writing and reading problem. First they had to construct and write the problem, then read and interpret it. Allen made clear to them the open-ended nature of the assignment. He could not have known what they would write—what data they would invent—so he could not have known whether students would create a function.

We examined the transcript of this interaction and noted how softly Ms. V and Ms. A both spoke, something a printed transcript could not convey. This was typical for Ms. V but not for Ms. A. Belenky et al. (1986) point out that "in a small room"—the room of the narrow academic world—"one tends to speak softly" (p. 87), for women may find that world "claustrophobic." The world of mathematics is even narrower than the general academic world. Perhaps Ms. A was reflecting her solidarity with Ms. V by being soft-spoken. Perhaps Ms. A did not want to dominate Ms. V, though at one point she ordered Ms. V to graph their answer since she had made up the data, saying, in effect, "I've made up the data, now it's your turn to do something." But Ms. V refused. Although the two women seemed to vacillate between speaking—having a voice—and silence, we found only two long pauses of eight seconds each. The two women spoke rapidly, even if quietly, frequently overlapping each other and completing each other's sentences. It was also significant that the utterances were usually short.

Despite the rapid turn taking and lack of pausing between Ms. A and Ms. V, the overall effect was one of women trying to overcome silence. They struggled to write a mathematical text, to become authors who take responsibility for their work, but they believed that their voices lacked authority, speaking as if they feared being heard, and seemed not to know what they ought to sound like. The struggle of Ms. A and Ms. V was, as we shall see, not much different from that of the women in the writing class who were also searching for their voice and authority.

The two women's discussions demonstrated the circularity of their discourse. They moved from discussions about answers, to equations, to ordered pairs, to graphs, back to equations, back to graphs. It appeared from the initial discussion that Ms. V interpreted the assignment literally as a request to find "the" answer, despite Allen's multiple and open-ended invitation to think about what makes a function and to write different data sets, some of which would represent a function and some of which would not. In other words, they could tell different stories, which required reading and interpretation. They had to determine how best to represent the narrative mathematically—how best to create a mathematical text out of that data. Allen had given them a "what if?" question demanding predictions. The women seemed to spend too much time trying to turn it into a closed task. They even ignored the hint Allen offered to focus on inventing their data.

At first Ms. V rejected the request for discussion and storytelling by simply wanting to get the "answer." This was often her approach, which we would argue is an aspect of *received knowledge*; previous math teachers had empha-sized getting the right answer as quickly as possible. She carried that approach with her into this class, despite nearly seven months of fairly open-ended discussion. For many students math is not something they should talk about, something social or socially constructed; it is a series of problems they *solve*, by themselves. But in Allen's class the students were instructed to focus on the process, not the product, to examine what turns data into a function.

Ms. A also tried to create a "narrative" text. Early in this session she wondered what Ms. V's "answer" meant and then asked, "Did you make up an equation?" She challenged Ms. V's answer by questioning both her process and role as narrator. Ms. A thought they needed an equation first, then an answer. For example, Ms. A insisted that they could not write heights and weights until they formulated an equation. But by the end of their discussion she had changed her mind: "How can you make an equation when you have two different things?" Before she reversed herself, however, she offered an equa-tion: "$y = 12x + 2$." We suspected that her equation also reflected her experience of received knowledge, for she made it look like a simple algebraic formula, fitting a particular and familiar genre. Ms. V and Ms. A spent several minutes floundering, as they tried to fit Ms. A's equation into the narration. Like a stubborn writer who refuses to revise, at first Ms. A would not give up her invention but worked hard to find a reasonable role for it in the narrative.

Ms. V suggested that they needed ordered pairs to make a graph—the appropriate language for their story: "If you want to glance at the height and weight you have to have an ordered pair." A graph provides a different repre-sentation of reality than does an equation.

We hope that all this talk of story, texts, and narrative voice doesn't sound too far-fetched. That they were constructing a narrative was suggested by some of the verbs they used: "Are you saying . . . ?"; "Did you make up . . . ?"; "We'll say that . . ."; "How do we guess . . . ?"; "Pretend that we can function . . ."; "It could be whatever . . ."; "So pretend . . . ."

Most of these phrases were uttered by Ms. A, though Ms. V twice used the verb *pretend*. As Ms. A tried to make sense of her equation, she finally realized that it wouldn't work. Ms. V offered an alternative plot: "Unless, it would be a function if you have a different ordered pair . . . ." She also tried to suggest a narrative strategy in which Ms. A's equation would play a role and even offered a possible revision of the equation: "Couldn't it be just . . . x plus . . .?" She began to risk invention, in contrast to her earlier statement "I don't think I know how to make up one." At that point she had rejected the role of mathe-matical writer, as she later rejected the role of mathematical recorder when she claimed she didn't know how to graph their data.

Both Ms. A and Ms. V hesitated, stopped, abruptly changed direction, re-versed themselves, agreed with each other only to undercut their agreement by raising questions. When Ms. V admitted that she didn't know how to graph their data, and Ms. A explained to her what to do, Ms. A offered some extended explanations. Ms. V suggested alternative writings only for Ms. A to reject them. Although Ms. V seemed to gain confidence, she said at the end of this excerpt, when she finally agreed to graph their data, "Oh, OK, well, I'm gonna wait for others to see how they're doing." She feared acting on her knowledge. To put something on the board is to author it, to own it, to claim responsibility and authority for it, and Ms. V was not convinced that she was ready. Later, as Allen explained some generic features about graphs, Ms. V said to herself, "Oh that's what I thought. I erased it." Again, she failed to trust herself and her instincts.

Ms. A, too, found it hard to trust herself and her instincts, as we saw in this brief exchange between Ms. A and Mr. C:

C: Would it be—five times five times seven times seven?
A: Well, first you do a combination problem and then you times it by the permutation problem, cause you have combinations . . .
C: Right.
A: . . . For the first, for the first five and then within those you have permutations. *I can't believe I'm saying this* [emphasis added].

Immediately preceeding the previous sentence, she paused, then laughed, thus discrediting her own mathematical voice.

Despite the attempts of Ms. A and Ms. V to create a mathematical narrative through their own voices and so make sense of the concept of a function, they were not entirely successful in this excerpt. Nevertheless, we found a few examples where the women used their own voice and language to talk about mathematics: Ms. A's statement that "You can't make it 'equationless,'" a mixture of her language and mathematical language; or Ms. V, "We can just 'function,'" where she turned the noun into a verb. This also demonstrated her thinking about mathematics as a process. Later in the discussion, as Ms. A read the graphs of the other groups, she analyzed them, and then put into her own words a description of why one of the other graphs "go like 'curved,' like it was 'possessed.'" Her metaphor revealed that she had found her voice; she wasn't using received, authorized knowledge. Rather, she was inventing, playing.

The women students in the second–semester, first–year writing course—Ms. J, Ms. L, and Ms. G—had spent some time discussing Ms. G's paper. Ms. G was in a precarious position because her colleagues knew that she has failed to turn in some previous essays. Although the current essay should have been the third of a four-part research project, it was only Ms. G's first submission. Ms. G, a Korean woman, had chosen to write about Asian American writers, their problems with identity, voice, and subjugation. For the most part the discussion focused on the cognitive—on what she had written—and had avoided the affective. Then Ms. J asked a question that galvanized the conversation. Whereas the previous conversation had been filled with long pauses and a style much more reminiscent of "male" discourse according to Tannen (1990), after Ms. J's question the three women shifted immediately into a "female" discourse style. The sequence was rapid, overlapping, collaborative. The women completed each other's statements. Ms. G gave numerous paralinguistic signals that she hated what she was reading: she employed a lethargic, bored tone; sighed; expressed reluctance to continue reading; gave monosyllabic responses (though she occasionally gave longer explanations to questions). Ms. J asked, "So what do you think of your paper?" because she sensed that her friend's strong negative feelings about her own essay were interfering with her work as a writer. The women's voices began to emerge as they allowed the affective and cognitive to enter the discussion together.

There were times prior to Ms. J's question when the discussion might have begun to focus on the affective, particularly when Ms. G began to talk about the tensions between immigrant generations, something she had experienced with her mother. However, rather than reveal her *own* story, which was embedded in her expository essay, she kept the discussion—and her paper—at a distance. Although Cheryl had encouraged her to include her own struggle as a Korean in America, and Ms. G had chosen to write about Asian American women writers because she identified with them, she resisted including her own voice and experience in her essay. It was almost as if the label *research* had triggered in her the received knowledge from high school about the "right" way to conduct and write research. She was not alone in her concern about following the rules. Some male students had complained that "this just doesn't seem like research." Cheryl encouraged them to move from received knowledge to constructed knowledge, the melding of subject and object, the knower and the known, for which there are no "handbook" rules. The lack of rules made many students—female and male—uncomfortable.

Ms. G tried to explain to her colleagues why the critics don't consider Asian American writers important—"They say they [Asian American women writers] cannot write with authority and authenticity." She believed that the writers with whom she identified (Amy Tan and Maxine Hong Kingston) had been marginalized or ostracized, that their voices had been silenced. She felt that no one listened to them and no one read them, or at least not the people who controlled the curriculum at her school. But she was really talking about herself. Why couldn't *she* write with authority and authenticity? Why couldn't *she* find her narrative voice? Why did she feel prevented from doing so?

Unlike most students who fail to meet deadlines, Ms. G had refused to turn in work because she hated what she had written. To her, it did not feel authentic, for she did not feel herself to be the author: "You can't even hear *me* in it. This is *not* my paper." She refused to take responsibility for texts that lacked her voice. Her colleagues, who had written and turned in three other essays, supported Ms. G and affirmed that she was valued and valuable, that her voice and views counted.

Few students were as articulate about a lack of voice as was Ms. G. Few students understood so clearly how alienating language becomes when you cannot locate yourself within it. The language that Ms. G used in her writing— the writing that she had been taught as "research language"—was alienating to her. The mathematical language that Ms. A and Ms. V tried to use seemed to alienate them, as well. Ms. G made this issue explicit, while it remained only implicit for the others. Ms. A came close to an explicit acknowledgment that mathematics sounded like a foreign language when she said, "I can't believe I'm saying this." She had been taught that she could not "speak" mathematics, that her voice was not to be trusted; her challenge was to unlearn the lesson.

In their logs, Ms. A and Ms. V explored their tenuous identities and voices within the field of mathematics. For example, Ms. V noted how she jumped back and forth in discussions, as she did above, finding it hard to settle in, circling, returning, exploring. This is the form of narrative, not of logico-scientific discourse.

Ms. A's story is particularly poignant:

The teachers could only think of one way to teach a lesson and I couldn't understand. . . . Then I had a teacher whose name I totally blocked from memory because he repeatedly called me "stupid" when I couldn't understand or finish an assignment. The only way I got through the class was have my book open & some answers in it during a test which is totally against what I believe in. I remember all of this because my mom always played number games w/me when I was young and I really enjoyed math and algebra till the last years of junior high.

At one time Ms. A, in the supportive relationship with her mother, had no difficulty with math and algebra. Not until her teacher insisted that there was only one right way and called her stupid because of the questions she asked did she stop talking. Because his comments changed her view of herself, which threatened her identity, she did more than withdraw: she violated her own moral code by cheating. She had to deny her self, her voice, her values.

Questions of voice and identity came up repeatedly for all the women we taped. Ms. A's story about her "bad" math teachers, which she contrasted with her positive learning experience with her mother, demonstrated that in supportive, encouraging relationships, where students are inventive and inventing, women like her and Ms. G can learn that they are not stupid. If teachers encourage women to explore open-ended questions, female students will not be alienated from their own voices, and they will find the language they need. Both mathematics and English have something to teach each other about "women's" language, about narrative voice, and about how to pose open-ended questions. As Witherell and Noddings (1991) said, "Even in the dread domain of mathematical story problems, we are beginning to realize that people learn from making up such stories. Getting into the mind of the story writer untangles some of the mystery" (p. 280). Witherell and Noddings are saying that even in math students need to become writers and tellers of tales.

What of the questions we raised at the beginning? We have not addressed each one explicitly. Rather, we have suggested that the ways women may approach both mathematics and English can be better understood by listening to and amplifying their individual voices as they join in the conversations of both disciplines—and as teachers in both disciplines hold conversations with each other.

NOTE

1. All quotations from transcripts or logs are as the students said or wrote them, without *sic*. For example, we use question marks only when a speaker's voice rises, regardless of the syntax.

REFERENCES

Belenky, M. F., B. M. Clinchy, N. R. Goldberger, and J. M. Tarule. 1986. *Women's Ways of Knowing: The Development of Self, Voice, and Mind*. New York: Basic.

Bruner, J. 1986. *Actual Minds, Possible Worlds*. Cambridge, MA: Harvard University Press.

Elbow, P. 1990. *What Is English?* New York: Modern Language Association of America; and Urbana, IL: National Council of Teachers of English.

Lakoff, R. T. 1990. *Talking Power: The Politics of Language*. New York: Basic.

Tannen, D. 1990. *You Just Don't Understand: Women and Men in Conversation*. New York: Ballantine.

Witherell, C., and N. Noddings, eds. 1991. *Stories Lives Tell: Narrative and Dialogue in Education*. New York: Teachers College Press.

FOR FURTHER READING

Artzt, A. F., and E. Armour-Thomas. 1992. Development of a Cognitive-Metacognitive Framework for Protocol Analysis of Mathematical Problem Solving in Small Groups." *Cognition and Instruction 9*: 137–175.

Barnes, D., J. Britton, and M. Torbe. 1990. *Language, the Learner, and the School*. Portsmouth, NH: Boynton/Cook.

Gilligan, C. 1982. *In a Different Voice: Psychological Theory and Women's Development*. Cambridge, MA: Harvard University Press.

Grumet, M. 1988. *Bitter Milk: Women and Teaching*. Amherst: University of Massachusetts Press.

National Council of Teachers of Mathematics. 1990. *Curriculum and Evaluation Standards for School Mathematics*. Reston, VA: Author.

Noddings, N. 1989. "Theoretical and Practical Concerns about Small Groups in Mathematics." *Elementary School Journal 89*: 607–623.

Pimm, D. 1987. *Speaking Mathematically: Communication in Mathematics Classrooms*. London: Routledge.

von Glasersfeld, E., ed. 1991. *Radical Constructivism in Mathematics Education*. Dordrecht, Germany: Kluwer.

Webb, N. M. 1984. "Sex Differences in Interaction and Achievement in Cooperative Small Groups." *Journal of Educational Psychology 76*: 33–34.

————. 1991. "Task-Related Verbal Interaction and Mathematics Learning in Small Groups." *Journal for Research in Mathematics Education 22*: 366–389.

Webb, N. M., and C. M. Kenderski. 1985. "Gender Differences in Small-Group Interaction and Achievement in High- and Low-Achieving Classes." In L. C. Wilkinson and C. B. Marrett, eds., *Gender Differences in Classroom Interaction*. New York: Academic Press, pp. 209–236.

16

Lab Coats and Little Girls: The Science Experiences of Women Majoring in Biology and Education at a Private University

Janice Koch

In this study I have examined the science experiences of two groups of women at the same private university. The focus was on the parallel experiences of college women majoring in biology and college women majoring in education. My purpose in doing this study was to gain a deeper insight into the science experiences, past and present, held by two distinctly different populations of women. One group of women chose careers in science and persisted in a science major throughout their undergraduate educations. The other group became science avoidant and persisted in this stance throughout their undergraduate educations. An assumption basic to this ethnographic study is that one develops beliefs about science and science-related careers through a complex web of experiences both in and outside of school.

My goal in this study was to examine the science stories of two groups of women, as well as observing them as science students in their university environments. The study was conducted over the course of three semesters through the exploration of two undergraduate environments: one environment was Dr. Samuels's animal physiology lab, a course open only to college seniors majoring in biology; the second environment was Dr. Howard's science education methods lab, a course open only to seniors majoring in elementary education. Both courses are required in the advanced sequence of the respective majors.

Toward the start of the first semester, the students in each group were requested to write their science autobiographies, personal narratives that described their science experiences from their earliest memories to the present time (Koch 1990). These science stories provided a context for describing the culture of each community of learners. There were three methods of data collection: the ongoing field observations and informal interviews, individual ethnographic interviews with selected participants, and science autobiographies.

I visited each lab weekly and kept a field log in which the events of each environment were recorded. I had one formal and several informal interviews with each professor and became familiar with their goals for each course. From each environment I selected three women to interview a minimum of four times each and met with each of these women periodically for about one year. I was seeking individuals who appeared excited about their chosen career paths and who were active and effective participants in their respective labs. For the biology women, in addition, I was interested in interviewing women whose career goals were different. Marlene is currently in medical school, Iris is headed toward a doctoral program in biology, and Diane is currently a secondary school biology teacher enrolled in a master of arts in education program.

This criterion did not apply to the education majors. In the science education methods lab, I was interested in interviewing women who had completed a full complement of precollege science courses and whose science autobiographies revealed that they were science avoidant despite being successful science students. These three women, Keri, Kristin, and Marla, are currently seeking elementary school teaching positions.

The findings reveal that these two environments represent two vastly different paradigms for teaching and learning. The pedagogy of the biology lab was strictly laissez-faire; the onus was on the students to come prepared, follow the rules, and do the lab. Although he was present, the biology lab professor acted as an overseer who made sure that the work of the students was up to par, that equipment was functioning, and that the basic premise of each lab was understood. The environment seemed inflexible, neutral, and technical.

The pedagogy in the science methods lab was powered by a professor who is collaborative and interested in promoting discourse about feelings. The methods lab offered students open-ended experiences with scientific materials and validated everyone's experiences as important to the whole view of the topic. There was an emphasis on open exploration.

The two labs differed drastically in appearance and resources. It is apparent that this university has invested many financial resources in the biology lab. The methods lab in the school of education, in contrast, is shabby, small, and old. The physical settings were a metaphor for the statuses that these two environments occupy in the university hierarchy.

The findings also revealed that competition for grades coexists with cooperation to get the job done much more significantly in the biology lab. Here, testing deliberately required that the students be graded on a curve. This system frequently pitted students against each other. There was little competition in the methods lab. Students tended to cooperate freely and supported one another's successes. Their grades were based on their performance on assigned papers, weekly lab exercises, final presentations, and the final exam.

The findings indicated a significant difference in the science experiences reported by the two groups of women. This was most distinctly expressed by the presence or absence of out-of-school experiences with science and nature as these women were growing up. Their science educations did not appear substantially very different, with the exception that the biology women each said that they had wonderful tenth-grade biology teachers. The presence of out-of-school science experiences was the major reported motivation for the biology women. The dynamic nature of science was communicated to the biology women mainly through these outside experiences. The education women could not recall science experiences outside of the confines of rigid school science environments. All but one of the women who were interviewed had attended parochial schools. Their educations were much more similar than different. Science was taught as static, textbook driven, and a collection of isolated facts.

Although both groups of women have a passion for their chosen careers, the biology women said they were consistently buoyed and motivated by the prestige of science that results in their "feeling special." The education women reported that they constantly fight a negative societal image, and they persist in their calling despite this lack of prestige.

The gender issues that informed the experiences of these women include issues of entitlement to doing science. For the education women, the scientist stereotype prevented them from seeing themselves as scientifically competent. Although they were fine science students, they did not associate with the dominant, popular image of scientists, an image that persists in excluding women. The biology women struggle with professional gender battles as they continue in their major. One of the women reported being ostracized by other students when her grades "broke the curve," and another woman, a returning mother of three, felt she was not taken seriously enough by those faculty who became aware that she had young children. The future teacher among the science majors felt that she was more accepted by other students outside of biology because of her education minor. Education is a traditional choice for a woman at this university.

METHODOLOGICAL CONSIDERATIONS

Discussion of Findings

The discussion that follows is the result of final data analysis about the two environments and the two groups of women described in this narrative. The stories of the participants offer a variety of lenses through which the dynamics of teaching and learning science may be considered. I have considered the major findings under two general headings: "The Two Labs: The Filter and the Pump" and "The Science Educations of Two Groups of Women."

It has been my intention throughout to present the meanings the participants made of their science experiences because it is my understanding that the ways in which these students perceive their reality offers possibilities for rethinking approaches to science education. Because the findings may have relevance to the practices of teaching and learning science, the implications for practice are embedded in the following discussion.

The Two Labs: The Filter and the Pump

The attributes of the pedagogy, the professors, the students, the language, the curricula, and the physical environments of the two laboratory settings are summarized in Table 1 and discussed below.

A Question of Pedagogy. In a recent study of undergraduate science, Tobias (1992) reported on several college-level programs that attract and retain students in natural science. One such program is at the University of Wisconsin—Eau Claire, where the chemistry department has a distinctive track record attracting and retaining first-generation college students, men and women, to chemistry.

The attributes of this chemistry program that contribute to its success are grounded in the fundamental relationships between the professors and their students. In this department, there is personal attention, an open-door policy, and recognition of students by name. The professor of the introductory course is also the professor of the lab. There are no separate lab and lecture midterm and final examinations. In addition, there is a research program that fosters professor and student collaborative research: "Faculty find that in the one-on-one setting, they can encourage their young research collaborators to pursue careers in science" (Tobias 1992, p. 25). One of the hallmarks of chemistry at the University of Wisconsin—Eau Claire is a dedication to teaching. The chemistry students at the University of Wisconsin—Eau Claire are nontraditional students of science and have to be taught and welcomed at the same time. This sort of invitation to science reminds me of Dr. Howard's lab, in which elementary education students engage in science. The pedagogy that characterizes Tobias's successful college science programs shares much with the elementary science methods course of the present study. It is collaborative, personal, caring, and welcoming. Although pedagogical techniques represent but one out of several attributes of successful college science programs, they are often the most immediately revised without additional cost to the college or university.

Dr. Howard's teaching style in the laboratory was central to the tone and effectiveness of the science methods lab. Many of these students seemed to need encouragement and an atmosphere of trust in order to feel capable with scientific processes and concepts. Dr. Howard furthered their understanding that science is something they do. He employed questioning techniques that he hoped the students would model when they become teachers. These techniques promoted thinking and discourse within the group. Dr. Howard was an active participant in the science methods lab. His personal style encouraged the students to try investigations in which they would otherwise be reluctant to engage. His primary agenda was to involve as many students as possible in each lab activity.

Dr. Samuels's pedagogy in the laboratory was a sharp contrast to this active and interactive teaching. He expected the students to come prepared and

Table 1
A Comparison of Characteristics of the Physiology Lab and the Science Methods Lab

Lab	Setting	Pedagogy	Language	Students	Implicit Objectives
Physiology	Modern; new high-tech facility; clean, well lit; abundant equipment; large space; tables and stools; beautiful	Opening minilecture; professor is peripheral; lab is manual driven; students teach themselves; professors and teaching assistants (TAs) are available for assistance	Technical; impersonal; scientific; third person; absence of personal discourse	Work well together, assist each other, ask many questions; compete for highest grades; strive to break the curve	Getting the job done; getting right; recording the data; keeping the lab notebook; following the rules
Science Methods	Dingy, musty, small, crowded; old lab tables and chairs; no science materials; shabby	Professor is at the center; professor drives the activities; professor is an active participant; professor explains science concepts; professor provides direction, no TA	Informal; non-technical; emotional; discourse about feelings	Interact freely; work well together; few questions; do not compete for grades	Making friends with science; interacting with materials; accomplishing new tasks; contacting one's feelings; understanding new concepts

perform the lab with minimal input from himself. He has been through under-graduate science himself, and he knew that by this time they would understand what to do and would ask him if they did not. Dr. Samuels appeared to consider it his responsibility to provide materials, check machinery, introduce the concepts, and then oversee the major portion of the lab. Although present during the entire lab, he assumed he had a group of students who knew the rules of the lab and were determined to follow them. They would tell him if something seemed unclear, and between Dr. Samuels and the teaching assis-tant, the students would receive the assistance they required. They had been properly trained in undergraduate science, and they also knew that if you do not ask questions, you will not get answers.

Traditional college science classrooms succeed in weeding out those who do not excel in large, impersonal lecture sections that permit little or no exchange between students and professors. The physiology lab represented what those select few can do by their senior year. This lab environment followed tradi-tional college science rules:

- If you do not understand the language, learn it.
- If you cannot work with animals, drop the course.
- If you are not successful, you are not tough enough.

Dr. Samuels conformed to the concept of science courses as filter by seem-ingly asking his students, "Are you good enough?" The pedagogy in the physi-ology lab reinforced a static, dualistic view of science: It is right or it is wrong; you know it or you don't. The science of the physiology lab was portrayed as a technical, mechanical process of learning concepts about physiology that were already embedded in textbooks. The students became adept at language that fosters the belief that you can know science by memorizing it. The rigid, lock-step procedures of the lab appeared to reinforce the view that scientific knowl-edge has already been established, and it is not likely to change. The pedagogy of the lab maintained science as isolated rather than integrated. There was an absence of discourse about feelings in the physiology lab. The experiences in the physiology lab were not designed to be personalized. No one asked how any individuals *felt* about the lab experience; they asked only that it be completed. Dr. Samuels did not ask what Dr. Howard consistently did ask: "How do you feel about what we are doing? What are you learning?" The lab notebook is standard; it is a third-person document. Students are required to record the objectives, procedures, results, and conclusions. There is no provision for the personal. Integrating the culture of Dr. Howard's environment would suggest that students would respond at the end of each lab write-up to the following questions:

- How did you feel about doing this lab?
- Were there parts that were particularly confusing or exciting?

- If you were able to repeat this lab, what might you do differently?
- Did you get any ideas you would like to explore further?

Tobias (1992) described an emphasis on personal communication as an essential component of successful undergraduate science programs. Such successful programs employ pedagogy that is more descriptive of the science methods lab environment than the environment of the human physiology lab. According to Tobias, the successful undergraduate programs are those that can recruit and retain students to science who may not represent the dominant science culture as we know it today. The new students whom we need to invite into the scientific enterprise may not have the self-confidence of the biology students in this study. They may be inexperienced in generating their own questions; they may need some assistance from the professor and an atmosphere that communicates that it is acceptable to experience uncertainty and doubt, even in the physiology lab.

By infusing more facets of student-centered pedagogy, the physiology lab could become a more interactive environment where students talk about the procedures with the professor and each other, try out other ways of doing the investigations, discuss their rationales for their designs and insights, and help move the curriculum forward. The students' work may result in data that differ from group to group, and the final collaborative whole may become the basis for the understanding of scientific principles. This would be more consistent with the principles of the scientific enterprise.

In a study of eighth-grade students, those who had a dynamic view of scientific knowledge stated that the goal of scientists was to try to identify a small number of ideas that are linked together to explain a large number of scientific phenomena (Songer and Linn 1991). This was in contrast to students who had a static view of science and believed that scientists collected isolated facts that did not apply to everyday life problems. Pedagogy like that of the science methods lab would encourage a more open-ended, investigative approach to the science material, would humanize the physiology lab, and would promote a more dynamic view of science.

Physical Messages. The modern, high-tech setting of the physiology lab contrasts sharply with the old, dusty basement science/art room site for the science methods lab. How does the physiology lab setting speak to the methods lab setting? What are the messages implicit in the appearance of each environment? What can the science methods lab learn from the physiology lab?

There is a clear message in the physiology lab. It appears to be very clean and well kept, reflecting a substantial monetary investment. This institution tends to invest large sums in the education of future scientists. The methods lab, however, doubles as the art room and is in need of new lighting, new fixtures, ventilation, and general repair. This environment also reflects the investment that this university makes in the science education of future teachers.

The life within the two settings cannot be considered out of the context of the physical settings. These labs are painful metaphors for the cultural image of scientist and educator. The scientists work on the top floor in a spacious, well-lighted modern facility, whereas the dusty, crowded basement facility is afforded to the science education course.

There is much debate about how to remedy elementary teachers' science deficiencies. Although Dr. Howard's course may be a first step, follow-up by continued study in natural science is an important consequence of the process of "making friends with science" described by science methods lab participants. Those responsible for the science methods lab might take the environment of the physiology lab to heart. More serious study of natural science might be invited here if the lab were afforded a well equipped setting with adequate space, materials, and media. Educators discuss the importance of science education at the elementary school level. In line with that, institutions of higher education must echo this importance in how they provide for the preparation of science teachers in appropriate facilities. This study suggests that if the science methods lab were updated, expanded, and supplied with appropriate materials and equipment, the learning that went on there might be further maximized. Assuming that the education students continue to work with Dr. Howard, consider the added impact of ample materials, a spacious lab, and beautiful, modern surroundings on the would be elementary science teachers. The message is one of importance, priority, and value. The conditions of the labs are a metaphor for the statuses of these two communities not only in society as a whole but also in this university.

Cooperation, Competition, and Grades. The community of students in the physiology lab appears to have learned and internalized that the road to graduate and medical schools must be paved with a high grade-point average. The participants in this study were generally very concerned about grades. Marlene reported that the examinations are set up to be excessively difficult, requiring the professor to grade the students on a curve. This resulted in pitting students against each other, and it made several of the students uncomfortable. Diane reported that the rigorous requirements for exams made it necessary for biology majors to work together in study groups in order to teach themselves the material that they did not understand. Diane experienced the competition for grades as motivating students to work together.

Iris worried that professors do not always give out the fairest grades. She had occasionally visited professors to ask them how they arrived at her grade. She was very insistent about standing up for herself if she believed that she had received an unfair grade. She discussed being constantly aware that her status as a returning student and mother of three small children places her image as a serious science student in jeopardy. Grades are very important to Iris because she wants to get funding for a graduate program.

In the physiology lab, students worked together and cooperated fully to achieve the desired ends in the lab activity. It was important to share ideas and materials and to copy printouts from the electrical recording devices in order for each student to have a copy in his/her lab notebook. All of the students were working toward the same goal, "getting it right" (see Table 1). The cooperative mode of the lab was always in tension with the competitive nature of testing and grading in this course. Although students needed to help each other to perform the required tasks, the undercurrent of competition for grades was also always there.

In the science methods lab, cooperation was the dominant mode of behavior. "Getting it right" may be different for different lab groups; however, all are quite willing to assist one another. The students in this lab were all women and they could be categorized into two groups: those who were more aggressively engaged in the activities and those who were more reluctant to participate. Each student was encouraged to personalize the science experience and explore activities in her own way. Those more capable assisted and encouraged those who were more reticent. On some occasions, they had to "get it right," and responses were freely communicated.

The professor informed the students that they would be assessed on the quality of their assignments, their engagement with each lab, the final presentation, and the final exam. The education women were aware that the final project contributed heavily to their final grade in the course. The quality of the final projects was high, attesting to a sincere desire on the part of these students to succeed. The final exam was all essay questions, and it was not graded on a curve. The essays asked the students to apply what they had learned about teaching science. It was the only formal test of the semester.

The Science Educations of Two Groups of Women

The women who participated in this study had strong commonalities and differences regarding their science educations, their outstanding attributes, and their choices of careers. These are summarized in Table 2. Both groups of women, the biology majors and the education majors, have a passion for their chosen careers and a strong desire to excel. They have been driven to get the best possible grades, and they have worked very diligently to that end. Neither group at this university can claim a monopoly on prolonged hours and tedious schedules. Although the biology majors require long and demanding lab time, elementary education majors require a second, liberal arts major and long hours in school field placements. As these women enter their senior year at this university, their schedules are grueling and tiresome.

At the center of this study is these women's stance toward natural science. My purpose has been to further understand why some college women are engaged by natural science to the point of pursuing careers in science, whereas others avoid natural science to the point of complete exclusion. Until they experienced the science education lab, Kristin, Keri, and Marla were most reluctant to teach science to their future students. They had been excellent high school science students but said they were completely disengaged by science, and Keri was intimidated by the subject. Their evolving passion for teaching children did not include science. This study offers insight into their avoidance.

Table 2
A Comparison of Characteristics of the Biology Women and the Education Women

Women	Science Education	Outstanding Attributes	Choice of Career
Biology	High school biology teachers were very influential; endured negative science experiences without losing interest in biology; took advanced placement biology in high school; had several out-of-school science experiences; always wanted to study biology	Goal-oriented; persevering; conscientious; independent; high self-esteem; will forego social life for studying; not conspicuous by their dress; gain prestige through their choice of major; hard working; genuine passion for biology	They always knew they loved biology; they have an inner calling to science; science gives them prestige; in the end, it is worth the work
Education	Dreaded science class; science was boring; impersonal rote memorization; science projects were fun; took biology, chemistry, and physics in high school; no out-of-school science experiences; dropped science at first opportunity	Conscientious; diligent; hard working; persevering; belong to sororities; dress similarly to one another and differently from other college students; no prestige in their choice of major; genuine passion for teaching	They have always loved being with children; they want to make a difference in children's self-image; there is little prestige in their choice; their rewards are personal; their major is worth it for the chance to make a difference

The avoidance of science that Keri, Marla, and Kristin reported is not uncommon among future elementary teachers. The absence of enthusiasm for science is a large loss, both personal and professional. There is a loss to their own personal understanding of the natural world and of scientific process and a professional loss to their desire to engage their future students in science.

For the education women, school science was largely oppressive and stifling. However, their science stories not only highlight what happened, they also reveal what did not happen. The biology women's science stories provide insight into what may have been missing for the education women in their evolving experiences with science. What the biology women and many of their cohort group experienced and the education women did not was the opportunity for outside of school, more informal science learning experiences. These experiences demonstrate a connection to scientific events outside of the formal school setting. They include, but are not limited to, visits to zoos and museums, working in hospitals and laboratories, watching television nature shows and natural history movies.

Out-of-School Science Experiences. As an elementary and secondary science educator, I have always hoped that doing science with young children was one way to engage their future interest in science. When Marlene, Iris, Diane, and their classmates overwhelmingly cited experiences outside of formal schooling that influenced their science career choices in ways that were more decisive than their school experiences, I was disappointed.

The early school experiences of the participants were not scientifically inspiring. Marlene, Iris, and Diane had early, rigid parochial school science where rote memorization was the norm. This was similar to the science experiences of Marla and Kristin in elementary school. Marla's and Keri's science project experiences salvaged an otherwise dismal early school science history.

In contrast to the biology women, the education women reported no memories of experiences connected to science outside of school (see Table 2). The women in Dr. Samuels's lab report of nature hikes, volunteering at a local hospital, working on an ambulance, regular visits to an extraordinary zoo, after-school clubs, and browsing through a father's old medical books.

These out-of-school experiences have implications for classroom science. First, they speak to the importance of making connections between classroom science and the outside world. Formal science education has become so far removed from daily experience that students are unaware that science is a way to make meaning of their natural world. The twentieth-century reductionist view of science that takes nature apart, bit by bit, in order to better understand it often neglects the process of putting it back together so that a holistic view may accompany the understanding of each of its parts.

Second, out-of-school science learning experiences speak to the value of participation. Actively engaging students in science as part of their world needs to be paramount for school science education. Field trips to recycling centers, zoos, plant nurseries, seashores, freshwater ponds, hospitals, and laboratories can provide needed informal science learning experiences. The findings in this

study indicate that science educators may want to study the attributes of informal science learning experiences that could be infused into science classrooms.
A model for translating informal science learning experiences into classroom
practice is already in place in many elementary school classrooms. The inclusion of activities that encourage children to extend their personal experiences
with nature to the classroom may be represented in the following ways:

- Invite the children to help raise pets and plants of their choice.
- Find or create a nature trail with the children.
- Encourage collections of rocks, seeds, shells, leaves, and any other natural objects
  with which the children are engaged.
- Explore the science materials with the children.
- Use science play as a means to construct new concepts.
- Invite a zookeeper, a research scientist, a lab technician, and a naturalist to chat with
  the children.

Out-of-school science includes the aspects of leisure and choice that are
difficult to access in the structured school day. I suggest, however, that whenever possible, a relaxed science atmosphere be encouraged. The only positive
science memories Marla and Keri recalled were their involvements with science
projects. These projects were constructed at home, usually with a family
member and friends, and have some attributes of informal science experiences.
They are done on leisure time, the process is not being judged, and there is
room for personal expression. Elementary science educators may consider
organizing occasions in which students can work on individual projects.

Of course, there will be those who remain disinterested in science despite
these more open activities. However, I suggest that such activities have the
potential to make important contributions to the rigid world of school science.

Feeling Special. Majoring in biology has been long and arduous, but in
addition to a sense of accomplishment, the biology women reported the prestige
of science is an extra benefit. Diane referred to it as "feeling special" from the
time she was chosen for an after-school science club to the present when she
was asked to be the organic chemistry teaching assistant. Diane's story reminds
me that her early interest was not in chemistry and that she was drawn to
chemistry in college because the professors really liked her and she felt important in the organic lab as a teaching assistant. Even now she says she would
have majored in chemistry if she realized how much more value is placed on
chemistry when you are looking for a teaching position. Feeling special was
definitely a reason for Diane to pursue a science major. It heightened her self-
esteem.

Iris called it the "prestige of science," which she considers the additional
perk to majoring in biology. Marlene called it "having a gift." Marlene believes
that she has a gift for the sciences. There is no doubt that successfully completing this major for these women is personally enhancing. This speaks to the
public prestige and authority of science. While this is a perk for Marlene, Iris,

and Diane, it created a mystique that was distancing for Marla, Keri, and Kristin.

Prestige is sorely lacking for the dedicated future teachers. Their long days and nights in a double major and at least ten hours per week of field placement for three semesters before student teaching leave them wishing for more recognition, but receiving precious little. The education women reported that they are frequently made fun of in their course of study; their colleagues believe that elementary education is easy. It has taken courage for them to pursue a course of study which offers no prestige and little opportunity for clout. They gave this as a reason why they frequently stick together in sororities. Their camaraderie enables them to endure a negative intellectual stigma, unearned and undeserved (see Table 2).

It should be noted that Kristin, Keri, and Marla reported that they felt like they "had a gift" for teaching children. Keri extended this concept by reporting that working with children was her "release." She described feeling so excited when she had the opportunity to interact with children. Kristin, Keri, and Marla reported feeling unacknowledged by society for their teaching gifts.

A Passion for Science. Marlene, Diane, and Iris were engaged by science; they liked biology at its guts! This was an important prerequisite for them to be successful. It also helped them to endure unhappy school science experiences without abandoning their larger biology major goal. For example, Diane's experience with high school chemistry made her feel as though she never wanted to see another chemical. She persevered to become a college chemistry minor. Iris both feared and hated physics. She took it twice in college before passing it in order to continue her biology major. Marlene's C in high school physics did not deter her from her college biology major. Once committed to majoring in biology, these women did not falter from their goal irrespective of the events in other science classes. Their career vision enabled them to dismiss and withstand oppressive science experiences in school for the larger goals toward which they were directed. Marlene, Iris, and Diane had exceptional high school biology experiences and consider their high school biology teachers to have been very influential in their decisions to pursue biology. These teachers modeled what it looks like to have a passion for biology.

A Passion for Teaching. Keri described herself as always having a burning desire to teach. As a high school student, she was engaged in student teaching and volunteer "read aloud" programs. Keri talked about loving the process of teaching and learning. She attributed her intellectual growth in college to fine teachers and to her emergence as a dedicated learner.

Kristin cannot remember a time when she did not want to teach. She is deeply sensitive and reported looking forward to the opportunity to help children gain confidence in themselves. She said that she feels that nothing can possibly be as rewarding as making a difference in a child's life (see Table 2). Marla's decision to teach was relatively recent, and her experience is with children in need. She stated that she finds the work most satisfying, but that it has been a struggle for her to look beyond the conventional, more prestigious jobs. The lack of prestige is frequently a deterrent for would-be teachers. Some return to education programs later in life because teaching was their calling, but public and family pressures diverted them to other fields.

The women in this study have worked diligently toward their career goals. They need support to follow their dreams and their passions. The support that the biology women said they could use would be found within the science culture of the university, manifested by more collegial, less competitive relationships among students. The education women expressed a genuine desire to be respected more for their energy and efforts in their program of study. This lack of consideration extends beyond the university to the larger culture where they are also held in low esteem, despite the importance of their work with children. These women's need to be highly regarded emerged clearly in this study.

Gender Issues. "In Eureka science, we get to do experiments every day and discuss and help our peers, but in school science, you can't talk among your friends about the work or you will get into trouble. You can't experiment every day in school because you have to cover a certain amount of work by the end of the year" (Latina middle school girl, 1992). For the elementary education women, both their experiences of school science and popular culture reinforced masculine images of science. These images were not only related to who does science but also to the process of science. For these women, the successful science student memorized isolated facts for exams. In their science educations, the goal was not understanding scientific principles but memorizing them. For these women, science did not apply to daily life. Their perception of scientific knowledge was a collection of isolated laws and ideas that had no meaning for them and no relation to each other. This sense that science seemed more disjointed from other subjects and more separate from their life was consistent with the stereotype of a scientist as an asocial man who works alone.

The biology women had experiences outside of school that spurred on their interest in nature, medicine, and animals. For Diane, the after-school exploration of unusual animals was enough to convince her that science was where she was heading. She explained that this experience preconditioned her to liking high school biology. Marlene and other women in her lab had mentors, most usually fathers, who encouraged their interest in science. Iris's experiences with the marine world and zoo visits were pivotal to her love of animals and her desire to work with them. The famous women veterinarians became her favorite role models as a young child. The biology women did not view science as foreign territory, culturally or intellectually. Each of them had creative and interesting women as high school biology teachers. The female biology teachers' enthusiasm for biology reinforced the interests that the biology women had already acquired. The education women did not remember any particular attributes of their high school science teachers of either gender.

The biology women's out-of-school science experiences helped them to see science in a more connected, dynamic way. Understanding science brought them pleasure and a sense of feeling special, and this raised their self-esteem.

This finding is consonant with the findings of the Girls, Inc., study written by Frederick and Nicholson (1991) that suggests that out-of-school science experiences, also referred to as informal science learning experiences, have strong possibilities for encouraging more positive attitudes toward science on the part of young women. The study supports the finding that women would benefit from more exposure to science in their everyday lives, thereby making connections with science that are currently missing in the traditional science education paradigm.

The recent report on girls and schools commissioned by the American Association of University Women (1992) and researched by the Wellesley College Center for Research on Women states that intervention programs that provide students with more real-life experiences with science and scientists may make a big difference. It reports that schools can learn much from out-of-school science programs that encourage girls in science (p. 32). The findings of these researchers indicate that girls respond well in relaxed environments where they work cooperatively and have equal access to science materials and tools. According to this report, the science methods lab in this study has attributes that work well for women.

This contrasts with the atmosphere of the physiology lab, which tended to be impersonal and mechanistic. Iris reported that Dr. Samuels communicated more frequently with the men than with the women. Dr. Samuels reported feeling cautious about getting too friendly with the women, so he tended to joke around only with the men. Iris reported feeling like she was taken less seriously by Dr. Samuels and her advisor when they learned that she was a young mother returning to school. Diane reported that the chemistry professors were very welcoming and made her feel very comfortable. This influenced her decision to minor in chemistry. Diane, Marlene, and Iris expressed the importance of good relationships with the professors in their major area of study.

Further support for this finding may be found in a study of college students who switch out of science majors. The study explored the science experiences of women at many universities who left mathematics, science, and engineering majors. Through interviews at these universities, Hewitt and Seymour (1991) learned that an impersonal, nonfacilitative, highly competitive atmosphere was largely responsible for women switching out of these majors. The researchers found that women who leave science majors did so because they were bothered by excessive competition and a sense of indifference on the part of professors of science courses. Their grades were actually higher than the men's who left the science major, but the affective environment was problematic (Hewitt and Seymour 1991). This present study suggests that the collaborative, personal atmosphere of the science methods lab would have positive consequences for the women in the natural science lab.

REFERENCES

American Association of University Women. 1992. *How Schools Shortchange Girls: A Study of Major Findings on Girls and Education.* Researched by the Wellesley College Center for Research on Women. Washington, DC: American Association of University Women Educational Foundation.

Fleury, S. C., and M. Bentley. 1991. "Educating Elementary Science Teachers: Alternative Conceptions of the Nature of Science." *Teaching Education 2*(2): 57–67.

Frederick, J., and H. J. Nicholson. 1991. *Explorer's Pass: A Report on the Study of Girls and Math, Science, and Technology.* Indianapolis, IN: Girls, Inc.

Guba, E., and Y. Lincoln. 1985. Naturalistic Inquiry. Beverly Hills, CA: Sage Publications.

Heilbrun, C. 1988. *Writing a Woman's Life.* New York: Ballantine Books.

Hewitt, N., and E. Seymour. 1991. *Factors Contributing to High Attrition Rates among Science, Mathematics, and Engineering Undergraduate Majors: Report to the Sloan Foundation.* Boulder, CO: Bureau of Sociological Research.

Kahle, J. B., and M. K. Lakes. 1983. "The Myth of Equality in Science Classrooms." *Journal of Research in Science Teaching 20*: 131–140.

Keller, E. F. 1985. *Reflections on Gender and Science.* New Haven, CT: Yale University Press.

Koch, J. 1987. *Science and Social Values.* Roslyn, NY: Publications, Inc.

———. 1990. "The Science Autobiography Project." *Science and Children 27*: 42–44.

———. 1991. "Elementary Science Education: A Multicultural and Gender Fair Perspective." Paper presented at the American Educational Research Association conference, April 4–7, Chicago, IL.

Lofland, J., and L. Lofland. 1984. *Analyzing Social Settings: A Guide to Qualitative Observation and Analysis,* 2nd ed. Belmont, CA: Wadsworth Publishing.

Mishler, E. 1979. "Meaning in Context: Is There any Other Kind?" *Harvard Educational Review 49*: 1–19.

National Science Foundation. 1990. *Women and Minorities in Science and Engineering.* NSF 90-301. Washington, DC: Author.

Rosser, S. 1990. *Female Friendly Science.* New York: Pergamon Press.

Rossiter, M. 1982. *Women Scientists in America: Struggles and Strategies to 1940.* Baltimore, MD: Johns Hopkins University Press.

Songer, N. B., and M. C. Linn. 1991. "How Do Students' Views of Science Influence Knowledge Integration?" *Journal of Research in Science Teaching 28*(9): 761–784.

Spradley, J. 1979. *The Ethnographic Interview.* New York: Holt, Rinehart and Winston.

Strauss, A. L. 1987. *Qualitative Analysis for Social Scientists.* New York: Cambridge University Press.

Task Force on Women, Minorities, and the Handicapped in Science and Technology. 1990. *Changing America: The New Face of Science and Engineering.* Washington, DC: National Science Foundation.

Tobias, S. 1990. *They're Not Dumb, They're Different: Stalking the Second Tier.* Tucson, AZ: Research Corporation.

———. 1992. *Revitalizing Undergraduate Science: Why Some Things Work and Most Don't.* Tucson, AZ: Research Corporation.

Tobias, S., and C. Tomizuka. 1992. *Breaking the Science Barrier: How to Explore and Understand the Sciences.* New York: College Board.

Ware, N. C., and V. Lee. 1988. "Sex Differences in Choice of College Science Major." *American Education Research Journal 25* (winter): 593–614.

Westerback, M. E. 1984. "Studies on Anxiety about Teaching Science in Preservice Elementary Teachers." *Journal of Research in Science Teaching*: 937–950.

Part V

Power and Relation at Home and at Work

Power arrangements are encoded in language and other systems of representation, as we have seen in the previous chapters. And they are also concretely inscribed in our relationships at home and at work. In the following section, we explore some dynamics of power and gender in public, semipublic, and private contexts. The three chapters in this section focus on some of the key relational environments in which we express, learn, and transform our gendered behavior. Most of the relationships that we observe express power as mastery, domination, and control—in short, "power over" others. Understanding how pervasively this conception of power as power over others has influenced our relationships enables us to begin to envision alternative ways of relating that instead emphasize cooperative "power-with" interactions regardless of the gender of the participants.

Much work on communication in the workplace investigates either the behavior of men or contrasts the communicative behavior of men and women. Amy S. Korpi's chapter examines the relationships of female coworkers and explores friendship as an alternative model of power relations. In her study of friendships in a formal work environment, Korpi observes ways in which horizontal, cooperative, affectional bonds can transform the communicative situation. She found that female coworkers experienced their friendships as cooperative, caring, egalitarian, and respectful rather than simply competitive and hierarchical.

R. J. Kivatisky studied the interactions of nurses and doctors, occupations that are gender stereotyped and afforded vastly different degrees of prestige and power. Kivatisky explores the ways in which the formal, organizational setting of the hospital is gendered in that "advantage and disadvantage, exploitation and control, action and emotion, meaning and identity, are patterned through, and in terms of, a distinction between male and female, masculine and feminine."[1]

For his analysis, Kivatisky draws on the five interacting processes that Acker identifies as constituting "gendering": (1) division of labor; (2) construction of symbols and images; (3) interaction patterns that enact dominance and submission; (4) choice of work, language use, clothing, and presentation of self as a gendered member of an organization; and (5) ongoing processes of creating and conceptualizing social structure. Kivatisky applies these categories to the gendered behavior of nurses and physicians. As he concludes, "If we are to strive for the ideal speech situation in organizational settings, then we must confront the deeply embedded aspects of culture and power." The verticality of the institution and the traditional avenues by which information is processed and power administered constrain the communication between male and female coworkers. Rather than encourage the self-disclosure that more egalitarian situations or relationships foster, the traditional roles played by doctors tend to reproduce impersonal, bureaucratic, self-concealing communication. New patterns of communication between doctors and nurses, occupations traditionally overrepresented by males and females respectively, can make communication more effective, meaningful, and pleasurable.

Gender-stereotyped patterns are also embedded in more private, informal interactions, as we see in chapter 19. In their descriptive study of ten married heterosexual couples, Deborah Ballard-Reisch, Mary Elton, and Daniel J. Weigel observe the communicative styles that these couples use to negotiate a problem-solving task. They then develop a typology in order to classify the various strategies that married partners use to achieve consensus and agreement or dominance and acquiescence. By dissecting the communication and decision-making processes in the relationships of married couples, the authors hope to reveal some of the underlying assumptions about gender roles and rules. Although they primarily report on the verbal exchanges between partners and use these as the basis of the transcripts, we recognize that power assumptions are not only coded in linguistic styles, but they also exist in the myriad nonverbal messages that comprise intimate, subtle, and highly personal communication. Fleeting nuances of intonation and emphasis are impossible to convey in the simple transcriptions of words alone. The relationship between couples, who may have charted their own highly specific communicative landscape full of subtext and metacommunication, is particularly difficult to map and points to possibilities for further study. Ballard-Reisch et al. have limited their study to heterosexual, middle-class couples, which delimits the extent to which we can draw implications about gender and power in the relationship of couples in general. Further research which examines a much broader spectrum of relationships in terms of socioeconomic status, ethnicity, and sexual orientation will help us to find out more about the ways in which power is inscribed in interpersonal interactions.

NOTE

1. J. Acker, "Hierarchies, Jobs, Bodies: A Theory of Gendered Organizations," *Gender and Society* 4(2) (1990): 136–158, at p. 146.

17

Women and Friends in the Workplace:
A Study of Coworker Relationships and the
Communication Within Them

Amy S. Korpi

For many people, work outside the home offers more than the opportunity to earn a living—it is a human activity that is virtually inseparable from other aspects of individuals' lives and the rest of their relationships. In many cases, employees identify with the mission of the organization for which they work, and develop ties to other members—people with whom they share ideas and experiences—as a greater community or as individuals (Baum 1990). Communication is seen as a critical factor in creating relationships among organizational members as well as between the organization and its employees (Falcione, Sussman, and Herden 1987).

One relationship which is created in organizations is coworker friendships. Friendship is a context within which a number of basic human needs are met. The importance of friendship is signified by the observation in much of the literature that not to have friends is to miss something in life, and that friendship is central to normal development and meaning (Davis and Todd 1985). In the research, individuals typically include acquaintances as well as intimates under the umbrella term *friend*, and cite communication as an important component within it.

Some research has claimed that the substance and process of women's friendships differs from men's experiences of friendship (e.g., Wright 1982), including the characteristic that women place a greater value on talking (Gouldner and Strong 1987; Hall 1990). Women may also have different experiences of work than men (e.g., Kanter 1977; Ragins 1989). But the literature remains inconclusive in both of these areas, and more research is clearly needed.

This paper explores women's work relationships and communication within them. I first review the applicable literature on communication and cognition in the contexts of work and friendship, especially for women; then I describe the results of an original study on women's work friendships and communication within them (with individual relationships—as perceived and reported by one partner); finally, I discuss the study in terms of its place in the research now and in the future.

SURVEY OF RELEVANT COMMUNICATION LITERATURE

Most research in the area of colleague relationships examines the organization as the unit of analysis, that is, investigates how jobs are structured, whether they offer opportunities for interaction, the extent to which organizational norms are conducive to intimacy and relationship development (Falcione et al. 1987), and relational communication at the group membership or network level (Monge and Eisenberg 1987). When the research does discuss relationships between organizational members, it generally involves superior-subordinate communication (e.g., Dansereau and Markham 1987; Jablin 1987), not relationships between colleague friends. Its focus is often diagnostic and management centered, and much of it views control as a fundamental dimension of relationships. A great deal of the study in this area has been developed from an economic approach, seeing friendship (especially at work) as an exchange of costs and rewards (e.g., Nelson 1989). Some other research takes a developmental approach (e.g., Maccoby 1990). The relevant literature which is examined here involves relationships in the workplace, women in the workplace, and friendship in general.

SCHEMATA AND PROTOTYPES:
TOWARD A CONCEPTUALIZATION OF FRIENDSHIP

One way to conceptualize friendship is according to the prototypes, or frameworks representing social knowledge that individuals use to classify their relationships (Davis and Todd 1985). In other words, a person may have a cognitive categorical structure such as "work friendship," which is attached to a list of attributes that are typical of such relationships.

One of the helpful aspects of the prototype perspective is its ability to compare relationship types. For example, when we distinguish the friendship archetype from the romantic relationship archetype, we learn what characteristics each has and does not have in common. (See Wilmot and Baxter, 1984, for a discussion of the criterial attributes of romantic and platonic relationships.) One such common trait is intimacy (Crary 1987). Through the course of working for an organization, people develop both intimate and casual relationships, often the result of physical closeness and interdependence (Baum 1990).

The literature offers several definitions for friendship, usually involving the concepts of mutuality, reciprocity, communication, and enjoyment. For example, Hall (1990) writes that friendship is a reciprocal relationship "where meaningful communications enhance awareness of self. Friends provide significant support for each other" (p. 197). Davis and Todd (1985) also write that in an archetypal case of friendship, "two individuals participate in a relationship which is mutual and reciprocal. They assign each other the status of friends" (p. 19). This voluntary aspect of friendship is echoed by Gouldner and Strong (1987), who define friendship according to their perception of the middle-class American view of the relationship: "Friendship . . . can be the best of relationships because it is free; it can be entered into voluntarily by people for the sheer joy of it. It can be engaged in and terminated without legal entanglements or institutional obligations" (p. 5). Because this study focuses on communication, the following definition for friendship was presented to respondents: a relationship between two individuals . . . wherein meaningful communication takes place.

Rules in domains such as respect for privacy, support, and intimate communication appear to be an extension of prototype attributes, and another way to characterize relationship types. People employ role schema and personal experience to develop their expectations of friendships as well as form rules for giving emotional support and assistance and for repaying debts or favors (Argyle and Henderson 1985; La Gaipa 1987). In work relationships, task support rules, such as those about cooperation, public criticism, and accepting a fair portion of the workload are also important—especially when involving a colleague with whom individuals share intimate communication. There is some merit to the application of such rule theories to friendships, as they are helpful in categorizing relationships, but as Gouldner and Strong (1987) point out, friendship is often considered friendship chiefly because there are no set rules or institutional restraints on the relationship.

WOMEN, FRIENDS, AND WORK

Women's experiences of friendship often appear to differ from those of men. Although women's relationships can also be activity oriented, talking is usually a central focus (Gouldner and Strong 1987). Many women want to share comments and speculations about their daily activities with the men to whom they are closest, but a commonly reported experience is that men do not value such talk. From Gouldner and Strong's (1987) point of view, there is a gender difference in the "universe of discourse" (p. 59) inhabited by men and women. They go so far as to suggest that women have a specific manner of discourse called "woman talk," a chief function of which is entertainment, yet it may focus on almost any subject matter. Greater intimacy as well as sharing of more mundane information characterizes such discourse. Gouldner and Strong (1987) write: "The relaxed conditions under which friends converse and the dynamic of woman talk encourage a gradual and uncensored revelation of information and feelings" (p. 68).

Hall (1990) indicates that women define who they are through friendship. She writes, "Self-revelation occurs through the many conversations and nonverbal interactions over long periods of time" (p. 118). In addition to self-revelation, communication between friends can foster a woman's self-discovery. Equal participation and full partnership are important components of Hall's conception of women's friendship: "Potential is developed through exchanges with others, and relationships allow us to lead meaningful and satisfying lives. We work towards goals and aspire to excellence through our social bonds" (p. 15).

According to Gouldner and Strong (1987), those in (societally) subordinate positions have historically watched their words and disguised their feelings around their "masters." Therefore, they argue, women turn to other women to share experiences on an equal footing. In the work world, this seems especially relevant, as women do not share leadership in many organizations. In addition, because so many waking hours are spent on the job, it would follow that women are better able to become acquainted with coworkers than with most other people. Most of Gouldner and Strong's (1987) respondents considered acquaintance interaction as an attractive part of working outside the home.

Women's work relationships are often valued for qualities distinct from relationships in which talking and activities are the focus (Gouldner and Strong 1987). Yet these friendships are often transformed into talking and activity-centered relationships as they develop in the daily accomplishment of the work. Some of Gouldner and Strong's (1987) respondents reported making "office associates the hub of their social lives, gradually extending the connections with workers beyond the confines of the work setting" (p. 60).

The greatest difficulties Gouldner and Strong (1987) found in work-related friendships was an "acute shortage of time and energy" (p. 86) and the norm of distance between supervisor and supervised. Others cited the need to separate work and home life, especially in a climate of competition or jealousy, where one would not want to make a colleague aware of personal flaws. Women in executive positions were especially prone to not make friends at work because they were isolated from peers of the same gender and were not able to interact closely with the men around them for fear of gossip regarding a sexual relationship. Even if other women were available in terms of proximity, they cited the risks of trusting a coworker with potentially damaging information about themselves. Gouldner and Strong (1987) claim that like many men, these women lose what they call the "purposeless" relationship (perhaps better described as the talking relationship, in which one meets with a friend just to talk, not to take part in another activity), and conduct their friendships on a segmental basis—relating to only one aspect of the other person, such as her interest in tennis or in a work project.

RESEARCH QUESTIONS

The present study conceptualized work friendships as a relationship between two individuals, begun in a work-related context, wherein meaningful communication takes place. Friendships were considered relationships which individuals could conceptualize as a prototype, and were studied on the basis of accounts offered by one member of the pair (more will be said about the benefits of studying comments from both partners later).

Unfortunately, it is often difficult to study women at work because of the likelihood that gender differences at work are due more to the structure of organizations rather than to the nature or socialization of women and men (Acker 1991; Kanter 1977). These methodological issues affect this study because it is attempting to examine an organization-related phenomenon. However, it is argued that the concept of friendship, although with someone met at work, transcends the organization, allowing women to think of it separately. Further, the research instrument was administered outside the workplace, hopefully maximizing respondents' ability to conceptually separate their friendship from their organization. As the literature in this area is by no means extensive, the present study is considered exploratory, and no hypotheses were developed. The following research questions were posed:

1. Why and how do women become friends with particular coworkers?
2. What characteristics define women's work relationships?
3. How do women communicate in the context of work friendships, that is, are there communication themes which characterize women's work friendships?

METHOD

Based on the preceding research questions, a questionnaire with open-ended and closed-ended questions was developed to collect data regarding perceptions of work friendships. Questionnaires were administered to sixty women in a professional organization in the Midwest. Data for this study were collected from a total of twenty-five usable surveys. A twenty-sixth potential respondent returned her uncompleted survey because she felt she did not make friends at work. This raises a question regarding the assumption that everyone develops friendships at work. As the survey was for exploratory purposes, the sample's lack of randomness was not a concern, but more will be said about this in the conclusion of this paper.

All of the relationships for which data were collected were currently intact, with eleven of the respondents reporting that the relationship was "very important—we're good friends," seven of the respondents indicating a value one level below the first category on the scale, and seven reporting an importance score of halfway between "very important" and "not very important." Only eight respondents reported any relationship difficulties. (Perhaps this finding lends support to Gouldner and Strong's, 1987, suggestion that subjects prefer to emphasize the positive aspects of their relationships, but more likely it is because respondents automatically thought of someone with whom they are still friends and with whom they have a good relationship, rather than someone who is now relatively unimportant to them or is no longer a friend.)

Qualitative research methods were employed in this study because participant interpretations surrounding the relationship were the data sought. Rather
than counting start-up events, characteristics, or communication behaviors in
order to generalize to a broader population, themes were identified to capture
respondents' salient perceptions of, explanations for, and discursive processes
within their relationships.

RESULTS AND DISCUSSION

Several themes emerged from respondents' answers to survey questions; for
presentation purposes, they are organized as responses to the research questions.

1. Why and how do women become friends with particular coworkers? In
remembering how they came to be friends, a number of those participating in
the study supported Gouldner and Strong's (1987) observation that they "just
became friends." Some remembered being at an orientation together, finding
out that they had common friends, or one of the partners sharing the "real
story" in the organization or office, but most seemed to be unable to explain a
definitive starting point of how and why, as illustrated in the words of one
respondent:

Looking back I'm not sure . . . you work in the same place . . . start sitting at the same
table during lunch . . . start talking about things besides work . . . and suddenly it
happens. It is not something I planned or said, "Gee, I want to become friends with her!"

Almost all of the respondents mentioned work specifically as a "reason" for the
relationship's initiation, suggesting that the context for the relationship may
make work friendships conceptually different from other types, and that these
people might not be friends if they met in other ways.

There was support for similarities as a basis for attraction. Several of the
respondents reported similarities in backgrounds, interests, career aspirations,
ways of thinking, and ways of communicating. Respondents gave several examples of conceptual and attitudinal similarities, including:

I think we're both the same kind of person and just naturally "clicked." . . . We approach
life in a similar frame of mind so we tend to know how the other person will react to
something. It is comfortable knowing that the other person will most likely share your
view or be sympathetic to your situation. . . . There's a kind of "kindred spirit" relationship.

Although similarities were cited as a basis for attraction by many, age was
not necessarily a factor. The average ages of both participants and their friends
were thirty years, but there was an age difference of ten or more years in twelve
(about half) of the relationships. A potential explanation for this finding is that,

although people differ in age and experience, work is a common link which overrides variance in chronological years.

2. What characteristics define women's work relationships? Qualities which were reported as important to the development of the friendship included: honesty, respect, fun/enjoyment, seeing each other socially, support in personal or professional matters, self-disclosure, affirmation, trust/discretion, answers to work questions, common interests/personality traits, work cooperation, reciprocity/equality, mutual friends, and intimacy—many of which are related to communication. The most commonly cited characteristics were personal and professional support, trust, seeing each other socially, and respect. There are some important reasons why trust, although important in all relationships, is especially important in work friendships. As Baum (1990) points out, organizational politics and intimacy do not mix well. Therefore, an individual must find a friend who she believes will not report her weaknesses to others. Although it may seem scientifically problematic to cluster personal and professional matters, this study's data indicate that respondents do so, although (in agreement with Gouldner and Strong's, 1987, findings) typically talk and support is about work first, and personal self-disclosure develops later in the relationship.

In addition, it appears that many respondents found that they enjoyed activities together at work first, then began to see each other socially away from work and talk on the telephone, again supporting Gouldner and Strong's (1987) assertions. It is also interesting to note that when respondents developed friendships at work, they felt as equals even if they were in a superior-subordinate position and were of different ages. A few of those surveyed specifically cited activities as the basis for their friendships. However, because work is an activity, it could be argued that more relationships involve activities than those specifically identified, and that more work relationships involve activities than other women's relationships as a whole.

3. How do women communicate in the context of work friendships, that is, are there communication themes which characterize women's work friendships? Communication was an important part of all the relationships in the study. It played a role in attraction; for example, one respondent wrote that she and her friend became friends because they are both "verbal people and share easily.? Communication was also cited as a regular activity during the course of the friendship: "We discuss much of what happens on a daily basis in our lives."

The development of most of the relationships in the study followed Gouldner and Strong's (1987) claims that work friendships begin with work and progress to greater levels of intimacy. One respondent chronicled her relationship's history as follows:

We had a great working cooperation. Even though we are different ages, we could connect with each other through the respect and trust that developed. The fact that she was my supervisor did not matter past the first week. . . . After a while we got together on a social basis.

Another responded that the work relationship about which she wrote "led to an increase in self-disclosure." "Becoming" (indicating a process) comfortable and closer was offered by some respondents as part of their relationship histories. Two respondents indicated:

You feel comfortable first talking about work and *then* personal things.

We started with only business/work issues, but as our friendship grew so did our range of topics.

Several respondents discussed the importance of their friendship as providing a sounding board for personal and professional issues, and four specifically mentioned "listening" as an important characteristic of their relationship.

A number of respondents commented on their friendships' ability to offer an opportunity to vent their frustrations regarding their work situation, which is in line with the assertion of Bates et al. (1983) that support among women and friends is critical to adjusting to a stressful life. Although almost all respondents cited being able to share daily work problems as topics for their talk, nine of those surveyed specifically indicated that blowing off steam or complaining about work was an important subject of communication. Other topics of communication included work and cooperation on projects, families and other relationships, personal issues, and activities. Humor was also cited by a number of respondents. Five mentioned humor specifically as part of their relationships. One respondent reported that she and her friend "frequently play off each other's comments and it gets quite funny!"

IMPLICATIONS AND SUGGESTIONS FOR FUTURE RESEARCH

This exploratory study has taken a type of relationship between two individuals in a work setting and ascertained how one participant perceives and interprets it. Evidence has been presented that women develop work relationships gradually that are mutual, reciprocal, and enjoyable. Demographic, attitudinal, and conceptual similarities were important to the formation of these friendships, but differences in age and experience did not seem to matter, except that they often helped to make the relationship richer in terms of a mentoring function. Communication was important in all of these relationships, including talk about work and personal lives. Several areas for further inquiry, in terms of topics and methods, are identified.

Cross-sex versus Same-sex Relationships

Davis and Todd (1985) found that both men and women were less likely to have opposite-sex than same-sex friends. Reasons they cite for this phenomenon include differences in perspectives and interests and the possibility that romantic partners would be threatened by the relationship. In this study, only five participants wrote about relationships with male friends; however, the title on the questionnaire (also found on this paper) might have biased women toward writing about relationships with other women. There were not many thematic differences in the responses about cross-sex friendships: two respondents mentioned the benefit of hearing the male perspective; two specifically stated that their relationships were platonic; and one wrote that she socialized with her friend outside of the work context "with our spouses, *of course*" (emphasis added). This might be a fruitful area for further research.

Turnover

Another interesting question is what turnover does to friendships and their communication behaviors in organizations. Jablin (1987) suggests that communications might be severed between the person leaving the organization and those left behind for two reasons: the person leaving might experience dissonance regarding the choice to leave a position or employer he/she did not dislike; and those left behind would not desire information about attractive alternatives to their present situations. Three of the respondents in this study indicated that their friendship would suffer or perhaps end if one member were to leave the organization of the relationship's origin, supporting Gouldner and Strong's (1987) finding that work relationships often cease after a colleague leaves for a new job. In five of this study's cases, one partner had already left, but the friendships were still intact. Another said that she would be moving soon, but that the friends would definitely stay in contact. A longitudinal study would determine the effects of turnover on work friendships.

Violations of Friendship

Turnover is not the only way work friendships might end. Another interesting course of study might focus on what happens when one relationship partner behaves in a manner inconsistent with her archetypal ideal of friendship. Davis and Todd (1985) indicate that resolutions of friendship violations are rare but that it is typically assumed that friendships end because individuals drift or grow apart. A potential avenue for researching the dissolution of friendships would be to study participants' accounts (Weber, Harvey, and Stanley 1987). However, Gouldner and Strong (1987) found that, when asked about relationship loss, respondents seemed to redefine the relationship in their accounts as a friendship that was not that important anyway; thus, information on how the relationship ended might be difficult to obtain.

What Don't You Talk About?

Friends also recognize that there are certain subjects which deserve the privilege of privacy, for example, finances (Gouldner and Strong 1987). Although they do not point to the work situation specifically, it would follow that not talking about money is especially critical when people are working for the same company. (One of the respondents in the present study did say that she and her friend talked about money, but she did not specifically identify salary as a topic of conversation.) Perhaps a future interview question is, "Are there subjects you specifically don't talk about?"

Family Issues

It is interesting to note that some of the women in Gouldner and Strong's (1987) sample felt that their coworkers did not sympathize with their efforts to be good mothers and wives while doing a good job at work until they became parents themselves. In the present study, about half of the respondents reported marital status differences, and ten reported demographic differences regarding having children. Although there was a general indication of talk about family within the friendship, respondents did not report the relationship issues found by Gouldner and Strong (1987). It would be interesting to see future research regarding the impact of partners' family status on the work friendship.

Methodological Improvements

A number of methodological concerns can be raised with regard to this study. First, the sample was not random, but one of convenience—those who were willing to write about their relationships—and thus its results are biased to the extent that respondents are persons who are relatively open about relatively private matters. Second, a questionnaire may not be an adequate instrument. Gouldner and Strong (1987) argue that data gathered in questionnaires are more prone to social desirability effects and self-deception because of U.S. society's and respondents' idealization of friendship. They suggest that interviews allow researchers to better capture how subjects really think and feel through feedback. Third, interviews with (or at least questionnaires administered to) both members of the relationship would also be helpful in order to compare relationship accounts and perhaps observe communication behaviors firsthand.

Personal Language

If interviews were conducted with both of the relationship participants, it would be interesting to note whether they exhibit similar speech patterns, how they engage in "Woman Talk" (Gouldner and Strong 1987), and whether they use idiosyncratic language for certain topics. Berger and Bradac (1982) report the use of personal idioms ("special terms to refer to each other and to their activities," p. 103) in romantic long-term relationships. They write that the degree of overlap between personal construct systems may be an indicator of length of relationship, and that cohesiveness may be facilitated by the use of such personal idioms. Some examples with relevance to the current study would be relationship participants' referents to work routines, work activities, organizational members, and organizational structures.

Mentoring Relationships

Finally, over half of the respondents (13) indicated that their work friendship is a mentoring relationship, which is a related relationship prototype (Baum 1990; Collins 1983; Zey 1984) and another subject for further study.

In conclusion, it appears that women may have a conceptual prototype for work friendships that includes both relatively casual and very important friends. However, this prototype also overlaps with other relationship types to encompass social and other activities. In all cases, talk appears to be important to the initiation and maintenance of the relationship.

Several authors argue that women's value hierarchies differ from those of men; generally, women place greater worth on nurturing, sometimes sacrificial, activity, and men value competition and dominance more (Gilligan 1982; Hall 1990). Currently, it appears that work organizations are structured to promote male values, causing Acker (1991) to write that, "to function at the top of male hierarchies requires women to render irrelevant everything that makes them women" (p. 174). If one accepts such a view, then if women are to succeed in business, must they adopt a competitive and "purpose-oriented" stance toward friendship? According to those surveyed for this study, women at work confide in and support each other, they enjoy each other's company, and they talk about daily as well as larger issues. Although social desirability may be a factor in respondents' answers, competition does not seem to be an issue for those surveyed. If these results are an indication of how women feel about their coworkers, perhaps organizations will evolve to encompass a more nurturing atmosphere as more women continue to excel in the workforce.

ACKNOWLEDGMENT

The author thanks Lynn Turner for her insightful comments on an earlier version of this paper.

REFERENCES

Acker, J. 1991. "Hierarchies, Jobs, Bodies: A Theory of Gendered Organizations." In J. Lorber and S. A. Farrell, eds., *The Social Construction of Gender*. Newbury Park, CA: Sage, pp. 162–179.

Argyle, M., and M. Henderson. 1985. "The Rules of Relationships." In S. Duck and D. Perlman, eds., *Understanding Personal Relationships: An Interdisciplinary Approach*. London: Sage, pp. 63–84.

Bates, U. U., F. L. Denmark, V. Held, D. O. Helly, S. H. Lees, S. B. Pomeroy, E. D. Smith, and S. R. Zalk. 1983. *Women's Realities, Women's Choices: An Introduction to Women's Studies*. New York: Oxford University Press.

Baum, H. S. 1990. *Organizational Membership: Personal Development in the Workplace*. Albany: State University of New York Press.

Berger, C. R., and J. J. Bradac. 1982. *Language and Social Knowledge: Uncertainty in Interpersonal Relations*. London: Edward Arnold.

Collins, N. W. 1983. *Professional Women and Their Mentors: A Practical Guide to Mentoring for the Woman Who Wants to Get Ahead*. Englewood Cliffs, NJ: Prentice-Hall.

Crary, M. 1987. "Managing Attraction and Intimacy at Work." *Organizational Dynamics 15*(1): 27–41.

Dansereau, F., and S. E. Markham. 1987. "Superior-Subordinate Communication: Multiple Levels of Analysis." In F. M. Jablin, L. L. Putnam, K. H. Roberts, and L. W. Porter, eds., *Handbook of Organizational Communication: An Interdisciplinary Perspective*. Newbury Park, CA: Sage, pp. 343–388.

Davis, K. E., and M. J. Todd. 1985. "Assessing Friendship: Prototypes, Paradigm Cases, and Relationship Description." In S. Duck and D. Perlman, eds., *Understanding Personal Relationships: An Interdisciplinary Approach*. London: Sage, pp. 17–38.

Falcione, R. L., L. Sussman, and R. P. Herden. 1987. "Communication Climate in Organizations." In F. M. Jablin, L. L. Putnam, K. H. Roberts, and L. W. Porter, eds., *Handbook of Organizational Communication: An Interdisciplinary Perspective*. Newbury Park, CA: Sage, pp. 195–227.

Gilligan, C. 1982. *In a Different Voice*. Cambridge, MA: Harvard University Press.

Gouldner, H., and M. S. Strong. 1987. *Speaking of Friendship: Middle-class Women and Their Friends*. Westport, CT: Greenwood Press.

Hall, C. M. 1990. *Women and Identity: Value Choices in a Changing World*. New York: Hemisphere.

Jablin, F. M. 1987. "Organizational Entry, Assimilation, and Exit." In F. M. Jablin, L. L. Putnam, K. H. Roberts, and L. W. Porter, eds., *Handbook of Organizational Communication: An Interdisciplinary Perspective*. Newbury Park, CA: Sage, pp. 679–740.

Kanter, R. M. 1977. *Men and Women of the Corporation*. New York: Basic Books.

La Gaipa, J. J. 1987. "Friendship Expectations." In R. Burnett, P. McGhee, and D. Clarke, eds., *Accounting for Relationships: Explanation, Representation, and Knowledge*. London: Methuen, pp. 134–157.

Maccoby, E. E. 1990. "Gender and Relationships: A Developmental Account." *American Psychologist 45*: 513–520.

Monge, P. R., and E. M. Eisenberg. 1987. "Emergent Communication Networks." In F. M. Jablin, L. L. Putnam, K. H. Roberts, and L. W. Porter, eds., *Handbook of*

Organizational Communication: An Interdisciplinary Perspective. Newbury Park, CA: Sage, pp. 304–342.

Nelson, G. W. 1989. "Factors of Friendship: Relevance of Significant Others to Female Business Owners." *Entrepreneurship: Theory and Practice* (summer): 7–18.

Ragins, B. R. 1989. "Gender and Power in Organizations: A Longitudinal Perspective." *Psychological Bulletin 105*(1): 51–88.

Weber, A. L., J. H. Harvey, and M. A. Stanley. 1987. "The Nature and Motivations of Accounts for Failed Relationships." In R. Burnett, P. McGhee, and D. Clarke, eds., *Accounting for Relationships: Explanation, Representation, and Knowledge.* London: Methuen, pp. 114–133.

Wilmot, W. W., and L. A. Baxter. 1984. "Defining Relationships: The Interplay of Cognitive Schemata and Communication." Paper presented at the annual convention of the Western Speech Communication Association, Seattle, WA.

Wright, P. H. 1982. "Men's Friendships, Women's Friendships, and the Alleged Inferiority of the Latter." *Sex Roles 8*: 1–20.

Zey, M. G. 1984. *The Mentor Connection.* Homewood, IL: Dow Jones-Irwin.

18

Case Management: Nurses and Physicians Confronting Gendered Organization

R. J. Kivatisky

This study presents initial findings from a longitudinal study of organizational change in a New England hospital. It covers the introduction of case management as a model for organizational change and traces the development of three case management teams (cardiology, pulmonary, and orthopedic) from a cultural-critical perspective (Burrell and Morgan 1979; Deetz 1992; Deetz and Kersten 1983; Frost, Moore, Louis, Lundberg, and Martin 1991; Geertz 1973). After two years, participating nurses and physicians appear to be confronting gendered organization (Acker 1990; Mills 1989). Acker (1990) elucidates, "To say that an organization, or any other analytic unit, is gendered means that advantage and disadvantage, exploitation and control, action and emotion, meaning and identity, are patterned through, and in terms of, a distinction between male and female, masculine and feminine" (p. 146). Acker believes these bipolar structural and behavior components rooted in gender confront most organizations. This study extends her thesis to the realm of organizational change in a health care setting.

The first of many modern approaches to organizational change emerged from the now famous Hawthorne experiments conducted by Elton Mayo at the Hawthorne plant of the Western Electric Company in Chicago. Mayo's findings began a human relations movement in management. The results of Mayo's research demonstrated that productivity could be improved in ways other than strict adherence to classical and scientific principles of management (Mayo 1933; Taylor 1911). The areas of motivation, morale, and job satisfaction became important avenues of inquiry for theorists. And practitioners became concerned about the human side of enterprise (McGregor 1960). Since Mayo's pioneering work, organization theory and approaches to organizational change have gone through a variety of transformations.

Morgan (1986) employs metaphors (e.g., machine, organic, cultural) to creatively illustrate these transformations in thought and to explain the theoretical underpinnings of organization theory. He lists the strengths and weaknesses of each metaphor and suggests using them as lenses to view and understand organizations. In contrast, Shafritz and Ott (1992) outline progressions in thought from a historical perspective (e.g., classical, human resource, systems) using exemplar essays by influential writers from each historical period. Though their approaches are different, Morgan and Shafritz and Ott agree on the evolution of organization theory and how practitioners implemented these ideas to make organizations more effective.

As organization theory evolved, practitioners moved through parallel approaches to organizational change (e.g., sensitivity groups, management by objectives, quality circles, total quality management). An interesting aspect of these change strategies, however, is brought to light by a cultural-critical perspective. Namely, the strategies were not necessarily due to progressive thinking, and they only dealt with surface change. They did not address organizational deep structure or the embedded power relations between organizational members (e.g., labor and management, women and men, nurses and physicians) (Clegg 1989; Conrad 1983; Deetz 1992; Geertz 1973). As a result, these strategies were not as effective as they could have been.

Case management is an approach to organizational change in health care settings. It is not a monolithic approach, and health organizations often adapt the basic principles to their own needs. The model adopted by the hospital in this study (Center for Nursing Case Management 1990) promotes nurse/physician collaborative practice teams and includes tools (e.g., Care Maps™ and Critical Paths™) to chart the variance between expected and obtained outcomes for certain conditions, such as heart attacks. Better patient care and education are also part of the case management model.

The major objective of this research was to explore and describe the effects of case management on the deep and surface social structures of the hospital over time. As mentioned earlier, preliminary findings place the focus of this paper on the power relations between nurses and physicians participating in the collaborative practice teams. The roles of nurse and physician are particularly intriguing because a majority of nurses are female and a majority of physicians male—the seam of power includes gender as well as role and status (Conrad 1983; Stein 1967; Stein, Watts, and Howell 1990).

At this point in the research process, Acker's (1990) theory of gendered organizations provides the best explanation of what nurses and physicians in this study are facing. Acker cites five interacting processes "that, although analytically distinct, are, in practice, parts of the same reality" (p. 146). These five processes describe and explain the deeply embedded power relations between nurses and physicians at the hospital and form the outline of the results section of this chapter.

METHODOLOGY

The research is taking place at a medium-sized, acute care teaching hospital located in a metropolitan area of New England. The methodology is qualitative (Marshall and Rossman 1989) as I have been a participant observer (Becker and Geer 1957) in the hospital since the introduction of case management in October 1990. I attend steering committee and case management team meetings and communicate with individual participants at least once a week.

The project began with the introduction of case management as a new approach to patient care. The model (Center for Nursing Care Management 1990) emphasizes collaborative practice teams with nurses in the role of case manager. The development of three case management teams (cardiology, pulmonary, and orthopedics) followed the introduction of the new approach. Each team took a separate route toward implementation of case management and, as will be discussed in the next section, some were more successful than others. Several steering committee meetings were held over time to check on the teams' progress and to collect feedback. In October 1992, a daylong retreat was held to discuss the future of case management in the hospital.

The data come from field notes and observations made over two years. Thus far, no audiotapes have been made because tape recorders appear to threaten some participants and would interfere with data collection and building trust. This is especially true for physicians, who see change as an erosion of their power.

RESULTS

The results of this study can best be understood by using Acker's description of five interacting processes that constitute gendering. Briefly, they include (1) divisions of labor; (2) construction of symbols and images; (3) interaction patterns that enact dominance and submission; (4) choice of work, language use, clothing, and presentation of self as a gendered member of an organization; and (5) ongoing processes of creating and conceptualizing social structure (Acker 1990). This section of the chapter examines the data through the prism of these five processes.

"First is the division of labor along lines of gender—divisions of labor, of allowed behaviors, of locations in physical space, of power" (Acker 1990, p. 146). The division of labor by gender in the hospital is quite obvious: most nurses are female and most physicians male. There are allowed behaviors associated with both their roles and their gender. Physicians, for example, "write orders" (medical instructions for patient care) and nurses carry them out. Most physicians are in private practice and not employed by the hospital. As a result, they have more control over how they spend their time and are free of the constraints of physical space. Nurses, by contrast, are employed by the hospital, are usually assigned to a particular unit, such as special care or pediatrics, and are generally confined to a certain floor or wing of the hospital for long periods of time.

In terms of division of power, only physicians can write orders. It is the physician's signature that releases the patient from the hospital. Nurses, as well as patients, must wait for these orders before proceeding with treatment or release. There is the strong influence of military history behind the relationship between nurses and physicians that continues to this day—obeying orders and discipline (Clegg and Dunkerly 1980) are a deeply embedded part of that heritage. A story about "the old days," when nurses would rise when physicians entered a room and would be required to give up their seats to physicians if none were available, is often told to me.

"Second is the construction of symbols and images that explain, express, reinforce, or sometimes oppose those divisions. These have many sources or forms in language, ideology, popular and high culture, dress, the press, television" (Acker 1990, p. 146). There is the language of medicine and the language of nursing. There is the mind-set of treating a disease or condition, and the mind-set of caring for the whole person. The first mind-set can be characterized as biosocial, the other as psychosocial. At both deep and surface levels, nurses and physicians live in two different worlds. The physician focuses on specific medical problems affecting the patient (biosocial), whereas the nurse takes care of almost everything else (psychosocial). Nurses have a more generalized and holistic view of the patient than physicians. Unfortunately, nurses have little power regarding treatment. One of the difficulties encountered by the nurses who serve as case managers is the fact that they have no real authority in the world of medicine. These two ideologies are compounded by other gender differences in "ways of knowing" (Belenky, Clinchy, Goldberger, and Tarule 1986) and "voice" (Gilligan 1982).

Differences in dress are also striking. Female nurses wear a variety of colored pants, lab coats, jumpsuits, and dresses. Physicians, who in this study are all men, usually wear dress shirts and ties under white lab coats. The one male nurse in the study dresses like the male physicians minus the tie. Using a continuum of formality in dress, physicians tended to dress toward the formal extreme and nurses toward the informal. It is easy to discern the "docs" (the term used by nurses to refer to physicians) from others in the hospital by their clothing.

Language and dress underscore the dominant power position of physicians in and out of the hospital. Throughout the implementation of the case management model, the major concern of the nurses has been how to get the "docs" to buy into it. From the very outset, social structure places nurses in a submissive position. Nurse interaction with physicians usually begins with the underlying assumption that physicians are in control. As Acker explains, "The third set of processes that produce gendered social structures, including organizations, are interactions between women and men, women and women, men and men, including all those patterns that enact dominance and submission" (Acker 1990, pp. 146–147).

Nurses and physicians have yet to develop an egalitarian discourse, an ideal speech situation as Habermas describes it (Habermas 1970a, 1970b, 1979). There are still clear lines of dominance and submission enacted in turn taking and in the number of interruptions between nurses and physicians, particularly as females and males (Stewart, Stewart, Friedley, and Cooper 1990). Everyone monitors the physicians; they are the ones who indicate when the discussion starts, where it goes, and when it ends. The one successful nurse/physician–female/male collaboration was the result of the nurse/female's assertive remark to the physician/male's question about a particular patient's care, and his thoughtful response. It came during the team's first meeting and set the stage for all following interactions. These two people were able to override system defects because of their willingness to collaborate on an individual level. Yet even their cooperation is shaded by the physician's underlying power and control of the situation.

"Fourth, these processes help to produce gendered components of individual identity, which may include consciousness of the existence of the other three aspects of gender, such as, in organizations, choice of appropriate work, language use, clothing, and the presentation of self as a gendered member of an organization" (Acker 1990, p. 147). Professional role behavior and clothing have already been mentioned; however, a poignant example of presenting oneself as a gendered member of an organization involved the selection of the nurse manager for the orthopedic collaborative team. The decision was made in an effort to pick the most influential person to "get the docs to buy in," and it was made solely on the basis of physical attractiveness. It was the only criteria used; the topics of motivation or competence were never brought up. Unfortunately, this particular nurse crumbled after being severely reprimanded by a physician, and this team no longer exists. Overall, though not as extreme as in the preceding example, nurses presented themselves in a gendered fashion, usually looking to appease or cajole physicians (Stein 1967; Stein, Watts, and Howell 1990).

"Finally, gender is implicated in the fundamental, ongoing processes of creating and conceptualizing social structures . . . underlying both academic theories and practical guides for managers is a gendered substructure that is reproduced daily in practical work activities" (Acker 1990, p. 147). Giddens's (1976, 1979) concept of the duality of structure, taken in tandem with Acker's theory of gendered organization, helps explain the relationship between deep and surface structures and how this relationship affects change. Simply stated, people simultaneously create, maintain, and modify social structure. Current structure is maintained when people use it as a guide for their behavior and can be modified when people act in ways different from the norm. The one successful example of nurse/physician collaboration occurs because it overrides dominant patterns of interaction between nurses and physicians. The other teams maintain the historical and cultural social structure by continuing to act and interpret patterns of behavior in the same old way. In experimental jargon, case management has had a weak treatment effect on them. The introduction of case management barely scratched their surface structure and has had little effect on their deep structure.

DISCUSSION

This research merges the theoretical concepts associated with a cultural-critical perspective with behaviors observed in the field in an effort to shed light on the process of organizational change. This study presents the results of two years of observation in a hospital where case management was introduced as a model of organizational change. The results were discussed using Acker's (1990) theory of gendered organizations. The results support the five interacting processes of Acker's theory and suggest nurses and physicians taking part in case management teams are confronting gendered organization.

Two other observations are also apparent. First, there is support for the notion that if real organizational change is to occur it will have to modify deep structures by challenging tacit assumptions about appropriate behaviors. Participants involved in the change process should be encouraged to consciously act in ways that do not fit recurring historical and cultural patterns of dominance and control. Second, female nurses bear a double burden because their role and their gender place them in a submissive and powerless position in the social structure of the hospital. Their gender linked with their role is at the heart of the problem. Research on male nurses and female physicians seems to verify this finding (Floge and Merrill 1986). Male nurses interact more easily and frequently with male physicians and climb the organizational hierarchy more quickly than women. Female physicians, on the other hand, are caught between their gender and the nonneutral gender (read male) role of physician (Hearns, Sheppard, Tancred-Sheriff, and Burrell 1989). In these cases, gender supersedes role and must be given special attention if the change process is to be successful.

As a case study, this research has obvious limitations. It is merely an example providing only qualitative data. However, it does provide some insights into the change process from the cultural-critical perspective and does offer support for Acker's theory of gendered organizations. In addition, it focuses attention on change in health care settings and may be helpful to those interested in this specific area of organizational behavior. More research from a cultural-critical perspective is needed, particularly on male nurses and female physicians involved in case management teams. These gender roles challenge current expectations and may provide excellent examples of the paradox (Quinn and Cameron 1988) inherent in gendered organizations. Further research might ask: What do people in these gender roles see as the major barriers to effective teams? How do others react to the paradox of their gender roles? And, what are the effects on organizational change?

If we are to strive for the ideal speech situation (Habermas 1970a, 1970b, 1979) in organizational settings, then we must confront the deeply embedded aspects of culture and power in them. A distortion-free dialogue will require change in the deep and surface structures of social reality. It will require dedication to unlocking the doors of perception that hold some members of our society in the perpetual bondage of a no-win situation—a situation in which they neither control the nature of the dialogue nor have the power to participate fully in it.

REFERENCES

Acker, J. 1990. "Hierarchies, Jobs, Bodies: A Theory of Gendered Organizations." *Gender and Society* 4(2): 136–158.

Becker, H., and B. Geer. 1957. "Participant Observation and Interviewing: A Comparison." *Human Organization* 17(2): 28–32.

Belenky, M. F., B. M. Clinchy, N. R. Goldberger and J. M. Tarule. 1986. *Women's Ways of Knowing: The Development of Self, Voice, and Mind*. New York: Basic Books.

Burrell, G., and G. Morgan. 1979. *Sociological Paradigms and Organizational Analysis*. London: Heinemann.

Center for Nursing Case Management. 1990. "Differentiating Managed Care and Case Management." *Definition* 5(2): 1.

Clegg, S. 1989. *Frameworks of Power*. London: Sage.

———. 1990. *Modern Organizations: Organization Studies in the Postmodern World*. London: Sage.

Clegg, S., and D. Dunkerly. 1980. *Organization, Class, and Control*. Boston: Routledge and Kegan Paul.

Conrad, C. 1983. "Organizational Power: Faces and Symbolic Forms." In L. Putnam and M. Pacanowsky, eds., *Communication and Organizations: An Interpretive Approach*. London: Sage.

Deetz, S. 1992. *Democracy in an Age of Corporate Colonization: Developments in Communication and the Politics of Everyday Life*. Albany: State University of New York Press.

Deetz, S., and A. Kersten. 1983. "Critical Models of Interpretive Research." In L. Putnam and M. Pacanowsky, eds., *Communication and Organizations: An Interpretive Approach*. London: Sage.

Floge, L., and L. Merrill. 1986. "Tokenism Reconsidered: Male Nurses and Female Physicians in a Hospital Setting." *Social Forces* 64(4): 925–947.

Frost, P., L. Moore, M. Louis, C. Lundberg, and J. Martin. 1991. *Reframing Organizational Culture*. London: Sage.

Geertz, C. 1973. *The Interpretation of Cultures*. New York: Basic Books.

Giddens, A. 1976. *New Rules of Sociological Method*. New York: Basic Books.

———. 1979. *Central Problems in Social Theory*. Berkeley: University of California Press.

Gilligan, C. 1982. *In a Different Voice: Psychological Theory and Women's Development*. Cambridge, MA: Harvard University Press.

Habermas, J. 1970a. "On Systematically Distorted Communication." *Inquiry 13*: 205–218.

————. 1970b. "Toward a Theory a Communicative Competency." *Inquiry 13*: 360–375.

————. 1979. *Communication and the Evolution of Society*, T. McCarthy, trans. Boston: Beacon Press.

Hearns, J., D. Sheppard, P. Tancred-Sheriff, and G. Burrell, eds. 1989. *The Sexuality of Organization*. London: Sage.

Marshall, C., and G. Rossman. 1989. *Designing Qualitative Research*. London: Sage.

Mills, A. 1989. "Gender, Sexuality, and Organization Theory." In J. Hearns, D. Sheppard, P. Tancred-Sheriff, and G. Burrell, eds., *The Sexuality of Organization*. London: Sage.

Mayo, Ed. 1933. *The Human Problems of an Industrial Civilization*. Boston: Harvard Business School, Division of Research.

Morgan, G. 1986. *Images of Organization*. London: Sage.

McGregor, D. 1960. *The Human Side of Enterprise*. New York: McGraw-Hill.

Quinn, R., and K. Cameron. 1988. *Paradox and Transformation: Toward a Theory of Change in Organization and Management*. Cambridge, MA: Ballinger.

Shafritz, J., and J. Ott. 1992. *Classics of Organization Theory*, 3rd ed. Pacific Grove: Brooks/Cole.

Stein, L. 1967. "The Doctor-Nurse Game." *Archives of General Psychiatry 16*: 699–703.

Stein, L., D. Watts, and T. Howell. 1990. "Sounding Board: The Doctor-Nurse Game Revisited." *New England Journal of Medicine 322*(8): 546–549.

Stewart, L., A. Stewart, S. Friedley, and P. Cooper. 1990. *Communication Between the Sexes: Sex Differences and Sex-Role Stereotypes*, 2nd ed. Scottsdale, AZ: Gorsuch Scarisbrick.

Taylor, F. 1911. *The Principles of Scientific Management*. New York: Harper and Row.

19

Communication Patterns and Decision Making: A Comparison of Third-Party Assessments and Couple Self-Reports

Deborah S. Ballard-Reisch, Mary Elton, and Daniel J. Weigel

Marital communication patterns and decision making are of utmost interest to researchers in the family domain. Decision making within marriages involves handling problem decisions for which partners have no immediate or agreed upon response alternatives (Thomas 1977). Krueger and Smith (1982) elaborated: "Some decisions are reached without any disagreement; others involve conflicting interests; most require at least the coordination of participants' actions or intentions in 'handling' the decision situation" (p. 121).

Scanzoni and Polonko (1980) argued that both context and process variables influence the outcome of marital decision making such that "current negotiations have inevitably been influenced by prior bargaining and outcomes" and "current negotiations and outcomes provide the context for future renegotiations" (p. 31). Based on this perspective, Scanzoni and Polonko (1980) developed, and Scanzoni and associates (Godwin and Scanzoni 1989a, 1989b; Hill and Scanzoni 1982; Scanzoni 1989; Scanzoni and Szinovacz 1980) refined, a model of marital decision making that divides the decision process into context, process, and outcome components.

Context includes the relational and structural characteristics that create the environment within which marital decision making occurs. Context variables fall into four categories: (1) compositional factors including age, length of marriage, first marriage or remarriage, number and age of children, and so on; (2) resource variables such as education, job status, income, negotiating experience, and instrumental skills; (3) orientations governing the use of bargaining power including self-esteem, sex-role preference, stake in the outcome, and decision salience; (4) orientation toward partner's past bargaining behaviors including expectations about how one's partner will negotiate the problem. Relevant issues include how cooperative or competitive the spouse expects the partner to be, trust, and fairness (Scanzoni and Polonko 1980). Godwin and Scanzoni (1989b) expanded this model to include the degree of loving/caring in the marital relationship, commitment, cooperativeness in past conflict, and modernity of sex-role orientation.

Process includes the strategies, moves, and countermoves couples use to negotiate decisions, their communicator styles, and the control each spouse exhibits over interaction (Godwin and Scanzoni 1989b). Pruitt (1981) identified four cognitive decision making styles which Scanzoni (1989) argued are key process variables in marital decision making. These styles, which lie on a continuum between competition and cooperation, are problem solving, compensatory, compromise, and competition. The style chosen in a particular decision-making situation depends on the perceived likelihood that it will be successful and the degree to which each participant is concerned about their own versus the other's or relationship outcomes (Fitzpatrick 1988; Scanzoni 1989). Process dynamics significantly impact decision outcomes.

Outcome, which has been the most frequently investigated component of heterosexual marital decision making, has been studied in a variety of ways including the examination of objective outcome behaviors—was a decision made, was it appropriate—to subjective perceptions of fairness, consensus, and satisfaction with the decision (Godwin and Scanzoni 1989b; Scanzoni 1989). The nature of the marital relationship and the individual moves and countermoves within a specific interaction will impact the outcome of decision making.

A second issue, when studying marital decision making, is that most researchers examine either couple self reports through the generation of questionnaire data (see Krueger 1985) or process analysis through the use of third-party observers (see Scanzoni 1989; Zietlow and Sillars 1988). Krueger (1982) argued that combined self-report and third-party analysis should give a fuller picture of the dynamics of marital decision making. This combined analysis would allow for the assessment of two of Scanzoni and Polonko's (1980) three components of decision making, context and process.

Previous research has indicated that decision salience influences the strategies couples use (Godwin and Scanzoni 1989a, 1989b; Krueger 1985; Webb and Pennington 1991). In this study, we chose to use a low-salience decision-making problem to access more basic "patterns of decision making" (Scanzoni and Polonko 1980). This chapter contrasts partner perceptions of their communication with behavioral observations of a low-salience decision-making conversation. Two research questions are addressed in this inquiry.

1. What patterns emerge within heterosexual, married couple decision-making sequences?
2. Does the couple's perception of their conflict styles correspond with observer interpretations of couple communication behaviors?

METHODS

Procedures

Subjects were ten heterosexual, nondistressed, married couples recruited by the authors and by graduate and undergraduate students from the speech communication department of a midsized university in the western United States. All couples took part in the study voluntarily and were not compensated for their time. Participants were asked to come to the communications lab, fill out questionnaires, including the Thomas-Kilmann Conflict Mode Instrument (Thomas and Kilmann 1974) and the Duran (1983) Communication Adaptability Scale (CAS) as both a self- and partner assessment, and take part in a videotaped decision-making activity and debriefing.

Upon completing the questionnaires, each member of the dyad independently completed the Desert Survival Activity, which involves rank ordering ten items in terms of their significance for survival in a desert setting in colonial America. Upon completion of the rankings, couples were asked to reach consensus on the ordering of the ten items. Their decision-making process was videotaped. Although couples took part in this phase of the study, the researchers calculated their scores on the conflict mode instrument.

When couples finished the decision-making activity, the researchers debriefed them, gave them the results of their conflict mode instruments, discussed the implications of their results, and asked the couples if their rankings on this instrument were an accurate reflection of the way they managed conflict and decision making in their relationship. All couples agreed that their classifications on the Thomas-Kilmann Conflict Mode Instrument were accurate within their relationship; this was generally the way they dealt with decisions.

Data Analysis

Couple videotapes were transcribed and qualitative assessments were made by observing the videotapes while referring to the transcripts. This method expedited the language action and lag sequential analyses. For the language action analysis, both coders reviewed the videotapes independently and then compared their global observations.

Language Action Analysis. Language action analysis is a global technique which offers a general, descriptive framework within which to analyze communication patterns in conversations. "The analysis describes the conversational sequence, identifies patterns, and explains how the interactants create decisions. The approach subordinates static, empirical objectivity to a more fluid, empirical, reflective, nonreductive interpretation" (Krueger 1982, p. 274). The language action paradigm (Frentz and Farrell 1976) contains three hierarchically ordered constructs: context, the interpersonal environment; topic sequences; and speech acts. Language action analysis has been widely used in the study of marital decision making and conflict management (Krueger 1985, 1982; Webb and Pennington 1991).

Lag Sequential Analysis. Language action analysis was supplemented by lag sequential analysis. Whereas language action analysis allows for the general description of communication patterns, lag sequential analysis permits the study of the actual communication process in conversations. Lag sequential analysis (Raush 1972, 1965; Raush, Barry, Hertel, and Swain 1974) explores sequential behavior in conversation and allows for the direct analysis of the process of decision making (Scanzoni and Polonko 1980), that is, the moves and countermoves couples made when negotiating a decision. The focus of analysis is on "speaking turns," defined as the uninterrupted talk of one person; it can range from one word to a lengthy monologue (Rogers and Farace 1975). Both patterns in the relationships among message categories (e.g., how often is a question followed by an answer) and in simple category frequencies (e.g., how often are proposals made) are interpreted. Krueger and Smith's (1982) coding scheme for decision making was utilized in this analysis. Coders categorized speaking turns into task and maintenance categories. Coders worked separately first and then compared their assessments and attempted to reach consensus on any variations in their perceptions. This method of coding was chosen as it was felt that with the large number of coding categories and their possible combinations, the collaborative check would lead to more consistent results. Act-by-act agreement was initially 85 percent to 90 percent with collaborative coding yielding approximately 98 percent agreement. Lag sequential analysis has also been used extensively in the study of marital decision making and conflict management (Krueger and Smith 1982; Raush 1972, 1965; Raush et al. 1974; Smith 1985).

Quantitative Analysis. To supplement the qualitative analysis of conversations, comparisons of these results were made with the couples' perceptions of their relational communication behaviors in general (marital conflict style, communicative competence). The Thomas-Kilmann Conflict Mode Instrument categorizes conflict style into five types: (1) collaborative, (2) competitive, (3) compromising, (4) accommodating, and (5) avoiding. These types correspond with Pruitt's (1981) decision-making styles. There are six dimensions in the CAS: social composure, wit, social confirmation, articulation, disclosure, and social experience. Used as both a self and partner assessment, the CAS allowed for the assessment of perceptions of both self- and partner competence as communicators. Finally, accuracy in the decision-making task was measured in terms of correspondence with the expert rankings on the Desert Survival Activity. The lower the score, the more accurate the decision.

RESULTS AND DISCUSSION

Following the patterns of Webb and Pennington (1991) and Krueger (1985), we discuss each couple globally in turn as well as the contributions of each spouse, and then we discuss the research questions.

Couple Characteristics

Couples have been married for between one and twenty-five years (a minimum of one year was required for participation). The average length of time married was 8.7 years and the mode was 6.5 years. For all couples, this is their first marriage.

Couple 1. Based on language action analysis, their decision-making style was male dominated—he controlled the process, set up and reinforced the rules and procedures. He was argumentative and disagreeing. He presented arguments for her and countered them.

In terms of lag sequential analysis, on the task side, he summarized, asked questions, and made rules. Maintenance wise, he was persuasive, rejected his partner's ideas, was coercive, made rules, and asked for support. With respect to task, she agreed, made extensions on proposals, and summarized. On the maintenance side, she attempted to persuade and was supportive of her partner's ideas. She played a more supportive role, agreeing with his ideas, extending on his proposals, and summarizing their views on issues.

Their questionnaire responses indicated that he viewed himself as competitive in conflict style and she viewed herself as collaborating. In terms of communication competence, both had pretty low perceptions of one another's competence and pretty high perceptions of their own. He saw himself as composed, confirming, experienced, and articulate. He saw her as articulate and disclosing. She saw herself as composed, confirming, and experienced. She saw him as articulate. Although he had more impact on the joint decision, she completed the activity more successfully.

Couple 2. Language action analysis revealed that their decision-making style was egalitarian/collaboration based. They completed each other's sentences and made each other's proposals, collaborating on the development of some arguments. Both explained their perspectives and acknowledged one another's ideas. Both referred to process, metacommunicated, used humor, and checked for agreement. Both listened well and were supportive of one another's ideas.

In terms of lag sequential analysis, both were cooperative on the maintenance level. On the task side, she agreed, advanced rules, and asked questions; he made proposals and advanced rules.

Their questionnaire results indicated that she used an accommodating and avoiding conflict style in this relationship. He reported himself as competitive. With respect to communication competence, both saw themselves and their partners as confirming. She viewed him as disclosing; he saw her as articulate. She impacted the final decision a bit more than he did. He pulled the couple score down a bit.

Couple 3. Their decision-making style was egalitarian and based on compromise according to the language action analysis. In fact, they ended up trading items; they agreed on the first, she gave him the second, he gave her the third, she gave him the fourth, and so on. Both negotiated process and assumptions.

Lag sequential analysis indicated that with respect to task, he asked a large number of questions (sometimes as proposals), agreed with her ideas, and summarized the discussion. On the maintenance level, he was cooperative and rules oriented. She focused on agreement and summarized task information and was rules oriented, persuasive, and cooperative with respect to maintenance.

On their questionnaires, his conflict style was equal in the areas of compromising, accommodating, and avoiding. Her conflict style was collaborative and avoiding. Both saw self and partner as highly competent communicators. They both reported competence in composure, confirmation, articulation, and disclosure. She also considered him witty. Although he agreed on the other three dimensions, he did not perceive her as composed as she saw herself. They worked well together on this task, significantly improving on their individual scores.

Couple 4. In terms of language action analysis, their decision-making style was egalitarian/collaborating. Both controlled the process and listened well. They set aside their original rankings and worked to discuss issues, manage disagreement, and seek agreement. He focused on deciding; she focused on understanding her partner's perspective and being understood.

Her approach to task, according to the lag sequential analysis, included giving opinions, negotiating rules, making proposals, and agreeing with her partner. She was cooperative, negotiated rules, and requested support on the maintenance level. With respect to task, he made proposals and gave opinions. On the maintenance level, he was cooperative and persuasive.

Her questionnaire responses indicated that she saw herself as competing and collaborating; he saw himself as avoiding and accommodating. With respect to communicator competence, both saw her as composed, disclosing, and experienced. She saw him as witty; he saw himself as articulate. They both did worse on the decision-making problem when they worked together.

Couple 5. Their language action analysis indicated an egalitarian decision-making style based on compromise. They had a lot of fun with this process and laughed a great deal. They listened well to one another. Both did process, he through questioning, she through summarizing and referring to procedures and rankings. If he appeared to acquiesce to her perspective, helped build a rationale, or showed understanding, she rewarded him by accepting his earlier proposal. Her communication style was more dominant, but he had more impact on the decision. She acted as recorder, reviewed their rankings, and asked for his consensus.

With respect to their lag sequential analysis, he agreed regularly with her but often only for a short time, and then he brought up the same issues later. In addition, he made a large number of proposals. With respect to maintenance, he was persuasive and cooperative. She took responsibility for the process, summarizing, agreeing, asking questions, and making proposals. With respect to maintenance, she was cooperative and persuasive.

Their conflict questionnaire results indicated that he saw himself as compromising and avoiding; she saw herself as compromising. He scored himself low on all communication competence dimensions. She saw him as confirming, articulate, and disclosing. Both saw her as articulate. He influenced decision making a bit more than she did. Her score was a bit better than the score they negotiated together.

Couple 6. Based on language action analysis, their decision-making style was male dominated/logic based. He advanced his perspective and pursued it persistently. He focused on deciding structure and logical approaches to issues. He was methodical and persistent. She was argumentative. She processed as she went, shifted logic and forgot her earlier arguments. She had no global approach and used incremental logic to justify her momentary position (arguing vs. argument).

The lag sequential analysis indicated that he summarized, sought agreement, asked questions, and extended on proposals. With respect to maintenance, he was persuasive, talked about rules, and was cooperative. She offered agreement, asserted rules, made proposals, and disagreed on the task level. She was cooperative, rejected her partner's ideas, and attempted to persuade on the maintenance level.

Data from their questionnaires indicated that both of them perceived themselves as collaborative. He perceived himself as a competent communicator, composed, confirming, articulate, disclosing, and experienced. He saw her as composed and articulate. She saw herself as confirming and him as confirming and articulate. He impacted decision making more than she did. When they worked together, they scored quite a bit better than she did individually. The couple score was a bit worse than his score.

Couple 7. Language action analysis indicated their decision-making style was egalitarian/accommodating. Both were concerned more with agreement than with rankings (relationship maintenance more than task). They started with shared decision making—"Who will write?"—and ended with the same— "Are you OK with this?" Both justified their final ranking on the basis of closeness. They spent little time discussing the use of the items.

In terms of the lag sequential analysis, on the task level, he used a lot of conventional remarks, expressed opinions and asked questions. On the maintenance level, he was cooperative, asked for support and was rules oriented. In terms of task, she gave agreement, made proposals, gave opinions and extended on proposals. Maintenance-wise, she was cooperative, she requested support for her ideas and was supportive of her partner's ideas.

He saw himself as compromising. She saw herself as collaborating. He scored them both low on the competence dimensions. She saw herself as composed, confirming, articulate, disclosing, and experienced. She saw him as confirming, articulate, and disclosing. He had a bit more influence on decision making than she did. Her score was better than his, which was the same as their couple score.

Couple 8. Their decision-making style was female dominated/control based in terms of language action analysis. She compromised once, early on in the discussion; he reciprocated and then expected her to continue the pattern. From then on, she was competitive. She tried to push her proposals; he disagreed. She resorted to the power of the recorder and indicated she had already "put a ranking down," thus ending discussion on that topic.

Lag sequential analysis indicated that on the task level, she used a lot of conventional remarks and summarized a great deal. Her summaries often distracted his attention away from a point he was trying to make. On the maintenance level, she rejected his ideas, was coercive, and cooperated. He made a lot of rules statements, summarized discussion, asked questions, and agreed with her perspective. On the maintenance level, he focused on rules, attempted to persuade, requested support, and was cooperative.

She viewed herself as avoiding and accommodating in terms of conflict style in their relationship. He viewed himself as avoiding with comparable competing and collaborating scores. With respect to communicative competence, she saw herself as confirming, articulate, and disclosing; he saw her as the same and added composed. Both saw him as articulate. She had more impact on decision making. The couple score was better than hers; his score was better than the couple score.

Couple 9. Language action analysis results indicated their decision-making process was male dominated/competitive. They could not agree on assumptions and did not try to negotiate them. They tried to constrain each other's choices by asserting rules. They asserted their perspectives and were unwilling to give in. Neither gave the other any credibility. Although they had significant initial agreement, they focused on disagreement. They were dogmatic and inflexible.

Their lag sequential analysis indicated that in terms of task, they both proposed rules and asked questions. He summarized and disagreed. She made proposals and gave opinions. In terms of maintenance, both were coercive and rejected the other's ideas and both tried to enforce their version of the rules. Both were competitive and evaluative.

He reported his conflict style in this relationship as avoiding and accommodating. She reported her conflict style as collaborating. He saw himself as articulate and experienced in terms of communicator competence. He viewed her as composed and articulate. She saw herself as composed, confirming, articulate, disclosing, and experienced. She reported him to be the same. Their couple score was quite a bit worse than his individual score and incrementally worse than her personal score. He steamrolled and focused more on win/loss than on the quality of their decision making.

Couple 10. Their decision-making pattern was egalitarian/competitive according to language action analysis. Both made proposals and acknowledged the other's perspective. They carried on simultaneous monologues and didn't listen well.

He focused on process and pushed his ideas. He was the recorder; therefore, he decided when to acknowledge her perspective, when to discuss, and when the discussion was over. He explained his perspective but agreed with many of her interpretations and acquiesced to her proposals. She stated her views but discounted them by giggling. She returned to agreement periodically. She was assertive in presenting her views.

Their lag sequential analysis indicated that on the task level, she summarized and advanced rules. On the maintenance level, she was coercive, rules oriented, and cooperative. He made proposals, disagreed with her ideas, agreed with her ideas and discussed rules on the task level. In terms of maintenance, he was coercive and rules oriented.

With respect to conflict styles, she viewed herself as avoiding and he saw himself as collaborative/compromising. She defined herself as high in five dimensions of communicative competence: composed, confirming, articulate, disclosing, and experienced; she saw him as witty, articulate, and disclosing. He perceived both of them as articulate. Both influenced the decision although he had a more significant impact on the outcome than she did. Their decision together was a bit better than his individual decision and significantly better than hers.

Process Results: Couple Decision-Making Patterns

Dominance versus shared decision making was determined by who controlled the process and content of decision making (see Webb and Pennington 1991). Consistent with previous research, we discuss the couples' patterns in terms of male-dominated, egalitarian, and female-dominated decision making.

Male Dominated. The three male-dominated discussions were characterized by very different behaviors. For couple 1, dominance was based on his control of the process. He accomplished dominance partly through the supportive behaviors of his wife. She was cooperative and supportive. His power came primarily from his assertiveness advancing his perspective, his unwillingness to negotiate, and his directive approach regarding process.

For couple 6, the male dominance arose from his focus on the task, and consistent, logical approach. She shifted focus and perspective throughout the discussion.

Husband: OK. The reason I, you have your water and you have your food but you need something, you're out in that ninety degree heat and you can't last, you can't last more than a couple of days out there without anything covering you up. Your, your skin will burn so quickly because you have no, no sun protection.

Wife: I could see a hat, but why would you need a coat?

H: Just something to put over, over your arms and . . .

W: Well, that's why I wanted to bring the blanket.

H: OK. But that still doesn't cover your head.
W: You can put it over your head.
H: Wouldn't a coat and hat be easier?
W: No, because it's extra luggage.
H: No.
W: Yeah. Do you understand what I'm saying? I think a shovel would be more important. [Note: The shovel had not yet been mentioned.]

For couple 9, the story was different. Both became so frustrated with the activity that they resorted to coercion, rejection, and attempts to constrain one another with rules. At the end of the activity, she was so frustrated that she removed herself from the task level and shifted to relational control issues. Their discussion was unproductive on the task level and they did a poor job, but the relationship dynamic was also highly negative. She was very angry when they left the encounter.

W: No, you can't. You cannot use a coat as a tent, so you're not going to get any sun. And the hat's useless because you can put the blanket over your head.
H: You can't see and it won't shade you from the sun.
W: You're being stupid.
H: I'm not being stupid.
W: Yes you are. Because you don't just don't want to give up on this one. And you know that I'm right. Uh-huh.
H: No . . . Come on, you're not going to get angry are you?
W: No. I just think you're stupid and I'm not going to go camping with you anymore.
H: OK, does that look good then to you?
W: Except for that gun and the blanket.
H: Well, Keri, you, you always made the point to say get the gun from your dad. And I'm sticking with that because your dad's . . .
W: But they're saying what's in order. . . . Well, my dad's not Grizzly Adams.
H: No. But we always bring the gun. I think this is a good set up. OK?
W: (moves her chair back, crosses her arms, and turns away) That's fine.

These results indicate that the simple conceptualization of a decision-making sequence as male dominated may obscure unique and important variations in patterns of communication within married couples. We have similar reservations about the egalitarian and female-dominated categorizations.

Egalitarian. Six of the ten couples studied engaged in egalitarian decision making. Two of the couples were egalitarian based on compromise, two were egalitarian based on collaboration, and one was egalitarian based on accommodation and relationship maintenance rather than out of any concern for task, and the last couple was egalitarian based on competition.

Couples 3 and 5 were egalitarian based on compromise. Their patterns expressed a strong focus on cooperation and agreement. These two couples spent a great deal of time negotiating assumptions as illustrated in the excerpt below from couple 3's discussion.

> *H*: Now, food that's number two.
> *W*: Well, I don't think food's number two. I put number two as, um, the knife. Because if we run out of food, we have to have a knife so we can kill animals.
> *H*: But we're assuming, it's food. Plenty of food to get you through the desert.
> *W*: Oh, more food than you, than you can eat. This isn't just a piece of beef jerky.
> *H*: Yeah. Yeah. Like water. You need water.
> *W*: OK. Assuming we have enough food to make it through the desert . . .

Couples 2 and 4 took a collaborative approach to egalitarian decision making. Their communication was characterized by cooperation and persuasion. One characteristic of these couples was a willingness to show understanding of their partner's perspective, as this excerpt from couple 4 illustrates.

> *W*: Which one did you have for one?
> *H*: Uh, water.
> *W*: Why? Well, I thought it was gun. Because, uh, then if someone comes to steal our stuff, we, then we could kill them.
> *H*: (laughs)
> *W*: And don't you think we'd come across water, like a river or something?
> *H*: Oh, I was just playing it safe. I said water, food as one and two. Because you could always go a couple days without food but you couldn't go without water. Those guys took everything they wanted, why would they come back?
> *W*: Well, I put like gun and knife as one and two just in case.
> *H*: That's because you were scared.
> *W*: Uh-huh. (Both laugh)
> *H*: I was hungry and thirsty.

Collaborating couples also worked together on generating agreement on the use of objects as couple 2 indicate in the following excerpt.

> *H*: OK. Then after knife you had blanket. And I had . . .
> *W*: You had small shovel?
> *H*: I had small shovel.
> *W*: Why shovel?
> *H*: You can, you can dig yourself a little . . .
> *W*: Hovel, or . . .
> *H*: A little area way up, you know . . .
> *W*: In the rock for water, basically.
> *H*: Right.

Couple 7 was egalitarian/accommodating. Although their communication was positive and full of agreement, they did little on the task level in terms of discussing the use of the objects. They continually focused on agreement as evidenced by the excerpt below which occurred in the middle of a discussion about whether or not the gun would be a good signaling device in the desert.

> *H*:   OK. So what do you have? Water first?
> *W*:   Mm-hmm.
> *H*:   OK. So blanket is going to be second. Right?
> *W*:   Yeah. Yeah, that's fine.
> *H*:   OK. So blanket. We agree on all that stuff so far.

Couple 10 was egalitarian/competitive. He controlled the process by acting as recorder, she controlled the process by articulating rules about the scenario. Interestingly, both acquiesced a significant amount.

> *H*:   Four, I have knife.
> *W*:   You have knife four?
> *H*:   I'm going to arm myself to the hilt.
> *W*:   You've got, you've got your knife and your gun before your blankets and any protection.
> *H*:   Yeah. Yeah. I've got the clothes on my back.
> *W*:   You haven't taken a survival course I can tell.
> *W*:   So do you want the gun before we want the food?
> *H*:   Well, no. I didn't but I was going to take food second.
> *W*:   Let's take the food third, the gun fourth.
> *H*:   No, well, OK. That makes sense.

Clearly, the dynamics of egalitarian decision making differ depending on the foundation for negotiation. The accommodation-, competition-, compromise-, and collaboration-based couples were very different from one another although strong similarities do exist within the categorizations.

Female Dominated. Couple 8 was female dominated. Their dynamics were quite different from those of the male dominated couples. The wife and husband both focused extensively on rules on the task level, he trying to get her to compromise and she trying to avoid giving in. This couple was defined as female dominated because she did not give in and, ultimately, he did. Once she wrote a ranking down, she was unwilling to change.

> *W*:   . . . eight as small shovel, nine as a rope, and coat and hat as number ten. If you have a blanket at night, you don't really need a coat and hat so that really can be the least, the least-important item.
> *H*:   Which one?
> *W*:   Coat and hat, that would be ten.
> *H*:   That would be eight. Oh, that would be ten?
> *W*:   I had it as ten.
> *H*:   All right.
> *W*:   I have that as the least-important item because you have a blanket and a scarf.
> *H*:   And small shovel is nine?
> *W*:   I had it as just number eight, just because it's already written down.

This pattern discussion clearly illustrated the danger in assuming couples that fit into a dominance-type category share common characteristics. Although dominance is a convenient measure of who influences decision making, focusing solely on dominance to the exclusion of process dynamics, which indicate how dominance is negotiated, obscures some very real differences.

Context by Process Results: Correspondence between Perceptions and Behavior

The second research question asked if couples' perceptions of their conflict styles correspond with observer interpretations of couple communication behaviors. For five of the husbands and two of the wives, their self-report measures of conflict style in this relationship corresponded with the assessments made in the language action analysis. The husbands in couples 1, 3, 5, 6, and 10 and the wives in couples 4 and 5 communicated consistently with how they viewed themselves in this relationship. Of the other participants, the differences were startling at times. For example, the husband in couple 9 indicated that he was avoiding and accommodating in this relationship and yet demonstrated a strong competitive pattern in this exercise, whereas the wife reported a collaborative style but approached the activity as a win/loss experience. Table 1 indicates each couple by number, their self reported conflict style in their relationship, the global assessment of their style and the lag sequential assessment based on the types of strategies the couple used.

There are a number of plausible explanations for why there was not a stronger correspondence between perceptions of conflict style within the relationship and performance in this decision-making discussion. These include the argument that there is a tenuous relationship between conflict style and problem-solving style; the notion that though individuals may have a preferred method for handling conflict in a given relationship, they may make unique choices in a specific decision-making interaction; that conflict style may be impacted by the salience of the issue for relationship partners, and finally that each decision-making sequence is unique and couple patterns cannot be predicted.

Another possibility arises. Self-report measures of conflict style and communication competence served as initial context perceptions going into this decision-making situation. The process interaction in the decision-making discussions themselves generated their own unique dynamics, often very different from the expectations and perceptions the couples expressed going into the discussion. This indicates that process may supersede context in regulating behavior in marital decision making.

Additionally, the combination of decision-making and conflict style assessments yielded some interesting combinations, for example, egalitarian/competitive. Although there has been a great deal of question about what conflict style has to offer decision making inquiry, the results of this study indicate that they

Table 1
Self Report versus Language Action and Lag Sequential Analyses

Couple No.	Partner H	W	Self-Report	Language	Lag
1	X		competitive	competitive	male-dominated-control
		X	collaborative	accommodating	
2	X		competitive	collaborative	egalitarian-collaborative
		X	avoiding/accommodating	collaborative	
3	X		compromise/avoiding/ accommodating	compromise	egalitarian-collaborative
		X	collaborative/avoiding	compromise	
4	X		accommodating/avoiding	collaborative	egalitarian-collaborative
		X	competitive/collaborative	collaborative	
5	X		compromise/avoiding	compromise	egalitarian-compromise
		X	compromise	compromise	
6	X		collaborative	collaborative	male-dominated-logic
		X	collaborative	competitive	
7	X		compromise	accommodating	egalitarian-accommodating
		X	collaborative	accommodating	
8	X		avoiding/competitive/ collaborative	compromise	female-dominated-control
		X	avoiding/accommodating	competitive	
9	X		avoiding/accommodating	competitive	male-dominated-win/loss
		X	collaborative	competitive	
10	X		collaborative/compromise	compromise	egalitarian-competitive
		X	avoiding	compromise	

may inform one another such that the conflict styles paradigm may be a useful tool in clarifying marital decision-making dynamics. As Troutman and Shanteau (1989) concluded, "When spouses agree on a judgment, the joint judgment follows directly; when there is disagreement, a unique conflict-resolution process is followed" (p. 142). Clearly a unique conflict resolution process occurred with a number of these couples.

CONCLUSION AND FUTURE RESEARCH

The findings of this study indicate the need for further research into the categorization of decision-making types into dominance categories, the traditional male-dominated, female-dominated, egalitarian model. The wide variation in process dynamics demonstrated by couples within these categories leads to significant questions regarding the information lost when couples are grouped together solely on the basis of dominance. Consistent with Scanzoni and Polonko (1980), results of this study indicate the importance of process dynamics for the analysis of decision making patterns. In this inquiry, the conflict styles paradigm offered useful information regarding unique process dynamics. Context, though not fully explored in this study, needs to be examined more fully as well for its impact on decision making.

The Scanzoni and Polonko (1980) model also offers explanation for the continued discrepancy between self-assessment and third-party assessment in marital decision making. When couple perceptions differ from those of observers, it is likely that couples are responding to context, process and outcome dynamics while observers, by nature of their activity, can only focus on process and outcome. Realizing that viewing decision making within a relationship is dynamic, whereas viewing it from outside is static, brings into question the notion that participants and observers should see things the same way. A more useful conceptualization would focus on how the observations of participants and observers inform one another.

Several avenues of future research seem promising based on the results of this study. First, this study could be modified such that decision-making activities could vary on the basis of issue salience so as to assess the impact of the issue on couple decision making. Second, this study could be replicated and extended such that following the decision-making activity, (1) couples filled out an inventory designed to measure their satisfaction with the process involved in their decision making, and (2) couples reassessed themselves and their partners in terms of conflict style and communicator competence. This would allow for a clearer understanding of how context impacts process and how process in turn impacts future context.

REFERENCES

Fitzpatrick, M. 1988. *Between Husbands and Wives*. Newbury Park, CA: Sage.

Frentz, T., and T. Farrell. 1976. "Language-Action: A Paradigm for Communication." *Quarterly Journal of Speech 62*: 333–349.

Godwin, D., and J. Scanzoni. 1989a. "Couple Consensus during Marital Joint Decision Making: A Context, Process, Outcome Model." *Journal of Marriage and the Family 51* (November): 943–956.

———. 1989b. "Couple Decision Making: Commonalities and Differences across Issues and Spouses." *Journal of Family Issues 10*(3): 291–310.

Hill, W., and J. Scanzoni. 1982. "An Approach for Assessing Marital Decision-Making Processes." *Journal of Marriage and the Family 44* (November): 927–941.

Krueger, D. L. 1982. "Marital Decision Making: A Language-Action Analysis." *Quarterly Journal of Speech 68*: 273–287.

———. 1985. "Communication Patterns and Egalitarian Decision Making in Dual-Career Couples." *Western Journal of Speech Communication 49*: 126–145.

Krueger, D. L., and P. Smith. 1982. "Decision Making Patterns of Couples: A Sequential Analysis." *Journal of Communication* (summer): 121–134.

Pruitt, D. 1981. *Negotiation Behavior*. New York: Academic Press.

Raush, H. 1965. "Interaction Sequences." *Journal of Personality and Social Psychology 2*: 487–499.

———. 1972. "Process and Change: A Markov Model for Interaction." *Family Process 13*: 275–298.

Raush, H., W. Barry, R. Hertel, and M. A. Swain. 1974. *Communication, Conflict and Marriage*. San Francisco, CA: Jossey-Bass.

Rogers, L. E., and R. V. Farace. 1975. "Relational Communication Analysis: New Measurement Procedures." *Human Communication Research 1*: 222–239.

Scanzoni, J. 1989. "Joint Decision Making in the Contemporary Sexually Based Primary Relationship." In D. Brinberg and J. Jaccard, eds., *Dyadic Decision Making*. New York: Springer-Verlag, pp. 251–267.

Scanzoni, J., and K. Polonko. 1980. "A Conceptual Approach to Explicit Marital Negotiation." *Journal of Marriage and the Family 42* (February): 31–44.

Scanzoni, J., and M. Szinovacz. 1980. *Family Decision-Making: A Developmental Sex Role Model*. Beverly Hills, CA: Sage.

Thomas, E. 1977. *Marital Communication and Decision Making*. New York: Free Press.

Thomas, K. S., and R. H. Kilmann. 1974. *Thomas-Kilmann Conflict Mode Instrument*. Tuxedo, NY: Xiacom.

Troutman, C., and J. Shanteau. 1989. "Information Integration in Husband-Wife Decision Making about Health-Care Services." In D. Brinberg and J. Jaccard, eds., *Dyadic Decision Making*. New York: Springer-Verlag, pp. 117–151.

Webb, L., and D. C. Pennington. 1991. "Decision Making in Dual-Career Couples: A Re-examination." Paper presented at the annual meeting of the Speech Communication Association, Atlanta, Georgia, November.

Zietlow, P. H., and A. L. Sillars. 1988. "Life Stage Differences in Communication during Marital Conflicts." *Journal of Social and Personal Relationships 5*: 223–245.

Part VI

Power and Empowerment

In this culminating section we explore the process and experience of empowerment, the ways in which people construe, acquire, and transform power. The chapters in this section explore psychological, physical, rhetorical, spiritual, and moral empowerment. Some of the chapters present, as a most desirable expression of empowerment, models based on traditional masculine values, whereas others question those values and posit a transformative notion of empowerment.

In chapter 20 Victoria DeFrancisco and Angela Allison-Faber examine the relationship between power and self-esteem. The authors raise the question of whether the very emphasis on self-esteem in our society is another reflection of the social construction of gender which favors the qualities and the values of masculinity. In identifying the social ideologies which influence the focus on self-esteem, DeFrancisco and Allison-Faber point to some of the following questions: How is self-esteem defined, and how is that definition presented as a generic concept rather than as framed by race, class, gender, and sexuality? Do women appear to be less powerful because they lack the type of self-esteem and the type of power that is "privileged" in our society? How does a focus on improving self-esteem "divert attention from the very social factors which helped to construct the low self-esteem, and particularly from men's abuse of power"? Perhaps we mistake egoism and selfishness for self-esteem and assume that domination and control are the most important types of power. We may need to ask different questions which do not just focus on the individual self and its assertions, accomplishments, and attitudes, but rather expand our understanding to include a more communal, relational, and ultimately more political definition of personal power.

Roberta L. Kosberg and Andrew S. Rancer explore the connection between power and a traditional male model of rhetoric interpreted as argumentativeness. Although Kosberg and Rancer differentiate between argumentativeness, which they characterize as constructive, and verbal aggressiveness, which they identify as destructive, their work rests on the assumption that some degree of argumentativeness is a trait or predisposition which individuals possess. The argumentativeness that is associated with masculinity is assumed to be a valuable skill, the acquisition of which can help to liberate and empower women. They examine the type of personal empowerment which they claim comes from training women to argue effectively. Their work leads us to question whether and why argumentative behaviors are culturally determined. Does argumentativeness privilege masculine attributes by defining power as the ability to win arguments? A further interrogation of rhetorical styles might go beyond the bipolar options of being either winners or losers of verbal contests in order to explore new roles, relationships, and forms of power for men and women.

Mary-Jeanette Smythe looks at the empowerment of women in terms of their physical, literal power over their own bodies in her research on women at a local health club. These women use "strategic storytelling" in order to motivate themselves to exercise; by shaping their bodies, they are constructing new selves. In Smythe's ethnographic study she explores the ways in which individual storytellers' narratives "defined a social reality and negotiated identity management." Personal narratives make meaning and organize experience. Smythe's research demonstrates the performative, collaborative, and sociopolitical dimensions of personal narratives which are co-constructed within a speech community. Smythe's description of the "Nautilus narratives" raises questions about the current cultural obsession with fitness and beauty which reflects the Cartesian need to "master" the physical self. Though the chapter does not directly address this issue, it provokes important questions about whether this emphasis on power over the body is necessarily liberating. Is the hidden assumption that women need to be more like men in exercising greater control over body and mind? Just as DeFrancisco and Allison-Faber interrogate the gendered notions of power in their examination of self-esteem, Smythe's ethnography of a fitness culture suggests questions about whether a particular type of physical power is itself socially constructed and gendered.

Linda A. M. Perry's chapter on women's spirituality describes her own concrete experience of empowerment in personal, intimate, and subjective terms. Perry contends that "one's ability to acquire emotional or physical health can be limited by overreliance on external agencies such as the medical field . . . [and] can be reclaimed through attitudinal change and visualization." She attempts to articulate an alternative model of healing which challenges the disembodied paradigm usually associated with a mechanistic model of health. In restoring her own health, she invokes the power of the women-centered goddess tradition in order to discover attitudes and images that are conducive to physical and psychic well-being. Although Perry points to the transformative power of what she describes as women's spirituality, it is important to remember that there are multiple paths outside of traditional religious and theological institutions to explore spiritual empowerment. Because religious and medical institutions tend to be patriarchal, hierarchical, and reductive, Perry's contribution helps us to envision new forms of believing and healing.

In the final chapter, Linda Longmire and Timothy H. Smith further explore an alternative, "postmodern" paradigm which sees our understanding of power as part of a larger set of modernist categories which have shaped discursive practices since the Enlightenment. This modernist paradigm has emphasized competitive individualism rather than community, narrow technical rationality rather than additional ways of knowing, and a mechanistic rather than organic view of the human condition. All of these categories imply a view of power that emphasizes domination, mastery, control—in short, power over self, others, and nature. In looking at moral development as a form of empowerment, many of these same modernist biases apply, according to the authors. An alternative view which emphasizes subtle, cooperative, and relational forms of power is more consistent with a feminist view of moral development. Genuine empowerment and transformation will require untying the knots that connect power and masculinity. Only by deconstructing gendered notions, institutions, and discourses of power can we create spaces from which alternative voices and visions can emerge.

20

A Feminist Guide to Studying
Self-Esteem in Communication

Victoria DeFrancisco and Angela Allison-Faber

Newsweek Magazine called self-esteem the "latest national elixir. . . . [It] is supposed to cure everything from poor grades to bad management" (Adler et al. 1992, p. 46). The authors of the article cite a range of applications of the concept with a variety of claims: a man sought in Montgomery County, Maryland, for a series of rapes was described as "in his 30s with a medium build and 'low self-esteem'" (p. 46). Churches have begun to use the phrase "low self-esteem" instead of sin because it's less likely to turn-off their members (p. 46). Businesses have found raising self-esteem is a "more effective" [read cheaper] way of raising productivity than providing financial incentives (p. 47). In education, the concept has been embraced as a cure-all to raise grades and lower drug abuse, teen pregnancies, and violence. In fact, California State Assembly representative, John Vasconcellos has promoted statewide task forces to raise self-esteem, similar plans have now been adopted by five other states.

Women, more than any other group, have become the primary target of this issue. The focus on women is particularly apparent in the popular self-help literature. Previous researchers have established that women are the target audience of this multi-million dollar-business, purchasing 75 percent to 85 percent of the products. This is apparent in everything from the titles (e.g., *Women Who Love Too Much* [Norwood 1985]), to the advice women are often given to essentially become more "masculine" (be independent, aggressive, etc., see De-Francisco 1995.) In these cases men are still portrayed as the norm of good mental health and women as sub-standard or deviant. Low self-esteem is blamed for everything from eating disorders, to codependency, to failure to get and keep a man. This is not to say women's eating disorders or failed relationships are unrelated to low self-esteem. What we *are* saying is that superficial analysis of these problems for women, as seems to be more and more prevalent, leads readers to the inevitable inference that it's "all the woman's fault." The focus is placed on the individual rather than the social forces that teach her to internalize a low self-image.

There are more in-depth studies of women and self-esteem, such as that conducted on young girls and education by the American Association of University Women (AAUW) (1992), which received national coverage and generated further essays, research and discussion in academic and public forums. Gilligan, Lyons, and Hamner's (1989) research on girls and how adolescence affects them differently (and generally more negatively) than boys has helped to raise awareness of the female relationship to self-esteem, as well as Steinem's (1992b) more popular depiction of the issue.

Given the great deal of attention focusing specifically on women's low self-esteem, and the more in-depth communication research which is still needed, we feel it is important to step back and reflect on the basic nature of this topic before we as researchers proceed under the assumption that the focus is inherently good. In our search for criteria to conduct this reflection and analysis we found an article by Lana Rakow (1987) raised relevant questions as she discussed feminist ethics in communication research: "If gender researchers do not undertake a self-conscious appraisal of what they are doing and why, gender research will continue to produce contradictory findings that shed little light on the means of women's oppression and the means for its transformation" (Rakow 1987, p. 79).

The questions she raised and the critical points she made have become our feminist consciousness, so to speak, and we would like to share those fundamental, wise words with others who strive as feminist scholars in the communication field. This chapter is not meant to be a comprehensive review of the self-esteem literature. Instead, we apply three basic questions Rakow used in her article to challenge feminist scholars in communication.[1] These questions allow us to identify social ideology which influence the focus on low self-esteem; common assumptions implicit in such a focus; and what a continued journey down this research path might hold in store.

"WHY AM I DOING THIS RESEARCH?"

In raising this question, Rakow (1987, p. 79) makes the point that feminist research is personally based, and the goal of such research should be to unveil social conditions which oppress women and to improve women's conditions. In research on self-esteem, the answer to this question may at first seem obvious. We know firsthand that self-esteem is at the heart of learned helplessness, internalized second class citizenship and justifications for oppression. Rakow points out that in gender research, "We are what we research" and "We should not try to disguise this connection or pretend it does not exist" (p. 79). We interpret this to mean that as researchers we should be ready to reveal our own personal experiences related to the topic. Researchers' so-called objectivity is to be questioned, not used to hide behind. When Gloria Steinem (1992b) attempted to write about women and self-esteem, she had to abandon her first impersonal attempts and put her history of struggles with body image and abuse center stage in her analysis. While many have criticized her focus and even suggested she "sold out" as a feminist (Sternhell 1992) by focusing on women's low self-esteem instead of men's abuse of power, her efforts to place herself in the focus of analysis are exemplary.

How many of us are examining self-esteem not just because we care about others, but because we have personal investments in the topic? As graduate students and teachers, we've heard countless women in academia voice words similar to: "I am waiting for someone to find out I'm a fake. I am not really as qualified as I sound." What are the implications of such personal investments in our research?

Before we began writing this chapter, we found it necessary to discuss our personal histories with self-esteem struggles and consider how these may influence not only the directions of our joint research and writing, but also how these struggles at times may create psychological barriers to considering other research and writing options. The irony of attempting to write about low self-esteem as we procrastinated and experienced writer's block was often hilarious and deadly.

As feminist theory informs us, these personal investments do not have to be obstacles in our work, they can actually be sources of knowledge and insights. For example, we know from a personal level that this topic *does* matter, and that our experience can offer guidance as we proceed. Our personal experiences make us acutely sensitive to popular interpretations that women's low self-esteem is portrayed as women's fault and women's responsibility to correct. Our experience makes us cautious of research which identifies discriminatory be-havior, yet fails to examine possible effects on the receivers' self-esteem or to explore solutions on a societal level. As Dale Spender noted, the causes of women's low self-esteem are all around us, what we need now is to identify strategies that work to improve it (personal correspondence, May 20, 1992).

"WHAT ARE MY ASSUMPTIONS THAT NEED TO BE QUESTIONED?"[2]

Definitions

There is a presumption that the concept of self-esteem is commonly defined and understood. Given this, we were surprised to find an apparent lack of comprehensive or consistent definitions of self-esteem. The inference seems to be that we all know what self-esteem is, we are all lacking it, so let's get to work improving it! Yet, in a survey conducted by the National Council of Self-Esteem (yes, there is one!), a pool of only 100 teachers reported using twenty-seven different definitions of self-esteem (Adler et al. 1992).

Most definitions of self-esteem are very brief and read like those in introductory textbooks. Pearson and Nelson (1991) provide one such definition: "self-image is descriptive, while our self-esteem includes evaluative feelings that bear some relationship to our self-image. Self-esteem is how we feel about ourselves, how well we like ourselves" (p. 53). Many definitions focus on self-esteem as the degree to which we are satisfied with ourselves, have confidence and pride in ourselves (Rubenstein 1992). Thus, though definitions are vague and vary, the concept tends to have a very individualistic, psychological focus. Common definitions fail to note that self-concept and self-esteem are largely derived from internalized social ideology. As with gender, race, age, ethnicity and social class, self-esteem is a social construction.

Characteristics of High Self-Esteem

Given that self-esteem is a cultural product, it is not surprising that the characteristics commonly associated with high self-esteem are considered masculine and reflective of white middle-class U.S. values. The concept can be traced back to the father of misogynist psychological therapy himself—Freud (although he used the term *ego-ideal* rather than *self-esteem*) (Adler et al. 1992). Since we now know that his concept of mental health was generally male biased, it follows that being female was seen as inconsistent with an ego-ideal. The way white middle-class U.S. men of European descent tend to answer the question of self-satisfaction has become the generic definition of self-esteem. In contrast, high self-esteem for many women has traditionally meant being "humble," and "self-effacing," otherwise women have been considered "vain" and "arrogant" (Sanford and Donovan 1984, p. 4). And in Japanese cultures, "American men's naked self-assurance" may be seen as immature and boastful (Rubenstein 1992).

Defining Adolescence

The Eurocentric male bias regarding high self-esteem means that our assumptions about adolescence—the process of developing self-image—are also biased. In white middle-class U.S. cultures, developing high self-esteem and becoming an adult are almost synonymous with independence (Allgood-Merten and Stockard 1991). Prior to Nancy Chodorow's (1978) and Carol Gilligan's (1982) theoretical work, maturity was commonly defined in male terms—growing toward independence. In contrast, Chodorow (1978), in her well-known work, explained this socialization process as different for males and females, according to their relationship with their mothers. Because mothers and daughters share more similarities than mothers and sons, the daughters experience more relationship continuity. Mothers and sons experience more difference, and thus self-definitions become a process of valuing individuality. The result is gendered differences in self-esteem. Women may view the self in a "collectiv-ist, ensembled or connected schema," and males may view the self in an "individualistic, independent or autonomous schema" (Josephs, Markus, and Tafarodi 1992, p. 391). Although not everyone agrees with Chodorow's expla-nation, the socially presumed alignment of men and independence versus women and relationship does exist. When researchers fail to recognize the likelihood of differing views of self, women are the ones who suffer, given the male model as the norm.

In a comparative study of self-esteem using fourth, ninth and twelfth graders, researchers found the younger participants associated both self-efficacy (masculinity) and relationality (femininity) with self esteem. However, the majority of older participants did not view relationality as a part of self-esteem (Allgood-Mertin and Stockard 1991). The researchers concluded that "coming of age for young women in postindustrial society brings with it a double-bind—a marked devastation of that which is female . . . which makes it very difficult to feel good about oneself" (p. 137).

The paradox of maturity for women is illustrated in Gilligan and associates' (1989) study of girls' psychological development over a three-year period of time. Based primarily on interview data, the researchers concluded that adolescent development for girls is a crisis of "connection," and not "separa-tion" as psychologists have traditionally described adolescence. "For girls to remain responsive to themselves, they must resist the conventions of feminine goodness, to remain responsive to others (and thus be feminine), they must resist the values placed on self-sufficiency and independence in North American culture" (p. 10). Gilligan and her associates then proceed to show through a series of interview studies how girls caught in this dilemma may "go underground"—repress their knowledge, disassociate from others, and buy into patriarchal definitions of what it means to be a feminine adult, risking depres-sion, eating disorders, and low self-esteem.

Self-Esteem a Universal Women's Problem?

Just as the definition of high self-esteem has been falsely presented as a generic concept, we question whether women's universal experience with low self-esteem has been just as falsely presented. For example, is the phenomenon as commonly studied primarily the experience of white middle-class women? The AAUW's (1992) study reported African American girls in elementary school maintained higher levels of self-esteem than girls of Northern European decent, and that Hispanic girls suffered most from low self-esteem. Unfor-tunately, the African American girls' so-called success with self-esteem seemed to be achieved by disassociating themselves from school. One explanation for these differing results is that, historically, African American women could not afford the "luxury" of self-effacement. In a culture where they are often single parents and face the double oppressions of racism and sexism, African American women have to present themselves as confident (Hawe 1991). Another explanation is that oppressed persons learn coping strategies to protect their self-esteem in a hostile environment through impression management, behavioral flexibility and/or shifting their point of comparison to a nondominant group (Crocker and Major 1989; Hawe 1991). This does not necessarily mean the members of socially oppressed group are free of low self-esteem (see for example, the Hispanic girls in the AAUW study), it may simply indicate more complex and varied explanations for low self-esteem than we may have realized (D'Souza 1991).

Feminists' Study of Self-Esteem

Given the false assumptions regarding definitions of high self-esteem, its characteristics, and development, an additional assumption comes into question. Should feminist research even be focusing on self-esteem?

Obviously, we do not want to contribute to a field of study where traditional masculine definitions yield research that portrays women as deficient and as individually responsible for self-improvement. Research that focuses on the individual may divert attention from the very social factors which helped to construct the low self-esteem and particularly from men's abuse of power. The challenge becomes one of how to avoid contributing to this view if we wish to study self-esteem. This question is particularly pertinent since Gloria Steinem received criticism of her analysis on the topic (see for example Sternhell 1992). We feel the difference between Steinem's book and so many of the more common self-help books is her documentation of the ways in which self-esteem is socially created and her identification of the institutional influences of media, education, government, family, religion, and business which create and maintain male dominance and power. Steinem's assessment clearly shows the reader that one's self-esteem is not created in an apolitical vacuum.

To take the question further regarding whether feminists should study self-esteem and exactly how we might do that, we ask why the research is focused on women's self-esteem while practically ignoring men's self-esteem? We know why a particular culture has focused on women's so-called problem, but perhaps it is time for feminists to unveil men's low self-esteem as well. It seems that generally when low self-esteem is discussed in relationship to men, it is discussed as a "human" problem, rather than as men's unique problem. In contrast, when low self-esteem is discussed in relationship to women, the assumption is the problem is unique to women. Women and men may benefit from documenting certain men's motives and vulnerabilities. It would reveal men's relative privilege to act out in violent ways—as ego defensive. Although women often internalize their feelings of inadequacy, Steinem (1992a) suggests hate crimes, dictatorships, and global politics in general may be linked to individual men's problems with low self-esteem, as was true with Nazi war criminal Adolf Eichmann, and his subsequent abuse of power. She has been criticized for reducing global problems to issues of self-esteem and for masking men's abuse of power behind a focus on low self-image. As Dianne Post (1992) wrote in response to Steinem's *Ms.* essay, "Men don't beat because they lack self-esteem, they beat because of excess power" (p. 6). We suggest both views may be correct. As with women's self-esteem, men's is also socially created, but that creation is one related to their social status as aggressor and dominator of women. Thus, acts of violence and domination are legitimized and depoliticized through social self-images of manhood. The construction of women *and* men's self esteems are patriarchal tools.

Another consideration is that implicit in the assumption that feminists should study self-esteem is the expectation that we can redefine the concept to more positively reflect women's values (see, for example, Mulqueen 1992). As researchers, we went down this road and read for example, with great pride that many women value relationship connections more than independence. Indeed, when self-esteem measures are created to assess this value instead of independence, women's self-esteem is found to be higher than men's (Rubenstein 1992). But in our soul searching and discussions with university women students, we were also reminded that connection is not the only primary value women hold which seems different from many men. And, it is not free of more powerful social constraints. In a survey of over 600 women across the United States, the four most significant factors which contributed to women's self-esteem were (in order of importance): satisfied with body and looks; have paid work; see work as a career; and rate self as very attractive, none of which were in the top four for the men surveyed. A feminine characterization of high self-esteem based on traditional values includes not only relationship skills, but comparisons of one's own body to social ideals, and women's internalization of capitalistic values (in the case of the United States). These values have been used as tools to oppress women (Wolfe 1991), but however problematic the values are, feminist attempts to exclude them in redefing self-esteem may risk alienating the very persons we intend to reach.

Finally, we must remember that even if we are able to redefine the concept, it is difficult to truly make it feminist—meaning to value different points of view and qualities. The very nature of the concept self-esteem is *prescriptive* as it is a socially constructed ideal on which we base personal evaluations. Robin Dillion (1992) is one feminist scholar who has attempted to address this dilemma with a related term, *self-respect*. She made the point that traditional connotations are also laiden with values of perfectionism, thus trapping women who aspire to attain traditional views of self-respect. Her reinterpretation calls for a woman to respect her "limitations and imperfections" rather than "pummel herself into likeness and commonality" (p. 60). She places self-understanding, acceptance, and relationship at the heart of a feminist conception of self-respect.

"WHAT IS THE BEST METHODOLOGY FOR ME TO USE?"

Rakow (1987) challenges feminist researchers to study "real women in their real contexts" (p. 81). In contrast, the vast majority of research on self-esteem has used psychological scales for assessment in laboratory settings. Related to the lack of a common definition, discussed previously, a review of research on self-esteem reveals that in over 10,000 scientific studies on the concept, more than 200 different instruments were used (Adler et al. 1992, p. 48). These scales use either a global assessment or are situation specific. The global refers to a person's general feelings of self-worth, goodness, health, attractiveness, and social competence in a single summary score (e.g., Rosenberg 1965), and has been criticized for producing ambiguous results (Harter 1990, pp. 365–366). Sex differences occur in scales that use situation specific indicators, but these results are largely stereotypic with women rating themselves higher on relationship and morality issues and men rating themselves higher on persuasiveness, dominance, capacity to withstand stress, and "giftedness" (Stake 1992, p. 351). One might ask, then, does a person's score have any meaning separate from traditional gender-role attributes, and do results simply measure how well one has internalized such gender expectations through the self-reports?

Critics have also pointed out that the actual rating method of standard scales may be sexist. Carin Rubenstein (1992) notes that asking women to rate how strongly they agree or disagree with a self-focused statement (e.g., "On the whole, I am satisfied with myself") is incompatible with the value of modesty that many women have been raised to express (p. 59). Thus studies which use such scales may inaccurately conclude women have lower self-esteem.

While we do realize the value of structured surveys, the studies we found most useful were informed by feminist theory and combined methodologies, in particular they utilized interview and ethnographic methods over a period of time (e.g., Gilligan et al. 1989; Holland and Eisenhart 1990). These methods allowed the participants to define the concept on their own terms and to render it more meaningful for themselves and the observers.

This chapter paper grew out of preparations to conduct our own study of women's self-esteem. Initially, we too intended to use established scales to be able to obtain a broader picture of the status of women on our campus. However, after reviewing this material, we began to question the proposed methods. Instead, we have begun the study by asking women students to talk with us confidentially about experiences they have had with discrimination or discomfort in the classroom. Thus far we have interviewed only a few, all of whom described discriminatory and discomforting behavior and how these experiences made them feel. Their descriptions tell a great deal more than scales could about how these women define self-esteem in a given context and the barriers they face in developing and maintaining positive self-esteem.

Common words mentioned were feelings of being "excluded," "ignored," and "put down." In discussing their responses to the sexism they stressed the need to "put up with it," "take it with a grain of salt." And their emotional responses were similarly inhibited, "It feels like [I'm] holding back," "a lack of confidence," "very hesitant, about like when we have stuff to turn in," "I write different for him" (because she knows his prejudice).

These few comments yield concrete pictures of how discriminatory behaviors may affect the receivers' self-esteem and what is the nature of these individuals' experiences with low self-esteem. They are context-dependent and relationship-specific definitions.

Results from another small qualitative study of women at two southern universities, one predominantly attended by white students, the other predominantly African American, remind us that the best methodologies for this research are ones that take into account not only the immediate social context, such as the classroom, but the participants' other realities. Holland and Eisenhart (1990) found that what happened in the classroom mattered relatively little to the women studied. Prestige (as defined by their peer group) was not gained from academic successes, involvement in student organizations or political causes, or from relations with other women; prestige came only from their success in romantic relations with men (p. 90). These findings suggest, for example, research on girls' self-esteem in education which focuses only on classroom interaction may yield narrow views and may, in fact, be a case of misplaced emphasis. This does not mean classroom experiences are totally unimportant. The point is, we as educators must be careful not to fool ourselves into thinking the classroom is the essence of a college student's experience. Instead, compulsory and "successful" heterosexuality is *central* in the problem of formal education failing women! Self-esteem is a multifaceted social construct.

When we begin to see such connections, we begin to recognize a wider variety of means to address the problem at hand. As Gilligan and associates' (1989) research points out, we must listen to what young girls and women have to tell us about their everyday strategies in psychological survival. When these researchers did so, they found young women were resolving the dilemma of connection/independence in adolescence. They were not only able to resolve the seeming contradictions between growing up feminine (connection) and becoming an adult (independence), they actually prospered psychologically through the seeming opposite values (Stern 1989). They described their ability to be independent as fostering their ability to care and monitor relationships with others. "In reducing preoccupation with receiving care, these women report a heightened capacity to look outside themselves and attend to others. At the same time, relationships provide the support one needs to push one's own development further" (p. 85). Contrary to common assumptions that independence and connection are presumed to be polar opposites, they viewed them as interdependent and mutually nurturing qualities. We believe research methods that elicit the participants' views of self-esteem will allow us to better identify the varied communicative acts which contribute to the development of positive self-esteem.

CONCLUSION

The process of developing this paper was a personal experience in the frustration of examining women's self-esteem. We hoped to find information which would help us in refining our own forthcoming research project. The process was disappointing in that we found no cure-alls for our personal struggles and other women's struggles with self-esteem. Furthermore, we found the dilemmas in this area of research resemble walking through a mine field of patriarchal tools!

The questions Lana Rakow (1987) posed forced us to examine not just the relevance of the topic, but our goals in such study, our methods of analysis, and where such research might lead. We discovered firsthand that one should not proceed with research in this area under the presumption that information gained will be inherently good. We hope the paper has served as a reminder that feminist research must be self-reflective and that the field of self-esteem is fraught with sexist, ethnocentric presumptions.

In general, we found the issue of women's self-esteem ripe for continued feminist analysis. The following are suggestions for this research. First, we must use methods which do not impose definitions of self-esteem on the individual. Second, we need methods which take into account the multiple, interdependent experiences and values which affect one's self-esteem. Third, we must keep in mind unique, yet interrelated influences according to one's race, ethnicity, sexuality, social class, age, and so on. Fourth, our research should make visible the power and danger of compulsory heterosexuality in individuals' evaluations of self-worth. And fifth, we should make visible links between communication acts of sexism and the potential damage they cause to girls' and women's self-esteem.

Perhaps most important, the assumptions examined in this chapter remind us that "it's not all our fault." It is understandable for women to struggle with low self-esteem in a culture where they are defined as "other." It *is* a hostile environment, as a student in our interviews illustrated in describing a class with one male instructor in accounting:

He used to be a football star. He uses lots of football examples. If the guy's in sports, he knows it. If girls are, he doesn't. . . . I feel like I shouldn't be taking the class. I'm not good enough for the class. I'm not meant to be in the class because I don't know how to play football. I get the feeling that he's putting up with the women being there cause they have to be there.

ACKNOWLEDGMENT

Special thanks to Cynthia Goatley of the University of Northern Iowa for her invaluable editing suggestions on an earlier draft of this paper.

NOTES

1. Lana F. Rakow, "Looking to the Future: Five Questions for Gender Research," *Women's Studies in Communication 10 (*1987): 80. Rakow raised five questions in her original piece. The two questions we do not discuss in this paper are "Is my research informed by feminist theory?" (p. 80), and "What are my own subjectivities?" (p. 81). We have integrated these issues throughout the paper.

2. Ibid., p. 80.

REFERENCES

Adler, Jerry, Pat Wingert, Lynda Wright, Patrick Houston, Howard Manly, and Alden D. Cohen. 1992. "Hey, I'm Terrific." *Newsweek* (February): 46–51.

Allgood-Merten, Betty, and Jean Stockard. 1991. "Sex Role Identity and Self-Esteem: A Composition of Children and Adolescents." *Sex Roles 25*(3/4): 129–139.

American Association of University Women. 1992. *Shortchanging Girls, Shortchanging America: A Call to Action*. Washington, DC: Author.

Chodorow, Nancy. 1978. *The Reproduction of Mothering*. Berkeley: University of California Press.

Crocker, Jennifer, and Brenda Major. 1989. "Social Stigma and Self-Esteem: The Self-Protective Properties of Stigma." *Psychological Review 96*(4): 608–630.

D'Souza, Dinesh. 1991. *Illiberal Education: The Politics of Race and Sex on Campus*. New York: Free Press.

DeFrancisco, Victoria. 1995. "A Feminist Critique of Self-Help in Heterosexual Romance: Read 'em and Weep." *Women's Studies in Communication 18* (fall): 217–227.

Dillon, Robin S. 1992. "Toward a Feminist Conception of Self-Respect." *Hypatia 7*(1): 52–69.

Gilligan, Carol. 1982. *In a Different Voice*. Cambridge, MA: Harvard University Press.

Gilligan, Carol, Nona P. Lyons, and Trudy J. Hanmer. 1989. *Making Connections: The Relational Worlds of Adolescent Girls at Emma Willard School*. Cambridge, MA: Harvard University Press.

Harter, Susan. 1990. "Self and Identity Development." In S. Shirley Feldman and Glen R. Elliott, eds., *At the Threshold: The Developing Adolescent*. Cambridge, MA: Harvard University Press, pp. 352–387.

Hawe, Kaye F. 1991. "Interactions of Gender and Race—A Problem for Teachers? A Review of the Emerging Literature." *Educational Research 33*(1): 12–21.

Holland, Dorothy, C., and Margaret A. Eisenhart. 1990. *Educated in Romance: Women, Achievement, and College Culture*. Chicago: University of Chicago Press.

Josephs, Robert A., Hazel Rose Markus, and Romin W. Tafarodi. 1992. "Gender and Self-Esteem." *Journal of Personality and Social Psychology 63*(3): 391–402.

Mulqueen, Maggie. 1992. *On Our Own Terms: Redefining Competence and Femininity*. Albany: State University of New York Press.

Norwood, Robin. 1985. *Women Who Love Too Much*. Los Angeles, CA: Jeremy P. Tarcher.

Pearson, Judy, and Paul Nelson. 1991. *Understanding and Sharing*. Dubuque, IA: Wm. C. Brown.

Post, Dianne. 1992. "Letter to the Editor." *Ms.* 2(5): 6–7.

Rakow, Lana F. 1987. "Looking to the Future: Five Questions for Gender Research." *Women's Studies in Communication 10*: 79–86.

Rosenberg, M. 1965. *Society and the Adolescent Self-Image.* Princeton, NJ: Princeton University Press.

Rubenstein, Carin. 1992. "New Woman's Report on Self-Esteem." *New Woman* (October): 58–66.

Sanford, Linda Tschirhart, and Mary Ellen Donovan. 1984. *Women and Self-Esteem: Understanding and Improving the Way We Think and Feel about Ourselves.* New York: Penguin Books.

Stake, Jayne E. 1992. "Gender Differences and Similarities in Self-Concept within Everyday Life Contexts." *Psychology of Women Quarterly 16*: 349–363.

Steinem, Gloria. 1992a. "Gross National Self-Esteem." *Ms. 11*(3): 24–30.

———. 1992b. *Revolution from Within: A Book of Self-Esteem.* Boston: Little, Brown.

Stern, Lori. 1989. "Conceptions of Separation and Connection in Female Adolescents." In Carol Gilligan, Nona P. Lyons, and Trudy J. Hanmer, eds., *Making Connections: The Relational Worlds of Adolescent Girls at Emma Willard School.* Cambridge, MA: Harvard University Press, pp. 73–87.

Sternhell, Carol. 1992. "Sic transit Gloria." *Women's Review of Books 9*(9): 5.

Wolfe, Naomi. 1991. *The Beauty Myth: How Images of Beauty Are Used against Women.* New York: William Morrow.

21

Enhancing Argumentativeness and Argumentative Behavior: The Influence of Gender and Training

Roberta L. Kosberg and Andrew S. Rancer

Argumentative communication has been a subject of study since antiquity. From Aristotle's *Rhetoric* to contemporary theoretical perspectives on argumentation, the communication discipline has considered arguing a constructive communication activity and has sought to understand argumentative behavior in the context of ongoing interpersonal, group, and organizational relationships.

ARGUMENTATIVENESS AND ARGUMENTATIVE BEHAVIOR

The predisposition "argumentativeness" has received considerable attention from communication scholars over the last decade. Dowling and Flint state, "Few concepts and measures have received as much attention in communication journals in recent years as Infante and Rancer's argumentativeness and its measure, the Argumentativeness Scale."[1]

One approach to understanding argumentative behavior is to focus on the underlying trait or predisposition to engage in argument. Argumentativeness is conceptualized as a form of aggressive communication, as is assertiveness, hostility, and verbal aggressiveness. Argumentativeness and assertiveness are placed on the constructive side of the aggressive communication continuum, whereas hostility and verbal aggressiveness are placed along the destructive side of the continuum. As argumentativeness is a subset of assertiveness, verbal aggressiveness is a subset of hostility.

Argumentativeness is defined as a generally stable trait which predisposes individuals in communicative situations to advocate positions on controversial issues and refute the positions others take on those issues.[2] The general trait "to be argumentative" (ARGgt) is conceptualized as a function of two competing motivational tendencies: motivation to approach arguments (ARGap) and motivation to avoid arguments (ARGav). The more the approach motivation exceeds the avoidance motivation, the more the individual is argumentative. Argumentativeness is conceptually and empirically distinguished from verbal aggressiveness.[3] In verbal aggression, the locus of the attack is on the individual, instead of, or in addition to, the controversial issue. Verbal aggression includes character or competence attacks, profanity, teasing, threats, and nonverbal emblems.

BENEFITS OF ARGUMENTATIVENESS

Research reveals several benefits of high motivation to argue. Arguing stimulates curiosity and increases learning because individuals tend to seek out information on the issues about which they argue. Arguing reduces egocentric thinking and forces individuals to explore issues from multiple perspectives.[4] Moreover, arguing enhances social perspective taking.[5]

Individuals high in argumentativeness, when compared with individuals low in argumentativeness, are perceived as more dynamic, more expert, and more interested in communication; these individuals also demonstrate more argumentative skill.[6] High argumentatives are less likely to be provoked into verbal aggression.[7] High motivation and skill in arguing have also been related to perceptions of communicative competence.[8] Perceived communicator credibility has been associated with higher levels of argumentativeness.[9] Infante found that influencing women to be more argumentative resulted in increased credibility.[10] Leadership in group situations has also been associated with high argumentativeness.[11]

Being high in trait argumentativeness also appears to have benefits in the organizational context. Subordinates report greater job satisfaction when they perceived their superiors to be high in argumentativeness and low in verbal aggressiveness.[12] Superiors who were higher in trait argumentativeness also reported higher salaries and more job satisfaction.[13]

A theory of independent-mindedness has emerged which suggests that argumentative communication can have benefits for both superiors and subordinates in organizations, as long as one argues organizational issues with an "affirming communication style."[14]

SEX, GENDER, AND ARGUMENTATIVENESS

Research reveals interesting and significant sex differences relating to argumentative behavior. Focusing more broadly on the modes of conflict resolution likely to be used by adolescent males and females, Roloff and Greenberg found that males reported that they were more likely to rely on antisocial modes of conflict resolution than females, including such behaviors as physical aggression, revenge (hate, lie, cheat, or take something from the person), and verbal aggression (trick, shout, insult, threaten the person); females were more likely to report preferences for prosocial (feel sorry, forgive, talk, persuade) and regression (cry, plead, worry) modes of conflict resolution than males.[15]

In a study examining the impact of gender on persuasive communication, Andrews found that females and males used different types of arguments; males more than females tended to advance established criterion-based arguments, whereas females often invented their own arguments, focusing on the theme of maintaining family relationships significantly more than men.[16] These results are consistent with Tannen's conclusions about differences between male and female behaviors. Tannen explains that women tend to argue from experience or argue propositions of value or policy, whereas males tend to argue propositions of fact and make categorical statements about right and wrong.[17]

It is significant to note that Andrews found that both males and females adapted to the gender of the confederate listener in selecting their arguments. This was supported by the research of Papa and Natalle, whose study on the effect of gender on strategy selection and satisfaction with conflict revealed that the gender composition of the research interactants during the argumentative discussion had a significant effect on the selection of argumentative strategies.[18]

As noted earlier, argumentativeness has been conceptualized as a construction and beneficial predisposition. Recent research in the specific area of trait argumentativeness reveals important and consistent sex differences. Several theoretical perspectives have been suggested to account for these sex differences in aggressive communication predispositions. The social learning paradigm suggests that males have been conditioned to be more dominant, assertive, and competitive than females. The influence of culture has also been suggested as a powerful factor influencing aggressive communication. Females may be discouraged from argumentative behavior because such behavior may be incompatible with prevailing cultural sex-role expectations and entrenched dominance-submission patterns. Burgoon, Dillard, and Doran note that because verbal aggression is less socially sanctioned for females, females may develop stronger inhibitions toward this form of aggressive communication. Bonaguro and Pearson speculate that females may view arguing as a stressful activity, thereby avoiding the behavior.[19]

Regardless of the explanation, the research reveals that women are significantly lower in trait argumentativeness. Infante found that males were significantly more argumentative than females.[20] Schultz and Anderson administered the argumentativeness scale in their study examining the role of argument in negotiation and found that women were consistently overrepresented in the low-argumentative tail of the normal distribution curve.[21] Rancer and Dierks-Stewart extended Infante's research and discovered that unlike previous research, their investigation did not find significant differences in trait argumentativeness when individuals were classified by biological sex. However, their finding focused on differences in argumentativeness when males and females were classified according to psychological gender orientation. Individuals classified as instrumental (masculine) were significantly higher in trait argumentativeness than individuals classified as expressive (feminine), androgynous, or undifferentiated.[22]

Rancer and Baukus sought to further explore the issue of sex differences by studying how the variables of sex and trait argumentativeness influence individuals' belief about arguing. They concluded that, in general, males and females differ in their belief structures about arguing; to a greater degree, females hold the belief that arguing is a hostile, combative communication activity. In addition, to a greater degree, females more than males believe that an argument is a strategy for controlling and/or dominating another individual.[23] Infante continued this line of investigating sex differences in trait argumentativeness by examining sex differences in response to an argumentative situation. He found that in an argumentative discussion, when an adversary responded argumentatively, male and female subjects did not differ in their preference for message strategies. However, when the adversary responded with verbal aggression, male and female subjects differed in their responses; female subjects were more likely to select an argumentative strategy, while male subjects were more likely to select verbally aggressive strategies.[24]

ENHANCING TRAIT ARGUMENTATIVENESS IN WOMEN

Given the differences between males and females in trait argumentativeness and the benefits of argumentativeness as suggested by research, researchers have explored means of increasing and enhancing the argumentative behavior of low argumentative females. Schultz and Anderson found that cognitive materials can affect changes in argumentativeness. Women showed significant changes in their motivation to engage in argument after exposure to material that emphasized its benefits.[25] A later study by Anderson, Schultz, and Courtney-Staley revealed that cognitive training in argumentativeness and conflict management positively influenced subjects to change their motivation to argue.[26] Infante used a cued argument procedure to induce less argumentative women to argue and found that the low argumentatives who were trained in the cueing procedure were perceived by both male and female observers more favorably on expertise and dynamism than low argumentatives who were not trained. Thus, inducing less argumentative women to argue had a significant effect in enhancing their credibility during an argument.[27]

From the research discussed, four conclusions can be drawn: (1) trait argumentativeness is a constructive predisposition, (2) there is a relationship between argumentativeness and argumentative behavior, (3) females are typically lower in trait argumentativeness than their male counterparts, and (4) training can positively affect attitudes toward argumentativeness.

Given these conclusions, it seems prudent to investigate instructional efforts designed to enhance trait argumentativeness. Efforts at enhancing argumentativeness, skill in argumentative communication, and conflict management have taken two major approaches. According to Deutsch, the cooperative orientation is "one in which the goals of the participants are so linked that any participant can attain his goal if, and only if, the others with whom he is linked can attain their goals." In the competitive orientation, "a participant can attain his goal if, and only if, the others with whom he is linked cannot attain their goals." It should be noted, however, that few real-life situations can be defined as pure cooperation or pure competition as defined. As Deutsch notes, most situations involve both cooperative and competitive aspects because of the complex set of goals and subgoals that individuals bring to these situations.[28]

Interpersonal conflict theorists who apply argumentation to the study of conflict management employ the traditional competitive argumentation model. Although this orientation has been criticized,[29] it is applied, in part, because it is the prevailing mode of conflict management adopted by American society. Thus, it was employed as the primary orientation of this study.

The three instructional approaches employed to enhance argumentativeness were: Wilson and Arnold's topical review, Infante's inventional system, and the multicognitive training in interpersonal conflict approach.

TRAINING METHODS

Wilson and Arnold's Topical System of Invention[30]

A cued argument procedure for the invention of arguments is the topical review. The topical review is a systematic method that uses a specific device of thought (*topos*, pl. *topoi*) to help generate ideas relevant to a subject. These topics are, according to Nelson, "labels for superordinate structures of conceptual categories."[31]

Wilson and Arnold developed a sixteen-item review system that is grounded in rhetorical theory, abstract in nature, and "especially adapted to assisting recall."[32] Wilson and Arnold's list of topics or places is as follows: existence, degree, spatial, time, motion, form, substance, capacity to change, potency, desirability, feasibility, causality, correlation, genus-species relationships, similarity or dissimilarity, and possibility or impossibility.

A series of empirical investigations on the role of topics in human recall using the rhetorical scheme developed by John Wilson and Carroll Arnold demonstrate the usefulness of this system. Nelson reported that when given one hour for recall, subjects using superordinate terms with a highly meaningful issue generated 17 percent more items than subjects using free recall. In addition, those subjects working with a less meaningful issue generated 10 percent more items.[33] In another study using groups of students assigned the task of solving a social problem, it was found that the groups using the topical review produced significantly more policy statements judged to be more thorough and practical than those generated by the groups working without a topical cueing system. Moreover, the developed solutions of the topical review groups were judged superior to those produced by the other groups.[34] The results of this study extend Nelson's original research and demonstrate the applicability of this self-cueing method of invention in the small group setting.

Infante's Inventional System[35]

The Infante inventional system is an integral part of his model of argumentative competence. The model involves five parts: stating the argument in propositional form; analyzing the argumentative proposition and inventing arguments; presenting and defending one's position; refuting the opponent's position; and managing effective interpersonal relations during an argument.

The Infante inventional system is specifically designed to enhance individuals' motivation and skill in interpersonal argument. Infante noted that the system is related to status in deliberative analysis, grounded in a problem-solution format.[36] This inventional system utilizes four superordinate structures (problem-blame-solution-consequences) and two or three subordinate cues (questions) for each topic. The system is as follows: "(1) *Problem*: What are the signs of a problem? What is the specific harm? How widespread is the harm?; (2) *Blame*: What causes the problem? Is the present system at fault? Should the present system be changed?; (3) *Solution*: What are the possible solutions? Which solution best solves the problem?; (4) *Consequences*: What good outcomes will result from the solutions? What bad outcomes will result from the solutions?"[37]

Infante reported that the system for inventing arguments has yielded favorable results in experimental research. In discussing a series of experiments on inventional systems, Infante concluded that "the observation by Nelson that subjects discover more when cued by topoi seems to hold while the topical systems are different."[38] Like Nelson, Infante consistently found that cued subjects generated more items than uncued subjects.

Cognitive Training in Interpersonal Conflict

Three assumptions are inherent in the cognitive training model:

1. conflict management requires a willingness to be argumentative;
2. substantial cognitive data must be presented in order to change unfavorable perceptions of conflict and argumentativeness; and
3. after negative perceptions are altered, skill in conflict management can be taught using a model drawing upon theories of argumentation and persuasion.[39]

The Schultz and Anderson model has been used in a series of lecture-discussion training sessions.[40] The training begins with cognitive material on perceptions of conflict and perceptions of argumentativeness, then focuses on a three-step procedure for managing conflict. Step one involves determining the issues of the dispute; step two involves the selection of direction (argument, persuasion, agitation) and a strategy (avoidance, diffusion, confrontation) to best achieve the goals; step three involves practice sessions in conflict management.

Anderson, Schultz, and Courtney-Staley report a study in which an experimental group received this cognitive training in argumentativeness and conflict management over a three-week period. The results of the study indicated that the cognitive training in argumentativeness and conflict management enhanced subjects' argumentativeness, with low argumentative females reporting the greatest change.[41]

PURPOSE OF THIS STUDY

Research studies have provided some empirical support for the utility of these programs in increasing willingness to argue and actual argumentative behavior. This study sought to test the impact of these three methods of training in argument and to determine if one method was superior to another. Further, this study sought to explore whether there were any significant differences between males and females who participated in these systematic training efforts. Finally, the study sought to investigate whether there were any interaction effects between sex of the trainee and the method of argumentative training on the dependent variables of argumentativeness, verbal aggressiveness, and argumentative behavior.

Specifically, the following hypotheses were posited:

H1: After training, there will be no significant differences between males and females in trait argumentativeness. The rationale for offering the null hypothesis as a research hypothesis was the presumption that the effects of the training would be potent enough to neutralize any sex differences in motivation to argue.

H2: There will be no significant differences between males and females in verbal aggressiveness after training in argument. Again, the rationale for offering the null hypothesis as a research hypothesis was the presumption that the effects of training would be potent enough to neutralize any differences between males and females on verbal aggressiveness.

H3: There will be no significant differences between males and females on the number of arguments generated prior to (and during) the actual argument. Again, it was hypothesized that the training would serve to neutralize any sex differences in actual argumentative behavior, as measured by the number of arguments generated by the participants.

H4: There will be no significant differences between the three training methods on the number of arguments generated by each method. It was hypothesized that the three methods of training in argument would be equally beneficial in enhancing individuals' ability to generate arguments.

METHODS AND PROCEDURES

Participants

Participants in the study were sixty-one male and seventy-one female students enrolled in the introductory interpersonal communication class at two small private northeastern colleges. Participation was voluntary. Subjects completed the instruments during class hours with the permission of the instructor.

Procedures

Beginning with the seventh week of the semester, each of the six groups participated in a training program in argumentativeness and conflict management over a two-week period. Each group was randomly assigned to a treatment condition: Wilson and Arnold's topical system, Infante's inventional system, and the cognitive training model. Each treatment condition was randomly assigned to two different groups.

During the first week of the training program, all participants received content information about the nature of interpersonal conflict. Topics included the nature of conflict, unprofitable and profitable conflict management, and attitudes consonant with effective conflict management (e.g., conflict is a normal aspect of interpersonal relations). Participants were then trained in one of three specific methods designed to enhance motivation and skill in argument. The training program included role-play practice sessions using simulated conflict situations, thereby providing participants with the opportunity to utilize the specific training method in the process of conflict management.

The third session constituted the actual experimental treatment. Participants were provided with a review (cue) sheet listing the major components of the specific training method. The purpose of this was to negate the impact of memory as an intervening variable. Participants were randomly paired for an argumentative discussion. Dyads were provided with a case, titled "The Roommate," to be used for the argument. The case involves a dispute between two roommates over the financial obligations of a long-term guest.[42] Each dyad partner received the same case information but from a different perspective. Participants were given ten minutes to formulate arguments in support of their position. The instructions called for participants to list and number, in writing, each argument they prepared for the argumentative discussion. Participants were then given twenty minutes to argue the issue using their prepared list of arguments. At the conclusion of the allotted time, the cue sheets and list of arguments generated were collected. All subjects then completed the Argumentativeness Scale and the Verbal Aggressiveness Scale.

Argumentativeness Scale

The Infante and Rancer Argumentativeness Scale contains twenty items—ten items for measuring general tendency to approach arguments (ARGap) and ten items for measuring general tendency to avoid arguments (ARGav). The difference between these two is called ARGgt, the general tendency (trait) to be argumentative. There is considerable evidence supporting the reliability and validity of the scale.[43] Coefficient alphas obtained for the argumentativeness scale in this study were 0.88 for the ARGap dimension and 0.82 for the ARGav dimension.

Verbal Aggressiveness Scale

Verbal aggressiveness was measured by the Verbal Aggressiveness Scale. This instrument contains twenty items and is unidimensional. There is considerable evidence supporting the validity and reliability of this scale.[44] Coefficient alpha obtained for the verbal aggressiveness measure in this study was 0.85.

RESULTS

To examine the influence of method of training and sex of participant on the dependent variables of argumentativeness, verbal aggressiveness, and the number of arguments generated by participants, three two-way analyses of variance were conducted (see Tables 1 and 2).

Table 1
Means for Dependent Variables by Sex of Participant

	ARGgt	*Verbal Aggressiveness*	*N* *Arguments*
Males	8.65	56.67*	8.48
Females	8.46	47.39	9.36

*$p < .01$.

Note: The higher the mean, the greater the argumentativeness, verbal aggressiveness, and number of arguments generated.

Table 2
Mean Number of Arguments Generated by Training Method

Wilson and Arnold's Topical System	Infante's Inventional System	Cognitive Training
10.27*	8.19	8.17

*$p < .05$.

Note: The higher the mean, the greater the number of arguments generated.

Hypothesis 1 predicted that as a result of the training in argument, any sex differences in motivation to argue that may have existed would be negated, that is, as a result of training in argument, there would be no significant differences between males and females in motivation to argue (ARGgt). Recall that previous research suggests that males are more motivated to argue than females. Results of the analysis of variance (ANOVA) supported this hypothesis. There were no significant differences between males and females on ARGgt ($F = .008$, $df = 1/123$, $p > .05$). Thus, if any differences in motivation to argue did exist between males and females prior to the training (as previous research suggested), these differences may have been negated by the training efforts.

Hypothesis 2 predicted that as a result of the training in argument, any sex differences in verbal aggressiveness would be eliminated, that is, as a result of training in argument, there would be no significant differences between males and females in verbal aggressiveness. Recall that previous research suggests that males are more verbally aggressive than females. Results of the ANOVA rejected this hypothesis. Even after the training in argument, males were significantly more verbally aggressive than females ($F = 29.12$, $df = 1/123$, $p < .01$). Thus, training in argument did little to negate previously observed sex differences in verbally aggressive behavior.

Hypothesis 3 predicted that as a result of the training in argument, there would be no significant differences in the number of arguments generated by males and females during the argumentative discussion, that is, the training received would enable males and females to generate an equivalent number of arguments for the argumentative discussion. Results of the ANOVA supported this hypothesis. There were no significant differences between males and females on the number of arguments generated during the argumentative discussion ($F = 1.30$, $df = 1/112$, $p > .05$).

Hypothesis 4 predicted that there would be no significant differences in the number of arguments generated by each training method, that is, participants in each method of training were expected to generate an equivalent number of arguments for the argumentative discussion. Results of the ANOVA rejected this hypothesis. Participants who received training in the Wilson and Arnold topical system of argument generated significantly more arguments than participants using the other two methods ($F = 3.60$, $df = 2/112$, $p < .05$).

DISCUSSION

Previous research has demonstrated the value of high motivation and skill in argumentative communication. Research has also revealed that females are typically lower in trait argumentativeness, as well as verbal aggressiveness, than their male counterparts. Finally, training has been shown to positively affect attitudes toward argumentativeness.

Kosberg and Rancer review several pedagogical methods that appear to result in enhanced motivation and skill in argumentative communication.[45] The purpose of the present study was to test these methods and examine whether training in argument can minimize or reduce the previously observed differences between males and females in motivation and skill in argumentative behavior.

This study found that after training, there were no significant differences between males and females in motivation to argue (ARGgt), as well as no significant differences in argumentative behavior (number of arguments generated during the argumentative discussion). There was, however, a significant difference in verbal aggressiveness. Consistent with previous research, after training, males were still more verbally aggressive than females. The study also found that subjects instructed in the Wilson and Arnold topical system generated significantly more arguments than participants trained in either of the other two methods.

The training program appears to have demonstrated some modest influence in reducing the differences in argumentative behavior between males and females. Thus, a two-week program focusing on skill building in generating arguments may have brought women into parity with men in increasing their motivation and skill in arguing. That same period did little, however, to diminish the differences in verbal aggressiveness between males and females. Even after the training, males were still more verbally aggressive than females. Although a two-week program may be beneficial in teaching skill development in argumentation and conflict management, it did little to diminish the force of cultural norms regarding predispositions to use verbal aggression. Thus, through training, it may be easier to make women more argumentative and more difficult to make men less verbally aggressive.

The results of the study also demonstrated that participants using the Wilson and Arnold topical system generated significantly more arguments than the other two methods. The usefulness of this system was revealed in previous research by Nelson. However, all three systems emerged as productive methods in providing participants with the tools to generate arguments. Participants generated an average of more than eight arguments during the brief preparatory period allocated for this behavior. These findings suggest that all three methods may be effectively utilized in both formal and informal training in argument and conflict management. One speculation for the relative success of Wilson and Arnold over the other methods may be the number of topics; Wilson and Arnold has sixteen topics, Infante has ten topics, and cognitive training has five topics. The number of categories (cues) in each method may be the underlying reason for the differences in argument generation for each method.

This study has implications in the areas of both sex difference findings and training. Significantly, as noted earlier, men have been conditioned to be more competitive than women, who have generally been trained in the cooperative mode of conflict management. Providing women with competitively focused conflict management skills enlarges their behavioral repertoires. According to Eagly, providing women with a range of options enables them to "encompass the behaviors that have traditionally allowed men to dominate and emerge as leaders in groups."[46]

To avail women of the educational opportunity to bring them into parity with men in increasing motivation and skill in argumentative behavior may work to augment both their argumentative competence and communicative confidence. The need for building confidence has been demonstrated in a study examining the impact of gender on persuasive communication by Andrews, who found that female subjects expressed less confidence than males in their ability to present persuasive arguments. Interestingly, female negative expectations in approaching the task did not seem to impair performance as trained communication confederates rated both males and females as having performed equally successfully. In addition to reporting varying degrees of self-confidence, males and females also rated themselves differently on their communication effectiveness. Regardless of confederate gender in presenting their arguments, males rated themselves higher than females in argumentative effectiveness.[47]

The present study also has consequences for training in relationship skills. Significantly, the current escalating incidence of familial violence underscores the relevance of training to increase motivation and skill in argumentative behavior. The problem of violence is not limited to the family unit. Research documents that approximately one in five college students, both male and female, has experienced violence (verbal and/or physical) in a dating relationship.[48] The statewide campaign in Massachusetts to reduce violence through the use of the Violence Prevention Curriculum for Adolescents is but one example of how conflict management practitioners and researchers in both academic and nonacademic settings have heeded the plea of public school administrators who are seeking methods of curtailing violence in inner city schools.[49]

The findings of this study also have implications for training in the area of relationship skills and marital distress. Communication scholars have long understood the relationship between communication processes and the development of marital (relational) distress. Communication patterns that discriminate between distressed and nondistressed couples have been investigated. Gottman and Levenson have identified negative affect reciprocity as the "signature" of relational stress.[50] Their findings are consistent with other observational studies of distressed and nondistressed couples. One such study by Notarius and Markman associates relationship stress with the presence of negative affect cycles. In addition to negative affective exchanges, nondistressed couples reveal higher rates of problem-solving strategies, as well as positive verbal and nonverbal behaviors, than distressed couples.[51] Margolin, Burman, and John also found that nondistressed, low conflict couples used more positive problem solving strategies.[52] Given the patterns of dysfunctional communication described and the demonstrated utility of the three methods used in this study in generating arguments, it would appear practicable to increase motivation and skill in arguing by utilizing one method or a combination in the training of distressed couples in problem-solving conflict management.

NOTES

1. R. E. Dowling and L. J. Flint, "The Argumentativeness Scale: Problems and Promise," *Communication Studies 41* (1990): 183.

2. D. A. Infante and A. S. Rancer, "A Conceptualization and Measure of Argumentativeness," *Journal of Personality Assessment 46* (1982): 72–80.

3. D. A. Infante and C. J. Wigley, "Verbal Aggressiveness: An Interpersonal Model and Measure," *Communication Monographs 53* (1986): 61–69.

4. D. W. Johnson and R. J. Johnson, "Conflict in the Classroom: Controversy and Learning," *Review of Educational Research 49* (1979): 51–70.

5. J. G. Delia, B. J. O'Keefe, and D. J. O'Keefe, "The Constructive Approach to Communication," in F. E. X. Dance, ed., *Human Communication Theory* (New York: Harper and Row, 1982).

6. D. A. Infante, "Trait Argumentativeness as a Predictor of Communicative Behavior in Situations Requiring Argument," *Central States Speech Journal 32* (1981): 265–272.

7. D. A. Infante, J. D. Trebing, P. E. Shepherd, and D. E. Seeds, "The Relationship of Argumentativeness to Verbal Aggression," *Southern Speech Communication Journal 50* (1984): 67–77.

8. D. A. Infante, "Influencing Women To Be More Argumentative: Source Credibility Effects," *Journal of Applied Communication Research 13* (1985): 33–44; E. O. Onyekwere, R. B. Rubin, and D. A. Infante, "Interpersonal Perception and Communication Satisfaction as a Function of Argumentativeness and Ego-Involvement," paper presented at the Speech Communication Association Convention, Boston, 1987.

9. B. Schultz, "Argumentativeness: Its Effect in Group Decision-Making and its Role in Leadership Perception," *Communication Quarterly 30* (1982): 368–375.

10. Infante, "Influencing Women To Be More Argumentative," pp. 33–44.

11. Schultz, "Argumentativeness: Its Effect in Group Decision-Making," pp. 368–375.

12. D. A. Infante and W. I. Gorden, "Superiors' Argumentativeness and Verbal Aggressiveness as Predictors of Subordinates' Satisfaction," *Human Communication Research 12* (1985): 117–125.

13. D. A. Infante and W. I. Gorden, "Benefits Versus Bias: An Investigation of Argumentativeness, Gender, and Organizational Communication Outcomes," *Communication Research Reports 2* (1985): 196–210.

14. D. A. Infante and W. I. Gorden, "Superior and Subordinate Communication Profiles: Implications for Independent-Mindedness and Upward Effectiveness," *Central States Speech Journal 38* (1987): 73–80.

15. M. E. Roloff and B. S. Greenberg, "Sex Differences in Choice of Modes of Conflict Resolution in Real-Life and Television," *Communication Quarterly 27* (1979): 3–12.

16. P. H. Andrews, "Gender Differences in Persuasive Communication and Attribution of Success and Failure," *Human Communication Research 13* (1987): 372–385.

17. D. Tannen, *You Just Don't Understand: Women and Men in Conversation* (New York: William Morrow, 1990).

18. M. J. Papa and E. J. Natalle, "Gender, Strategy Selection, and Discussion Satisfaction in Interpersonal Conflict," *Western Journal of Speech Communication 53* (1989): 260–272.

19. Infante, "Influencing Women to be More Argumentative," pp. 33–44; M. Burgoon, J. P. Dillard, and N. E. Doran, "Friendly or Unfriendly Persuasion: The Effects of Violations of Expectations by Males and Females," *Human Communication Research 10* (1983): 283–294; E. W. Bonaguro and J. C. Pearson, "The Relationship Bewteen Communicator Style, Argumentativeness, and Gender," paper presented at the Speech Communication Association Convention, Chicago, IL, 1986.

20. D. A. Infante, "The Argumentative Student in the Speech Communication Classroom: An Investigation and Implications," *Communication Education 31* (1982): 141–48.

21. B. Schultz and J. Anderson, "Learning to Negotiate: The Role of Argument," paper presented at the Eastern Communication Association Convention, Hartford, CT, 1982.

22. A. S. Rancer and K. J. Dierks-Stewart, "The Influence of Sex and Sex-Role Orientation on Trait Argumentativeness," *Journal of Personality Assessment 49* (1985): 69–70.

23. A. S. Rancer and R. A. Baukus, "Discriminating Males and Females on Belief Structures about Arguing," in L. B. Nadler, M. K. Nadler, and W. R. Todd-Mancillas, eds., *Advances in Gender and Communication Research* (Lanham, MD: University Press of America, 1987), pp. 155–173.

24. D. A. Infante, "Response to High Argumentatives: Message and Sex Differences," *Southern Speech Communication Journal 54* (1989): 159–170.

25. Schultz and Anderson, "Learning to Negotiate."

26. J. Anderson, B. Schultz, and C. Courtney-Staley, "Training in Argumentativeness: New Hope for Non-Assertive Women," *Women's Studies in Communication 10* (1987): 58–66.

27. Infante, "Influencing Women To Be More Argumentative," pp. 33–44.

28. M. Deutsch, *The Resolution of Conflict: Constructive and Destructive Processes* (New Haven, CT: Yale University Press, 1973), pp. 20, 21.

29. See, for example, M. Solomon, "A Prolegomenon to Research on Gender Role Communication," *Women's Studies in Communication 7* (1984): 98.

30. J. F. Wilson and C. C. Arnold, *Public Speaking as a Liberal Art*, 5th ed. (Boston: Allyn and Bacon, 1983), pp. 83–88.

31. W. F. Nelson, "*Topoi*: Functional in Human Recall," *Speech Monographs 37* (1970): 122.

32. Ibid., p. 124.

33. Ibid., pp. 121–126.

34. W. F. Nelson, J. L. Petelle, and C. Monroe, "A Revised Strategy for Idea Generation in Small Group Decision Making," *Speech Teacher 23* (1974): 191–196.

35. D. A. Infante, *Arguing Constructively* (Prospect Heights, IL: Waveland Press, 1988), pp. 45–54.

36. D. A. Infante, "The Influence of a Topical System on the Discovery of Arguments," *Speech Monographs 38*(1971): 125.

37. Infante, *Arguing Constructively*, p. 47.

38. Infante, "Influence of a Topical System," p. 128.

39. Anderson, Schultz, and Courtney-Staley, "Training in Argumentativeness," pp. 58–66.

40. B. Schultz and J. Anderson, "Training in Management of Conflict: A Communicative Theory Perspective," *Small Group Behavior 15* (1984): 333–348.

41. Anderson, Schultz, and Courtney-Staley, "Training in Argumentativeness," pp. 58–66.

42. A copy of this case can be obtained by contacting either author.

43. Infante, "Trait Argumentativeness as a Predictor of Communicative Behavior," pp. 265–272; Infante and Rancer, "Conceptualization and Measure of Argumentativeness," pp. 72–80; V. P. Richmond, J. C. McCroskey, and L. L. McCroskey, "An Investigation of Self-Perceived Communication Competence and Personality Orientations," *Communication Research Reports 6* (1989): 28–36.

44. Infante and Wigley, "Verbal Aggressiveness," pp. 61-69; D. A. Infante, T. A. Chandler, and J. E. Rudd, "Test of an Argumentative Skill Deficiency Model of Interspousal Violence," *Communication Monographs 56* (1989): 163–177.

45. R. L. Kosberg and A. S. Rancer, "Approaches to Training in Argumentativeness," *Speech Communication Annual 5* (1991): 97–107.

46. A. H. Eagly, "On the Advantages of Reporting Sex Comparisons," *American Psychologist 45* (1990): 561.

47. Andrews, "Gender Differences in Persuasive Communication," pp. 372–385.

48. S. S. Torrey and R. M. Lee, "Curbing Date Violence: Campus-Wide Strategies," *Journal of the National Association for Women Deans, Administrators, and Counselors 51* (1987): 3–8.

49. D. Prothrow-Stith, *Violence Prevention Curriculum for Adolescents* (Newton, MA: Education Development Center, 1987).

50. J. M. Gottman and R. W. Levenson, "Assessing the Role of Emotion in Marriage," *Behavioral Assessment 8* (1986): 31–48.

51. C. I. Notarius and H. J. Markman, "Coding Marital Interaction: A Sampling and Discussion of Current Issues," *Behavioral Assessment 11* (1989): 1–11.

52. G. Margolin, B. Burman, and R. S. John, "Home Observations of Married Couples Re-enacting Naturalistic Conflicts," *Behavioral Assessment 11* (1989): 101–118.

22

Strategic Storytelling: Constructing Self through Narrative and Nautilus

Mary-Jeanette Smythe

Comparatively few ethnographies of language communities have appeared in scholarly journals of communication research. Yet such naturalistic approaches are uniquely suited for capturing the subtle and often elusive relationships among language, gender, and community. Too often our research on these relationships is contrived and linear, dependent on placing individuals into prepared scenarios and painstakingly recording their behaviors. In so doing, many valuable insights concerning the patterns and techniques of communicating in naturally occurring situations are lost. This investigation focuses on the role of discourse among women within one such natural setting, a fitness facility called Bodyworks. Their stories, and the interpretive themes emerging from them, are the results of seven months of continuous participant observation.

STORYTELLING AS A COMMUNICATION STRATEGY

Telling stories about personal experiences has been identified as a "prominent part of everyday discourse" (Robinson 1981, p. 580). Stories may be told to satisfy a range of communication goals, including a desire to inform, frighten, incite others to action, obscure (Askam 1982), and to create identities (Georges 1982). It is the latter instance that Labov and Waletzsky (1967) describe in terms of self-aggrandizement, the desire of the narrator to create the best possible image of himself by showing that "the narrator was unusually brave, intelligent, insightful, or some other quality appropriate to the situation in the story" (Watson 1973, p. 254). Robinson (1981) claims that in addition to the apparent intent to enhance self-esteem, stories of personal experiences are "semi-ritualized means of reaffirming both one's personal identity and the socially sanctioned beliefs and values, particularly those that ascribe responsibility" (p. 64). This perspective emphasizes the role of the listener in

providing confirmation to the narrator's efforts, and points toward the importance of the attributions contained within a storytelling episode.

A number of feminist scholars have hypothesized that conversations among
women are characteristically distinct from conversations among men or those
of mixed-sex groups, using labels such as "collaborative" and "competitive" to
capture the essence of the distinctions perceived as relevant and descriptive
(see, e.g., Kalcik 1975; McConnell-Ginet 1983; Thorne, Kramerae, and Henley
1983). Comparatively little empirical data have been gathered that reveals
much about the precision of these labels, but there are a number of specific
behaviors which presumably define and distinguish either a "collaborative" or
"competitive" communication style. Both structural elements of conversation
and strategic choices that interactants make are included. For instance, the
mutuality of "interaction work" (Fishman 1978), described as active listening,
building upon the utterances of others, flexible leadership, and overlapping
conversational turns in women's conversations with other women are markers
of the collaborative style. A competitive style is built around elements including
frequent interruptions, dysfluent speech forms, and strong, clearly defined
conversational turns. In terms of strategic choices, conversations among women
are more likely to incorporate mutual sharing of emotions and personal
knowledge. Topic control, depersonalized content, and low disclosure characterize conversations among men. Research reported by Dindia (1987), Smythe
and Huddleston (1991), and others has provided clarification of the notion of
gender-based linguistic styles.

Gender styles research suggests that narrative analysis of conversational
behaviors such as storytelling would shed information on at least two key
issues. First, stories may be examined as units of discourse which either conform to or belie the patterns of language cues associated with language styles
like those described earlier. In addition, the actual content of the stories and
their strategic placement in the larger context of conversations may provide
insights about how men and women create and project identities during interactions.

That stories are essentially interactional phenomena, subject to negotiation
within discourse, has been emphasized by Jefferson (1978), Robinson (1981),
and Polyani (1979). In many respects, storytelling episodes may provide one of
the most revealing venues for a naturalistic examination of conversation.
Defined as "the linguistic encoding of past experience in order to explain
something about, or by means of, the events or states described" (Polyani 1979,
p. 208), stories may come in various forms. Personal experience narratives are
first personal recapitulations of actual events and are distinguished from those
vicarious accounts which describe the activities of others, or folklore and joke
telling (Watson 1973). Both stories and narratives have internal structures.
Labov and Waletzky (1967) describe five components: (1) orientation (describing persons, places, times, and situations), (2) complication (the series of
events), (3) evaluation (the point of the account), (4) resolution (the portion that
follows the evaluation), and (5) code (the return to the present of the ongoing

discourse). Similar structures have been identified by others (Askam 1982; Stimson and Webb 1975; van Dijk 1975).

Another impetus to examine storytelling as a form of sex-role display derives from the contexted nature of storytelling units. Conversational analysts have turned their attention toward the extended nature of stories as discrete from turn-by-turn talk and describe storytelling as a sequential unfolding of mutually negotiated units which define individual identities and interpersonal relationships (Benoit 1985; Jefferson 1978; Sacks 1972). Stories in conversations are often chained into a series of stories, and some analysts (Ryave 1978) have scrutinized the coherence of the series in relation to the larger conversational structure. "Next stories," for example, have been found to illustrate the same point made by the previous speaker or may show application in another, similar situation. In this way interactants appear to negotiate the point of stories so that they may eventually introduce their stories as coherently as possible.

A final intersection of storytelling and the study of sex-role display emerges from the essentially collaborative nature of storytelling—emphasizing the role of the recipient. Listeners are expected to be "attentive, appreciative, to give overt indications of interest, to show that they grasp the point of the story, and to agree with the narrator about its meaning" (Robinson 1981, p. 71). Listeners display these expectations through their behaviors (posture, gesture, speech). Listeners also offer tokens of special interest to signal their alignment as a recipient of a story (Jefferson 1978). When listeners follow expectations, they affirm the meaning of the story and the identity of the narrator as it is illustrated through the vehicle of a story. This promotes the relationships between the interactants as well as the smooth and orderly flow of the conversation.

To date, little work on storytelling has appeared. Even less has been concerned with narrative analysis. Based on the early works of Sacks (1974) and Jefferson (1978), McLaughlin, Cody, Kane, and Robey (1981) undertook an empirical investigation of sex differences in story receipt and story sequencing behaviors during initial dyadic interactions. These researchers hypothesized that women would spend more time than men as story recipients, would tell more sequential stories than men, and employ more story sequencing devices than men. Based on a review of the sex differences in language literature, McLaughlin and associates hypothesized that men and women would also differ on a number of specific story receipt behaviors. Their findings provided only partial support for their hypotheses. Women did receive more stories than men, but few differences in sequencing behaviors emerged. McLaughlin and colleagues noted that the strategic and content dimensions of storytelling might be more meaningful indicators of gender differences in conversation. Exploring this possibility therefore became one goal of the current ethnography.

SETTING

As is the case in aesthetic ethnographies, the focus in this investigation was on the characters, scene, and actions that defined the group. The social situation in which the Bodyworks' members located themselves was equally important. Their discourse was as much influenced by the specific physical locale as it was by the nature of the relationships among the women comprising the group. The basic descriptions of key elements in this ethnography follow.

Scene

Bodyworks was a fitness center located in Columbia, Missouri. Membership was by subscription and is predominantly female. The layout of the club was particularly important, in that this center offered only aerobic workouts and free-weight classes. Hence the physical environment has two interaction areas: the dance floor and the adjoining weight area. Each area was mirrored on two sides and was bisected by a walkway leading from the entrance, by the registration desk, to the locker room and shower area. Immediately in front of the locker and shower area was a small counter and set of eight stools where individuals congregated while waiting for classes to begin, or when preparing to depart after completing a workout. These three areas constitute the interaction arenas at Bodyworks: the aerobics floor, the weight room, and the counter area.

Characters

Membership at Bodyworks largely comprised women whose ages range from eighteen to sixty-four. The majority of members fall into one of two demographic categories. The eighteen- to twenty-four-year-old college group and another equally active, long-standing membership group ranging in ages from thirty-two to forty-eight define the major constituencies. As is often the case, some members are more faithful in their attendance than others, and as a consequence are more integrated into the social network of the club. These members received various social status tokens associated with their longevity. Examples included the obvious, such as being greeted by name by the staff, and more subtle concessions, such as "ownership" of specific spots on the aerobics floor. This ownership of space was widely acknowledged and others deferred these more desirable locations without question or dispute. Occasional or transient members of classes, by contrast, did not routinely claim spaces or even attempt to engage the "regulars" in conversation. Both metaphorically and physically, these individuals operated on the fringes of Bodyworks.

Some fifty-three women and six men were consistently prominent members of the Bodyworks social network systems. These individuals for the most part held unlimited memberships, meaning that they could attend as many sessions as they chose during a specified time period (month, semester, year, etc.). Across membership categories, it also became apparent that certain classes were consistently populated by the same individuals. Over time, these groups assumed the characteristics of subcultures, with fully developed social networks independent of the larger Bodyworks culture.

For instance, a class labeled "Step-Low Aerobic Circuit" met on Tuesday and Thursday mornings at 9:10. The population of this class was singularly homogenous and consisted of a nucleus of six central figures and a rotating cast of another nine women whose appearances were less consistent, but whose membership and participation in the group was firmly and frequently validated. This group emerged as a primary focus for the analysis in this study for two reasons. First, the composition of the group was enduring and stable. Women in this class had been attending sessions for as long as ten years, dating from the opening of the facility and through two location shifts, numerous fee changes, and one complete ownership and management shake-up. In addition, the women in the class displayed many of the cues associated with particular speech communities, functioning as an intact subset of the larger fitness culture of the community with an established network of relationships revealed through their discourse.

Activities

The stated purpose of all activities at Bodyworks was health and fitness related. There was no juice bar, whirlpool, or other amenities characterizing other local clubs and blurring the focus of the establishment for the members and the general public alike. At Bodyworks, most communication events were embedded within physical activities—aerobic classes, whether high or low impact, step or interval workouts, or circuits, aerogility, and weight classes. This was not a place that facilitated lengthy or extensive interactions. Talk was not the dominant activity. In fact, talk during classes was an informally, but very directly, sanctioned violation of prevailing behavioral norms. Talk that disrupted the concentration of others during a workout was a serious breach of etiquette. Thus, the ways in which interactions were formed and managed in these often strenuous circumstances contributed to the unique patterns of relating that members developed.

This investigation focused on three interrelated issues. First, the actual recounting of stories in conversations. Questions such as who initiated the storytelling, what topics were introduced, and the relationship of storytelling episodes to the total conversational context were of primary interest. In addition, story receipt behaviors, a series of specific cues designed to serve several communication functions, including the display of collaborative intent, revealing listener comprehension, and indicating acceptance of the teller's interpretation, were observed. Interpretative themes, based on recurring patterns of interactions and defined through the form and content of stories told, were derived from the field notes kept for each session attended. Finally, and more important, this ethnography sought to uncover the nature of relationships among women in a single fitness class, as revealed through their shared conversations. Through the narrative of this loose-knit group, it was possible to explore the ways in which these individuals defined a social reality and negotiated identity management.

METHOD

Methodologies in ethnographies are comparatively straightforward. Participant observation was the mode of study employed in this investigation. As a member of Bodyworks for many years, it was not difficult for me to conduct observations. In the initial phases of the observation (November 1, 1991 to July 1, 1992), I maintained extensive field notes on the interactions observed in each session attended. Covert observation was deemed essential at this phase to ensure that "typical" interaction behaviors were observed and recorded. At the conclusion of the initial observation, a series of "guided conversations" (Lofland 1971) were completed with key members of the group. Rather than objectifying members of the group through an empirical recounting of their various characteristics, the purpose of this phase of the analysis was to allow the Bodyworks' members to suggest their own interpretive framework for their shared experiences. Thus, this approach was ahypothetical and focused on the descriptive elements of women's storytelling rather than on an analytical or evaluative rendering of their discourse.

The corpus of data was composed of the extensive field notes concerning the interactions and stories, in particular, shared among members of the Bodyworks community. These field notes have provided the initial interpretive themes for the study—identity management and therapeutic discourse. Members' own narratives concerning their histories with the club and perceptions of its place in their lives and relationships formed a second major category of data. These interviews gauged the level of importance and commitment members felt toward the activities and relationships associated with their participation at Bodyworks.

Entry into the social system was reasonably easily effected. My own membership profile with Bodyworks made my presence quite usual and typical. It is important to note, however, that prior to the onset of this investigation, my participation had been limited to the late-afternoon and early-evening classes. My exposure to the culture of daytime classes was initially incidental, but in a very short time, the distinctive aspects of the morning class culture were apparent. Initially, the disparities among the subcultures of Bodyworkers (Lipsticks versus Bookpacks) invited obvious comparisons. Lengthier exposure, however, made the unique flavor of the morning group a focus of the ethnography.

Two characteristics of the observational record warrant attention here. A variety of circumstances, including the ambient noise level (stereo music is the invariable accompaniment to any class), the desire for unobtrusive measurement, and the variable movements of interactants made reliance on field notes the only realistic choice for record keeping. Although the advantages of a tape recording for verbatim transcripts of storytelling episodes were obvious, that option was simply infeasible. Rather, extensive notes were made immediately following each session. Information recorded included a reconstruction of the communication exchanges, detailing the content of specific interactions, the individuals involved, approximate length, topics, and responses. Regarding participants, all relevant demographic and sociometric information was recorded.

A note concerning the role of the researcher seems in order. While ethnographers and conversational analysts have argued (Carbaugh 1990; Pomerantz 1987) that direct involvement does not hinder accurate record keeping, a conscious effort to minimize personal participation evolved over time in this study. This reflected an impulse to allow the discourse among the participants to emerge as it would, absent an investigator's intentional or inadvertent prompts. The pragmatic rationale for maintaining a low profile was simple. The opportunities for interactions were sharply limited by the time available during the Step-Low Circuit class. With only forty- to sixty-second intervals in the weight area, there was little enough time to gather discourse samples. Further reductions associated with personal contributions from the researcher seemed unnecessarily intrusive. Therefore, a strategy that included minimal verbal contributions but active nonverbal participation (e.g., cashing interest tokens in response to others' comments by laughter, groans, or exclamations) was adopted.

TALK AT BODYWORKS

In most ethnographies the researcher's first task involves contexting the discourse or narrative of a specific speech community under investigation. One initial task was to recognize and codify recurrent patterns within the discourse. Of particular interest were those patterns that either regulated interactions or gave meaning and/or structure to talk among participants. Following Crawford (1986), Carbaugh (1990), and others, the first patterns sought in this study were the communication rules that were relevant to discourse at Bodyworks. In addition to the field notes and unstructured interviews with members and nonmember observers of the fitness culture, a number of commentaries on American speech habits and cultural predilections were used as reference points. Rules were evaluated and revised on the basis of explanatory adequacy. In general, the rules possessed the following attributes:

1. Rules were reportable by members of Bodyworks. Thus, the actors in this setting exhibited variations upon the communication rules during typical communication events.
2. Rules were clearly intelligible to members of the Bodyworks community. These were accepted and acknowledged (e.g., no one needed to question the appropriateness of

the communication rule in that context, or required an interpretation of the conduct) widely. In this regard, it was significant that in the postobservation interviews with participants, virtually all of the interviewees articulated one or more of the rules in their spontaneous descriptions of their experiences.

3. Rules reflected recurrent, stable patterns in the discourse of Bodyworks' members. Conversational analysts (Pomerantz 1987) sometimes disagree about the minimum number of times a behavior should appear to warrant inclusion in a taxonomy. In this study, the rules were characterized by high repeatability.

4. Rules were used as repair mechanisms to deal with the unexpected, atypical, or inappropriate discourse.

Although the rules generated through these observations were not universal, they embodied a set of subtle agreements among participants that had pervasive effects upon the nature of communication events that unfolded during classes. Conversations taking place during the workout sessions were structured within the boundaries defined by the rules.

THE 9:10 AM STEP-LOW CIRCUIT CLASS

The 9:10 AM Step-Low Circuit class was led by one of the original Bodyworks instructors, a popular and enduring individual who was a professional dancer/choreographer at Stephens College as well as a fitness trainer. She was among the first female instructors in the city to incorporate weight work with the basic aerobic dance, calisthenics routines. The instructor, M, was a key element in the dynamic of the group. The population of the group varied somewhat, but from among the fifteen to twenty quasi-regular attendees, a core group of ten women attended nearly every Tuesday-Thursday session. This group included L, a professional artist who created jewelry for local shops; Mi, a Ph.D. candidate at the University of Missouri who is also a published poet; Ja, a homemaker involved in community service activities; BB, a homemaker and mother of three small children; N, a homemaker, nurse, and mother of two; K, a computer technician, mother, and avid weight lifter; Ly, a realtor; J, a hair stylist; Sz, a homemaker and mother; and G, a former teacher.

The empirical profile for the discourse observed within this class was generally consistent with that of other groups observed during this study. The numbers of stories (843 for this group), story topics, and frequencies of teller and listener roles have been summarized elsewhere (Smythe 1993). Conversations involving these individuals were distinctive, however, in terms of the interpretive themes that emerged from their discourse. The two themes that predominated concerned identity management and problem solving. These themes, and the rules associated with each, were the focus of this recounting.

Self-Presentation

As Carbaugh (1990) noted, the business of impression management—the construction of self for public consumption—has been a distinctively American phenomenon and may be contrasted with a number of cultures in which silence, rather than speech, regarding the self is the interaction norm. A key element of impression management involved claims of personal uniqueness, particularly in terms of abilities, experiences, traits, or possessions. Regarding the bases for this impulse in impression management, Schlenker (1980) has noted:

Many personality theorists hypothesize that people require a sense of individual unique-ness to allow them to stand out from members of their own groups and other groups. . . . People want to feel as if they have special attributes or gifts that distinguish them from the crowd . . . claiming such attractive special qualities also allows a claim to the image of uniqueness. Being unable to make any claims to special attributes makes one appear to be ordinary, common, or mediocre—highly unattractive images. (p. 18)

Clearly, then, one salient motivation in impression management was the desire to shape the attributions others make concerning the actor's character, experiences, and qualities. Individuals were rightly concerned with providing self-relevant information to others that would generate positive impressions. The rule associated with this aspect of discourse was stated as follows:

Rule 1: In conversations at Bodyworks, presentations of self are among the preferred communication activities.

The discourse of the women at Bodyworks reflected what Labov and Waletzky (1967) described as self-aggrandizement. Narrators used the vehicle of a story to construct a favorable image of self. In its most basic form, this story type contained the following elements. Tellers describe a predicament they confronted and overcame through personal effort and/or skill. Not surpris-ingly, one of the most common variations on this story concerned the struggle to maintain a desired level of fitness, often at considerable emotional expense. On one occasion, BB, recently a mother for the third time, lamented the difficulties of losing the "baby fat," compounded by the inability of her immediate family and coworkers to understand her frustration or support her need to set the time aside for herself to come to Bodyworks and exercise. Her affirmation of the importance of fitness despite the sacrifices required cast her plight as an ennobling struggle against difficult odds. Countless other stories of this sort, centering on the problem spots targeted by toning programs, weight regimes, and the like, filled a similar function. Casting the teller in the role of a diligent, even dogged devotee of good health was a recurrent theme of stories told. Interestingly enough, these were not stories about the pursuit of some elusive standard of perfection. Rather, these stories were about effort rather than outcome. Even K, arguably the most physically conditioned of the core group, emphasized the process. To the poet, Mi, these were "rituals of purification." To the feminist J, these stories were about the empowering experience of "taking control through physicality and making my body my very own . . . *for* me and *about* me."

Rule 2: In conversations at Bodyworks, actors are permitted to present self-descriptive information without challenge.

Although rule 1 was concerned with the salience of impression management stories, the second rule asserted a sort of right or privilege that was assured each participant in the situation. In such instances, recipients of stories were expected to accept the self descriptions without question. For the most part, these stories were positive in nature, and reflected two types of general acclaiming tactics that appeared to be used in an effort to influence the ways in which listeners might make attributions about the teller of the stories. The first acclaiming strategy entailed enhancements, or enlargements, upon the positive or unique qualities of a story. When, for instance, Mi had a poem appear in print, she not only brought a copy of the publication along to class for individuals to peruse but also provided specific, unsolicited details about the quality of the periodical; the intense level of emotional investment required by her simultaneously juggling graduate work, marriage, and teaching in addition to her writing; and the gratification experienced through her achievement. All of the extra story details, which incidentally extended across more than three classes, had the effect of enriching both the narrative and the impressions others formed of her abilities and accomplishments.

A second strategy for impression management appeared through entitilings, those additional details incorporated into a story which serve to maximize the teller's responsibility for an experience, a quality, or an outcome. Quite often stories included explicit descriptions of the severity of challenges tellers were forced to meet and ultimately proved able to overcome. In tellings of this sort, J was particularly likely to elaborate on the difficulties of obstacles faced in coping with the contrary demands of professional and personal life. In one instance, she appeared to be on the verge of losing a major promotion because she was "so stressed about family problems" that she was unable to perform well at work. She was genuinely concerned that she might be fired. Then, with virtually no rest and very little lead time, she was able to pull a presentation together that garnered overwhelmingly positive reviews from her boss and co-workers. Another variation on this theme placed the teller in situations in which others were aligned against them, or in situations in which they had no previous skills or experiences to guide them. Yet even in the face of this adversity, these women described many more outcomes featuring successes than failures.

Taken together, these rules and related stories appeared to be strategic attempts to secure positive evaluations of self from others. Such self-aware stories were not, however, the only sorts of narratives that dominated the conversations. Another recurring theme was therapeutic discourse, or the use of stories as vehicles to seek or administer recommendations, validations, or solutions to life's problems from the group.

Therapeutic Discourse

Use of the label *therapeutic* in this context implied no clinical or diagnostic judgments. Rather, it was employed as a characterization of the actions and outcomes of the discourse shared by this particular group of women. As such the label should be viewed as purely descriptive and provisional.

Rule 3: In conversations at Bodyworks, recommendations and advice are expressed in terms of individual options rather than societal or situational norms.

Certainly one dominant feature of the interactions among the women in the Bodyworks class was a reliance on the input of selected others when confronting problems or dilemmas in one's own life. Here there were clear stratifications among the core group, with certain individuals chosen as recipients for problem-based stories. Some of the choices were obviously related to age and experience levels claimed by individuals. L, the professional artist, drew on a long and varied experience as a classroom teacher, designer/decorator, and entrepreneur as well as wife, mother, and president of her area's country club. Her advice was often sought through both subtle and direct tactics. On the other hand, Mi laid claim to a wide range of experiences that belied her comparative youth within this core group. Nonetheless, she frequently inserted herself into interactions and shared her stories whether invited or not. On one occasion, she literally placed herself physically in front of a retreating J in order to complete an account Mi considered relevant. What was striking about stories of this type, however, had little to do with the specific content of the stories, which was often rather predictable (e.g., family disputes, job problems, generalized angst, interpersonal relationships, health). Rather, what was notable was the way in which individuals scrupulously avoided advancing opinions or recommendations without couching these in terms of individual options. Prevailing societal norms, or assertions that might be perceived as impositions upon the "rights" of an individual to act in a manner consistent with her own code, were avoided.

This pattern was demonstrated when J was distraught about her lover's alleged infidelities. Stories offered by L, Ja, M, and even Mi in response to J's bid for attention were consistently phrased as expressions of their own preferences, without comment about the applicability of the decisions described in the stories to J's situation. Prefatory comments in particular often distanced the example described in the story from the recipient. This framing of recommendations through what Carbaugh (1990) calls nonimpositional or negative face rules applied in a wide range of personal topics.

Rule 4: In conversations at Bodyworks, the personal is public.

One of the more intriguing characteristics of the discourse shared by the women in this group was the high level of self-disclosure it contained. Deeply personal information and topics were shared as routinely as complaints about the vagaries of the weather. The level of candor and acceptance of that candor on the part of the listener(s) was striking. This therapeutic discourse was characterized most by a singular absence of self-consciousness surrounding self-disclosures. Eavesdropping on these conversations was highly revealing and spoke in some ways to the degree of trust afforded by the observance of the communication rules in this setting. A telling commentary on this aspect of the discourse was offered by N, who opined that "the women here remind me of that hokey TV show *Sisters* . . . y'know the part at the beginning, where all of 'em are sittin' in the steam bath and saying just whatever, no matter who can hear them. I mean, it really does." The characterization was indeed apt. These women were willing risk takers who made public those details of their lives that were absolutely unavailable otherwise.

In summary, then, it appeared that the four communication rules served a variety of self-related conversational functions. These included the public presentation and management of self-images, the exchange of social tokens and expressions of good will, and the resolution of topical or personal problems. This group of women used stories as primary vehicles for the impression management and therapeutic functions of communication in ways that reflected at once uniquely cultural (the American emphasis upon an individualistic orientation and the notion of the self) yet richly individual experiences. Theirs was an evolving saga that extended well beyond the obvious bonds forged by sweat and struggle. Their stories seemed to enrich, empower, and ultimately define these women and their relationships with one another.

On a more conceptual level, the frequency and centrality of storytelling during conversations were revealing and significant. The observations reported here added to our understanding of how naturally occurring storytellings proceed and described key goals individuals attempt to accomplish through this dimension of discourse.

REFERENCES

Askam, J. 1982. "Telling Stories." *Sociological Review 30*: 555–573.
Benoit, P. 1985. "Story-telling and the Negotiation of Social Identities." Paper presented at the annual conference of the Speech Communication Association, Denver, CO.
Carbaugh, D. 1990. *Cultural Communication and Intercultural Contact*. Hillsdale, NJ: Lawrence Erlbaum.
Crawford, L. 1986. "Reluctant Communitarians: Personal Stories and Commune Behavior." *Communication Quarterly 43*: 286–305.

Dindia, K. 1987. "The Effects of Sex of Subject and Sex of Partner on Interruptions." *Human Communication Research 13*: 345–372.

Fishman, Pamela. 1978. "Interaction: The Work Women Do." *Social Problems 25*: 397–406.

Georges, R. 1982. "Toward an Understanding of Storytelling Events." *Journal of American Folklore 95*: 313–328.

Hall, J. 1984. *Nonverbal Sex Differences*. Baltimore, MD: Johns Hopkins Press.

Jefferson, G. 1978. "Sequential Aspects of Storytelling in Conversation." In J. Schenkein, ed., *Studies in the Organization of Conversational Interaction*. New York: Academic Press, pp. 219–248.

Kalcik, S. 1975. "'. . . Like Ann's Gynecologist or the Time I Was Almost Raped': Personal Narration in Women's Rap Groups." *Journal of American Folklore 88*: 3–11.

Labov, W., and J. Waletzky. 1967. "Narrative Analysis: Oral Versions of Personal Experience." In J. Helm, ed., *Essays on the Visual and the Verbal Arts*. Seattle: University of Washington Press, pp. 12–44.

Lofland, J. 1981. *Analyzing Social Settings: A Guide to Qualitative Observation and Analysis*. Belmont, CA: Wadsworth.

McConnell-Ginet, S. 1983. "Review Article." *Language 59*: 373–391.

McLaughlin, M., M. Cody, M. Kane, and C. Robey. 1981. "Sex Differences in Story Receipt and Story Sequencing Behaviors in Dyadic Conversations." *Human Communication Research 7*: 99–116.

Perry, L. 1989. "Weaving the Web: Oral Histories and Women's Communication." In C. Lont and S. Friedley, eds., *Beyond Boundaries: Sex and Gender Diversity in Communication*. Fairfax, VA: George Mason University Press, pp. 3–14.

Polyani, L. 1979. "So What's the Point?" *Semiotica 25*: 207–241.

Pomerantz, A. 1987. "Conversation Analytic Claims." *Communication Monographs 57*: 231–236.

Robinson, J. 1981. "Personal Narratives Reconsidered." *Journal of American Folklore 94*: 58–85.

Ryave, A. 1978. "On the Achievement of a Series of Stories." In J. Schenkein, ed., *Studies in the Organization of Conversational Interaction*. New York: Academic Press, pp. 113–132.

Sacks, R. 1972. "On the Analysability of Stories by Children." In J. Gumpers and D. Hymes, eds., *Directions in Sociolinguistics*. New York: Holt, Rinehart, and Winston.

Schlenker, B. 1980. *Impression Management: The Self-Concept, Social Identity, and Interpersonal Relations*. Monterey, CA: Brooks/Cole.

Smythe, M. J. 1993. "Talking Bodies: Women's Narratives on Fitness." Unpublished manuscript, University of Missouri—Columbia.

Smythe, M. J., and B. Huddleston. 1991. "Competitive and Collaborative Communication Styles." In L. Parry, H. Sterk, and L. Turner, eds., *Constructing and Reconstructing Gender*. Albany: State University of New York Press.

Smythe, M. J., and D. W. Schlueter. 1989. "Can We Talk? A Meta-analysis of the Sex Differences in Language Literature." In C. Long and S. Friedley, eds., *Beyond Boundaries: Sex and Gender Diversity in Communication*. Fairfax, VA: George Mason University Press, pp. 31–48.

Stimson, G., and B. Webb. 1975. *Going to See the Doctor*. London: Routledge and Kegan-Paul.

Thorne, B., C. Kramerae, and N. Henley. 1983. *Language, Gender, and Society.* Reading, MA: Newbury House.

Van Dijk, T. 1975. "Action, Action Description, and Narrative." *New Literary History* 6: 273–294.

Watson, K. 1973. "A Rhetorical and Sociolinguistic Model for the Analysis of Narrative." *American Anthropologist 75*: 243–264.

23

Women's Spirituality: Attitudes, Visions, and Health

Linda A. M. Perry

Spirituality can take many forms. For some, spirituality is religion (Baptist, for example)—one believes the "right" thing; for others, spirituality is philosophy (Buddhism, for example)—one searches for an ultimate truth; and, for still others, spirituality is a connectedness between the self, others, and the planet—one sees spirit internally as well externally. This is my understanding of women's spirituality.

Stein (1987) notes that the women's spirituality movement stems from the goddess tradition:

Women have always been healers of ourselves and others, and are reclaiming that empowerment as part of the women's spirituality movement today. Connecting the earliest midwives, witches and wisewomen to today's medical activists, body workers, herbalists, psychics and crystal/gemstone healers is a long line of women's healing tradition. This tradition, going back to ancient Egypt and Samurai, and suppressed by the male establishment since patriarchy's takeover of the goddess, is a known and vital fact of herstory. (p. xvii)

There is great diversity within the women's spirituality movement, but all varieties stem from the belief that all things are connected. From a general systems perspective, women's spirituality can be defined by "wholeness" and the "emergent quality" of systems. Wholeness suggests that a change in a part of the system reverberates throughout the system (Bertalanfy 1968). Spiritually, this means that the way one behaves and believes will have consequences for the self, others, and the planet at large (Capra 1982). For example, if I pollute the planet, I breathe in the pollution; if I treat my colleagues badly, I exist in "sick" relationships.

The emergent quality of interaction within systems shows that the whole is more than the sum of the parts—that is, there are attributes of the system that cannot be accounted for by simply analyzing the parts (Watzlawick, Bavalas, and Jackson 1967). Women's spirituality, like new physics, suggests that the emergent quality of humans interacting with each other and with the planet creates a collective consciousness (Capra 1982). As more of us collectively work for internal and external health, the collective consciousness of the planet will be altered in ways we cannot foresee. A healthy, positive collective consciousness could bring us closer to world peace.

Although women's spirituality takes many forms, in this essay, I focus on attitudinal change and visualization. Attitudinal change means adopting holistic, positive attitudes; visualization is a method for imagining an internal or external way of being such that the imagined, becomes reality. "Simply put, [visualization] is the mind thinking pictures" (Epstein 1989).

Most spiritual orientations purport that prayer or meditation can alleviate, if not eliminate, poor emotional or physical health. In this essay I discuss women's spirituality for healing emotional and physical pain. First, I argue that one's ability to acquire emotional or physical health can be limited by overreliance on external agencies such as the medical field. Then, I discuss some ways in which one's responsibility for one's health can be reclaimed through attitudinal change and visualization.

MEDICAL MODEL LIMITATIONS

For the last five thousand years of earth HIStory, women's power, wholeness, goddess values, learning and healing have been repressed, denied and partially lost to patriarchal power-over that's brought harm and dehumanization on women and men alike. Modern patriarchal medicine, with its fragmentation of body and spirit and its heavy handed "cures" is not a positive experience for women's bodies, for anyone's well being. Women's healing, by contrast, with its emphasis on wholeness and gentleness, on the unity of body, emotions, mind and spirit, on the seen and unseen and on choice, is a powerful and hopeful alternative. (Stein 1987, pp. xvii–xviii)

The medical field has done a good job prolonging and improving life. However, there are some ways the medical field limits personal health. The traditional medical model overrelies on cause and effect, separates body from soul, denies the patient dignity of her own experience, and resists alternate healing methods.

Overreliance on Cause and Effect

The medical model relies almost exclusively on cause and effect to describe and prescribe. From this stem such metaphors as "the brain works like a computer." No it doesn't. If the brain worked like a machine (cause-and-effect links), we could cure every disease that afflicts it and the rest of the body.

If we see the human body as a series of interlocking random actions, we cannot compare it to a machine and we cannot describe illnesses and cures in cause-effect terms. The mistaken identity of the body-as-machine myth stems from the dissection of body from soul.

Separation of Body from Soul

The separation of body from soul by the medical field places physicians in the position of ultimate control and the patient in the position of subservience. Stein (1987) notes that

[m]ale medicine and patriarchy fragment the parts of woman's Be-ing. They not only separate the seen from the unseen whole, but separate the physical self. The power-over system denies the non-physical, the non-scientifically measurable, the psychic and irrational, as it denies the female with her connection to these things. It refuses to acknowledge, derides and represses the emotions, mind and spirit in healing, and cuts itself off from studying or making use of them. (p. 5)

The separation of body from soul plays out in two ways. First, it means that health providers become overly responsible for the individual's health because the physical body takes precedent over the integrated whole. And physicians are almost exclusively interested in the body and not the spirit, or soul. Second, the ability for self-healing becomes taboo—one who believes in self-healing (or focusing on the connection between the body and the soul) is stereotyped as unstable at best, and insane at worst.

Denial of the Patient's Dignity of Her Own Experience

I recently ran a visualization training session with a nursing group. I asked them what problems they saw with the traditional medical model. One of their responses was that traditional medicine overestimated doctors' expertise and underrepresented patients' experiences. For example, I took a family member to a doctor because she had several symptoms: aching joints and muscles and hair loss resulting in a significant bald spot. The doctor gave two recommendations: take a drug that induces hair growth, or leave the spot alone to see if the hair would grow back by itself. He did not consider her family history or her emotional state; he did not question the relationship between the bald spot and the aches and pains; he simply focused on one symptom.

There is a family history of arthritis and Systemic Lupus Erythematosus (SLE) for which hair loss and aching joints and muscles are symptoms. I asked the doctor why he wasn't interested in family history or the patient's emotional condition. He responded that there is no reason to believe that a person has a disease simply because others in the family have it and, in his opinion, these few symptoms were not enough reason to do diagnostic tests. You might be saying, "Well, this is just a lousy doctor"; certainly I agree. However, this is not an uncommon response. If the doctor is the one with expertise, then the patients' knowledge about her body or family history takes a back seat.

Resistance to Alternate Healing Methods

Next, the traditional medical model does not acknowledge alternate healing methods. Most doctors are not trained in nutrition, exercise therapy, massage therapy, or relaxation therapy. In fact, most doctors are not usually even introduced to these therapies. Further complicating the problem, the American Medical Association and insurance companies do not support alternative therapies. This lack of information and support is ironic in so far as many studies show the primary deciding factor in getting an illness or disease and recovering is directly related to stress. These diseases include everything from heart diseases to cancer. Although a person may have a propensity to acquire a disease through heredity, she may not get the disease unless her stress level is raised. The alternative therapies listed above all work to decrease stress.

One way to counter the limitations of the medical field is to become more personally responsible for one's own emotional and physical health. We, along with the health care providers we select, must (1) not see health (or the lack of it) in terms of cause and effect, (2) reconnect the body with the soul, (3) be willing to acknowledge our experience with and knowledge about our own bodies, and (4) incorporate alternate therapies.

TAKING RESPONSIBILITY

Diane Stein (1987), in *The Women's Book of Healing*, presents several women's spiritual healing orientations in which attitudes and beliefs condition one's health. These orientations include laying on of hands, meditation, color work, crystals and gemstones, attitudinal change, and visualization. All of these orientations integrate the body and soul through spirituality. As Richard Bach (1977) points out in *Illusions*, "Within each of us lies the power of our consent to health and to sickness, to riches and to poverty, to freedom and to slavery. It is we who control these and not another" (p. 13).

Spiritually based healing methods are gaining more attention and acceptance because researchers are beginning to look at the connections between body and soul—head and heart. The research findings from studies done since the work and experiences of Norman Cousins (1979) shows many ties between emotional health and physical health. In Norman Cousins's video (1985), he cites case after case where lives were extended or diseases cured through spiritual therapies of attitudinal change and visualization.

Attitudinal Change

Jerry Jampolsky (1981) describes several ways in which we limit our lives or do not take responsibility for them. Also, he says that we replay the past and depend on what we are told will happen, to happen. We can, however, choose our reality and retrain our minds. During a lecture, Jampolsky (1988) explained that he and others at the Center for Attitudinal Healing are helping cancer and AIDS patients alter thinking patterns to improve their life experiences. He overviews these with the following list:

1. The essence of being is love.
2. Health is an inner peace. Healing is letting go of fear.
3. Giving and receiving are the same.
4. We can let go of the past and the future.
5. Now is the only time there is and each instant is for giving.
6. We can learn to love ourselves and others by forgiving rather than judging.
7. We can become love finders rather than fault finders.
8. We can choose and direct ourselves to be peaceful inside regardless of what is happening outside.
9. We are students and teachers to each other.
10. We can focus on the whole of life rather than the fragments.
11. Since love is eternal, death need not be viewed as fearful.
12. We can always perceive others as either extending love or giving a call for help.

The key espoused by Jampolsky is to take responsibility and use the above attitudinal changes to let go of the stressors that limit life experiences and endanger health.

I personally began using attitudinal healing long before I read Jampolsky's book or heard him speak. I was very ill at one time. I have SLE and the disease was in a progressive state that included high fevers, constant infections, and uncontrollable shivering. Although many medications were used, my condition did not improve. At one point, my primary care doctor told me that I should "get my life in order and make arrangements for my children's care." At the rate the disease was progressing, he believed I might pass on as soon as two weeks. Painkillers in hand, I opted to spend my final days at my parent's house. I stretched out on the couch and committed myself to dying for about one week. (I depended on what I was told would happen to happen.) One day my children came rushing in all excited about a trip to the beach from which they had returned. As I listened to them, I realized I couldn't possibly leave them. I got up from my "deathbed," packed my children's and my bags, and returned to our own home. That was seventeen years ago, and I truly believe that deciding to live and acting as though I could saved my life.

As previously mentioned, the medical model separates the body from the soul, the physical from the spiritual. Thus, we become estranged from our experience. Starhawk (1982) says in *Dreaming the Dark*:

Estrangement permeates our society so strongly that to us it seems to be consciousness itself. Even the language for other possibilities has disappeared or been deliberately twisted. Yet another form of consciousness is possible. Indeed, it has existed from earliest times, underlies other cultures, and has survived even in the West in hidden streams. This is the consciousness I call immanence—the awareness of the world and everything in it as alive, dynamic, interdependent, interacting, and infused with moving energies: a living being, weaving a dance. (p. 9)

Once we decide not to be estranged from our own experience, we begin to heal the separation between body and soul, the physical and the spiritual—to weave a dance of life.

A personal example of reconnecting body and soul again comes from dealing with SLE and arthritis. I have had six separate operations in as many years. Early on I decided that I would not allow general anesthesia so I could be equally responsible for the surgical outcome and, on an internal level, participate in the process. One method I use is a form of biofeedback in which I concentrate on the blood pressure and vital signs machine readouts. After concentrating for a few minutes, I imagine the numbers to be lower. As the numbers go down, my blood pressure decreases and relaxation increases. Stein (1987) describes this as a form of meditation in which "[c]hanges are made intentionally, via woman's will, knowledge and power-within, via the goddess and the goddess-within. Entering a trance state does not mean losing contact with reality; it means taking power over inner and outer realities by choice" (p. 67).

Cousins (1979) delineates his own experiences as an ill person who laughed himself to health in *Anatomy of an Illness as Perceived by the Patient*. The Power of Laughter and Play conference is an outgrowth of Cousins's work and is attended primarily by medical practitioners who are waking up to spirituality as a form of consciousness and connectedness. At this conference, the emphasis is on alternate healing methods such as attitudinal change (which may be as simple as Cousins's laughing "therapy") and visualization.

Visualization

Creative visualization is the technique of using your imagination to create what you want in your life. There is nothing at all new, strange, or unusual about creative visualization. You are already using it every day, every minute in fact. It is your natural power of imagination, the basic creative energy of the universe which you use constantly, whether or not you are aware of it. (Gawain 1985, p. 2)

Visualization can be used in specific situations such as healing an illness or disease or for opening oneself up to peace and self-love. Visualization is the use of imagination to relieve stress, decrease pain, or improve life in general.

The primary process entailed in visualization is to think of something that is a symbolic representation for what you are trying to achieve. Stein (1987) says:

"Creative visualization is the conscious, planned impressioning (programming) of the emotional body with an idea to be transmitted above it to the mind and below it to the physical level—to cause healing changes" (p. 16).

In *Love, Medicine and Miracles*, Bernie Siegel (1986) discusses the physical and emotional outcomes of creative visualization: reduced cancer cells in patients, fewer coronary attacks by previous type A personalities, and improvements in lives if not extended lives. There are real-life consequences when the body and soul are reconnected. The changes created through visualization were once thought to be simply the "power of positive thinking." Now there is medical evidence that shows there are tangible reasons visualization and attitudinal change work. For example, studies have shown that emotional activities such as laughing and crying stimulate the production of endorphenes, which in turn boost the immune system.

One example of visualization demonstrated at The Power of Laughter and Play conference are before and after slides of a little boy's cancer cells. Chemotherapy and radiation he was undergoing showed limited success. The health care providers then created an image that helped the boy to fight the disease. The boy loved to play Pac-Man, so that was the image he was trained to visualize. He was first taught to relax and focus on the image of the Pac-Men running around in his body eating up the cancer cells. Then, once he became proficient with this image, he set aside a certain amount of time each day to let his personal Pac-Men "eat up cancer cells." The result was that the cancer cell count went down dramatically. As a result, his more traditional therapies then had a chance to work.

I use visualization to counter pain and stress. For example, I had an operation with one surgeon in which local anesthesia was used. I refused all painkillers and relaxants except the local anesthesia. Instead, I imagined myself floating in beautiful lavender-colored air—air that protected me from pain. The next time I was wheeled into the operating room with this surgeon, no anesthesiologist was present. The doctor decided that the local anesthesia that she administered combined with my use of visualization made having an attending anesthesiologist unnecessary. As the doctor said, "What's the point, you won't let him do anything anyway."

CONCLUSION

Women's spirituality is based on connectedness. As a healing orientation, that means one looks inward for health and peace before moving outward. To do so reclaims responsibility for one's emotional and physical health.

The methods emphasized in this essay are attitudinal change and visualization. Women's spirituality, however, includes many more approaches to healing. All of these approaches stem from the goddess tradition, although many medical practitioners and laypeople using these methods do not recognize that fact. Through women's spirituality, limitations of the traditional medical model are overcome: one begins to experience health as dynamic and not dependent upon cause and effect; body and soul are reunited; and one's own reality and experience of his/her body is dignified. Stein (1987) reminds us that

If, in our current state of knowledge, women's healing is not total health care for everyone, then neither is male/traditional medicine. A balance between the two would be an ideal state, using the best parts of science in a humane, respectful, woman-oriented/people-oriented way along with women's skills for total health. Such a combination and synthesis of knowledge and a concentrated effort to gain more understanding is for the benefit of all, for women, children, and men, for animals and the planet. (p. 270)

REFERENCES

Bach, Richard. 1977. *Illusions: The Adventures of a Reluctant Messiah*. New York: Dell Publishing Company.

Bertalanfy, Ludwig von. 1968. *General Systems Theory: Foundations, Development, Applications*. New York: George Braziller.

Capra, Fritjof. 1982. *The Turning Point: Science, Society, and the Rising Culture*. Toronto: Bantam Books.

Cousins, Norman. 1979. *Anatomy of an Illness as Perceived by the Patient*. New York: Norton Press.

Cousins, Norman (Speaker). 1985. *Norman Cousins: Self-Love and Healing*. Film shown at The Power of Laughter and Play Conference, Long Beach, CA.

Epstein, Gerald. 1989. *Healing Visualizations: Creating Health through Imagery*. New York: Bantam Books.

Gawain, Shakti. 1985. *Creative Visualization*. New York: Bantam Books.

Jampolsky, Gerald G. 1981. *Love is Letting Go of Fear*. New York: Bantam Books.

———. 1988. *Attitudinal Change*. Public address, The Power of Laughter and Play Conference, San Francisco, CA.

———. n.d. "The Principles of Attitudinal Healing." Handout, Gerald G. Jampolsky, ed. San Francisco: Center for Attitudinal Change.

Siegal, Bernie S. 1986. *Love, Medicine, and Miracles*. New York: Harper and Row.

Starhawk. 1982. *Dreaming the Dark: Magic, Sex, and Politics*. Boston, MA: Beacon Press.

Stein, Diane. 1987. *The Women's Book of Healing*. St. Paul, MN: Llewellyn Publications.

Watzlawick, Paul, Janet Bavalas, and Don Jackson. 1967. *Pragmatics of Human Communication: A Study of Interactional Patterns, Pathologies, and Paradoxes*. New York: W. W. Norton.

24

Postmodern Possibilities: Gender, Power, and Moral Development

Linda Longmire and Timothy H. Smith

A profound paradigm shift in thinking has evolved in the last several decades. This shift began in the natural sciences, expanded to the social sciences and humanities, and has now begun to influence our thinking about gender and moral development. Labels characterizing this new paradigm thinking include "postmodern," "postliberal," "poststructural," and "postpositivistic." These terms collectively suggest a body of meanings which question the most fundamental assumptions of modernity. The modernist paradigm has tended to privilege rationality, predictability, and certainty, which in this century has meant a nearly unqualified faith in science and technology. This faith in turn has reinforced the assumption that progress, usually defined by material well-being, industrialization, and modernization, is inevitable and constructive. Finally, and most important for the purposes of this chapter, the modernist paradigm has reified individualism and minimized the importance of relationships and communities. Power has increasingly come to be expressed as "power over" others, self, or nature in the form of domination and control rather than as "power with" expressed as cooperation, equality, caring. Though discursive practices which emphasize power over and against others have dominated our experience in the West since the Enlightenment, the contours of this new paradigm are emerging. This chapter explores the meaning and significance of this postmodern paradigm in terms of its holistic, systemic, and relational orientation, along with some of its implications for our understanding of gender relations and moral development.

One of the major reconstructions implied by a postmodern paradigm is a reconceptualization of the notion of power embedded in modern thought and practice. The modern view of power is central to a cluster of Enlightenment notions about human nature, historical progress, scientific method, and linear causality. The modernist sense of power also tends to be associated with masculinity and patriarchy. As previously mentioned, this description of power emphasizes domination, control, prediction, mastery, and conquest—in short, what can be called "power over."[1] According to this prevailing notion of power in the modern world, human nature tends to be seen as primarily aggressive, competitive, violent, and selfish. In this bleak formulation, life is, as Hobbes describes it, nasty, brutish, and short. According to this view, the state of nature is fundamentally a state of war, and therefore absolute sovereignty is necessary to control the behavior of unruly individuals. Only concentrated collective power over these atomistic, anarchic, and self-interested individuals will compel them to obey and thereby provide social stability and security. The transition from the state of nature to civil society may be formalized through contractual relations, but ultimately it is primarily upheld by power over subjects.

In similar fashion, since the seventeenth century science and technology have increasingly been utilized in order to assert control and power over nature. Indeed, since the Enlightenment, the primary tendency has been to see nature as a threat, an irrational and destructive force which must be fought and overcome. This attitude also has encouraged Western society to treat nature as a resource, a commodity to be appropriated and exploited. This is yet another expression of power over that fails to acknowledge our interdependence with nature and our need to cooperate with it.

In contrast, the shift to a postmodern orientation is characterized by the emergence of a new understanding of power which can be described as "power with." Power with is characterized by relationships of cooperation rather than repression, aggression, and hierarchy. In this connection, Richard Falk has noted that a "postmodern sensibility helps emancipate us from colonizing forms of knowledge associated with evident and disguised structures of domination: statism, nuclearism, patriarchy."[2] This new conception of power is understood and experienced as potentiality, creativity, and relational capacity in ways that fundamentally challenge the modern version of power over. Power with is not simply a difference in emphasis or a qualification of power over; it represents a qualitatively different way of seeing the self and relationships. In Kreisberg's exploration of the distinction between power over and power with, he advises that

"power with" . . . is not a concept that can or should simply be incorporated into existing theories of power and domination—rather it challenges us to rethink our categories, our frameworks, our underlying assumptions, and ultimately our grand analyses of how power functions—both for domination and for liberation.[3]

This radical and far-reaching reconstruction of our understanding of power as power with has of course been explored by many feminist thinkers. These constructions of power with emphasize connectedness, interdependence, and sharing in relationships rather than isolation, domination, and aggression. According to this view, power is not inherently destructive, but it must be reinterpreted and reclaimed in order to create space for new meaning. In fact, the original meanings of power evoke images of capacity, effectiveness, potency, creativity, fertility—in short, of "power to" rather than suppression and control. This positive and expansive view of power can fundamentally change the character of relationships; they become rich, intertwined webs and organic networks rather than hierarchies of control which resemble rigid pyramids. Accordingly, the feminization of power recasts relationships as mutually enhancing, synergistic, and cooperative. Rather than assuming an inevitable, built-in scarcity of power and unbridled conflict over a limited resource, the notion of power with emphasizes abundance, sharing, and empowerment.

This view of power, what with its emphasis on relationship and connection, also implies different institutional relationships and forms of life. As new expressions of spiritual and ethical consciousness emerge, challenges develop to alter the political and economic status quo. Postmodern and feminist insights emphasize this alternative experience of power with as mutualistic, plentiful, and cooperative[4]—in short, as a feminization of politics. Richard Falk, for example, in writing about international relations, describes the implications of this postmodern vision of power with for societal and political life in the following way:

The postmodern . . . implies the rediscovery of normative and spiritual ground upon which to find meaning in human existence. It does not imply a return to the past. . . . The postmodern . . . proceeds on a different basis: *a dispersion of spiritual energy that is associated with the sacredness of the whole universe and a related feminization of political life that find power in relations rather than in capabilities for dominance and destruction, in earthborne more than skyborne energy.* Unity with centralization or hierarchy provides the only firm constraint upon the design of desirable world-order arrangements for the future.[5]

This new conception of power as relationship makes it possible to reconnect ethics, politics, and spirituality in ways which are decentralized, egalitarian, and rooted in more authentic, or "earthborne," democratic practice.

Correspondingly, the emphasis in Carol Gilligan's thinking about relationship, social embeddedness, and responsibility to others conveys in both ethical and epistemological terms key elements expressed in the message of the postmodern critique. In her writings exploring a postmodern vision, egalitarian, nonhierarchical imagery is commonly employed to articulate a pluralistic and relational perspective; and this orientation also characterizes Gilligan's formulation of the roots of ethical intuition and deliberation. As she wisely envisions the larger issue, "the promise in joining women and moral theory lies in the fact that human survival, in the late twentieth century, may depend less on formal agreement than on human connection."[6]

Since the publication of her first book, *In a Different Voice,*[7] Gilligan has exerted an increasingly wider impact on thinking and research relating to psychological, relational, and moral development. Although for many years her work was seen as reflecting primarily the life experience of girls and women, elaboration of her original research has earned attention for its capacity to address more adequately both male and female moral development. In short, while even much of her recent work continues to focus on female adolescent change and experience of identity,[8] Gilligan's theoretical framework for conceptualizing growth and development is gender inclusive.

An illustration of this framework is provided in her discussion of a high school student, Anne, who is confronted with a moral conflict over whether or not to buy cigarettes for a close friend.[9] The conflict Anne experiences helps to clarify the basis for the two different world views presented to us by Gilligan and Lawrence Kohlberg. Whereas Kohlberg emphasizes justice reasoning and an abstract sense of "duty" and "rights," Gilligan associates moral deliberation with an ethic of care or responsibility. In this account Anne decides not to buy cigarettes for her friend; when interviewed, she reasons, in Kohlbergian fashion, that to do so would be "illogical," since she herself believes strongly that smoking is simply harmful and wrong. But pressed to consider whether another interpretation is possible, Anne acknowledges a tension rooted in her relationship to her friend. Although she continues to maintain that she was right not to buy the cigarettes, she admits to an ambivalence stemming from her not seeming to be open and responsive to her friend. Accordingly, as Gilligan views it, "The dilemma or tension she faces is not [simply] of peer pressure—how to say 'no' to her friends or classmates. Instead, it stems from a different way of thinking about herself in relation to others, a way that leads into the question of what relationship, or in this instance friendship, means."[10]

As Gilligan indicates, moreover, there is a corresponding shift in what Anne describes as her sense of autonomy in relation to her decision. On the one hand, her refusal to buy the cigarettes clearly makes her feel autonomous in the sense of confronting directly the ethical issue and doing her duty even at the risk of alienating or losing her friend. On the other hand, her recognition that right and wrong cannot always be reduced to a simple equation or to one moral perspective—that relationships, in other words, inherently involve constraints upon impersonal detached autonomy—compels her to speak in a different voice, albeit a quieter one.

This example clearly illustrates how meaningful relationships require authentic selves, and how true caring must be accompanied by healthy autonomy. But this is no easy task in a society which makes it hard to achieve either. In their recent book, *Women's Psychology and Girls' Development*,[11] Gilligan and Lyn Mikel Brown explore the disheartening ways in which adolescent females learn to truncate their own power and mold themselves into compliant, accommodating "good little girls," silencing the honest, forthright, and creative youngsters they were at an earlier moment in their development. They learn to idealize relationships, to hand over power to fantasy, rather than deal with the messy and confusing relationships that reality offers. Girls may learn to care too much about their opinions of others, thereby sacrificing or repressing their own feelings and perceptions. By overemphasizing their connections to others, they may even lose precious parts of themselves. Somehow the nature of these bonds threatens to deny them their own autonomous subjectivity and also damages the quality of their relationships to others. Though one of the strengths of women lies in their ability to care, it also reflects their weakness when it undermines personal autonomy. The initially confident, spontaneous voices of young girls are often silenced as they come to endow external authority with increasing power.[12] They begin to become passive, more apt to listen than to speak authoritatively. Later they may reject, sometimes very forcefully, these external voices in order to discover their own subjective truth. The following moment may find them reacting against this overemphasis on their own personal truth in order once again to search outside themselves for other voices that connect in some way with their own experience. They come to realize that there is some knowledge that is separate and personal and some which involves connection to others. In the last analysis, there is hopefully the full integration of the voices, one's own separate and unique experience and those which honor and recognize the external voices. Likewise, finding one's own voice cannot ultimately be accomplished in an interpersonal vacuum; it implies a rich intersubjective world in which the self is connected to a diversity of others. Clearly there are different forms of autonomy, just as there are different forms of connection and relationship, out of which gender related experiences and distinctions emerge. However,

Like concerns about yielding to pressure from others, concerns about not listening or becoming cut off from others are also vital. The ability to create and to sustain human connection . . . may, however, hinge on the ability to differentiate true from false relationship, to read the signs that distinguish authentic from inauthentic forms of connection. . . . The capacity for detachment . . . prized as the hallmark of cognitive and moral development, is thus double-edged. . . . Although detachment connotes the dispassion which signifies fairness in justice reasoning, . . . detachment also connotes the absence of connection and has the potential to create the conditions for carelessness or violation, for violence toward others or toward oneself.[13]

Gilligan's account of Anne's moral conflict is instructive insofar as it incorporates Kohlberg's ethic of justice into a theoretical framework that also acknowledges the ethic of care. What Gilligan recognized early on in her work is the universal experience of interdependence and its association with gender; this experience more commonly and easily gives rise in turn to care reasoning among girls and women who are invited to talk about their moral conflicts. The reality of human interdependence on a global scale can thus be more readily acknowledged if connection and relationship are personally experienced as a meaningful and shared dimension of growing up. Males, on the other hand, are customarily provided early in their development with the experience of separation from their mothers, or primary caregivers, and are encouraged as a rule to experience independence as a primary fact of life. But as Gilligan has often observed, young boys do commonly experience inequality, which in turn facilitates the emergence in them of a disposition to see fairness as a basic dimension of life. This disposition shows up later in their moral propensity to employ justice reasoning to resolve ethical conflict precisely because of its ostensible abstract independence freedom from compromising relationship and emotional connection. To the extent that the culture remains patriarchal and applauds and rewards justice reasoning as morally superior to care reasoning, male adults are given little incentive to acknowledge even the relevance of care reasoning; correspondingly, adolescent and adult women, as Gilligan and her coresearchers have found, become easily confused about their moral identity and their ways of thinking to the extent that care reasoning appears to be institutionally inappropriate and not culturally sanctioned in the public sphere. Accordingly, while there may be universality in both the experience of interdependence and of inequality, a culture biased toward patriarchy will not accord equal validity to each; and an ethical orientation rooted in connection and relationship will be seen as inferior to that which emphasizes a detached concern for fairness and justice.

It is equally evident, however, that cultural change is occurring. While it is too soon to predict the emergence of a nonpatriarchal society and world, what are developing on the horizon are signs—theoretical and institutional—that point in the direction of such change. In medicine, law, and education, for example, institutional changes seem to be underway which reflect the thrust of new paradigm thinking that originally began in the field of physics. Prompted by Einstein's discovery of relativity theory, but given stronger impetus by quantum theory and, more recently, chaos theory, the field of physics—the hallmark of science—has undergone revolutionary change in the twentieth century. As Kuhn observed some time ago,[14] a paradigm shift that was occurring in physics signaled a profound epistemological change in the way scientist think and behave. Such a shift involves change not only in the basic assumptions, beliefs, values, and traditions of scientists but also in how and what problems are determined and framed.

The dimensions of this paradigm shift relating to our discussion here are complex but can be sketched briefly. For the past four hundred years the world of physics was postulated on the existence of an independent, orderly world. For much of this time, Newton's laws of gravity were thought to embody the way nature really is; and nature itself could be described as a mechanical clock governed by eternal unchanging laws. The validity of these laws was assumed to be completely independent of human volition or thought, rooted in a sharp separation between knower and known. This independent orderly mechanical world was, in Newton's view, divinely created in accord with predetermined patterns and directions that imposed order on nature's chaos. Indeed, as Einstein himself is alleged once to say, God did not "play dice" with the universe, reflecting Newton's sense of certainty about the creation and workings of the universe.

The paradigm shift that has recently emerged, however, embedded as it is in both experimental and theoretical research, questions this entire picture of nature in its macroscopic and microscopic dimensions. Chaos theory and fractal geometry have enabled scientists to see the disorderly aspects of nature more clearly and have compelled them to accept the fact that random behavior in nature is as much a part of the "real world" as the orderly patterns that appear on the surface. Heisenberg's uncertainty principle, firmly established in theory and in the laboratory, reminds us as well that knowledge of the world is, in principle, intrinsically dependent on participant observation. And quantum theory stands as a challenging reminder that linear mechanistic formulations of subatomic life are simply inadequate as ways to describe the mystical dance of mass and energy and the chaotic and complex relationships among subatomic particles.[15] Reflecting upon her lifelong research in natural science, Ruth Bleier has summarized the normative significance of this paradigm shift as follows:

[S]cience is not the neutral, dispassionate, value-free pursuit of Truth; . . . [and] scientists are not objective, disinterested, or culturally disengaged from the questions they ask of nature or the methods they use to frame their answers. It is, furthermore, impossible for science or scientists to be otherwise, since science is a social activity and a cultural product created by persons who live in the world of science as well as in the societies that bred them.[16]

As previously mentioned, this new paradigm in natural science underlies and precedes a parallel shift in the social sciences which are more closely aligned with Gilligan's focus on human development. In this connection, it is instructive to note specific philosophical convergences between the "hard" science of physics as it has recently evolved and the work of Gilligan in psychological and moral development.

First of all, it is apparent that Gilligan's theoretical framework reflects directly the epistemological orientation emerging from the new paradigm of modern physics. Gilligan's model suggests that moral decision making utilizing both the ethic of justice and the ethic of care more adequately characterizes the actual "messy" world in which we live. This is a more holistic approach to moral conflict transcending the subjective-objective disjunctions and the moral reductionism historically accompanying dualistic thinking. New paradigm physics is rooted in a similar epistemological orientation, acknowledging a relationship between the physicist and the object studied, where the observed and the observer are interdependent as a necessary condition of knowing. Moral wisdom and lack of certainty in ethical matters are no more in opposition than the limits to knowledge reflected in chaos or quantum theory. And an interdisciplinary approach[17] to problems inherent in physical reality is increasingly recognized to be as necessary as it is to confronting moral dilemmas. There is a place for analytic and technical reasoning in both physics and morality, but integrative and systemic thinking are equally crucial. How parts are connected to the whole and the dynamic patterns of relationship among parts are as basic to the accumulation of moral knowledge as they are to inquiry into subatomic reality.

The meaning of these philosophical distinctions can be better appreciated perhaps if we attempt to see how they are beginning to be applied in medicine, law, and education. In the field of medicine, for instance, we can recall that Norman Cousins over a decade ago helped to found the movement to change dramatically the way that doctors approach their work. Motivated by a diagnosis of a terminal illness, Cousins challenged the reductionist ways of specialized medicine, along with its biased orientation to prescribe drugs for nearly everything. In the process he not only saved his own life, but in addition his criticisms of medical practice were considered legitimate enough to be published in the prestigious *New England Journal of Medicine*. Subsequently, Cousins was hired to teach at the medical school of UCLA, where he helped develop a more holistic approach to medicine, including new emphases on nutrition, diet, exercise, and healthy lifestyle as an important part of the responsibilities of doctors to their patients. In line with Cousins's belief in the need for genuinely close power-with relationships between doctor and patient, Levine, among others, has recently welcomed the insights of Gilligan to the practice of medicine in a journal widely subscribed to by medical practitioners. In brief, Levine argues that medical ethics has been grounded more in an "ethics of strangers" than in an "ethics of intimacy,"[18] and that the former is more in accord with an ethics of justice with its emphasis on individual rights and duties and legally circumscribed responsibilities. But an ethic of care—and care-oriented reasoning—are equally essential to the practice of medicine. The care ethic is needed to help doctors transcend the language of rights and duties and to humanize the technical, mechanical relationship commonly experienced between patients and medical specialists. Like Gilligan, Levine concludes that doctor-patient relationships built upon trust and intimacy must be included in medical training to reflect both the ethic of justice and care. He writes:

Clearly our society requires norms grounded in the justice orientation in order to deal with the potentials for abuse that exist in the doctor-patient relationship. However, unless we balance our teaching of these norms by supplementing them with norms reflecting the priorities of care-oriented reasoning, we shall be self-defeating in our goals of developing caring personal doctors.[19]

In law as in medicine, moreover, there are abstract as well as concrete connections to be recognized as essential. Here again Gilligan's groundbreaking work on moral and human development has been cited as sparking a fundamental reassessment of the law by feminist legal scholars.[20] Lewin, in this connection, notes, "The traditional body of law . . . was developed by men, and reflects the male emphasis on rights and abstractions. It thus fails . . . to take account of women's real-life experiences . . . even in redefining such fundamental legal concepts as [to] what . . . [constitutes] an injury."[21]

In point of fact, a significant redefinition of criminal law has emerged in response to increasing involvement of the legal system in spouse abuse cases.[22] In particular, some battered wives who have killed their husbands have been found not guilty "on grounds of self-defense even where they seemed to flout the traditional rule that deadly force may be used only where there is an imminent threat."[23] Now such cases are not only increasingly important in social terms, but they point as well to the fact that the law itself needs to go beyond defining rights in relationships in the abstract terms of justice reasoning if it is to address the reality of legally connected lives in a patriarchal society in which much violence is personally administered. Indeed, as Lawrence Tribe has recently argued, we can also look to the paradigm shift in physics not only as an aid to "our comprehension of social and legal issues,"[24] but also to better appreciate, as feminist scholars have argued, that "the law cannot extract itself from social structures; it cannot 'step back,' establish an 'Archimedean' reference point of detached neutrality, and selectively reach in, as though from the outside, to make fine-tuned adjustments to highly particularized conflicts."[25] In advancing such insights, Tribe directly connects Gilligan's moral development framework emphasizing, in the ethic of care, the crucial significance of concrete context in moral reasoning, with the metaphors and concepts that have become central to the meaning of new paradigm thinking in natural and social science.

Perhaps more than in any other field, Gilligan's work has extended to and influenced the world of education and schooling. This observation is not surprising in that the focus of much of her research during the past ten years has centered upon developmental psychology and human development. Her insights, however, have not only cast light on important differences in development of males and females. Of more general significance, she has contributed directly to the intellectual movement that acknowledges the need to reassess the entire field of developmental psychology previously dominated by Freud, Erikson, and Piaget, among others, who collectively mirror a distinctly male—and limited—perspective. In her own quiet and unassuming voice, Heilbrun writes, Gilligan has "challenged the way psychologists ask questions, and their tendency . . . to end up learning what they thought they already knew."[26]

Within the institution of schooling, in particular, the ethic of care has emerged in recent years as a significant dimension of the educational restructuring movement. In their book *Responsive Teaching*, Bowers and Flinders illustrate the ways in which Gilligan's assessment of human development joins hands with new paradigm thinking emanating from natural science and forming the epistemological basis of the postmodern perspective we characterized at the beginning of our analysis. As the subtitle of their book, "An Ecological Approach to Classroom Patterns of Language, Culture, and Thought," intimates, the classroom, in their view, needs to be regarded in its own way as a kind of "ecosystem," displaying dynamic patterns and power-with relationships. Students' interactions and behaviors, they argue, have to be responded to in holistic and systemic terms, acknowledging the profound ways in which human nature is embedded in culture and human communication is encoded in metaphorical language. Such a classroom reflects an ecological paradigm and is contrasted with the management-oriented power-over paradigm typically characterizing teacher-student environments. Bowers and Flinders suggest that the management paradigm model reflects the more mechanical and manipulative orientation originally deriving from Newton's seventeenth-century Enlightenment view that the world itself is like a clock with independently functioning parts. This model of the teaching-learning process rests in turn upon an atomistic conception of human nature and characteristically places emphasis upon individual achievement based in competition among students and one-way power over, and manipulation of, students' behavior. The ecologically run classroom, in contrast, rooted in an ethic of care, is more organically orches-trated and can only succeed in the context of meaningfully functional relationships and connections between and among students and teachers.[27]

Recent analyses of moral development provide confirmation for the argu-ment provided here that attempts to connect the work of Gilligan and others with the emerging postmodern critique. In relation to the issues of em-powerment, a postmodern sensibility encourages us to understand and experi-ence power in significantly new ways. Rather than conceiving of power as domination or control, a postmodern formulation of power envisions moral evolution in ways congruent with Gilligan's conception of the moral develop-ment of women; and rather than seeing moral development simply as a move-ment toward a detached sense of duty or abstract rights transcending and overpowering the complicated world of personal relationships, feelings, and intimacy, a postmodern vision would emphasize, as well, moral empowerment as connection, care, and concrete solidarity with others. Power is thus redefined and expressed in more systemic and subtle ways that affirm the feminized, more eastern sensibility captured in the poetic description of the Tao as follows:

The Tao produces;
Its Power supports;
Its Natural Law forms;
Its influence completes.

Thus All Things without exception
Respect the Tao and value its Power.
To respect the Tao and value its Power—
No one demands this, and it comes naturally.

Therefore the Tao produces and its Power supports;
It advances, cultivates, comforts, matures, nourishes, and protects.

Produce but do not possess.
Act without expectation.
Advance without dominating.
These are called the Subtle Powers.[28]

NOTES

1. Seth Kriesberg, *Transforming Power: Domination, Empowerment, and Education* (Albany: State University of New York Press, 1992).

2. Richard A. Falk, "In Pursuit of the Postmodern," in David Ray Griffin, ed., *Spirituality and Society* (Albany: State University of New York Press, 1988), p. 82.

3. Kriesberg, *Transforming Power*, p. 61.

4. See Charlene Spretnak, ed., *The Politics of Women's Spirituality* (New York: Anchor, 1994).

5. Ibid., p. 83.

6. Carol Gilligan, "Moral Orientation and Moral Development," in Eva Feder Kitaay and Diana T. Myers, eds., *Women and Moral Theory* (Savage, MD: Rowman and Littlefield, 1987), p. 31.

7. Carol Gilligan, *In a Different Voice* (Cambridge, MA: Harvard University Press, 1982).

8. Carol Gilligan, Nona P. Lyons, Trudy J. Hanmer, eds., *Making Connections: The Relational Worlds of Adolescent Girls at Emma Willard School* (Troy, NY: Emma Willard School Press, 1989). See also Carol Gilligan, Janie Victoria Ward, and Jill McLean Taylor, eds., *Mapping the Moral Domain* (Cambridge, MA: Harvard University Press, 1988).

9. Gilligan et al., *Mapping the Moral Domain*, pp. xxiv–xxix.

10. Ibid., p. xxvi.

11. Carol Gilligan and Lyn Mikel Brown, *Women's Psychology and Girls' Development* (Cambridge, MA: Harvard University Press, 1992).

12. Similar insights are expressed in Mary Field Belenky, Blythe McVicker Clinchy, Nancy Rule Goldberger, and Jill Mattuck Tarule, *Women's Ways of Knowing: The Development of Self, Voice, and Mind* (New York: Basic Books, 1986).

13. Carol Gilligan, "Adolescent Development Reconsidered," in Gilligan et al., *Mapping the Moral Domain*, pp. xxvii–xxviii.

14. Thomas Kuhn, *The Structure of Scientific Revolutions* (Chicago: University of Chicago, 1962).

15. Fritjof Capra, *The Turning Point* (New York: Simon and Schuster, 1982), chap. 3.

16. Ruth Bleier, *Science and Gender* (New York: Pergamon Press, 1984), p. 193.

17. James Gleick, *Chaos: Making a New Science* (New York: Penguin, 1988).

18. Robert J. Levine, "Medical Ethics and Personal Doctors: Conflicts between What We Teach and What We Want," *Journal of Clinical Ethics 1*(1) (spring 1990): 27.

19. Ibid., p. 28.

20. Tamar Lewin, "Feminist Scholars Spurring a Rethinking of Law," *New York Times*, September 30, 1988, p. B9.

21. Ibid.

22. Deborah Rhode, *Justice and Gender* (Cambridge, MA: Harvard University Press, 1989), pp. 242–244.

23. Lewin, "Feminist Scholars Spurring a Rethinking of Law," p. B9.

24. Laurence Tribe, "The Curvature of Constitutional Space," *Harvard Law Review 103*(1) (November 1989): 2.

25. Ibid., pp. 7-8.

26. Carolyn Heilbrun, "Making Connections," *New York Times Book Review*, October 4, 1992, p. 13.

27. C. A. Bowers and David J. Flinders, *Responsive Teaching: An Ecological Approach to Classroom Patterns of Language, Culture, and Thought* (New York: Teachers College, 1990), chap. 1.

28. Lao Tzu, *The Tao of Power*, trans. R. L. Wing (New York: Doubleday, 1986), p. 51.

Index

About the Contributors

ANGELA ALLISON-FABER graduated from the University of Northern Iowa with a master's degree in Communication Studies in 1993. Since that time she has worked in the human resources field, primarily focusing on employment and legal issues.

DEBORAH S. BALLARD-REISCH is Associate Professor of Communication and Assistant Director of the honors program at the University of Nevada. Her research interests include gender, marital decision making, communication dynamics in families coping with cancer, and participative decision making for patients and health care providers.

PATRICIA A. BRIESCHKE is Associate Professor of Educational Administration in the Department of Administration and Policy Studies at Hofstra University's School of Education. She is currently at work on "Race Narratives," a study of how people experience race, and "Imagining Iraci," a conceptual paper on the relationship between fact and fiction in writing.

VICTORIA DEFRANCISCO is Associate Professor in Communication Studies and Director of Women's Studies at the University of Northern Iowa.

MARY ELTON is involved in training and development for a western regional medical center. Her primary research interest is in the area of interdepartmental communication in organizations, with a focus on improving efficiency and aiding in quality improvement efforts.

ALLEN EMERSON does his research on male-female discourse in mathematics, develops curriculum using the graphing calculator, and offers seminars and workshops for mathematics teachers on the role of technology in transforming the mathematics classroom.

CHERYL FORBES is Assistant Professor of Writing and Rhetoric at Hobart and William Smith College in Geneva, New York. Her article "Reading Portfolios Conversationally" appeared in *New Directions in Portfolio Assessment* (1994).

MICHAEL P. KELLEY is Professor of Communication Studies in the Department of Communication Studies at California State University, Los Angeles. He was the inaugural editor of the *National Forensic Journal* from 1983 to 1986 and President of the National Forensic Association from 1977 to 1980.

R. J. KIVATISKY is Assistant Professor of Communication at the University of Southern Maine. Dr. Kivatisky's area of expertise is organizational behavior, and he has been conducting research in health care settings for the past five years.

JANICE KOCH is Associate Professor in the Department of Curriculum and Teaching at Hofstra University. Her area of specialization is science education, where her research focuses on encouraging the participation of women in science and engineering.

AMY S. KORPI completed research for her contribution to this volume while a graduate student at Marquette University in Milwaukee, Wisconsin. Since then, she has taught at Cardinal Stritch College in Milwaukee. In addition, she is a Strategic Communications Project Manager for Allen-Bradley Company, Inc., and a freelance consultant.

ROBERTA L. KOSBERG is Associate Professor of Communication at Curry College in Milton, Massachusetts. Her current research focus is on the study of interpersonal cooperation and conflict management. Her research has appeared in such journals as *Communication Education* and *Communication Research Reports*.

LINDA LONGMIRE is Associate Professor of Political Science, the Director of Women's Studies, and the Coordinator of International Studies at Hofstra University's interdisciplinary New College. Her publication and teaching focus on feminist, environmental, and international politics.

LOU ANN MATOSSIAN, a doctoral candidate in linguistics at the University of Pennsylvania, is completing her dissertation on generic pronouns in contemporary urban speech while working as a freelance writer, editor, and community activist. She lives in Minneapolis.

LISA MERRILL is Associate Professor of Speech Communication and Rhetorical Studies at Hofstra University's School of Communication. She is coauthor (with Deborah Borisoff) of *The Power to Communicate: Gender Differences as Barriers* (3rd ed., 1998). Her publication, teaching, and research interests focus on gender and performance studies.

HUANG PANG has focused academically on Sinological culture and linguistics and applied anthropology. She is currently employed at AT&T in Boston.

LINDA A. M. PERRY is Chair of the Department of Communication Studies, the University of San Diego, California, and a consultant for LampLight Productions. She has edited three anthologies and authored publications on gender socialization theory, gender and education, women in management, and women in film.

DEBORAH PETERSEN-PERLMAN is Director of the Office of Equal Opportunity at the University of Minnesota, Duluth where she is Associate Professor of Communication. Her research interests include children and television, radio history, and criticism of television.

ANDREW S. RANCER is Associate Professor of Communication in the School of Communication at the University of Akron in Ohio. His research focuses on the aggressive communication predispositions of argumentativeness and verbal aggressiveness. He is the coauthor of *Building Communication Theory*.

PHYLLIS R. RANDALL was formerly Professor of English at North Carolina Central University, where she taught courses including Fundamentals of Speech Communication, Advanced Composition, and Contemporary Drama. She is an editor of *Caryl Churchill: A Case Book* (1988).

GAIL M. SCHWAB is a professor of French at Hofstra University. She is interested in feminist theory and is writing a book on Luce Irigaray.

DANIEL J. SHEA is Coordinator of Instruction and Advising at Community College of Vermont where he also teaches Introduction to Women's Studies, Psychology of Women, Gender Issues in the Classroom, and Feminist Theory and Practice.

SYLVIA BAILEY SHURBUTT is Chair of the Department of English at Shepherd College in Shepherdtown, West Virginia. She has published articles in *Victorian Poetry, Southern Literary Journal, Women's Studies,* and other scholarly journals.

TIMOTHY H. SMITH is Professor of Foundations of Education and Director of the Master's Program in Foundations of Education in the Department of Administration and Policy Studies of Hofstra University's School of Education. His research interests and publications center on ethics and education, especially in relation to gender and ecological issues.

MARY-JEANETTE SMYTHE is Chair of the Department of Communication at the University of Missouri, Columbia. Her current research focuses on women's narratives of life experiences, particularly embodiment and success stories.

KATHERINE STEPHENSON is Associate Professor of French and Women's Studies at the University of North Carolina at Charlotte. She has published articles on twentieth-century French women writers of fiction, on Luce Irigaray, and on her collaborative linguistic research with Irigaray.

PATRICIA A. SULLIVAN is Associate Professor of Communication at the State University of New York at New Paltz. She is coeditor (with Carole Levin) of *Political Rhetoric, Power, and Renaissance Women* (1995).

LYNN H. TURNER is Associate Professor of Communication Studies at Marquette University. She is the coauthor of *Gender and Communication* (1991) and coeditor of *Constructing and Reconstructing Gender* (1992) and *Differences That Make a Difference* (1994), two collections of essays concerning gender, language, and communication.

DANIEL J. WEIGEL is Associate Professor with the University of Nevada Cooperative Extension. His research interests include communication dynamics impacting marital commitment, family decision making, and determinants of family satisfaction.

RICHARD WEST is Associate Professor and Chair of the Department of Communication at the University of Southern Maine. He has published a number of resource manuals and articles in communication and education journals and is the coauthor of *Gender and Communication* (1995) and *Perspectives on Family Communication* (1998).

KATHLEEN G. WILLIAMSON is currently employed as a Judge Pro Tempore, teaches feminist Jurisprudence as Adjunct Professor of Law, and is a doctoral student of anthropology at the University of Arizona.

ISBN 0-313-30686-9

90000>

EAN

9 780313 306860

HARDCOVER BAR CODE